THE LIFE AND TIMES

OF

COTTON MATHER, D.D., F.R.S.

Cotton Mather.

THE LIFE AND TIMES

OF

COTTON MATHER, D.D., F.R.S.

OR

A Boston Minister of Two Centuries Ago

1663-1728

BY REV. ABIJAH P. MARVIN

HASKELL HOUSE PUBLISHERS Ltd.
Publishers of Scarce Scholarly Books
NEW YORK, N. Y. 10012
1973

HASKELL HOUSE PUBLISHERS Ltd.

Publishers of Scarce Scholarly Books

280 LAFAYETTE STREET

NEW YORK. N. Y. 10012

Library of Congress Cataloging in Publication Data

Marvin, Abijah Perkins.
  The life and times of Cotton Mather.

  1. Mather, Cotton, 1663-1728. I. Title.
F67.M426 1973   973.2'092'4 [B]   72-1979
ISBN 0-8383-1454-6

Printed in the United States of America

CONTENTS

Increase Mather.

LIFE AND TIMES OF COTTON MATHER.

CHAPTER I.

FROM BIRTH TO GRADUATION : 1663–1679.

COTTON MATHER was born in Boston on the twelfth day of February, 1663. He was the eldest child of Increase and Maria (Cotton) Mather. His grandfather, Rev. Richard Mather, was one of the oldest and wisest of the early settlers of Massachusetts Bay. He was born in Lowton, county of Lancashire, and was a graduate of Brasenose College, Oxford. At Cotton Mather's birth the old patriarch was yet alive, and continued active in the ministry six years longer, when he died, being worn out with toils, dangers, privations, study, prayer, preaching, and all the exhausting though blessed duties of a parish minister. His very presence was a blessing to the opening mind and eyes of the quick-witted boy. Calm, sedate, studious, ever busy, devout, yet pleasant withal, he was an embodiment of the best form of godliness, and from such prayers as his flowed priceless blessings to his grandchild.

The grandmother, Katharine Holt, of gentle ancestry, had been taken to heaven. But though one grandmother was gone another had taken her place, for the aged minister had married the widow of the famous John Cotton. She was indeed a mother in Israel. She had a daughter who became the wife of Increase Mather, and so was the mother of our boy, and such a mother as few were ever

blessed with. Maria Cotton was the helpmeet of her
husband. Humble, intelligent, discreet, a notable house-
wife, a companion of learned and able men, the trusted
wife of the greatest of them all, she gave her soul to the
training of her children in the nurture and admonition of
the Lord. No wife ever had a finer tribute from her husband than Increase Mather wrote in his diary late in life,
for the eyes of his children. She gave her son to God
and his service as the best thing her heart could conceive
for his welfare. To this may be added that he had a
father who never forgot the duties of home. His company was a school for his son ; his example was an education; his position was an inspiration, and his piety was an
incitement to a holy life.

Having glanced at the parentage of the child, we will
now take a view of his birthplace. Boston had been settled about thirty-three years, and had become not only
the capital of the " Bay," but the leading seaport of all
the northern colonies. There were many ports and havens
on our coast, but Boston had then the preëminence' which
has been kept in all the years of our history. Her sailors
went up and down our long-extended coast, to the West
India Islands, to Europe and Africa, and sometimes to the
far east of the Indian seas. Boston was a busy, bustling,
town, the center of navigation, the metropolis of trade
for a large section of country, and the seat of power.
The officials of the colony from the first had the air and
self-respect of statesmen and generals. With modesty
and firmness they went forward as if conscious of the
greatness of the future. The merchants were enterprising and thrifty; the mechanics and farmers were intelligent and industrious ; the leading men were endowed with
education and discretion, and the clergy ranked with the
most accomplished of Old England, where ·most of them
had first seen the light and received their education.

At this time (1663) there were about forty towns in the colony of Massachusetts Bay and not far from ten in Plymouth Colony. The number of churches in both colonies was fifty. Many of the towns were flourishing. Those near the coast united fishing and commerce to the cultivation of the land, and grew in population and wealth more rapidly than the inland towns and those on the Indian frontier. But in forty-three years from the landing of the Pilgrims and thirty-five from the first settlement of the Bay, in Salem, great progress had been made in various branches of business, in education, and in religion.

The New England colonies had become important. They were growing and becoming more and more efficient in government; they had learned how to maintain their rights in relation to the imperial government, and their children grew up in the school of intelligence, liberty and law, morality and piety. Perhaps it may be said with some show of truth that New England was, on the whole, the best place in the whole British dominions at that time in which to be born, and to be educated into the privileges and duties of a freeborn Englishman. A child of bright mind and good parentage, born here any time between 1660 and 1688, had no occasion to envy one born in England or Scotland, of any rank, during that period. If of a dissenting family, his condition and prospects were in many respects preferable. His chances for success in business and the secure possession of his gains, for education, for position, for power, and for the enjoyment of religious rights, were better, as a general rule, than that of the child born in the mother country. The lowliest youth was not held down by caste or public opinion or exclusive privilege. The school was open to him and the college beckoned him upward. As a farmer, he was more honorable than the English yeoman; as a mechanic, his children could associate with the highest in the schools ; as a trader or a navigator, he could acquire a competency, and often wealth. He could vote in town, parish, and colony affairs. The way was open to him to minor offices, to the magistracy, to military promotion, to the general court, to the council, and even to the office of governor, as in the case of Sir William Phips.

If a boy desired learning, fame, or a field of usefulness, he need not cross the ocean, enter the university, or seek the honors of public life. Cotton Mather here in the wilderness became one of the most learned men of the age, and that in no narrow sense. He "intermeddled with all knowledge," and that in the most thorough manner. Though thousands of miles from the great capitals and illustrious universities of Europe, his name became a household word among the dispensers of fame. His foreign correspondence was so extensive that his son and biographer writes : "I have known him, at one time, to have above fifty correspondents beyond sea." Among these were some of the most learned and famous men in Europe. In the same line is the testimony of Rev. Dr. Thomas Prince, in these words : "Dr. Cotton Mather, though born and constantly residing in this remote corner of America, has yet, for near these forty years (1688–1728), made so rising and great a figure in the learned world, as has attracted to him, while alive, the eyes of many at the farthest distance ; and now deceased, can't but raise a very general wish to see the series, and more especially the domestic part of so distinguished a life exhibited. His printed writings, so full of piety and various erudition, his vast correspondence and the continual reports of travelers who had conversed with him, had spread his reputation into other countries. And when, about fourteen years ago (1714), I traveled abroad,

I could not but admire to what extent his fame had reached, and how inquisitive were gentlemen of letters to hear and know of the most particular and lively manner, both of his private conversation and public performances among us." The fame thus acquired was enduring. Though it has been the fashion in some quarters to sneer at Cotton Mather, his name, always *clarum et venerabile*, is becoming more resplendent as receding time hides all but his greatest contemporaries, and leaves him conspicuous.

If we consider his position for usefulness, it will be hard to name one, in the new world or the old, who surpassed him in his generation. Baxter and Howe exerted a mighty influence for good in their day, and afterwards Owen and Jeremy Taylor, in far different directions, upheld the cause of learning and piety. Tillotson, as a parish priest and as archbishop of Canterbury, was a great power for righteousness among the people and the nobility, and in the closet of King William and Queen Mary; but not one of them, or of their renowned contemporaries, surpassed the humble pastor of the North Church in Boston in all the ways of secular and Christian beneficence. Every moment of a most busy life was devoted to the welfare of others.

The boy thus born and placed began his education at home. He was almost preternaturally bright and thoughtful. His perceptive faculties were keen, and every object presented to sight or hearing secured attention. He drank in knowledge as the thirsty earth imbibes water. When quite young he entered school under the tuition and mastership of the once famous and still honored Benjamin Thompson, a very learned man, a wit, and a poet after a fashion, and a man who had withal a rare gift of teaching. Thompson was familiar with Latin and

Greek literature, and taught with great thoroughness. Next young Mather came under the tuition of the more famous Ezekiel Cheever, one of the ablest educators in the annals of New England.

His religious education went on while he was preparing for college. His son tells us that "he began to pray almost as soon as to speak." He continued to "pray while a schoolboy. He used no forms in secret, but wrote some prayers for the use of his schoolfellows. Very early in life he wrote notes of sermons after returning from meeting." He was so fond of the Bible that he read fifteen chapters a day, in three courses of five at a time; nothing less could satisfy him.

He also joined a society of youths who met on Sabbath evenings. It is said that it was in these meetings that he took "his first rise in the art of speaking and praying." When very young he thought it his duty "to give unto the Lord of all some part of the small substance which was afforded him."

At the age of twelve years and about six months (1675) he was admitted to the freshman class in Harvard College. Though a mere boy in years and stature, he was well prepared. He had written many Latin exercises, and, in the words of his son, "had conversed with Tully, Terence, Ovid, and Virgil. He had gone through the Greek Testament, and had entered upon Socrates and Homer." In those days candidates were required to read the classic authors at sight. In addition, he had begun the Hebrew grammar, a study unknown, in recent times, in most colleges in any part of the course except in an extra class of seniors who have the ministry in view. His pace was rapid after entering college, being impelled forward by his native love of learning and by the influences that surrounded him. He was a boy of great expectations. His son Samuel writes: "If what some great men have hinted be true, 'Nemo vir magnus sine afflatu,' while he was yet young he bade fair to be great, for he believed he should be so; he expected it; and therefore (*multa tulit, fecit,* etc.) he bore and did many things, and disregarded all the difficulties that would encompass him."

His intimate friends and the president of the college fostered these high expectations. At the beginning of his college course, President Hoar prophesied his future eminence by giving for his first declamation the following motto from the great Latin poet: —

"Telemacho veniet, vivat modo, fortior aetas."

We are told that he mastered the Hebrew perfectly; that he digested " Richardson's Tables," and transcribed them; that he composed systems of logic and physics which other students used afterwards; and in short, "described the circle of all the academical studies." But his studies were not confined to the college course. He read many books with care, and made " ingenuous remarks upon them in his diary." In this respect he left college different from many graduates who are marked high for scholarship, but who are shamefully ignorant of general literature.

Young Mather entered college in 1675, when Leonard Hoar was at the head, and took his first degree in the summer of 1679, from the hands of Rev. Urian Oakes. Both were men of ability and character, though the first, for unexplained reasons, was unpopular, and therefore resigned. This was the period of the great Indian, or King Philip's, War, which began in the summer of 1675 and continued into the middle of 1677. It resulted in the death of Philip and the overthrow of the aboriginal power in New England. It was a stirring time, when student life must have partaken of the general spirit and excitement. Probably half the students came from towns which suffered from fire, pillage, or massacre, and perhaps from all these forms of Indian violence.

The reputation of our student rose steadily through his whole college course. He was "pretty healthy," had a "capacity for learning," and a "modest inquisitiveness," all of which conduced to high scholarship. When he took his degree, President Oakes, in a Latin oration, spoke of him in terms of eulogy which nothing could justify but the most extraordinary degree of character and culture; terms which would have turned the head of any but a remarkable youth of sixteen. These are his words: "Mather is named Cotton Mather. What a name! My hearers, I mistake; I ought to have said what names! I shall not speak of his father, for I dare not praise him to his face. But should he resemble his venerable grandfathers, John Cotton and Richard Mather, in piety, learning, splendor of intellect, solidity of judgment, prudence, and wisdom, he will indeed bear the palm. And I have confidence that in this young man Cotton and Mather will be united and flourish again."

It is worthy of note that young Mather's religious character seems to have developed while he was in college, though he was not received into the church until about the time of his graduation. From the church records it appears that John Cotton and Cotton Mather united with the North Church "31 d., 6 m., 1679" (August 31, 1679). For this solemn service he had been preparing for years. It has been already stated that he prayed in secret and read the Bible with absorbing interest in boyhood, and that he wrote prayers for some of his comrades to use in private. It may be added that he sometimes spoke to his playmates on religious duties. His son writes that "at fourteen he kept his days of fasting and prayer; at fifteen he studied Dr. Hall on Meditation and other books, and formed a *Method* of Meditating." This he drew out at length, and by following his method not only made his mental acquisitions secure, but had them at command whenever needed.

At the time of uniting with the church he was past sixteen years of age. Before doing so, he went through a process of thorough self-examination, of which this was the record : —

1. *Concerning my faith.*

I am convinced of the utter insufficiency, in my own righteousness, to procure my salvation. . . .

I perceive now no other way for my salvation, but only by the Lord Jesus Christ. Refuge fails elsewhere on every hand.

I behold a fulness and a beauty in Jesus Christ; he is worth loving, worth prizing, worth following.

2. *Concerning my repentance.*

I abhor sin, because it is abhorred by God and contrary to him.

Sin is my heavy burden; death itself would be welcome to me to free me from such a burden.

3. *Concerning my love.*

I long to see and know the favor of God unto me; the sight of that would make all my afflictions light.

I desire to be as active as may be in promoting the honor of God; and I seldom come into any company without contriving whether I may not act or speak something for that in it, before I leave it.

I am sorry that I love God no more.

With such views and feelings the student, just as he was leaving college and stepping into the world, entered into covenant with Christ and his Church. The recorded evidence of spiritual growth in his diary, and the numerous products of his pen, and the almost incredible amount of work done by him in all forms of Christian effort show how well he kept his vows.

The following letter, written in the early part of young

Mather's senior year, finds its place here. It has been truly said that this was a remarkable letter for one of the writer's age. It is interesting also in the facts stated. The other children referred to in it as having escaped the smallpox were Elizabeth, Samuel, and Abigail. Three other children were born in following years. The *luto sata* refers to the muddy streets near the dock. The letter was addressed to his uncle, young John Cotton, at Plymouth, and dated November, 1678.

I should fling a "*prob pudor*" upon my delayes of doing you that service that duty does as much oblige as you desire, but that I am made brazen-faced by excuses sufficient to bear me out.

I wonder what you impute my non-transmission of those things of yours which are in my hands to. I know your candor will not charge me with Idleness. Your courtesy will not Implead me for forgetfulness, & most of all, you, without reason, will not accuse mee of unwillingness to serve you in what I may, even *usqᵉ ad aras*, and if possible, there. But if I am of age to speak for myself, sickness, which had the first part in hindrance, was succeeded by uncertainty of conveyance, and that again seconded by other avocations. How frequently and unweariedly I have been engaged in seeking Plymouth boat, if noth. else, yet my old shooes wil testify, who, in this time, when Boston is become an other *Lutelia* (*cf. Luto sata*) do proclaim that they wanted a pair of Golo-shooes when traveling near the Dock-head. I would bee more frequent in *Letters Testimonial* of my gratitude, if I could but either fling salt on the tail of Time, or get the wind and tide to be favorable to my designs, which possibly may in a sense bee before the Greek Calends.

Never was it such a time in Boston. Boston burying places never filled so fast. It is easy to tell the time wherein we did not use to have the bells tolling for burials on a sabbath day morning by sunrise; to have 7 buried on a sabbath day night, after Meeting, — To have coffins crossing each other as they have been carried in the streets, — To have, I know not how many corpses following each other close at their heels, — To have 38 dye in one week — 6, 7, 8, or 9 in a day; yet thus hath it lately been; and thus it is at this day. Above 340 have died of the Small Pox in Boston since it first assaulted the place. To attempt a Bill of Mortality and number the very spires of grass in a Burying Place seem to have a parity of difficulty and in accomplishment. . . . At first the gradual mercy of God to my father's family was observable and remarkable. First, my Brother Nath. gently smitten, and I more gently than hee, and my Sr. Sarah yet more gently than I. But the order is broken on my sister Maria wº, on the same month & day of the month that my father was visited with the same disease 21 years agoe, was taken very ill; the symptoms grievous, and our fears grᵗ. Sometimes light-headed, but her father prayed down mercy for her and her pox having turned a day or 2 agoe, shee is now so *inter spemque metumque locata*, that *spes* bears down the scales. So that of my father's septenary of childr: 4 have been visited. God fit and prepare for the 3 strokes that are yet behind.

Sir. Let us not want the help of your prayers for all of us, especially for him who is

Not more your Nephew than desirous to be

Your . . . & servant, C. M.

CHAPTER II.

SOME graduates leave a traditional fame behind them, and their sayings, their attainments, or their exploits are heard of and repeated by following classes for a generation. Mather not only left such a reputation, but some of his manuscripts were used by students who came after him. He had begun to make a name already, and expectations of future eminence were high. One of his friends wrote of him in his seventeenth year in this strain: —

> For grace and art, and an illustrious fame,
> Who would not look from such an ominous name:
> Where two great names their sanctuary take,
> And in a third combined a greater make?

One of the first public services of the youthful graduate was an address on "Religious Societies, — Proposals for the Revival of Dying Religion, by well-ordered Societies for that purpose; with a brief discourse unto a religious Society on the first day of their meeting." This might have been called a sermon, only it was spoken two years before the author was approbated to preach. What is curious about it is the fact that it was not published until 1724, with this note: —

"In this essay there is one thing a little singular. The sermon in it is one that I entertained my neighbors withal before I was a public preacher, when I was but sixteen years of age. It may be this is the first sermon from one of that age that has been published."

After graduation, Mather seems to have studied with

redoubled energy. We find nothing in his journals, diaries, or letters, giving a hint of vacation or recreations, except an occasional visit to Plymouth, Lynn, or some other place not remote from his home. His delight was in reading, studying, writing, teaching, and preaching in the years preceding his approbation, in 1682, when a little over nineteen years of age. He had been reared under the idea of being a minister. That was the wish of his parents, and on that his own heart had been fixed; but a serious impediment in his speech almost forced him to abandon the hope of entering the pastorate and becoming a public speaker. A troublesome stutter prevented ready and distinct utterance. He therefore devoted some time to the study of medicine, with a view to the life and calling of a physician. In this pursuit he doubtless exhibited his usual energy and persistence, and probably learned all that could be gleaned from medical books at the time, and more than entered into the curriculum of the majority of young doctors in those days.

Writers who were not aware of this episode in his life, or who have ignored it, have left the impression that he dabbled in what he was entirely ignorant of, and what was outside of his province, when he wrote on medical subjects, and also when he introduced inoculation for the smallpox. His writings on the healing art have furnished some merriment for the doctors of recent times, because of the curious and ridiculous remedies prescribed, but these were not invented by him. He was merely the exponent of medical science in his day, which fact Dr. Samuel A. Green has recognized in his Historical Discourse.

But though Cotton Mather the youth was interested in the study of medicine, and seemed to have in him the elements of a close, accurate student, and of an enlightened practitioner, the bent of his genius and the aspiration of his heart bore him, as on a tidal wave, into the pulpit. He prayed for relief from his impediment and made efforts to overcome it; but what set him on the practical course of improvement was the advice of " good old schoolmaster Mr. Corlet," who said to him : " Sir, I should be glad if you should oblige yourself to a dilated deliberation in speaking, for as in singing there is no one who stammers, so by prolonging your pronunciation you will get an habit of speaking without hesitation." He followed this advice with advantage, and though he had, " with great application studied physic for some time," he now turned with no less ardor to prepare for the duties of the sacred office. By constant effort he became a ready and, in time, a powerful speaker.

Some of his time was devoted to teaching. Among his scholars were his two younger brothers, Nathaniel and Samuel, and those of his sisters who were of suitable age, probably Maria, Elizabeth, and Sarah, the latter of whom was in her ninth year. Besides these, he had other pupils in various stages of their education. As a teacher he was accurate, enthusiastic, and inspiring.

But in the course of a year or two, in 1680, preaching was added to his other pursuits. While in college he had become an uncommonly accurate student in the Hebrew language, for one so young. Besides, some of his reading had a direct bearing on his preparation for the ministry. Following his grandfather and father, he discarded some of the physics and metaphysics of Aristotle (preferring the dialectics of Peter Ramus), and thus gained clearer views of the nature and character of God and of the relations of mankind to the moral Governor of the universe.

At the commencement, in 1681, his father being then president, when about eighteen years and a half old, he proceeded Master of Arts. For his thesis he maintained that the vowel points are of divine origin. This opinion he laid aside as he became more familiar with Hebrew, for he learned to read the language without points, like a native Jew, and thereat concluded that they were not of supernatural origin, but were the invention of men for the sake of convenience.

But previous to this time, even as early as August 22, 1680, he preached in the meetinghouse in Dorchester, where his grandfather had officiated more than thirty years. His first text was: "The Spirit of the Lord is upon me, because he hath anointed me to preach the gospel to the poor; he hath sent me to heal the broken-hearted, to preach deliverance to the captives, and recovering of sight to the blind, to set at liberty them that are bruised" (Luke 4: 18). The next Sunday he preached for his father in Boston, and the Sunday following he was in the pulpit of the First Church, where his grandfather Cotton had ministered with great distinction.

Mr. Mather began a diary very early in life, but none of it is extant earlier than 1681, February 12, when he was eighteen years of age. The following was written on that day, or soon after, and it is copied here, as it shows the spirit and intentions of the writer when he began his public career: —

This day was filled with the devotions and enjoyments of a raised soul. But there were especially two things whereabout the sallies of my soul were considerable, not only on this day, but at many other times in this part of my life. One thing wherein I was more forcibly concerned, was that great thing of a *Closure* with the Lord Jesus Christ. In the prosecution of this matter I may truly say, 't was the Spirit of God that was my Teacher. No man or book showed me the way of pressing this glorious transaction; but this day I used such words as these, among others, before the Redeemer of my soul. Oh! my dear Lord: thy Father hath committed my soul into thy hands. There 's a Covenant of Redemption wherein I am concerned. I know my election by my vocation, and my concernment in that Covenant, by my being made willing to come under the shadow of thy wings, in the Covenant of grace. Now, in that Covenant, the Father said unto the Son: Such an elect son there is that I will bring into thy fold, and thou shalt undertake for that soul as a sufficient and an eternal Saviour. Therefore I am now in thy hands, O my Lord. Thy Father hath put me there, and I have put myself there. O save me! O heal me! O work for me! Work in me the good pleasure of thy goodness! And afterwards I said, Lord, I have been leaving my soul, this day, with Jesus Christ, for thou hast bid me to believe that I shall be saved by him. Lord, I do believe that there never came a poor soul to the Lord Jesus Christ in vain; I do believe that I myself shall not find it in vain. He will do great things for me. He has already done enough to leave me without any cause of repenting that I have, through so much agony of soul, come unto him. Yea, but I believe that he has more still to do for me. Having been the Author, he will be the Finisher of my faith.

Though he had improved in his speech so far as to be encouraged, yet the impediment was not wholly overcome. He adds: —

Another thing that much exercised me was, that I might not be left without necessary supplies of *speech* for my ministry. God may please so far to let my infirmity remain, that, although by a careful deliberation, my public services were freed from any blemish by it, yet I was, by his wisdom, kept in continual *care* and *fear* and *faith* concerning it. How many thousands of solicitous thoughts I underwent concerning it, is best known to him, who by those thoughts, drew me and kept me nearer to himself.

As the design of this memoir is, in part at least, to exhibit the character and views of the subject of it, another passage will be given. It is evident in this case that no miraculous cure was wrought upon the vocal organs, but that constant care in speaking with "dilated deliberation" was crowned with success. But he made his infirmity the subject of prayer, and his very act of prayer would serve to keep him firm in his purpose to coerce his vocal mechanism into obedience to the desires

of his heart.   But for the glimpse they give into his heart
we will read his words : —

On this day particularly, I resolved, Lord, thou art he that made
man's mouth.   Thou wast angry with Moses because he would not
make that consideration an argument for faith that thou wouldest be
with his mouth.   And now, because I would not so sin, therefore I
trust in thee.   Thou dost send me forth as thou didst Moses, in
service for thy name, among thy people ; and thou who didst make
man's mouth, and make my mouth, wilt be with my mouth.   It was
also once used as a bottom for faith.   The Lord hath, and therefore
the Lord will.   Now for a blessed experience which I have already had
of the help ; yea, such an experience as hath caused me to promise that
I would never distrust more.   Thou sayest, none of them who trust in
thee shall be desolate.   But how desolate shall I be, if I am left without speech for thy work?   I trust in thee, and therefore I shall not be.
Thou sayest, thou wilt never forsake them that seek thee.   But I have
sought thee, and I will seek thee, as long as I have a day to live.
And now, O Lord, I will believingly wait on thee.   I shall see a token
for good.   Thy people also shall be witnesses of the token.

The reader cannot fail to notice how near to God this
young man was trying to live.   With awful reverence and
childlike fear he talked with God, as it were, face to face.
At the time the above lines were written he drew up
some resolutions which related, not merely to his gift of
speech, but which covered his whole course of living.
They will serve to evince his spirit, and may afford an
example to other youth who are studying how to live
a life of active holiness.   Here follow the resolutions : —

As to my walk with God ; Lord, thou makest me to *will*; help me to
resolve : —
   I.   As to my Thoughts.
   1.   Keep God, and Christ, and heaven much in my thoughts.
   2.   Watch and pray against lascivious thoughts, ambitious thoughts,
and wandering thoughts in the times of devotion.
   II.   As to my Words.
   1.   Words few and deliberate.
   2.   My tongue is the Lord's, and to be used for him.

3. Pray before speaking, or answering a weighty question.
4. Speak ill of no man except on a good ground, and a right end.
5. In visits, consider what I may do for God.
III. As to my Course of Duties.
  1. Pray at least three times a day.
  2. Meditate once a day; *doctrinal* and *practical*.
These Questions at night.
  1. What has been the mercy of God to me to-day?
  2. What my carriage before God?
  3. Is my immortal spirit safe if I die this night?

He resolved also "to lead a life of heavenly ejaculations; to be diligent in observing and recording illustrious
providences"; and in all "continually going unto Christ
as the only physician and Redeemer of my soul." He
adds that the "singular assistances which the God of
heaven gave unto me, in my public ministrations on the
following Sabbath were such as caused me to draw up this
conclusion: I believe I shall have a glorious presence of
God with me through my whole ministry." This certainly
proved true, to an extraordinary degree, in the course of
a long and fruitful pastorate; and yet we often meet with
entries in the diary which indicate a desire to have evident "tokens" on which his "assurances" might rest.

The evidence of the people's approbation was emphatic,
for "God so strangely inclined the hearts of the people
in the congregation, that, besides their weekly collections
every Lord's day, they did about this time, subscribe
about seventy pounds for my encouragement in my public
service the ensuing year."

The above subscription was in close connection with
a vote of the church, on the twenty-third of February,
1681, inviting him to be the assistant of his father in
the ministry.

The disposition of the man at this time is shown by
the following detached sentences: "I am of Melanch-

thon's mind, who said, 'Let who will abound and increase
in riches ; they may for all me. I look upon my work as
my treasure.'" Then Mather added : "That a power and
opportunity to do good, not only gives a right to the doing
of it, but also makes the doing of it a duty."

At the close of the Lord's day, March 23, he wrote as
follows in his diary : "Coming home from the public service wherein I had enjoyed the special assistance of God,
I wrote these words. I believe that I am a chosen vessel,
and that the Lord will pour mercy unto me till I have
arrived unto a fullness of eternal glory ! Lord, help me
to serve thee, love thee, glorify thy name. Fill me with
thy Spirit. It will be so ! Oh, who am I that I should
be filled with the Spirit of the holy God ! But it will be
so ! (Is. 44 : 3.) This day in the assurances, the glorious and ravishing assurances of the divine love, my
joys were almost insupportable."

It must be kept in mind that these words were not
printed for the public to read, or spoken to the ear of a
most intimate friend. They were simply the delightful
thoughts of his own secret soul. Remembering this fact,
the charges of pride, conceit, and vanity sometimes made
against the writer seem not only baseless, but unkind.

Mather spent much time in devotions, and in these his
whole soul was so engaged that he was almost exhausted.
He also, at times, found himself under strong distempers,
and especially in an idle frame of soul, fearing God would
"take a farewell of him." But prayer was a resort in all
these spiritual trials. "When I can't pray," he said, "I'll
groan." In his dependence on God, he wrote : "Though
thou grindest me to powder, I will never leave thee;
though thou killest me, I will put my trust in thee." He
was willing to die if the Lord called, but anxious to do
something and also to "write something that might do

good to young persons when he was dead and gone."
These two desires or passions characterized him through
life. He wanted to do and write in the way of usefulness,
and his heart was drawn to the young. To extreme old
age he felt special interest in the children and youth of
his flock and of the whole town.

The following incident gives us a view of his way of
improving every occasion to recover men from a life of
neglected duty : —

> There was an honest man in the town whom I lovingly and fre-
> quently rebuked for his neglecting to join himself unto some church of
> the Lord Jesus Christ. His indisposition thereto continuing, I told
> him, " Well, the God of heaven hath by his *word* been calling upon
> you; expect now to have him speak unto you by a *blow*." A few
> days after this, the honest man fell down from the top of a house, and
> received a blow whereof he lay for some time as dead. But, coming
> to himself, one of the first things he thought on was what I had said
> unto him, under the sense whereof he quickly went and joined himself
> with the South Church.

Of this event Mather inquires: "What shall I make
of it ? "

Rather frequent citations will be made from the diary,
because it lets us into the inner life of the writer in his
youth, and the beginning of his ministry. The rest of
his life was but the unfolding and expanding of what was
here in the bud. It will be seen how early he was beset
by the temptations which assail rising young men, and
with what unusual effort he tried to discipline his heart.
He spent the fourteenth day of May in fasting, with
prayer, on account of "old iniquities and late impurities," and was much grieved about his "proud, wanton,
and slothful heart." The day closed with high enjoyments. His heart was melted with a marvelous assurance
that he should enjoy much of the divine presence in his
ministry.

An unsympathizing critic, not in the habit of chastising his own imperfection, might infer that the writer was a man of exceptional proneness to sin. But when such an indefatigable worker bewails his sloth, it is easy to see that he used the same merciless severity in regard to "wanton and proud thoughts."

Ten days later, in the morning, he went into the meetinghouse for "some convenience of study," when a strong impression on his mind led him to go into the pew of a gentleman of good fashion and quality and earnestly pray that the "Lord would work thoroughly and savingly on his heart"; and he felt assured that at some time his prayer would be answered. About eleven years afterwards the man was converted, and became a worthy member of the church and a great blessing and comfort to Mr. Mather. From this it is inferred that he sometimes reviewed his diary, and made insertions like the above, showing answers to prayer, or results from former endeavors.

A sermon from his father, on the sin of pride, much affected him. He speaks of this as the sin of young ministers, and he humbled himself before God for the pride of his heart.

This battle with pride, as he calls it, which had a flavor of gratified vanity, perhaps, and on that account was the more noxious, was carried on vigorously, and there was need of it. No young minister, in all the years since Boston was founded, has met greater or more discriminating applause : and as approbation was very pleasing to him, he was in danger of being swollen with self-conceit. Many young men in public life, with half the breeze of popularity that filled his sails, have become vain and insolent ; but young Mather was led to a deeper sense of his unworthiness by this dangerous show of public favor.

Vast audiences greeted him at home and wherever he went. The hearers, old and young, female and male, unlearned and educated, hung upon his speech, whether one hour or two hours long, even if preceded by an hour of prayer. He could not help inhaling the fragrance from the cloud of incense which ensphered him, but he struggled manfully and prayerfully to nullify its baneful effects.

It is instructive to read of this contest and victory. Vanity and pride are besetments that can be cast out only by prayer with fasting. This is especially true when favor swells to adulation, and comes from the wise and the beautiful alike. Mather saw his danger, and set himself to overcome his easily besetting sin. On the eleventh of June he fasted and prayed, "fighting with pride." He found himself "wofully guilty in two respects": 1. Self-applause, when he had been successful in "preaching or praying with enlargement," or answering questions "presently and suitably." 2. "Affectation of preëminency far above what can belong to my own age or worth, and above others that are far more deserving than myself." It was a determined struggle within his soul. And yet the record of this contest with pride has been made the occasion of censure and ridicule, as being itself a proof of the writer's conceit.

Seven days later, on Saturday, which was always a day of self-communing and of communion with God, Mather drew out his experience at some length. He kept this day as a time of thanksgiving before the Lord. He had never heard of but one person — his grandfather, John Cotton — who had been accustomed to keep such days. The day was spent in "recollecting merciful dispensations." The "greatness and fulness of them" were registered in his Memorials, and he gratefully acknowledged them in prayer.

the following week.   His or
reception of the Master's de
ing Tuesday, the ninth, and,
degree was received from h
when I am yet about half a
age; and all the circumst
were ordered by a very sens
theme, about the Hebrew
mentioned.

In September he began
called *rising thoughts*.   "
Scripture; sometimes on s
quence to eternal interests
thoughts placed on divine
"better disposed unto fea
These truths would sanc
ariah 13: 1: "In that
opened to the house of
Jerusalem for sin and f
observations:— 1. "Th
fitly compared to a foun
3. It is for the washing
In this way he went o
the Bible in these morr
multitudes of cases ref
Christianitie."   The
much rich thought wo
ing scraps of time wh
paper, they would s
public use.

Next we are introd
ful preacher.   He b
poor, and also of the
of September "thre

Under date of the nineteenth, being Lord's day, he writes: "About this time I bought a *Spanish Indian*, and bestowed him for a servant on my father, with the impression that some special and signal return will follow. (Now see a record in the thirty-fourth year of my life.) This will come in due time." The query may here arise, whether he were in the habit of giving, on the ground of his hope that he would thereby secure some mark of divine favor. His thrifty charity has excited what seems like a sneer in some quarters. Such a thought would have been indignantly spurned. In fact he held that all giving should be without the hope of reward as the motive for benevolence, though he believed, without doubt, that filial piety would be pleasing to his heavenly Father. In the case before us there is no proof that the gift was inspired by the hope of reward. It is written merely that he had an "impression" that such would be the case, when he made the present; but the act of kindness to his father sprang from his filial regard.

His desire to be useful, which was one of the consuming passions of his life, is shown by lines written on the seventh of July. He proposed *reform* in regard to several things: 1. "In respect to myself: laboring after a greater sense of the *Realities* of the *Invisibles*." 2. To improve his time in general. 3. "In respect of my father's family." That is, to induce his brothers and sisters, as many as were capable thereof, to take their Bibles, "when the Scripture was read, morning and evening, before prayer, and attentively accompany the vocal reader." In respect to his sisters, to "set as many of them as he could to spend an hour together every day: half of it in writing, and half of it furnishing themselves with knowledge about the matter of religion." At this time he had five brothers and sisters old enough to derive great benefit

from such a practice.
and the eldest sixteen y
sisters as they grew up
if not instruction.

About the middle of
pain in the teeth and
to the cause or design
had sinned by "sin
and by evil speaking,
speaking.

There is more re
Mather's writings —
usual in pulpit lit
Here is a brief exa
looked through the
if the Lord meant
would he have ever
to glorify him on e

We have already
in the education a
and sisters, and a
good of the young
interest continue
of the vigorous
the sixth of A
though he had
same exercise, in
ing at which h
different parts o
Probably this s
junior pastor.

The special
humiliation an
be carried thr

one for rape, and two negroes for burning a house, and persons therein." Mather "had a feeling of deep humiliation for the sin of his own heart, which might have led him into such sins, if God's grace had not kept him," and for this grace he was thankful. It soon became a habit with him to visit the poor and devise means for helping them. Poor debtors in prison had his sympathy, prayers, and pecuniary aid. And while yet young he became, as it were, the minister of the criminal classes, as thieves, incendiaries, pirates, and murderers. No man could be more faithful, and at the same time kind-hearted, in dealing with them.

The working of his mind on the third of October will be read with different feelings by different persons. One class may suspect that the young man was stirred by burning ambition to equal or excel his ancestors; while another class, more charitable and possibly more correct, may regard him as moved to a holy emulation by the example of such men as his father and his two grandfathers. It is certainly natural as well as praiseworthy for noble youth to be fired with resolution to attain to the excellence of their predecessors. After a day spent in "sowing the tears of repentance and supplication in agonies and prayers," the record closed with these words: "Lord, I know that thou wilt be with me. Lord, I know that thou wilt improve me in eminent service for thy name. Lord, I know thou wilt signalize me, as thou hast my father, my grandfathers, and my uncles before me. Hallelujah." His uncles Samuel and Nathaniel were eminent among the ministers of England.

The ninth of October was a day of usual devotion in preparation for the Lord's day, in reference to which Mather writes: "The Lord made me somewhat an instrument of his praise, to endeavor to his praise yesterday.

I went this day into the pulpit of my old grandfather Cotton, in the Old Church of Boston, and there, being thereto called, I preached with a very singular assistance of the Lord; yea, such was his powerful presence with me, that some afterwards declared their melted and broken hearts could hardly forbear crying out aloud in the assembly."

About this time he kept a private fast before the Lord on account of "temptations to slothfulness, and some degree of wantonness"; and this when he was working like a fast-driven engine.

The entries in the diary in November are interesting, as will be seen in what follows: "It was proposed among many devout persons in this country to keep a concert of prayer in private every Monday, between eleven and twelve A.M., to pray purely on behalf of the church abroad, withering under grievous persecutions, and our own land now in many threatening circumstances. A similar practice had been agreed among many in Great Britain and Ireland, and thence came here. Many good men held aloof from it, as having somewhat of superstition in it." Mather favored it, and many other pious people in this country came into this fellowship of prayer. He adds that "many good men did afterwards highly bless God for the proposal." We here notice a characteristic trait of his, all his life, which was to know a good thing when he saw it, and to promote it, from whatever source it might come. He followed up this plan of prayer in private for a long while. Perhaps the practice lingered along in a quiet way till the time of Edwards, when Christians in Scotland and New England agreed to keep a similar concert of prayer, which is now superseded by our regular concert of prayer for foreign missions.

In this same month of November the first overture

from a distant people came to our youthful preacher, which
he notices in these words : "Messengers came from the
ancient and famous church of New Haven, desiring me
to become their pastor." He was now three months less
than nineteen years old, and it seems strange that such
a church should have invited a boy, so to speak, to settle
with them. This was the church of John Davenport, and
the "call" was a striking proof of the reputation of the
youthful preacher. That church would prefer none but
the best, and New Haven was a very desirable place of
residence. But he does not seem at first to have felt any
desire to remove thither, and the invitation was declined.

His own church took immediate measures to fix his
abode with them. On the twenty-eighth of December
they renewed their vote for the continuance of his public
labors among them, adding that it "should be in order to
his settlement as their pastor." They also voted a salary
of £70 per annum. In view of this state of things he
set apart a day to "humble himself before the Lord, and
implore favor in two regards," 1. "the freedom of my
speech, which for some difficulties upon it was become a
matter of more than ordinary thoughtfulness unto me ;
and, 2. the *guidance* of all concerned between our church
and myself." His impediment seems to have returned in
a measure, and he now took urgent means by prayer, and
by strict attention to utterance, to conquer the difficulty.
Gradually he succeeded and, perhaps through the grave
deliberation necessary to distinctness, became a more
effective speaker than if he had been naturally fluent.

On the second of February, 1682, the church in New
Haven, six days before his birthday, "renewed their addresses," so he writes in his diary, "unto poor, vile me to
become their pastor ; but this day I wrote unto them the
indisposition which I had unto the thing which I desired.

My reason was, because the church of North Boston would have entertained uncomfortable dissatisfactions at my father, if after so many importunate votes of theirs for my settlement here, he had any way permitted my removal from them."

From this it may be inferred that the renewed invitation from New Haven, a town second to none in the colonies for the intelligence, taste, and piety of its people, appealed with some force to his feelings; but the love of his own congregation, with his filial regard to his father's wishes, decided him to remain. We shall find proof later that Mr. Mather had a warm place in his heart for New Haven, Yale College, and the state of Connecticut.

CHAPTER III.

THE invitation to settle in New Haven as the pastor of the First Church was noted in the last chapter. Mr. Mather continued as his father's assistant through the year 1682. There is no diary of this year extant, though doubtless one was kept. Since he had not yet begun to publish, and was not involved in any way in public affairs, as he became in maturer years, there are no materials for filling out the record of this year. It is known, however, that he was diligent in writing sermons, preaching, visiting in the parish, looking after the poor and the criminals, holding meetings of the young, and in intense study. Many hours were also given to secret devotions. He was laying the deep, broad, and solid foundations of his vast superstructure of learning in all branches of human science and divine knowledge.

It is worthy of note that Mather never, in his whole life, showed any desire to go abroad, or to seek any abode away from Boston. Several young men born here went to England as ministers or were employed there in some public business. His father was there on two occasions: the first, about a year after his graduation in 1657, when he remained nearly four years; and the second in 1688. His sojourn was drawn out till 1692. Two of his uncles, Samuel and Nathaniel, spent almost the whole of their ministerial life in England or Ireland, and his youngest brother, Samuel, was settled many years in Witney, Oxfordshire. But Cotton Mather loved Boston; he loved

the North Church, he loved his country, and he delighted
to serve his Master here. Therefore in that service he
wore himself out in his native town.

The following extract from his diary, though belonging
to the next year by date, is inserted here because it shows
his activity, and the nature of his engagements, except in
pastoral work, during several years before and after. It is
dated August 28, 1683.

> Legi Exod. 34, 35, 36. Oravi. Examinavi adoloscentulos. Legi
> Cartesium. Legi Commentatores in — 6: 37. Paravi concionem.
> Orationi interfui domesticae. Audivi pupillos recitantes. Legi Salmon
> Pharmacop. Pransus sum. Visitavi pluros amicos. Legi varia.
> Paravi concionem. Audivi pupillos recitantes.[1] Meditat. on the
> exceeding willingness of the Lord Jesus to do good unto them that
> come unto him.

After a few words in English, he goes on to say in
Latin that he prayed, taught, worked on a sermon, and
was present at family prayers. We have thus a glimpse
of a scholar's life for a series of years; in fact, from the
time of graduation in 1679 to the time of ordination
in 1685.

On the eighth of January, 1683, he was unanimously
chosen to the office of pastor by the church. He declined
the invitation, but was willing to continue his connection
as assistant to his father, who was the teacher of the
church. One reason was that his father was in the vigor
of his strength, being but forty-three years old; but perhaps the chief cause of his declining was a humble view
of himself. He writes that it caused an "earthquake in
him" to read the words: "They watch for your souls as
those who must give account." It would seem that the

---

[1] I read Exodus 34, 35, 36; prayed; examined the children; read Des Cartes;
read Commentators on — 6: 37; prepared a sermon; took part in family worship;
heard my pupils recite; read Salmon's Pharmacopea; dined; called on a number
of friends; read various books; prepared a sermon; heard pupils recite.

fact of his being not quite twenty years old was an all-sufficient reason for his shrinking from such an onerous position as his father's colleague.

On the twelfth of February, 1683, his birthday, the diary for the ensuing twelve months began with these words: "I am this day twenty years old; but alas, how little have I done for the glory of God all this while! I would this day resolve, especially, two things: 1. To be more diligent in searching the Scriptures. 2. To be more concerned for the welfare of the church whereto I am related."

A week later he recorded a noble and generous purpose which would furnish a good example for any young minister whose parish contains men of means. His entry concerning it is as follows: "A purpose. There are some gentlemen and merchants in whom the good God hath given me an interest; and shall I not improve that interest? I may do well to engage them in agreement together, to single out some godly but needy ministers in the country for the objects of their charity, unto whom their bounty may so express itself that God may be glorified and they themselves gloriously rewarded." Thus had Mather already begun that system of *good devices* for the benefit of others which made his progress through life a path of beneficent light. And his "devices" never appear to have had a reflex look to his own advantage.

March 4, Lord's day. The preaching of his father this day, on the eighth commandment, recalled to Cotton's mind that several years before he had borrowed three small books from a schoolmate with a promise to return them when his friend should call for them. The friend left the country, leaving the books. Now he resolved to lay out ten times their value in good books to give away, not knowing how else, he writes, to have peace in his own mind.

He early learned the true way to make advances in the Christian life. The principle of spiritual goodness being laid in a renewed heart, it was necessary to take definite steps in the way of improvement. Thinking it would glorify God to regulate his tongue, he made these "rules of speech ": —

O Lord God, in Jesus Christ, help me.

1. Let me, in a solemn way, give my speech up unto God as a faculty to be entertainingly improved for him. ,

2. Let my future care in and of my words declare the sincerity of such a dedication.

And therefore let me seek rules of right speaking, 1. By praying daily to God : Lord, let my mouth show forth thy praise. 2. By reading both of exemplary men, and of profitable books, which may teach me the government of my tongue.

Let me then use the rules which I have sought, 1. By being a person of but few words. 2. By being deliberate in the use of my tongue and lips. 3. By avoiding all expressions which I apprehend will trespass on the commandments of God. 4. By rarely coming into company without seeking of useful discourse in the company. 5. By so doing, the tongue of the stammerer shall speak plainly.

Some time before his ordination, but having settlement in view, he planned about "visits to be religiously performed." He set apart one afternoon in the week to visit all the families in the neighborhood, with the design of "bringing persons of all ages and sexes into an acquaintance with God."

The following, dated March 30, may stand for many other passages as indicating the source and the depth of his piety : —

In prayer, the Lord filled me with faith and joy, when I considered that amiable clause in the new covenant: "I will not turn away from them to do them good"; and when I professed unto the Lord, that since the covenant, and all the indescribable blessings of it were offered unto my acceptance, I deliberately lay hold thereon. And I desire not only an interest in all that salvation which the covenant proposed; and

above all, that highest blessedness of being made like unto God and
Jesus Christ : but also I considered that Jesus Christ, the surety of the
covenant, should be the way in which all mercy should be communicated unto me.

And in the same strain he wrote a few days later :
" Let me be abundant in secret prayer. Let me read
some excellent books which my Saviour in his infinite
faithfulness has bestowed on me, and among the rest,
' Howe's Blessedness of the Righteous.' "

The third of May was spent in prayer and fasting,
"upon many calls thereunto." He records : " I will give
one instructive instance unto my few friends with whom I
leave these papers, and particularly recite the method of
my proceedings from the beginning to the conclusion of
the day." It is such passages as these that let us into
his interior character : —

1. I began the day with expressing before the Lord my belief of his
being a rewarder of them who diligently seek him, and my request
that he would now strengthen me to seek him.

2. I then read the chapters of the Bible which occurred unto me in
the course of reading, and those chapters I largely turned into prayers
before the Lord.

3. Afterwards I essayed in meditation, to affect my own heart with
a sense of the manifold vileness wherewith I have provoked God; my
old sins and my *late sins ;* especially my woful unfruitfulness under my
marvelous enjoyments, privileges and advantages ; all which I then
confessed and bewailed upon my knees before God.

4. This done, I sang unto the Lord that hymn of Burton's which is
called Confession of Sin.

5. Hereupon I spent some time in pondering of a profitable and a
seasonable question ; and then in forming of some occasional reflections.

6. I then went again unto my supplications, wherein I considered
that after all my vileness, the Lord is willing to deal with me in the
covenant of grace ; and for that end offered unto me such a surety and
a Saviour as the blessed Jesus ; wherefore I now stirred up myself to
take hold of him, earnestly putting my soul into the hands of the
Mediator, crying unto him that he would convey unto me not only
pardon of sin, but also power against it, and make me a happy subject
of all his redeeming work.

7. Now I sang unto the Lord that hymn — Burton — which is entitled " Humble Petitions and Supplications." And I set myself by further meditation to establish myself in the use of such *rules of speech* as might render me a perfect man.

8. From which I betook myself unto prayer; and my prayer now was especially for such a degree of utterance as from time to time, in my ministry, I might have occasion for. And I had a full assurance that I was heard in this petition.

9. I then sang part of the 51st psalm, and so proceeded unto another prayer, which I presented before the Lord — the desire of Solomon for wisdom — and for the presence of God with me in all the concerns of my ministry.

10. Which being finished, I sang part of the 103d psalm. And then I examined myself by the signs of a *state* of *nature* and a *state* of *grace* given in Mr. N. Vincent's *True Touchstone,* and found joyful causes to hope.

11. In the next place, I made another prayer to recommend unto the blessing of God, my particular friends, and all his people.

12. So I went unto a meeting of Christians that were preparing for the communion to-morrow, and prayed and preached with them.

13. Leaving them, I visited a sick neighbor, and prayed with him.

14. And last of all, I shut up the day, renouncing all apprehension of merit in my own duties, and relying upon the Lord Jesus Christ alone for acceptance and salvation.

If the reader is weary in perusing this record of a day's experience, what must have been the endurance of the youth who actually went through it all ! But this was the spiritual and mental discipline of a person not yet of age ; and it enables us to see the real working cause of those wonderful attainments made by him not only in Christian character, but in becoming the most intelligent, instructive, and delightful converser of his time.

Seven days later we find another entry quite as helpful in laying open his heart to us, and showing the indefatigable pains he took to become an able minister of the New Testament. It was at the close of May 12 that the following lines were written : —

This evening I had much satisfaction of mind in considering what *noble attainments* I should be continually pursuing of. And while I was lying on my couch, in the dark of the evening, I *ex tempore* composed the following hymn, which I then sang unto the Lord.

HIGH ATTAINMENTS.

Lord, what shall I return unto
Him, from whom all my mercies flow?
(1) To me to *live*, it Christ shall be,
For all I do, I 'll do for thee.
(2) My question shall be oft beside,
How Thou mayst most be glorified?
(3) I will not any creature *love*
But in the love of Thee above.
(4) Thy *will* I shall embrace for mine,
And every management of Thine
Shall please me.   (5) A conformity
To Thee shall be my *aim* and *eye*.
(6) Ejaculations shall ascend
Not seldom from me.   (7) I 'll attend
Occasional *reflections*, and
Turn all to gold that comes to hand.
(8) And in particular, among
My cares, I 'll try to make my tongue
A *tree of life*, by speaking all
As be accommodable who shall.
(9) But *last*: yea *first* of all, I will
Thy Son my surety make, and still
Implore Him that He will me bless
With strength as well as righteousness.

He adds: "I designed rather *pietie* than *poetry* in these lines." And the reader will agree that he accomplished his design. Then follow nine notes on the lines, each explicating the sense of one of the numbers. I give one, referring to the last number (9) : —

The former *honest purposes* are amiable, are necessary; but the *Things* are too great for me and I cannot do them myself alone; wherefore my dependence must be upon the Lord Jesus Christ for the *pardon* of my *defects*, and for a supply of *grace* that shall be sufficient unto me.

It was the custom in former times, and it continued in vogue as late as the middle of the present century, to offer prayers in public for those in affliction and to give thanks for special mercies. Mather had many requests sent to him, but he was not satisfied with praying for the afflicted in public. He took the "bills that were put up for prayer" to his study and prayed for each person separately. He also used to ask himself who had shown him any kindness during the day, and supplicate the God of heaven that he would "bestow spiritual and eternal favors on such."

Near this time he enters his lament for failing to "record particular providences," and goes on to relate the following : —

I was owner of a *watch* whereof I was very fond for the variety of motions in it. My father was desirous of this watch, and I, in a manner, gave it him, with the thoughts, "I owe him a great deal more than this": and "the observation of the fifth commandment never wants a recompense." Quickly after this, there came to me a gentlewoman, from whom I had no reason to expect so much as a visit, but in her visit she, to my surprise, prayed me to accept, as a present from her, a watch which was indeed preferable unto that I had before parted with. I resolved therefore to stir up in my neighbors, dutifulness unto parents more than ever, and redeem the time I was helped thus to measure.

A former biographer has drawn attention to this record as showing the selfish element in the son's gift to his father, but the cavil was anticipated by Mather himself in the phrase, "in a manner," thus intimating that the gift was made in expectation of a return in some shape or from some source. We can only admire the honesty which inspired the record. The thought and the record of it require no apology, for since God has promised a ·blessing upon filial duty, the motive for filial conduct is pure as well as strong.

The first death in the family of Increase Mather occurred on the eleventh of June. The family seems to
have been remarkably healthy, as this little Katharine,
less than a year old, who was the ninth child, was the first
to be taken away. Cotton calls her his "little sister
Katharine," and there is pathos in the expression.

One of his ways of doing good was to employ an "old
hawker," who would fill the country with "devout and
useful books" if directed, wherefore he writes, "I will
direct him and assist him, as far as I can, in doing so."

Resolves were made by him that in parting with friends
he would "contrive to commend unto them some suitable
text of Scripture; and that he would rise early that he
might more glorify God in his studies."

In this same month of June he was much interested
in reading Mr. Corlet's "Self-Employment," from which
work he copied some excellent resolutions. As these
became a part of young Mather's spiritual being, I give
them a place. They will be helpful to any one who
observes them.

1. In arguing, watch against inordinate heat.
2. If neglected or slighted, care not for it, yet observe it.
3. Reckon any trial a gain.
4. Subject *delights of sense* to spiritual ends.
5. If the talk in company is *vain*, watch to put in a word for edification.
6. If any one despise or neglect you, bear no grudge against them.
7. Uphold the reputation of thy colleague as thine own.
8. Watch against all secret pleasure in the lessening of another for
the advantage of thyself.
9. Be not bitter against malignant opposers; for meekness of spirit
and behavior is more according to Christ than wrathful zeal.
10. After public service be not concerned about the opinions of sinful men, but inquire how acceptable it is to God.
11. Watch to put in a saving word for the good of a soul. Pray for
others as heartily as for thyself.

12. Value others more according to their true worth, and not according to their value of thyself.

13. Suppress the expectation of hearing your own praises.

14. Put down inordinate delights in eating and drinking.

15. By no means let pride set thee to study, or preach, or pray, or carry thee on in any service.

In July he undertook to start a "pious and praying meeting" among the young people in the southern part of the town for the "prevention of the mischief arising from vain company" and as a nursery of the church. The effort was not successful at first, but in subsequent years it grew into a great means of good. The number of members from the south[1] who joined those at the north end was so great that it was necessary to have two separate meetings. At the origin of this movement the pastor gave them a sermon.

In looking over the addresses of persons proposing to join the church, he found above thirty seals of his ministry in the place. He inferred that many more had been blessed in Boston and elsewhere of whom he had received no definite information.

The north part of Boston was then populous, and when walking in the evening Mather was impressed with the number of people living there. He was moved with a more than ordinary desire for their salvation, and as he walked his "soul was transported with prayer for such a mercy."

Probably one experience was not peculiar to our young minister so far as the anticipation is concerned. He had the habit of reading in the morning, before rising, a verse at a time, with meditation, and when dwelling on the story of Isaac being blessed with Rebecca, he thought that perhaps he might be blessed in the same way with such a consort.

[1] That is, south of the water way, now Blackstone Street.

In August, in company with his father, he spent about a fortnight in Lynn and had many "happy hours in the country retirement of the fields." Increase Mather had resorted to the waters in Lynn in the early days of his ministry for his health, and it seems to have been a favorite residence in the warm season. At this time the young minister had "strong and strange assurances that God would not only bless him but also make him a blessing to others."

The defect in his speech still troubled him, and on the twenty-seventh of August he made "a most explicit address unto the Lord Jesus Christ as having all keyes in his hands," for his speech, praying that he might have such supplies of it in his ministry as he might need. He wrote : "I exceedingly bewailed the sins of my tongue. I declared I asked for a tongue only to serve him and bespeak the love and lives of my neighbors for him ; and I concluded with the assurance that the tongue of the stammerer should speak plainly."

This is followed by the extract from the diary in Latin which has been cited already to show the range of his studies and his mental activity. He then informs us that he had kept a "very full diary," and that he had noted his sins till his "heart was weary of it." In consequence, he resolved to change his course and throw his notes, "as useless paper, into the fire." This was wise. It was the way with Christians in his time, as well as before and after, to explore all the nooks and corners of their souls to find how sinful they were and to seek for marks of true piety. The first might have been assumed as a fact, and in regard to the second, they might have looked for evidence in doing good. Introspection was carried to excess. It was well that Mather changed his course, but the diaries kept after this date were so full as to excite curiosity to know how voluminous the former had been.

He adopted a singular way of binding himself to duty. It was by paying a piece of money as a forfeit for every neglect. In this way he did good even if he failed in duty, because his forfeit went to the poor, over and above his tithes. The happy result was that he soon found himself so pleased with his duties as to need no reminder in the form of a penalty.

Of the good resolutions adopted about this time the following may be noted. One was to inquire at night what had been God's providence towards himself during the day under three heads : — " 1. My interior ; 2. my exterior ; and 3. my friends about me." He inquired : II. "What has been my behavior towards God in eight particulars. And III. Am I in a state or frame to die this night, if called ? " He resolved also : " I will never hear or see that any person has wronged me, or slighted me, but I will immediately, before him that sees in secret, pray for the welfare of that person by name." This appears to have been a ruling principle of his life ; and yet he has been accused of being revengeful. I believe he was strictly truthful in this resolve and faithful in the keeping of it. There does not appear to be any proof that he ever willfully wronged any one, even his bitterest maligners, during his whole life.

His diary at October 20 reveals the gratitude to God which he habitually cherished. He devoted the day to thanksgiving in private for the marvelous "mercies on every side, which he enjoyed." For all these blessings, enumerating them, he says : " I offered up my thanks unto the Lord, longing to be brought into the land of the Hallelujahs." Later in the exercises he considered some further mercies of God : —

1. My improvement [employment] in the ministry of the gospel, after I have been the vilest creature in the world.

2. The many advantages which I have to convenience me in that improvement.

3. The miraculous freedom of my speech.

4. A library exceeding that of any man's in the land.

5. A discoverable acceptance among the people of God.

6. A happy success of my labors, both public and private, upon hundreds of souls.

We would be glad to know how it came to pass that while so young he became the possessor of a library "exceeding that of any man's in the land." Possibly some volumes came from the library of his uncle Samuel, a very learned man, who died in Dublin in 1671, leaving no son. Possibly he devoted some of the money received from teaching to the purchase of books. Besides, to one craving for books, they accumulate with surprising rapidity.

In the autumn a gentleman procured from England a very valuable seal to be given him. Unhappily it was lost, among other goods, in a great fire among the warehouses. He felt called to see the hand of God in what befell him, and he held by that consideration; and he adds: "I prayed herewithal, that by no fire, whether the fire of lust here, or the fire of hell hereafter, I might miss of the promises which the blood of the Lord Jesus Christ hath sealed." Several months later the seal was found, unhurt by the fire, and came into his possession.

Several passages in the diary towards the close of the year prove that he was "exceedingly tried and vexed with evil imaginations." He resorted to prayer with fasting that they might be excluded from his mind. He went so far in self-denial as to injure his health. His "main weapon of defense" was prayer, and he resolved that he would never leave crying unto the Lord until he had obtained from him the grace to secure therewith such holiness that so much as an ugly thought should not ever dare to effect any lodging in his soul. The alleged fall of an aged and eminent minister into a sin which gave a "most infamous wound unto religion" caused him to fear for himself and to pray for preserving grace. It is pleasant to add that this minister was either found to be innocent or was so exemplary afterwards that he was restored to the ministry and filled out his life with useful and honorable labors.

We will enter upon the year 1684 by noticing Mr. Mather's habit of *ejaculatory prayer*, which was begun thus early and continued through life. He offered up his short petitions in his study or wherever he might do so without attracting notice or violating any of the rules of propriety. One specimen may be given of his course at a table, where, being the youngest of the company, it was not proper for him to speak, and where the discourses of others were too trivial to be worthy of attention : —

Casting my eyes upon the gentlewoman who carved for us.	Lord, carve of thy graces and comforts, a rich portion unto that person.
A gentlewoman stricken in years.	Lord, adorn that person with the virtues which thou prescribest for aged matrons, and prepare her for approaching dissolution.
A gentlewoman lately married.	Lord, espouse and marry the soul of that person unto thyself, in a covenant never to be broken.
A gentlewoman very beautiful.	Lord, beautify the soul of that person with thy comeliness.

And so on to the number of thirty, including a magistrate, a minister, a man unhappy in his children, a physician, one who had met with great losses, and a servant in attendance.

In the street he prayed for a *tall* man whom he met, that he "might have high attainments"; a *lame* man, that he "might walk uprightly"; a *negro*, that his "soul might be made white in the blood of the Lamb"; for *young people:* "Help them to remember their Creator in the days of their youth"; for *young gentlewomen:* "Make them wise virgins; and as the polished stones of thy temple."

He writes: "It would be *endless* as well as *needless* to exemplify a hundredth part of the ejaculations which a person may dart up without any loss of time." But in Boston to-day he would have to take people in groups as they crowd the streets. And why should not a Christian pray for his fellow travelers as he threads his way through the crowd? All need his prayers, and more than he knows would be thankful if they were aware of it. Doubtless there is much praying in the streets, and the "fleet angels of God" can go up and down in the thronged places of concourse as well as at Bethel.

The opening of the year 1684 was a time of stirring interest to the people of Boston and all New England. Charles II demanded the surrender of the charter of the Massachusetts Bay. Edward Randolph, well styled the "evil genius of New England," came over with the writ of *quo warranto*, bringing also a declaration from the king to the effect that "if the colony, before the prosecution of the *quo warranto*," would make full submission and entire resignation to his pleasure, he would regulate their charter for his service and their good. "The proceedings of the king in England were well understood here, and the people knew that he was vacating charters and giving new ones in the interest of arbitrary government." The Bay Colony was to be deprived of its chartered rights and its God-given freedom, in matters secular and religious.

No young man in the colony was more alive than

Cotton Mather to all that concerned its growth and prosperity. He was a true son of the soil, and from the first
intimation we have of his political sentiments he was on
the popular side, in distinction from that of the court.
This was true of him through all his life, and in this he
followed the example of his father and grandfather. In
this also he was followed by his son, Dr. Samuel Mather,
down to the time of the Revolution, when, leaving the
family of his wife, — who was a Hutchinson, — he acted
as a bold and uncompromising "son of liberty."

There was close and warm sympathy between the
colonists and the friends of freedom in England ; and
young Mather, in unison with his father, was already a
keen politician from a sense of religious duty. As there
was no man on our side of the water who understood the
principles of government in general, and the rights of the
colonies in particular, better than Increase Mather, so
there was no young man more thoroughly imbued with
the views and sentiments of the English Independents
than his learned and brilliant son. Contemporary politics
in England were as familiar to the people of Boston then
as they are now, though news was longer in coming.
The opinions and movements of Halifax and Sydney ; of
Shaftesbury and Nottingham ; of the second Hampden ;
of Maynard, Danby, Russell, Somers, and Locke, were dis-
cussed as freely as are now those of Gladstone and Salis-
bury, and with a deeper personal interest, in consequence
of the connection between the mother country and the
colony. The lessons learned in childhood and youth in
this line affected all his future life, and made him a
stanch friend of his country and of the free principles of
the Bible in every crisis, from the forfeiture of the charter
on June 18, 1684, to the establishment of the House of
Brunswick on the throne.

The scene in the Old South Church, January 21, 1684, was of great historic interest. The council, with Governor Bradstreet at their head, fearing the implied threat of the king, yielded to the demand for the charter, and voted that they would not contend but "would humbly lay themselves at his feet." The House of Deputies, representing the people, refused to concur. The people of Boston took up the matter in town meeting, and after discussion, their own delegates being present, sustained the deputies. When this meeting was in session a request was sent to Increase Mather to attend and address them. A condensed form of his speech is given in his autobiography. A few sentences follow. The question was, Shall we give up our charter? He said : —

"I verily believe we shall sin against the God of heaven if we vote an affirmative unto it. The Scripture teacheth us otherwise. 'That which the Lord our God has given us, shall we not possess it?' If we make a submission, we fall into the hands of men immediately : but if we do not, we still keep ourselves in the hands of God. The loyal citizens of London would not surrender their charter lest their posterity should curse them for it. Shall we then do such a thing?" He epigrammatically added that it was "better to die by the hands of others than by their own."

The people listened intently and then voted "No" without a dissenting voice. Then aged men took him by the hand and, with tears on their solemn faces, said: "We thank you, sir; we thank you, sir." The lesson of this event was never forgotten by Cotton Mather.

There is but a scrap of diary for this year, but we know that the year, like the last, was filled with manifold labors. In addition to his preaching, for which he made thorough preparation both by study and prayer, he was faithful in all parochial duties, making calls, visiting the sick, attending funerals, and assisting the needy ; moreover he continued his work of teaching as heretofore. In this service he. covered a wide range. Besides guiding the studies of brothers and sisters, he instructed young men in the ancient languages and in theology. Nor was his own studying confined to the branches he was teaching ; nor indeed to what specially belonged to a theological course. He was a universal scholar and had a marvelous faculty of acquiring and digesting knowledge in every branch of science and literature. Whatever book came in his way was made to yield its quota, whether of fact, or anecdote, or of inspiration. He conversed with older men and learned of them. By this means he gathered up more knowledge of the early history of New England than any other man possessed. All sorts of men were laid under contribution, each in his own sphere, whether landsman or sailor, mechanic, trader, or soldier, scholar or statesman ; and every item took its place in the vast storehouse of his memory. And what is of more consequence, everything in his mind came at his call when wanted. In reading and observing, his attention was so fixed that inerasable impressions were made on his mind. Nor was he overloaded and weighed down by his acquisitions like a plodding pack horse. He was alert, handy, strong in all his mental movements. He could walk and not faint ; he could run and not be weary ; he could mount up as on wings of eagles.

What notice the younger Mather took of the invitation to become their permanent pastor, by the North Church, is not known ; but he continued to perform the duties of the office, except the administration of the sacraments, as if he expected to abide with them. Perhaps he felt a natural shrinking from assuming the position of pastor

while so young, being only twenty-one in the preceding
February; and possibly he wished to prosecute his studies
farther in certain directions before becoming a Congregational minister. It is not known that he ever had any
doubts about the validity of Congregational or Presbyterian ordination; but we are informed that he made a
thorough study of the Episcopal or prelatical question
before taking ordination vows. In this examination his
mind was settled that the New Testament knew of no
distinction as to rank, honor, or duties between bishops
and elders. He found no authority for the claim of apos-
tolical and prelatical succession as held by the Roman or
the Anglican churches; and from this time he always,
when referring to the subject, speaks like one familiar with
the details of the controversy, and with the history of
the Christian Church in all generations.

The North Church, satisfied by long trial that Mr.
Mather was the man they wanted, renewed their "call" on
the third of August. This invitation was unanimous and,
according to Dr. Sibley,[1] "rather impatient." It is supposed that his acceptance was made known at the time,
but the young candidate was in no haste for formal in-
duction into the sacred office, and so worked on through
the year and into the following spring before the ceremony was performed.

The death of Charles II, February 6, 1685, occurred six
days before the diary of Mather begins for the same year,
on the twelfth, which was his birthday. Very soon we
find him referring to the changes in England, and it is
plain, from the record, that he understood the character
of Charles as a bad man, and also felt a distrust of the
new king. But the first entry in his diary refers to his
own spiritual state: "Hitherto my God hath helped me."

[1] vol. iii, H. G., p. 8.

February 12 : " Humble me, O Lord, that I have done
so little for thee, all this while. Oh ! how much of my
short life is gone, most unaccountably. Lord, help me
now unto the redeeming of time, and the spending as
much as I can of it, in a perpetual exercise of grace."

At this time he set apart half an hour between twelve
and one o'clock every day of the week, except the fifth
and seventh, for prayer ; and " spent the whole afternoon
of his Saturdays in *peculiar transactions* between the Most
high God and his own soul." The time was filled with
praises, prayers, converse with God, renewal of covenant,
and " petitions in regard to his ministerial capacitie,"
besides the " reading of books and singing of psalms."

Mather was as careful to keep rubbish and trivialities
out of his mind as to fill it with useful knowledge and
beautiful thoughts. His soul was " vexed to hear, in the
most venerable company, the whole hour together, little
but idle chat, whereby holes were picked in the coats of
others." He resolved to be silent or turn the discourse
into other channels. " Lord, make my tongue a tree of
life ! "

The fact is mentioned that " divers ministers had it in
heart " in the early spring of this year to address the general court with proposals for a " reformation, and for the
deliverance of the land." The last clause had reference
to expected and dreaded measures of the new popish king.
He writes : " Little can be done by so little a person as
I am ; but three things may I do. 1. Confer with my
father. 2. Excite Christians who are meeting privately
for the object. 3. Spend a great part of Lecture day in
secret prayers." Praying for a moral and spiritual reformation among the people, and for divine guidance in
regard to public affairs, prepared the people to maintain
their rights.

The time of ordination drew near and he made special preparation for that important even*, feeling as he did the solemnity of that service.

On the twenty-third of March, while praying and fasting, he resolved, " 1. To be exemplary in his charities; 2. considerate in his speeches ; 3. to build up the church with an umblemished reputation." He was willing to bear any reproach for himself; but not that he might cause the name of God to be reproached. " Oh ! let that cup pass from me."

He was somewhat perplexed by two things, for the moment, before the time set for the ordination. One was a thinner congregation on a certain Sunday ; but he soon learned that such a thing might occur to any minister. The other was "some apprehension about the ability of the society to raise money enough to support both pastor and teacher." To prevent division he was willing that God should "take him out of the world, if necessary to harmony." He continues however: "The design of Satan to embarrass the designs of my settlement were soon disappointed by a most uniting work of God upon the hearts of the people."

On another day, having his ministry in view, he made a solemn covenant with God "to be wholly devoted to the service of the Lord Jesus Christ." This was written, and signed in large hand, COTTON MATHER.

As the time drew on he was, like other ingenuous youth, "often overwhelmed with melancholy apprehensions" of his unfitness for the work of the ministry.

The ceremony of ordination took place on the fifteenth of May. The account must be given in his own words : —

This day is appointed, (because Thou, O Lord art stronger than I, and hast prevailed,) for my ORDINATION to the office of a Pastor over the North Church in Boston.

In the morning, while I was alone, meditating on the work which the call of the Lord Jesus Christ hath now put me upon, and of the *support* and *rewards* which he has therein assured unto me, I was, diverse times, melted into tears. And the Spirit of my glorious Master gave me such rapturous *touches* and *prospects*, as that I was forced most unwillingly to shake them off. They would have been too hard for me, and I would not have others take notice of any effect thereby left upon me.

With a soul inexpressibly irradiated from on high, I went into one of the vastest congregations that has ever been seen in these parts of the world, where I prayed about an hour and a quarter, and preached (on John 21 : 17) about an hour and three quarters, with such assistance from heaven, that exceeded all that my poor faith could have imagined.

This sermon was the keynote to the whole ministry of Mr. Mather. The discourse would naturally explain the duty and privilege of loving Christ with supreme devotion ; and the other duty and blessedness of being an undershepherd to his disciples — his flock.

In the afternoon, my father having prayed, and preached (on Acts 13 : 2) the ordination was performed with more than ordinary solemnity, producing a greater number of moved hearts and weeping eyes, than perhaps have, at any time, been seen together. My father, with Mr. Allen [pastor of the First Church], and Mr. Willard [of the South Church], the other two ministers of the town, imposed hands on me. My father gave me my Charge, (which I have transcribed at the beginning of my Bible,) and good old Mr. Eliot gave me the Right Hand of Fellowship.

This was John Eliot, pastor of the church in Roxbury' and the " apostle to the Indians," now eighty-one years of age. In modern usage the right hand is often given by one of the younger ministers in the council ; but here we have the venerable saint of fourscore and one years welcoming the stripling of twenty-two. It was common in early times for the preacher to address the people and charge the candidate, and this usage continued as late as the time of the younger Edwards and perhaps later. It might be well to revert to the ancient practice, as the sermon would naturally, if adapted to the occasion, furnish an application to the people and also to their new minister. On this occasion the preacher put the Charge into a distinct service. It is inserted here as a model on account of its fullness, its scriptural spirit, and the brevity and terseness of its language : —

Whereas, you, upon whom we impose our hands, are called to the work of the ministry, and to the office of a Pastor in this church of Christ, we charge you before God, and the Lord Jesus Christ, and in the presence of elect angels, That you take heed to the ministry which you have received in the Lord, to fulfill it ; and that you feed the whole flock of God over which the Holy Ghost hath made you overseer. That you study to show yourself approved of God, as a workman that need not be ashamed. That you give yourself to reading, and to meditation ; to exhortation and to doctrine ; and that you endeavor to show yourself an example of the believers in Faith, in Spirit, in Purity, in Charity, and in Conversation.

And if you heed this Charge, we pronounce unto you, that the Lord Jesus Christ will give you a place among his holy angels that stand by as witnesses of this day's solemnity, and of your being thus solemnly set apart to the special service of God, and of Jesus Christ. And if you do thus, when the Lord Jesus shall appear, you shall appear with him in glory. He who is the Chief Shepherd, will then give unto you a Crown of Glory, which shall never fade away.

CHAPTER IV.

COTTON MATHER was ordained as the pastor of the North Church, and as colleague with his father, when he was twenty-two years, three months, and one day old. The narrative may be arrested here for a little while to take a look at his position and surroundings.

In regard to the first, he had little to desire. He was associated with his father, with whom he acted in perfect harmony. His congregation was large, intelligent, and able to give a comfortable support to both its ministers. For his duties he was as fully equipped as a man could be at his early age. He was a general favorite with scholars, gentlemen, and the mass of the people. Physical energy, tireless activity, capacity to do, as well as facility to plan, warranted the hope of a fruitful and happy pastorate. No man of his years stood so high or looked out on such bright prospects as smiled upon him.

There were three churches in the town. The meeting-house of the First Church was on the west side of Washington Street, a little above the head of King, now State, Street. That of the second, or North Church, was on the north side of North Square. The population of the northern section of Boston has almost entirely changed within the memory of living men. In 1685 it was occupied by a people, almost without exception, of English blood. They were engaged in all branches of business, including seafaring. Among them were merchants, graduates of the college, and several members of noted families. They lived in comfortable houses, with yards in front and gardens behind them. The third church was the South, and its sanctuary was on the spot now occupied by the old Old South. The senior ministers were Rev. James Allen, Rev. Increase Mather, and Rev. Samuel Willard. The colleague of Mr. Allen was Rev. Joshua Moodey. In the whole colony, including Plymouth, there were sixty-seven churches, most of which enjoyed the regular preaching of the Word. Most of the pastors were educated men, and their reputation for godliness and fidelity in their duties was high.

The college at Cambridge, which was founded for the purpose of training men for the ministry, for the magistracy, and for the teaching of youth, was flourishing. "About one half of the graduates under President Chauncy, who died in 1672, became ministers of the gospel, and several others held posts of distinction in civil life." Two able and learned men filled the office of president during the next eight or nine years, Rev. Leonard Hoar and Rev. Urian Oakes. Mr. John Rogers, of Ipswich, educated for the ministry, but never ordained, was elected in 1681. He had studied medicine, and was a man of general knowledge and amiable temper, and well fitted to win the good will of students, but he held the post only two years. The Rev. Increase Mather was then invited to become the head of the institution, and he presided at commencement a year or two before becoming president. There was no man in the colony so qualified for the position, but he could not be induced to move to Cambridge and give his whole time to the duties of the office. He presided at commencement, had a general supervision of the college, gave instruction once a week, part of the year, and sometimes preached to the students; but the teaching and management were to a great extent in the hands of competent tutors. Mr. Mather held connection with the college till 1701, though absent in England, as agent of the Colony and Province, about four years (1688–1692). But while abroad he had the interest of the institution on his heart, and secured many present and prospective benefits for it. Cotton Mather felt a deep interest in the college from the time of admission, when twelve years old, to the end of his life.

Boston was a populous and busy town. For a long time it took the lead of all others in the colonies in commerce and in political influence. In 1674 the number of families was 1,500. As families then were, there might have been between 8,000 and 9,000 souls. In 1679 there were about 800 freemen and in 1680 there were about 868 taxable polls. Small as this seems at this time, no other town in New England could rival Boston in those years, and by its connections its influence was paramount. It was the center of business, of political power, and of religious propagandism to all the eastern colonies.

In 1674 the estimated population of all New England was 120,000. Three fourths of the whole, or 90,000, were supposed to be in the three " provinces of Boston, Maine, and New Hampshire," the whole three being ruled from Boston. The far larger part of this number belonged to the Bay and Plymouth colonies. Simon Bradstreet was governor of Massachusetts from 1679 to 1685. The charter was then vacated, and Joseph Dudley was president of New England about one year, when Sir Edmund Andros succeeded and went through the farce of ruling an abused and unwilling people till the early part of 1689, when the people cast him out.

Governor Bradstreet, with the old council, carried on a sort of provincial government till the charter of the province was granted in 1692, and Sir William Phips became governor by appointment of William and Mary.

remain in my posture, for some time, noting down what hints occur to me, fit for my improvement [use]. If I do it with ejaculations, I would intermingle my writing with my prayer, so far and so long as may be convenient.

The secret of Mather's power in the pulpit is revealed in this extract. We see the cause why he became the greatest pulpit power in his day, and unsurpassed since, unless, perhaps, by a very few in later generations. During the week he made the most faithful preparation by reading, meditation, prayer, and writing. Study of the Bible in the original languages kept his mind fresh and unhackneyed. Praying as he wrote, he went into the house of God surcharged with God's truth and spirit. Nothing was left till Saturday night or Sunday morning to tax his strength by way of mental toil and worry over a sermon. Saturday evening and Sunday morning were sacred to devotions. He went to the sanctuary as to the "gate of heaven." Full of matter and fervent in prayer, he was like a charged battery, and he represented Christ as he stood before his auditory. They were instructed, they were aroused, their consciences were quickened, their affections were kindled, their reason was satisfied by the words spoken, and all was sent home by the intense spiritual energy with which he spoke and prayed.

Mr. Mather felt the need of guarding against temptation. He reflected that when "our Lord Jesus Christ was entering upon his public ministry, very sore temptations assaulted him," and he said to himself, " It may be, now I am safely ordained, I shall not want my temptations." To prevent his "dishonoring of God under them," he resolved to read immediately a "profitable book or two concerning temptations," and also to forecast what might be the temptation by which he was now most of all endangered. " Forewarned is forearmed."

One day near the end of May, it being a day set apart
for secret thanksgiving, he went into the meetinghouse,
probably because it gave him more privacy than his home,
full of brothers, sisters, and servants. While there he
thought of mercies received, and also took singular pains
to celebrate and magnify the Lord for his attributes
and perfections, and his wondrous works in creation and
providence. He also blessed God for afflictions, and
then contrived how to "glorify God more particularly
by strengthening the hands of the tithing men to
promote reformation, and by reviving the young men's
meetings on Sabbath evenings, and by studying to speak
with more exactness, watchfulness, and truthfulness."

From this and previous citations, it appears that
"young men's meetings on Sabbath evenings" had been
held before his ordination, and it is often a pleasant surprise to find in these old records proof that the ancient
ministers anticipated nearly all the methods devised for
doing good that are most approved at the present day.
We are not to understand by his use of the word "truthfulness" that he was used to falsifying his word, but that
he had the same meaning as President Edwards had in
the next generation, when he resolved never to embellish
a story for the sake of effect, but to be exactly truthful in
relating facts or dialogues. Such a resolution is called for
now by multitudes of speakers and writers of good reputation. Scarcely a paper is opened, however valuable,
that does not contain one or more examples of this kind
of inaccuracy. Either the relation is incorrect, or the
story is told of the wrong person, or the witty remark is
ascribed to one who never made it. What is true in substance is made untrue by exaggeration. It will be found
by candid readers that Cotton Mather acted up to his
resolution beyond most authors, notwithstanding the hasty

accusations of some critics. In printing as many names
and dates as are found in his works, omniscience would
be necessary to keep out all mistakes.

On the seventh of June, he met with a sudden and
great affliction, which is thus reported in his own words:
"My dear friend, Mr. Shepherd, of Charlestown, being
taken suddenly ill, I preached for him in the forenoon.
At noon he said unto me, 'My hopes are built on the free
mercy of God and the merit of Christ, and I do believe,
if I am taken out of the world, I shall only change my
place; I shall neither change my company nor my communion. And as for you, Sir, I beg the Lord Jesus to be
with you to the end of the world.' At night, unto the
consternation of me and all his friends, he died." This
Mr. Shepherd was one of an eminent family of ministers,
who were remarkable for ability, scholarship, and holy
zeal in their sacred calling.

On the first Sunday in June he baptized the first child
that he ever "washed in the name of the glorious Trinity," and the preceding Sabbath was the first time of his
"administering the Lord's Supper, which he did, after
preaching on John 3 : 16, with comfortable assistance
from heaven." It is a text full of love and theology.
"For God so loved the world, that he gave his only be-
gotten Son, that whosoever believeth in him should not
perish, but have everlasting life." Four days later he
preached his "first country lecture," — the regular Thursday lecture, — wherein the Lord gave him "extraordinary
assistance." He was now fairly engaged in the work of
the ministry, in all its various requirements, and from this
time his course was like the shining light, shining with
increasing brilliancy and power till its happy close, over
forty years later.

About this time he kept a private thanksgiving, when

he "sang, read, and thought on his knees." He wrote:
"I blessed the Lord, 1. for his gracious work in my
hands; 2. for my improvement in the work of the gospel; 3. for my acceptance among the people; 4. for the
success of my labors, being very manifold and visible;
5. for my free utterance; 6. for my large library." He
records that the Lord "invigorated his design" to visit
the families of his flock.

In July he began a practice that he considered the most
holy and useful that the good Spirit of the Lord had ever
inspired him with. It was a course of reading the Scriptures with such devout attention as to fetch at least one
observation and one supplication; "a note and a wish,
out of every verse in all the Bible." He adds, in relation
to this plan, "I have a prospect of, who can tell how
much truth and grace to pass through my soul, in this
waiting upon God." He also took the same way of singing, so that the "singing of Psalms," became to him a
"most delicious, entertaining, profitable exercise, that
't is, perhaps, to many of them that practice it." Such
an habitual practice would fit a man for every ministerial
exigency.

In this month he made a visit to Plymouth, where his
uncle, John Cotton, Jr., was for some time minister, as
well as a devoted laborer for the welfare of the Indians,
whose language he understood better than any man in
America, not excepting Mr. Eliot.

In August young Mather's "musings" about Isaac and
Rebekah began to take more definite form. He was now
settled in the ministry, and according to immemorial
usage a Congregational pastor is expected to become a
married man. August 25, he writes: "I spent the day in
secret humiliation and supplications, especially to seek for
the guidance and blessing of God in what concerns the

change of my condition in the world from single to married, whereto I have now many incitations." He was evidently considered a desirable match.

His method of working upon individuals in his pastoral labor is illustrated by the following entry: "Much interested in the religious welfare of a young gentleman, Mr. Samuel Royse. Prevailed with him to spend the day with me in my study." The day was principally "laid out for the gaining of one precious and immortal soul unto the Lord Jesus Christ," and he trusted that he had prospered in the effort. This man afterwards joined the North Church, and lived and died a serious Christian.

James II had now begun to reveal his despotic designs, and his purpose to bring Roman Catholics into places of honor and power, contrary to law. Fearful apprehensions took possession of Protestants in England, Episcopalians and Dissenters alike, and the interest in this great change appealed directly to the churches of New England. We are not surprised to learn that Mather was much distressed in September on account of the calamities and confusions of the English nation under James. The ill-starred rising of Monmouth had been crushed at Sedgemoor. Jeffreys had ridden his bloody circuit and Kirke, the butcher, had loaded the gallows with victims. The cruel temper of the king was disclosed. No wonder that men like Mather betook themselves to "sighs and prayers for the distressed churches of God," and for the imperiled liberties of Englishmen. The king had come to the throne as a bigoted papist, with the old notions of arbitrary power, and with settled revengeful hate of the party which had sought in the late reign to exclude him from the throne or to curtail his power, if allowed to reign. He went beyond the fears of those who distrusted him, and hastened to a bitter and disastrous end.

Among Mather's "designs to do good," were these : When "praying with a sick person," he would try to do good in his prayer to those in the room. In his *rising* thoughts on Lord's day morning, he would consider what special service he could do for the flock. While hearing a sermon he would send up ejaculations that the truth might do good to himself. When any in his flock suffered from afflictions or temptations, he would seek opportunities to assist them. Being deeply · interested in the students of Harvard College, he would study to suggest profitable things to his father, the rector or president, especially as to settling them in good principles.

His lifelong interest in the education of the young was expressed in a resolution made at this time, that he would never be at rest while our island here (the north part of Boston) is without a good school master and a flourishing school. He also in this month (September) promoted and assisted in the publication of a book by his father about "Faith, Repentance, and the Day of Judgment."

On the seventh of November, which was devoted to religious uses, he prayed that he might be hindered from doing anything displeasing to God. He averred that if God would have him "embrace a celibacy, he would evermore take contentment in it," but subjoined, "since his inclinations and invitations did now seem to recommend a married state, he begged that God would lead him in the way wherein he should go."

He kept a list of all the communicants in his church, and in secret prayers would "sometimes go over the catalogue by parcels at a time, praying for suitable blessings upon them all."

The following relates his experience at the Lord's Supper, on the tenth of December : —

I came at last, unto these passages before the Lord. Lord, I am willing to part with all that thou wouldst have me to forego, for an interest in the Lord Jesus Christ. I am willing to forego my righteousnesses. And I confess unto thee, after all that I have done, or can do for thee, if thou shouldest break me sore in the place of dragons, for ever, I could not say there were any injustice in thy proceedings. I am willing to forego my corruptions too, and I do profess unto thee I wish every sin were made bitter unto my soul.

Similar passages occur in other writings of Mather, and they may be taken as expressing what has been caricatured as "being willing to be damned for the glory of God." The real meaning of the words above quoted was probably this : that his sins deserved punishment and if God could not safely screen him from suffering, he would acquiesce, and even glorify God in thus upholding his holy law. But that he, or any other New England divine, was willing to be damned, in the sense of being condemned to a sinful future, is too absurd to be believed.

We often hear that ministers are worked harder now than in former generations, but it is certain that few men in these days have exceeded Cotton Mather in the labors of the pastorate. In the last week of December, this year, he preached Sunday, Monday, Tuesday, Wednesday, and Thursday. In several weeks he preached as many as five times. When two preaching days came together, he sometimes preached twice each day. In preaching, he would fetch an ejaculation out of every head and every text, sending up these silent and *obiter* prayers for his hearers.

This closes the year 1685 (New Style), but as Mr. Mather dated his diary from his birthday, six weeks remain, from the records of which a few items will be taken.

On the twenty-seventh of January he kept a day of thanksgiving in his study. He cultivated the grace of gratitude. But in the forenoon he searched his heart and lamented his vileness and unworthiness. For making such records he has been censured as insincere and overstating his sins and his report of them. Those who have not been used to examine themselves in the light of God's holy law and Christ's perfect character cannot of course, understand the workings of his mind on this and similar occasions. The patriarch Job did not abhor himself in dust and ashes until he had had a vision of God. After humbling himself before God, Mr. Mather devoted the time to "contemplating the glories of the great God" until his heart was rapt into heavenly frames. In the afternoon he dwelt upon the specific blessings he had enjoyed, with grateful love. He then considered what he should do for God. 1. He gave himself — all, soul and body — to the Lord. 2. He would contrive how to honor God.

He next called to mind answers to prayers. He had prayed that the suspected designs of the king might be defeated. The diary reads: "The glorious assurances I have enjoyed and uttered, very many times for now some years together, about the Lord's appearing to deliver his people from impending desolations, are now answered. That monster, Kirke, who was coming to New England with a regiment of *red coats* to sacrifice the best lives among us, diverted from coming hither by the death of that greater monster, King Charles II." The design of sending Kirke here is an historical fact. This was before his great infamy in suppressing Monmouth's insurrection, but he had already acquired an infamous fame by his brutal cruelties in Tangier. It is refreshing to read Mather's just characterization of Charles II, whom many have glorified as the "merry monarch."

On the twenty-third of February he had a special season of devotion, and in conclusion he writes: "I begged the Most High that he would bestow on me a *companion for my life*, by whose prudence, virtue and good nature, I might be assisted in the service of my Master, and whose company I might also at length have in the heaven of heavens forever." He also prayed for direction in his choice, and for divine guidance in every step.

The deceptive movement of King James to entrap the Dissenters into his support, by the offer of religious liberty, seems to have made some impression upon the mind of young Mather, as it did upon others here, as well as a small section of the Nonconformist party in England. Mr. Danforth, the leading man on the popular side, had no faith in the king; perhaps Increase Mather had as little, but he made most adroit use of the king's professions in favor of religious liberty when admitted to the royal closet in 1688. For a short time there was "liberty of worship." This had been taken away in the reign of Charles II by the "five-mile act," and the " conventicle act," by which public worship by Dissenters could only be performed at extreme peril. James suspended these laws, in hopes of gaining the favor of the Nonconformists, while carrying out his purpose of setting up his own religion.

In February the young pastor, though it would cost a very bitter trial, planned to find the *" evil humors"* that abounded in the town, and to "pray that those devils might be cast out." He spent much time this winter in visiting families, catechizing, praying, and instructing, and in the undertaking "enjoyed a most wonderful presence of God."

Another method of benefiting others, while improving himself, was started early in 1686. He singled out a number of students who were graduates, and capable, and they met in his study every forenoon. Here in the

"seven commonplace heads in discourse," in reference
to any "notable controversy that had been managed in
the church of God, ve had a solemn disputation on the
controverted question." Mr. Mather was the moderator
of the company, and summed up the conclusion. He
adds : " Thus we resolved upon going through a body of
divinity, and it is incredible how much we advantaged ourselves by these exercises."

Some writers have asserted that the volume called
"Memorable Providences relating to 'Vitchcraft'" was
published in 1685. This is a mistake of several years,
as the Goodwin children, to whom it relates principally,
were not afflicted before 1688.

The year 1686, upon which we have now entered, was
memorable in the history of Massachusetts, and of other
colonies, including New York. Before its close, Sir
Edmund Andros appeared on the stage as governor, or
president ; and Edward Randolph continued his baleful
activity. But the treatment of this matter belongs
properly to the Life of Increase Mather, or the history
of the colony, and is alluded to here only because the son
was deeply interested in the labors of his father, and in
all the affairs which involved the welfare of the colony
and the churches.

The first entry in the diary, February 12, Mather's
twenty-third birthday, was characteristic, and it marks
an important step in the progress of his life.

This day, through the good hand of God upon me, I finish the
twenty-third year of my age. And this day I gave one of my first
visits unto a young gentlewoman, the daughter of most worthy, pious
and credible parents, — Abigail, the happy daughter of John and
Katharin Phillips, of Charlestown, unto an acquaintance of whom the
wonderful providence of God, in answer to prayers, conducted me. I
propounded unto myself the methods, the divine and sacred methods,
wherein the glorious Lord Jesus Christ engages our immortal souls

unto himself, and I studied how to make my addresses unto my friend analogous unto those. But alas, wherewithal shall a young man cleanse his way?

For a whole quarter of a year, he tells us, he "made the affair a subject of prayer, and never any sinful man saw more sensible answers to prayers than poor C. M. did in this matter." Later, he writes of the lady as a "comely, ingenious woman, and an agreeable consort."

While he was in this "conversation," it befell him to be desired by a poor, condemned malefactor, on the fifth of March, to preach a suitable sermon for him on the day following. In compliance with the request, he preached to a "vast congregation" at Boston, and administered the Lord's Supper on the same day. The sermon was printed and "sold exceedingly." This therefore, contrary to some authorities, was Cotton Mather's first acknowledged publication.

Other writings of his, however, had been given to the press, but without his name. This seems to be the proper place to refer to them. For information in regard to these firstfruits of his mind, and to many other of his works, I am greatly indebted to Dr. Sibley's "Graduates of Harvard University," a most valuable work (vol. iii). It may be stated also that I have examined nearly every volume of Mather's to be found in the libraries of Boston, Worcester, and Harvard College.

The first "composure" (to use his own word) of Cotton Mather which had the honor of type, so far as known, was "A Poem dedicated to the Memory of the reverend and excellent Mr. Urian Oakes, the late Pastor to Christ's flock, and President of Harvard College," etc., with other matters. The letters N. R. subscribed to the poem are the last letters of the names of Cotton Mather. The only known copy was in the library of the late Mr. Brinley, of Hartford. Though printed without the author's name, there is no doubt of the authorship. The Rev. Nathaniel Mather wrote from Dublin, in 1683, to his brother Increase: "The last I had from you were two of your son's poems on Mr. Oaks." The date of this publication was 1682.

The second publication was an almanac, in 1683. A part of the long title was: "The Boston Ephemeris. An Almanack for the Dionysian Year of ·the Christian Æra, M.DC.LXXXIII.," etc., in a long title, with a motto in English and Latin: "Redeeming the Time." "Damna fleo rerum, sed plus fleo Damna Dierum ; Quisq : potest rebus succurrere; nemo Diebus." No name is attached, but Judge Sewall wrote on his copy, "By Mr. Cotton Mather."

The third writing, which was printed in 1685, was "An elegy on the much-to-be-deplored Death of that never-to-be-forgotten Person, The Rev. Mr. Nathanael Collins," of Middletown, Conn. He died on the twenty-eighth of December, 1684. This was anonymous, but has always been ascribed to Cotton Mather. Mr. Brinley writes: "Not in any public library; have never heard of another copy."

But we are curious to learn how the young minister prospered in his "addresses," which were so carefully "studied." Passing several dates, it becomes evident that the "course of true love" ran smooth, in this case, because in May we find him praying that he might have a "comfortable habitation." He was evidently preparing a home. He had never yet "spoken to his people about salary," and it would seem from his diary that he never departed from this reticence. During most of his life he was provided for, either by his people, his books, or his personal friends. At one time, when old, he was involved

in debt by connection with others and suffered severely;
but from a proper self-respect, or, it may be, natural pride,
kept his peace until friends, made aware of the state of
things, most generously raised several hundred pounds
for his aid. This was done in a manner so kind and
delicate as to awaken lasting gratitude. In regard to
money matters no man was ever more disinterested and
at the same time honest and honorable. He gave away
with a discriminating and liberal hand.

The record of his marriage demands notice. This took
place on May 4, 1686, when he was twenty-three years and
nearly three months old. He writes: " I was married,
and the good providence of God caused my wedding to be
attended with many circumstances of respect and honor,
afore most that ever have been in these parts of the
world." 'There was probably a large and distinguished
company, and much of the state which was affected by
genteel families in those early times, on festive occasions,
as well as funerals and inaugurations.

He continues the record: " In the morning of my
wedding-day, the Lord filled my soul, while secretly at
prayer, before him, with celestial and unutterable satisfactions, flowing from the sealed assurances of his love
unto me. And my heart was particularly melted unto
tears, upon my further assurance that in my married state
he had resources of rich and great blessings for me."
This exercise was in Boston, in the morning; later, he
went over to Charlestown, the home of the young bride
elect, almost sixteen, in her blushing beauty. We will
now see how he spent the time while the lady was getting
ready for the ceremony : —

After going over to Charlestown, and having some leisure time there
before the arrival of the neighboring ministers, and other persons of
quality expected, I carried my Bible with me into the garden, where

I singled out the story of the wedding in the second chapter of John, and fetched for myself one *observation* and one *supplication*, out of every verse in that story. In the doing whereof I received further assurances from the Spirit of my heavenly Lord, that I was blessed and should be blessed, by him forever.

These "assurances" are not to be understood as differing from those enjoyed by all rational Christians, in lesser or greater degree, when resting in the hope that they are reconciled to God and have a right to believe in his promises. It does not imply that they expect to be exempt from sickness, bereavements, misfortunes, and wrongs, but that they shall be blessed, nevertheless, not only in spite of, but even through, these evils and sufferings.

On the next Sabbath he preached in Charlestown, from Psalm 17 : 14, and showed that he did not wish to be among those who "have their portion in this life." He informs us that he applied the truth unto himself, "under the fear of being put off with a *portion here*, now he had received so good an one *in*, as well as *with* his consort." Of course he did not speak these words to the congregation, but he did, "in the whole exercise, freely profess unto his hearers," that, for his own part, all the delights he had ever enjoyed in three and twenty years in the world were not comparable to those which had come to him through a chapter in the Bible.

Though keenly alive to the lawful enjoyments which a kind and bountiful providence provides, he valued far higher those which came from the use of his spiritual faculties. He thought this a peculiarly fit time to enforce this truth, and from his tact and delicacy he could do it without violating the sense of propriety in the most fastidious. Accordingly, on the next Sunday, preaching in Boston, he took Psalm 119 : 14 : "I have rejoiced in

the way of thy testimonies as much as in all riches," for
his text.   The subject was "Divine Delights."   One passage will show the spirit and drift of the discourse : —

Oh! that the God of heaven would effectually persuade every
person here, every day, without fail, to read a portion in the Bible.
But I wish that you would read it, not customarily, but with suitable
observations, and *applications*, and *ejaculations*.

He resided several months after marriage with his
"dear consort," in the house of his father-in-law, but
later in the season removed to Boston and took the house
where his father had lived, and wherein, he says : "My
childish age had made many hundred prayers unto the God
of heaven."

In September he had a singular dream, but not more
remarkable than many that are occurring to thousands
of others.   I give it a place as showing the workings of
his mind when not under the control of his will.   He
dreamed of meeting Mr. Shepherd, of Cambridge, deceased, with other gentlemen.   He felt shy of Mr.
Shepherd, realizing that he was dead, and was "contriving to step out of the room," when his friend came nimbly
up to him, and took him by the hand saying, "Sir, you
need not be so shy of me, for you shall quickly be as
I am."   Mather was soon taken with a violent fit of
ephialtes, or nightmare ; then came on a cold, and he was
threatened with a violent fever.   If he had died, the
dream would have been regarded as a supernatural warning.   Probably the fever was already in his system and
was the cause of his dream.   One good result attended
this attack.   The Lord "overcame for him the fear of
death."

Two things, exactly as we might expect, followed the
settlement in his own house.   (The house, by the way, is
supposed to have been the one owned and occupied by

his grandfather Cotton, near the entrance to Pemberton Square from Tremont Street, south side.) The first was the "keeping of a day of thanksgiving." The other was one of his "devices to do good." He set up a meeting at his own house, to entertain his neighbors on Sunday evenings. This went on for some time, until his father's departure for England in 1688, when other labors prevented him from holding them.

At this time there was a small company of French reformed people in Boston. They were not in very flourishing circumstances, and their condition enlisted the interest of Mr. Mather. He exerted his influence also in order to secure a better observance of the Lord's day among them. It is probable that they had some of the continental laxity in regard to the keeping of holy time.

In the latter part of this year he persuaded several gentlemen belonging to the congregation to combine into a private meeting once a fortnight, to seek the fear, and hear the Word of God, in their several families together, as they lived in order. At a general meeting, either at stated or occasional times, the pastor was to be present and carry on the meeting for them. This seems to have been a most effective mode of bringing the whole church into social Christian life and activity. It is unknown at the present day, instead of which we have a general weekly prayer meeting; but here we see a whole church, divided up into sections according to locality, meeting once in two weeks; in addition, a general meeting brought all together under the guidance and inspiration of their minister. The exercises at these meetings were prayer, reading the Scriptures, conversation, and reading selections from authors. Later in the season he notes that several religious families had not yet joined any of the private meetings in their neighborhood. These he would endeavor to bring into the scheme.

It is evident that the brethren led in prayer when he was present, for he observed from their prayers that they were led to copy his when they led the devotions. By this he was inspired to be more *long, argumentative*, and *instructive* in praying with them. He was, it seems, anxious to have *good* prayers rather than *many* prayers, except as all present were expected to make the prayer of the leader their own.

The record of the year was closed by stating that it was his practice, in morning family prayers, to read a chapter, or part of one, and "compose his prayer out of it"; and in evening worship, he "meditated on a text." And thus, he writes, "the good hand of God brought me to the end of my twenty-fourth year."

There is a hiatus in the diaries, including five years, 1687–1691. The life of Mr. Mather has to be filled out by reference to the records of the North or Second Church, by looking up his connection with public affairs, especially the overthrow of Andros, and by consulting the occasional sermons and other writings published by him, — several each year, — and a few letters may find a place as we advance in the work.

The sermon preached in 1686, and "applied unto a condemned malefactor," was perhaps given to the press in the same year, but as the only copy to be found bears date 1687, it will be placed in the annals of this year. The title is, "The Call of the Gospel, applied unto all in general, and unto a condemned Malefactor in particular; a sermon preached on the seventh day of March, 1686, at the request, and in the hearing of a man under a just sentence of death for the horrid sin of Murder. Second edition." The reader may be pleased to see how a sermon was fixed up for the press with mottoes in English and Latin from the Bible and the classics, besides a text, in those ancient days. We have in this specimen, first, one verse from a psalm, "I will sing of the mercies of the Lord for ever; with my mouth will I make known thy faithfulness to all generations" (Ps. 89: 1). The Latin motto or sentiment is from Origen, as follows: "Nulla species peccati tanta est qua non sit superior Jesus (There is no kind of sin so great but that Jesus is greater)." The author remarks that peculiar circumstances made it necessary to prepare the discourse in haste, but that it was published at the "urgent importunity of others." Then comes the text from Isaiah 45: 22, "Look unto me, and be ye saved, all the ends of the earth." The way being clear, the young preacher opens as follows:—

These words give unto us the most joyful sound that ever the children of death had the favor of. Some of us, doubtless, can with a most distinguishing and experimental relish, profess concerning this oracle of God, as some other persons have concerning some other passages, we would not have this sentence left out of our Bibles, for the riches of both the Indies. Yea, who among us all, at the reading of these glad tidings, can forbear joining with the rapturous shouts of heaven; with that angelical and evangelical outcry in Luke 2: 14, "Glory to God in the highest; on earth peace, good will towards men"? Behold, the Saviour of the world is this day speaking unto you, ye congregation of the Lord, arrayed in his white garments. He looks through the windows of his bright, ivory palace, and uttereth an invitation to you which blessed are your ears that hear this day.

The offer of salvation is unfolded in all its freeness and fullness and applied to the prisoner. As one who had confessed his guilt, and evinced deep penitence therefor, he was encouraged to hope for mercy. The style of the sermon is vivacious. There is not a sleepy line in it, and it must have been full of life to the hearers. It was admirably adapted to the occasion, and, what may seem incredible to those who have formed their opinion of Mather's style from the statements of others, there are no Greek or Latin quotations in the discourse, and no quips or oddities to mar its solemn effect. And what is better, the poor malefactor is treated with tenderness, and doubtless felt that the preacher was his friend.

The activity of Mr. Mather in pastoral duties had its reward in additions to the church. During several years the average admissions appear to have been over twenty-five. This covers the time between 1681, when he began to "assist" his father, and 1688, when the latter sailed for England.

Another sermon, though preached in 1686, belongs to the literary record of this year, as the date on the title-page is 1687. It was spoken to the Middlesex Artillery Company, then holding nearly the same rank as the Ancient and Honorable Artillery Company of Boston. The service was on the seventh of September, in a "very great assembly," in Charlestown, and as the whole affair, parade, sermon, and all, was redolent of the times when Indian warfare raged in New England, and dread apprehensions were felt about the action of the home government under James, the reader will not object to a brief glance at the sermon.

The text was Psalm 144: 1: "Blessed be the Lord my strength, which teacheth my hands to war, and my fingers to fight." One of the titles was " Military Duties laid before a Trained Band." In the introduction he argues against war, except for just cause, and inculcates the spirit of peace. He considers, (1) What God was to David ; and (2) What he had *done* for him. He goes on: " God is to be acknowledged as the author of whatsoever

military skill or strength any children of men do excel in."
"It is the privilege of some to excel in these respects,
namely, 1. Some excel in military *skill*."

There is such a happy unhappy art used among Adam's wrangling
posterity in the world, as that of *Tactics*, or the art of war; and there
we may find those who have the honor of being excellently well-skilled
therein . . . persons that understand all the *figures* and *postures*
which a soldier is to use in the handling of his arms; persons that are
well-acquainted with all the *motions* and *orders* which a soldier may be
called to; all the various *facings* and numerous *doublings* and intricate
countermarchings and comely *wheelings* which are customary; and all
the *chargings* which the many sorts and shapes of *battaile* do admit,
with innumerable *stratagems* of war; persons, in a word, who can
handsomely apply all the *instruments* of *defense* which a soldier may,
cap-a-pie, be furnished with; and all the *instruments* of *offense* which
a soldier's hand can be put unto, from the handspike unto the granado,
and the roaring cannon.

He then remarks that some men are excellent for their
military *strength*, and gives examples of those who were
endowed with great strength of *body*, as Samson, Iron-
side, king of England, Scanderbeg, who could "make his
sword strike through iron," and "through the neck of a
mighty wild bull," and also of Milo and Maximus.

Others have *strength* of *spirit*, as David's band, who
were all "mighty men of valor." Again: "We may see
men whose blood chills not when they are called out to
die alone in cold blood; men that, with a steady countenance can take grim death, arrayed with all its pompous
horrors, by the cold, clammy hand, and cheerfully say,
'*Friend*, do thy worst!' Such skill and such strength
many mortals have."

In his second division he shows that God is the author
of skill and of strength. Therefore it is the duty of men
to acknowledge God as the author of these, as of all other
mercies. In the way of *uses*, he shows that military dis-

cipline is a very "lawful thing" and a "very needful thing." He appreciated the value of a good soldier. "Men expert in military discipline are to be had in high account by us as the great blessings of the great God."

The last topic is the "holy, individual warfare" of every soul against sin. The "godly man is never free with wars with some soul enemies; therefore soldiers should put on the whole armor of God." The whole sermon is full of thought, rich in illustration, and instinct with life and force.

Mr. Mather's firstborn child, named Abigail, from her mother, first saw the light on the twenty-second of August, 1687. There is no complete list of the children in print. Mr. S. G. Drake states that there were fifteen sons and daughters, but gives the names of only thirteen. The dates of birth and death are not in all cases accurate. He places Katharine first in the list, without giving the date of her birth. He then gives the birth of Abigail as above. This proves that the latter was the firstborn, as her parents were married in the preceding year. I have found, in reading the diaries and several funeral sermons, the order in which all the fifteen children were born, as well as their names, but the list will be reserved for a later chapter. This child was short-lived, as will be seen from the sermon preached by her father on the occasion of her death. It was entitled, "Right Thoughts in Sad Hours," and presented the comforts and the duties of good men under all their afflictions, and particularly that of the untimely death of children. "Unto the upright there ariseth light in darkness." "Mercatura est pauca amittere, ut majora luseris."[1] When preached, he had no second child, but Katharine was born in 1689. Thus these pas-

---

[1] "It is good exchange to lose a few things that you may enjoy greater." — *Tertullian.*

sages show that this was the firstborn, and as yet the only child in the family. It is dedicated to S. S., probably Judge Sewall, as follows : " To my worthy friend : ever-honored Sir. The ensuing sermon, delivered . . . under afflictive impressions from the sudden death of an only child, with a bestowal of some correction and enlargement since upon it, I know no fitter person than yourself to present unto. Yourself, I say, who have had several infants carried hence unto the Father of spirits, in the chariot of the same distemper that fecht mine away."

From Genesis 42 : 36 he proceeds to show that the loss of children is *not* against us, but *for* us, and *for* them. He says : " I have often felt the power, and almost the sweetness of that persuasion, my God will never hurt me. So far as the loss is a dealing of God, it is intended for our good, and does work for the good of them that love him. And, in regard to the children, they are taken from the evil to come, and received the sooner to glory." The sermon is full of sweet, comforting thoughts. He felt keenly the anguish of a bereaved parent. He says : " Of outward, earthly anguishes, none equal unto these. The dying of a child is like to the tearing of a limb unto us." He proceeds : —

Was the infant whose decease we do deplore, one that was very pretty, or that had pretty features, pretty speeches, pretty actions? Well, at the resurrection of the just we shall see the dear lambs again. The Lord Jesus will deal with our dead children, as the prophets Elijah and Elisha did by those whom they raised of old ; he will bring them to us, recovered from the pale jaws of death ; and how amiable, how beautiful, how comely they will then be, no tongue is able to express, or heart conceive. Though their beauty do consume in the grave, yet it shall be restored ; it shall be advanced, when they shall put off their bedclothes in the morning of the day of God. . . . The fit epitaph of such infants is : " Of such is the kingdom of heaven." Have we any doubts about the eternal salvation of the children which we have buried out of our sight? . . . As to young children, the fear of God will take [away] all matter of scruple in the owners of them. Parents, can you not sincerely say, that you have given, as yourselves, so your children unto God, in a covenant never to be forgotten? . . . Then be of good cheer, your children are in a better place, a better state, than you yourselves are yet attained unto. . . . Those dear children are gone from your kind arms unto the sweet bosom of Jesus. And this is by far the best of all, to have children, this day in heaven.

Thus did he learn by early experience to comfort the afflicted. The bereavement this death occasioned was the first one in a long series which came to grieve the heart, while kindling the graces, of the father. Of fifteen children, nine died in infancy or early childhood.

CHAPTER V.

IN the spring of this year President Mather went to
England on business of the colony and with special
reference to the charter. He sailed April 7, and reached
the coast of England on the sixth of May. His son
Samuel, then fourteen years old, went with him, and
continued his education in the old country. As the father
was detained in England about four years, the whole care
of the church and parish fell upon the son, with perhaps
occasional help. The second son, Nathaniel, remained at
home, pursuing his studies with unremitting diligence and
fervor. The intense application of this marvelous scholar
was more than a mortal body could endure, and he died,
it would seem, from sheer exhaustion. The day of his
decease was October 17. He died in Salem, and was
buried there. As a genius, a scholar, and a Christian, he
rivaled his older brother at the same age, and inspired
the highest hopes of future eminence and usefulness.

One of the sermons that marked this year was preached
on the twenty-eighth of October, eleven days after 'the
decease of this brother, and was occasioned by that event.
The general subject was: "The Walk of holy and happy
Men." Text: "Enoch walked with God."

In the first place, he describes that walk; then he tells
the grand end of a good walk: "God took him." In the
third place, he points out the interest and duty of youth:
or the "Thoughts of an elder on the Death of a younger
brother." There is no special mention of Nathanael in

the discourse ; no biographical facts, and no expression of personal feelings in view of his loss.   It was character-istic of Mather not to obtrude, or even suggest, his own personal feelings or griefs ; but it is evident, all through, that he spoke from a full and chastened heart ; and as remembering a brother who remembered his Creator, and walked with God in the days of his youth.   The sub-text was from Ecclesiastes 12 : 1.   The following paragraph is a specimen of an old-time sermon.   Speaking of the many *conveniences* a young man has to excite and assist his remembrance of the Lord, the preacher says : —

There seems to be a sort of correspondence between youth and grace.   Youth seems mightily adapted and agreeable to the exercise of that lovely thing.   A quick wit is one prerogative of the young man. Well, how can he lay it out better than by doing like that young man in Psalm 119 : 9, by taking heed to the word of God?   The young man has a tenacious memory.   What can he do better with it, than fill it with Divine treasures?   Warm affections are stirring in the young man. Where should he set them than on the things above?   The spirits of young men are mettlesome.   Why should they not be fervent, serving the Lord?   The bodies of young men are vigorous.   Why should they not be a living sacrifice unto God?   There is a brave courage in youth. How can it better show itself than by overcoming the wicked one? Youth is a merry age.   Let it then rejoice in the Lord.   O, nothing is more comely and natural than that young men should remember God.

Several editions of this sermon have been published, one or more of them by the Congregational Publishing Society.

The church seems to have enjoyed the presence of the Spirit in the year 1689, as twenty-six were received to full communion, among whom was Abigail Mather, probably the wife of the pastor.

Several events which began in 1688 extended into the next year.   In fact, the Indian war in the eastern regions broke out in 1687, when, by the instigation of the French, the savages entered on aggressions which did not end in ten years, except for short intervals. The occasion and origin of this war cannot be given in this place exactly, even if it could be discovered. The Indians made complaints against the English, and the French followed them with accusations. The English, in reply, complained of insults and injuries, and added that if the enemy had suffered any wrong, they ought to have sought satisfaction in a lawful way, before resorting to hostilities.

Sir Edmund Andros was summoned from New York, and coming to the Bay he raised an army of a thousand men, with whom he marched to the eastward; but as winter came on, the enemy retired to the woods and so escaped. The expedition served no good purpose. Many more of our soldiers died from exposure than were killed or taken from the enemy.

It was a season of great hardship. Houses were burned; cattle were killed or driven off; women and children were taken captive, and men were slain. To encourage the people in this time of suffering and gloom, Mr. Mather preached a sermon on the first of September, 1689, entitled: "Soldiers counselled and comforted: a Discourse delivered unto some of the forces engaged in the late war of New England against the northern and eastern Indians." It was addressed "To my much honored friends, the pious and valiant commanders of the forces engaged against our Indian enemies." The sermon was published by request. The author wrote: "The reasons for preaching and printing this little sermon are, a desire to save the souls, and mend the lives, and promote the edification of those for whom my heart's desire and prayer to God is, that they may be happy; my ambition to encounter and abolish, what I can, the unchristian temper of those who take advantage from the other difficulties and entanglements of the country, to refuse doing their part in carrying on the Indian war." He gave the officers and soldiers this assurance: "It is the war of the Lord which you are engaged in, and it is the help of the Lord that we are at home affectionately imploring for you." He then addressed the officers as follows: —

Gentlemen: your forces are happy in you; none of you being that debauched sort of captains, which will drink, and swear, and curse, and profane the Sabbath; and at the same time, give out that perilous word of command, "Follow your leaders." Alas, whither do they lead them? But I assure myself you are such as have long since listed yourselves under the banner of the Lord Jesus Christ.

After these addresses, he comes to the text (Psalm 119: 109): "My soul is continually in my hand; yet do I not forget thy law." From these words he deduces four weighty suggestions: —

1. The remembrance of God's law is a thing of no small importance to them that have their lives continually in their hands. 2. The direction proper for them that have their lives in their hands, is to remember the law of God. 3. Our having our lives in our hands, ought not to affright us from anything that the law of God makes incumbent on us. 4. Don't part with your lives out of your hands, without such demonstrations of courage as may confound your adversaries.

The first connection of Cotton Mather with the witchcraft calamity began in 1688, when he received the children of the Goodwin family into his house, and kept them until they were cured of "whatsoever disease they had." His book styled "Memorable Providences," about which there has been much mistake and misrepresentation, was not given to the press until the following year. But the facts of this sad experience, as they are detailed in that and other publications, will be reserved till we come to the final horror in 1692. Here it is only necessary to mark the time when Mr. Mather was drawn into connec-

tion with the witchcraft phenomena by the importunity of
the father, Mr. Goodwin, in 1688, and to note the date of
the publication, in 1689.

At this time, Mr. Mather, though still younger than
most ministers at their settlement in modern years, had
become one of the most able, learned, and devoted pastors
in the American colonies. His reputation had extended
through New England, and beyond, but up to this time
his name had not been prominently connected with public affairs. There was now, however, a call for such a
man, and he readily gave his hearty coöperation to the
mature and able men who had been a few years before
superseded by Andros, Randolph, and their subordinates.
Though earnestly devoted to his work as a parish minister, with the whole care of a very large congregation, he
soon became conspicuous for his zeal and ability in the
guidance of public affairs at a critical crisis.

The charter had been demanded in 1683 by Charles
II. The colony refused to surrender it. It was vacated
in 1685 by the Court of Common Pleas, and that without
giving the colony an opportunity to be heard by its
agents, who were on their way to England. Soon after,
Sir Edmund Andros had been appointed president by
the king, and his jurisdiction included the rest of New
England (excepting Rhode Island) and New York. In
taking away the charter, the design was, without doubt,
to bring the colony under the direct government of the
king and to subvert its liberties and its property rights.
This was the common purpose of Charles and James, but
the latter had a further plan, there is reason to believe,
which was to interfere with the religious rights and privileges of the Protestant colonies as well as with those of
his Protestant subjects in England and Scotland.

Andros had no sympathy, political or religious, with the

Puritan colonies, and so far as their rights were in peril he was a willing servant of the king. This was made evident by his actions and his neglects. He was soon suspected of being hostile to the constitution of the colonies and to the general sentiment of the people. It was reported that he and his satellites had given voice to the opinion that the inhabitants must give place to a new immigration. It was dangerous to English despotism to have a free republic grow upon these shores, although a colony under the crown.

The common people in Boston and throughout the colony of the Bay and of Plymouth, with that political discernment which seems to be an unerring instinct of Anglo-Saxons, appear to have taken an accurate measure of Andros sooner than their leaders. Discontent grew apace, and in the year 1688, before William of Orange had sailed for England, there was a rapid maturing of the public mind in favor of resistance to unjust demands. There was no outbreak, however, until news came from England that the Revolution had been successful. This event had been foreshadowed by advices from the mother country. Doubtless Increase Mather, who was in the midst of the excitement in London during the summer and autumn, had kept his friends informed of the state of things and of the great design of the Prince. From the time the report came of the sailing of William on his perilous undertaking till Mr. Winslow brought authentic intelligence of his triumphal entrance into London, the people waited with intense anxiety. From every pulpit and from thousands of family altars prayers ascended to heaven that the Prince might be prospered in " maintaining the liberties of England."

When word reached Boston, early in April, that William and Mary were seated on the throne, the governor demanded of the messenger the paper containing the intelligence, and because it was not yielded threw him into prison. He also issued a proclamation commanding all people to use their endeavors to prevent any person, whom the new king might send, from landing. Vain were his efforts, for the hearts of the people were averted from James; they hated Andros and his tools and they had strong confidence in the new sovereigns. The people of Boston and the towns adjacent formed clubs and resolved to stand by each other in defense of their rights. It is clear that there was already an organization, like that which appeared nearly a hundred years later, at the opening of the Revolution of 1776, which embraced the bulk of the population, because the town was soon in arms, and in an almost incredibly brief time soldiers in large numbers had hurried on from towns in Middlesex and Essex counties. They were massed at Charlestown, and ready to cross the Charles at the word of command. Some of the wary leaders and experienced men of affairs were at first disposed to let things remain as they were until word came from the new government in England, fearing lest violence here might be resented at court. They were ready, however, if the people were resolute for a change, to put themselves at the head of the movement, and, as far as possible, direct it so as to prevent any unseemly and sanguinary outbreak.

The sentiments of the people were not long in finding expression. They demanded the deposition of Andros and the setting up of a provisional government until word should come from England. A company of soldiers, under Captain Hill, conducted ex-Governor Bradstreet, eighty-five years old, Mr. Danforth, Major Richards, Dr. Cook, and Mr. Addington to the council house. In the meantime the people had seized Randolph, Justice Bullivant, and several other enemies of the colony, and having superseded the gaoler by another man, whom they could trust, put them all in prison.

By noon the gentlemen in the council house to the number of fifteen, including, besides those already mentioned, William Stoughton, two Winthrops (Adam and Waite), and other men of standing, had prepared a summons to President Andros that he should "forthwith surrender and deliver up the government and fortifications, to be preserved and disposed according to ordered directions from the crown of England, which suddenly is expected, may arrive ; promising all security to yourself, or any of your gentlemen or soldiers, in person and estate. Otherwise we are assured they will endeavor the taking of the fortification by storm, if any opposition be made."

Andros, having castled himself at the fort, at first refused to surrender and sent to a frigate in the harbor for means of defense ; but a second summons came ·with such emphasis that he gave himself up as a prisoner and put the fort into the hands of the patriots.

This being done, the gentlemen in the council chamber ordered a declaration to be read to a vast concourse of people from the gallery. This document was drawn up by Cotton Mather, and is quite remarkable in its way. It is headed : " The Declaration of the Gentlemen, Merchants and Inhabitants of Boston, and the country adjacent, April 18, 1689," and then proceeds under twelve heads, giving the facts and reasons on which the Revolution was founded.

This has always been considered an able state paper, and the reader will find it so, on perusal, though not in the style of the present day. Though the phraseology was already going out of fashion in England, yet it smacks of the days of John Pym and of the other great statesmen of the Long Parliament; while for its array of facts, its methods, and its cogency, it belongs to all time. Some have doubted that it could have been written on the spur of the moment, and because Mather states that the leading men laid their plans beforehand to guide the populace it has been inferred by some, contrary to general opinion, that the manifesto was prepared in anticipation of a public necessity. But there is no occasion to question that it was put to paper rapidly when the crisis came. All the facts of our early history were familiar to the author; probably more so than to any other man except his father, who was then in England. Besides, the writer had a wonderful faculty in arranging facts and putting arguments. In his mind they all sprang to their place, and his facility in expressing them was unrivaled by that of any man in the colony. It seems to have been his office in all sorts of assemblies, great as well as small, to embody the general sentiment in lucid and forceful sentences.

The gentlemen who issued this address took measures to have a general assembly meet as soon as possible, by appealing to the towns for the choice of delegates, and took upon themselves the temporary duties of a provisional government, under the title of a "Committee of Safety." The assembly met towards the end of May, and must have been composed of earnest and determined men, if we may judge from the results of their deliberations as exhibited in the Declaration sent out to the people, dated May 24. In it they declare in favor of settling the government on their charter rights and privileges, "devolving the full power of government upon, and intrusting it in the hands of those in office when the charter government was vacated."

But Bradstreet and the old members of the council

were wary men, and chose to act as a merely temporary
provisional government, until they could learn the temper
and designs of the new sovereigns. In this way society
was held together for several months (though there were
some who did not respect the authorities), and in this way
they avoided being censured for acting under a vacated
charter. In the autumn a letter, dated August 12, came
from the king and queen, giving "allowance and approbation" of the proceedings of the extemporized administration and continuing their authority till further orders
from the home government.

The author of the Declaration made by the assembly
is not known, but we may reasonably conjecture from
expressions in it that it was revised, if not written, by the
author of the former paper. In either case the sovereigns and their ministers in England could not fail to be
convinced that the colonists had suffered great insults,
indignities, and hardships, and that they knew how to
redress their grievances and defend their actions.

Though it has taken time and space to relate the
service rendered to the public by Mr. Mather in the first
half of the year 1689, it really occupied but a little of
his time and attention, as his duties to his people were
done with great assiduity. This was his vocation, to be
a parish minister; his avocations held him but a short
time from his life work. In the way of parish duty he
preached four sermons which were published by the request and at the expense of his father-in-law, Captain
Phillips. The general title of the book, of 128 pages,
was "Small Offers towards the Service of the Tabernacle
in the Wilderness; four sermons accommodated to the
design of practical godliness." Mr. Phillips had lately
"been restored from threatening sickness," and he secured the publication of this volume "as an humble essay

to serve the interests of religion, in gratitude to God for his recovery." Their practical nature is expressed by their titles and texts: — I. "Methods wherein Men ought to engage both Themselves and their Houses in the Service of God." *Joshua* 24: 15. II. "The Right and Best Ways of Redeeming Time in the World." *Eccles.* 8: 5. III. "The Carriage We should have under Trials used by God upon us." *Job* 23: 10. IV. "Concerning the End which in our Desires of Life we should propound unto ourselves." *Psalms* 119: 175.

The year 1690 was marked by the usual activity of Mr. Mather. His congregation was large; probably the largest in New England or in all the colonies; and its demands on him as pastor were severe and unceasing. Besides, no week passed without giving many hours to prayer and fasting.

The increase of the church went on steadily, the additions being far above the average in Christian churches. Among those who united by confession this year were two of his sisters, Elizabeth and Sarah. The former, who became Mrs. Greenleaf, and later, Mrs. Byles, was twenty-five years old; Sarah, afterwards Mrs. Walter, was nineteen; Mary, or Mariah, the eldest sister, had been a member since 1682. The famous William Phips, already knighted, came into the church this year. The personal attachment between him and his pastor was very strong, and continued through life. After the death of Phips, Mather wrote his life — one of the finest pieces of biography in the language. It is pertinent to notice the fact in this place that Mary Goodwin, the girl who had been taken to Mr. Mather's house two years before while suffering under supposed witchcraft machinations, and there cured, became a member of the church at this time. And we may anticipate by stating that this trophy, who lived many years to be a reputable Christian, always maintained that there was no trickery or deception in her strange conduct while at his house.

The sermons delivered before the general court have been, in all generations down to the time of their discontinuance in 1884, by ministers of prominence in their profession. A few only have been heard on more than one occasion; but Mr. Mather was invited to this duty several times. Besides, the Thursday Lecture was sometimes attended by the general court, when in session; and at times special fasts were appointed by the council, when the members attended. On occasions of this kind the young pastor of the North Church was heard many times, and his sermons were always adapted to the occasion. Two sermons that were given to the press this year (1690), though preached the year before, are in point. One was entitled "The Way to Prosperity," and the subject was treated in a masterly manner. He referred to causes which hindered prosperity, and then pointed out the principles and methods by which prosperity may be attained. As was his wont, he was intensely practical in exposing evils and applying the remedies. The sermon was printed by general desire.

The other discourse was preached to the general court on public Thanksgiving, December 19. "The Wonderful Works of God commemorated, in Creation and Redemption," was his theme. He also referred to "remarkable resolutions of providence, especially in connection with the success of King William." His divisions were:— 1. Happy things in creation; 2. Happy things in redemption; 3. Happy things in providence. In conclusion, he urged the repeal of wicked laws. All true sons of the soil desired to have every trace of Andros, Randolph, and company, erased from the statute book.

The sermon, with other matters, made a volume of sixty-four pages, which throw light on the state of affairs at that time.

All classes of men sought the interest and services of our young minister, and those in all stages of life. In this year (1690) he preached and published addresses to "Old Men, and young men, and little children." They were affectionate, earnest, and singularly well adapted to each class. See the significance and beauty of the titles : I. "The old man's Honor ; or, the Hoary Head found in the Way of Righteousness ; recommending unto old men a saving acquaintance with the Lord Jesus Christ." II. "The Young Man's Glory ; or, a Wreath of graces for the Head of youths; recommending unto young men a blessed victory over the devil." III. "The Little Child's lesson ; or, a Child Wise unto Salvation ; a discourse instructing and inviting little children to the exercises of early piety." A brief catechism was added, adapted to the capacity of children. At the end, the ten commandments were condensed into verse, as follows:

> Worship thou shalt no God but me,
> No graven image make to thee,
> The Lord's name take thou not in **vain,**
> The Sabbath do thou not profane.
> Lend to thy parents honor due,
> And see that thou no murder do.
> Commit thou no adulterie;
> Moreover from all stealing flee.
> No false thing of thy neighbor say
> And covet not in any way.

A late celebrated Connecticut divine had a way, when he could not find a hymn that was needed, of writing one for the occasion ; and I suppose the reason why Cotton Mather printed so many sermons and small books was that the supply of such " composures " was so limited in those days. There were many books in the seventeenth century, but few comparatively that were adapted to the wants of the common people and of portable size for the pocket. He became a sort of "Book and Publishing Society," and supplied a want. The "Companion for Communicants" was in this line, and was made up of "discourses upon the nature, the design, and the subject of the Lord's Supper, with devout methods of preparing for, and approaching to that blessed ordinance." The dedication and prefatory paragraph recall the past: "To the church of the Lord Jesus in the north part of Boston; particularly to the Honorable Sir William Phips, Kt.; to the Worshipful John Richards, Esq., and to my honored and worthy friends, Mr. Adam Winthrop, Mr. John Foster, Dr. John Clark. Invitations to the supper of the Lord; preparations for the supper of the Lord; devotions at the supper of the Lord." 136 pp.

"An Order by the governor and general court, for the work of reformation," came out March 13. On the 20th Mr. Mather preached a lecture on "The Present State of New England, considered in a discourse on the necessities and advantages of a public spirit in every man, especially at such times as this, — upon the news of an invasion by the bloody Indians and Frenchmen, begun upon us." It was addressed to Governor Bradstreet. The text was Esther 4: 14, and the topic drawn from it was that "every Christian should readily and cheerfully venture his all to serve the people of God, when a time of distress and danger calleth for it." Such discourses, in those days, raised the spirits of the people, gave a tone to the public mind, and greatly helped the government to act with vigor in meeting the enemy.

A small volume of 156 pages came out at this time, with a preface signed by several Boston ministers, with the title : " The Principles of the Protestant Religion maintained, and Churches of New England, in the profession and exercise thereof, defended, against all the calumnies of one George Fox, a Quaker." Fox had written a book in Pennsylvania, assailing the churches. Dr. Sibley suggests that Mather was the principal author of this reply.

On the twenty-eighth of May, before the general court, at the election anniversary, was presented " The Serviceable Man." A vote of thanks was passed and the discourse was requested for publication. Taking the words of Nehemiah : " Think upon me, my God, for good, according to all that which I have done for this people," he described a *good man*, and then proceeded to show that " the God of heaven had good thoughts for those men whose good works render them serviceable to his people." This was a speech for the times, and, like all his productions, evinced the clear-headed insight of Mather and the adaptation of his words to the wants of the public. He was not the forward, meddlesome man who has been described to us by writers, following each other in ignorant repetitions ; but one who spoke what the general good demanded, and who published what was desired. IIe grasped the fact that a New England pastor, like an ancient prophet of the Hebrews, was a "tribune of the people " as well as a minister of the New Testament. In his day, when what is now called " the press " was an unknown factor in political life, such an office was specially needed, and the speeches and writings of such a man were helpful for men in public as well as in private station. In this discourse, after giving the points of the serviceable man, he stimulates all to be serviceable men, and presents, among other motives, the highest possible ; that is, the favor of God to such men. Quakers and others who were not serviceable, who withheld their aid, tried to discourage the loyal and true ; but he opposed all persecuting measures against those who were derelict in duty to the state.

The year 1691 was filled with labors and prayers. The affairs of his church, as well as those of his family, absorbed Mr. Mather's chief attention. His little daughter Katharine, born in 1689, was an engaging child, and to her a little sister was born in November of this year. Her Christian name is not found in any genealogical sketch of the family, but I find in the diary for 1693, October 6, that the child Mary died, and that she was "near a month short of two years old."

There must have been uncommon religious interest in the congregation this year, as the number added to the church was forty-nine. His father being still in England, struggling for a charter against formidable odds, and with feeble support from some of his colleagues, the son had to bear the full burden of pulpit work and pastoral supervision. The care in training the candidates for admission ; the attendance on many funerals ; the strain on the nervous system from sympathy with the sick and the bereaved ; the preparation of works for the press, with special reference to the needs of his own flock, and his duties to the poor and those in prison, pressed heavily upon him. The witchcraft trouble pursued him, and he gave much time to the wholesome regimen of diet and prayer, in behalf of the suffering and the deluded. Nor was his interest in public affairs remitted. The Indian raids, exasperated by the French, were a serious drain upon the life and resources of the colony, and the influence of the clergy was needed to keep hope alive in rulers and people.

The works prepared for, and put through, the press this

year would have consumed most of the time of an ordinary worker. Altogether they would have made a book of over eight hundred pages, 12mo., in type suitable for that sized volume. Some of these publications were sermons, adapted for the press after delivery;' others, like the "Life of Eliot" (pp. 168), required extra writing. Another of these larger volumes (pp. 92) had the title "Balsamum Vulnerarium e Scriptura," "a balsam for wounds, drawn from Scripture; or, the cause and cure of a wounded spirit." A volume kindred in spirit (pp. 93) was entitled "Fair Weather; or, Considerations to dispel the Clouds and allay the Storms of Discontent." The former seems intended for the solace of private griefs, while this is adapted to allay the evils of public complaints. It was a "discourse, which, with an entertaining variety, both of argument and history, lays open the nature and evil of that pernicious vice, and offers divers antidotes against it." The author gives a list of sins against all the commandments, and calls for honest repentance and confession before the Lord. There was a second edition in 1694.

"Good Soldiers a Great Blessing" was preached by request, it is presumed, of the Artillery Company, which desired a copy for the press. Mr. Sibley states that no correct copy has been found. The fact that such a sermon was solicited shows that the times demanded trained soldiers, and exhibits the sympathy between the clergy and the defenders of the country in the field.

A book relating to witchcrafts and possessions, entitled "Late Memorable Providences," was printed in 1690, but another edition came out in London this year, recommended by Richard Baxter and "three or four other ministers in Boston and vicinity." Other discourses were added, making a large collection of facts, or supposed facts, relating to the witchcraft epidemic.

The work numbered 28, in the list of Dr. Sibley, must be referred to, as it is in its title and matter eminently characteristic of its author. "Little Flocks guarded against Grievous Wolves ; an address unto those parts of New England which are most exposed unto assaults from the modern teachers of the misled Quakers; in a letter which impartially discovers the manifold heresies and blasphemies, and the strong delusions of even the most refined Quakerism ; and therefrom demonstrates the truth of those principles and assertions which are most opposite thereunto ; with just reflections upon the extreme ignorance and wickedness of George Keith, of Penn., who is the seducer that now most ravines upon the churches in this wilderness." This Keith afterwards entered the Episcopal ministry in England and became a strong opposer of Quakerism.

One of the happiest efforts of Mr. Mather was his "Ornaments for the Daughters of Zion; or, the character and happiness of a vertuous woman, in a discourse which directs the female sex how to express the fear of God in every age and state of their life, and obtain both temporal and eternal blessedness." Another edition came out in Cambridge in 1692 ; one in London in 1694, and two others in Boston, the last as late as 1741. It has a motto from Lactantius : " Go ye forth now, arrayed with such ornaments as the apostles have provided for you; clothe yourselves with the silk of piety, the satin of sanctity, the purple of modesty ; so the Almighty God will be a lover of you." The text was Proverbs 31 : 30: "Favour is deceitful, and beauty is vain, but a woman that feareth the Lord, she shall be praised." He takes the ancient view as to the authorship of Solomon, and speaks of Bathsheba, his mother, as the wise woman who is supposed to speak the words of the text. These are the "words of Bathsheba to Solomon." He then refers to several women whose " wise words" are recorded in the Bible; as, Deborah, Hannah, Huldah, Miriam, Mary. Under the first division, he treats of the "character of the vertuous woman." She "counts the best female favor to be deceitful; the best female beauty to be vain." He explains that " by favor is meant a comely presence, a handsome carriage, a decent gesture, a ready wit, expressing itself with all other graceful motions, and whatsoever procures favor for a woman among her neighbors. The vertuous woman is willing to have this favor so far as is consistent with virtue. She counts it a favor of God for one to be graced with it; still, she looks upon it as a deceitful thing. She is careful that she do not hereby deceive herself into proud imaginations, and into an humor conceited of herself, and contemptuous of others." After an excellent description of the virtuous woman, he speaks, in the second place, of the virtuous woman's happiness. The book is so full, so sensible and entertaining that it would bear republication.

"Expectanda; or, Things to be looked for," a 12mo of 83 pages, was printed this year, bearing the running title of " Discourses on the glorious characters, with conjectures on the speedy approaches of that state which is reserved for the church of God in the latter days; together with an inculcation of several duties which the undoubted characters and approaches of that state invite us unto." This was "delivered unto the Artillery company" at the annual election of officers.

A more important work followed, of about 160 pages, which passed through four editions in Boston and London, besides being in all the editions of the *Magnalia*. This was styled "The Triumphs of the Christian Religion in America; The Life of the renowned John Eliot, a person justly famous in the church of God, not only as an eminent Christian, and an excellent minister among the English, but also as a memorable evangelist among the Indians of New England." Later editions have an account of the "many strange customs of the pagan Indians." I give a passage from the Introduction, showing the spirit of the biographer. Having implored the acceptance and assistance of that God "whose blessed word has told us 'the righteous shall be held in everlasting remembrance,'" he continues : —

I am attempting to write the life of a righteous person, concerning whom all things but the meanness of the writer, invite the reader to expect nothing but what is truly *extraordinary*. It is the life of one who has better and greater things to be affirmed of him, than could ever be reported concerning any of those famous men which have been celebrated by the pens of a Plutarch, a Pliny, a Laertius, an Eurapius, or in any pagan histories. It is the life of one whose character might very agreeably be looked for among the collections of a Dorotheus, or the orations of a Nazianzen ; or is worthy at least of nothing less than the exquisite stile of a Melchior Adam to eternise it.

The remaining publication of this year to be noticed was "A Scriptural Catechism," which is chiefly valuable now for its historical character, as it is one of the few compendiums of Christian doctrine which have come down from the fathers of New England theology.

We catch a glimpse of the ways of the "olden time," in the fact that near the beginning of the year the church chose a committee of four, to "take care of seating persons in the meetinghouse," and a committee "to see to repairs of the meetinghouse." Also, voted, that the "pastor be desired to take what care he shall judge proper in choosing persons for the inspection of children in the meetinghouse."

CHAPTER VI.

HALFWAY COVENANT. — AUTHORSHIP. — WITCHCRAFT. —
THE GOODWIN CHILDREN : 1691–1692.

THE year 1692 was memorable in the life of Cotton
Mather, made specially so by the culmination of
the witchcraft horror in the trial and execution of nineteen persons in the summer months. The excitement
began before this year, and continued after its close; but
that which has made a dark and sad page in our history
belongs to 1692. In this sad chapter Mr. Mather has a
large space by right, because of the prominent part taken
by him to extirpate the evil, and a still larger, because of
the false charges made against him a few years later;
charges that have been repeated and amplified in more
recent times. Yet the witch enchantment occupied but
a small portion of his time during this troubled year.

He was very weak in the early months of the year.
The troubles caused by witchcraft drew him to Salem in
the spring, but, contrary to the popular belief, he did not
attend a single trial during the summer. Notwithstanding severe illness, his activity as a student, as a pastor,
preacher, friend of education, and author was unabated.
No form of benevolent action asked for his aid in vain;
though in all this tireless activity he was fettered by
bodily weakness which seemed to portend an early death.

Under date of February 7, it is recorded as follows:
"This day our congregation gathered seventy-two pounds,
odd shillings, for the redemption of our captives in the
hands of the Indians." Liberal contributions for similar
objects of charity were often made by the church.

One person was admitted to the church this year on the halfway covenant, so called, and her son was baptized. It is singular that this was the first instance of the kind in the North Church since Increase Mather was influential in promoting that innovation many years before. The change was opposed by leading members of the church, the most active of whom was the Honorable John Richards, who came over in 1644, and settled in Boston, where he became a rich merchant. His standing in the colony is shown by the fact that he was Speaker of the House, an assistant in 1680, and agent of the colony in England. He was also one of the judges in 1692, before whom the cases of witchcraft were tried. The church was led into the adoption of the new plan by the address of the pastor, while the teacher was in England, but with his concurrence. The following letter to Major Richards will let us into the manner by which the change was secured : —

February 13, 1692.

My Dear Major, — You are doubtless, as well as I, convinced, that it is a time for churches to do some remarkable thing, in the matter of returning unto God ; and perhaps you have lately read, what I have writ upon that Article.

I now send you a recognition of the duties to which our Covenant has obliged us ; and of the evils wherein we are most in danger to forget our covenant.

The voting of such recognitions, in such terms as are here laid before you, dos most effectually obtain the ends of a renewed covenant, and yet it is a thing so agreeable to the sense of even the weakest Christian, that I cannot imagine where those persons that have needlessly scrupled renewal of covenant, can here find any objections. . . .

I put it first into your hands, because my value for your person and judgment (which I have in print everlastingly signalized unto the world) will cause me either to proceed or desist, in the design which lies much upon my heart. And I desire you to use the more exact thought upon it, because, if I have your countenance, I am sure I shall have the immediate concurrence of *all this people*, to do a thing that would be as great a compliance with the loud calls of God, as any that I am capable of devising; and *I think also that I am somewhat awake*.

The method by which he induced the church to come into the new plan was characteristic. He did nothing by authority of his position. Instead of bringing the matter up at first in a meeting of the church and having a discussion, he sent a copy of the "Recognition of the Duties," of the church, in relation to the subject, and "the reasons for it," to all the members, requesting them to send their answers to him. In this way he secured general concurrence and avoided all irritation or division. It appears that a few did not approve of the measure, and with them he patiently labored until they gave their approbation, or in a kindly spirit agreed not to oppose its adoption.

On the tenth of April, he records: "Our church unanimously signified their acceptance of an Instrument which I laid before them, as containing the acknowledgments and protestations of their souls, and a recognition of their obligations, by their covenant laid upon them, for the revival of practical godliness among us." The day after he wrote a letter, or "little book," which was printed and sent to every communicant. The agreement to the "plan" was signified by written answers, instead of a vote in general meeting.

While this measure was thus before the members, the pastor wrote a longer letter to Major Richards which gives the most favorable view of the "halfway covenant" plan that I have ever seen. Perhaps the explanation was not the general one, but peculiar to a class of ministers, of which Mr. Mather was a leader. Citations will be made from this letter, dated December 14, 1692 : —

Many months are now past, since I laid before your hono:, my judgment, my desire, and with God's leave, my purpose, to administer the
baptism of our Lord, unto such as were instructed and orthodox in the
Christian religion, and should bring testimony signed by more than
one among the people of God, that they are of a vertuous conversation,
and should, after their names have been publicly propounded (and
objection cannot be made against them,) openly and seriously give
themselves up to God in Christ, according to the terms of the covenant
of grace, with a declaration of their study to prepare themselves further
for the table of the Lord.

I have intimated unto you, that I look upon such persons as visible
subjects in the kingdom of our Lord Jesus Christ, although they have
not proceeded so far in Christianity, as to be constituent members of
the corporations, the particular churches in that kingdom; and I have
intimated that baptism is an ordinance that belongs to visible Christians, or those that are visibly of the catholic church, before, and in
order to, their joining to a particular.

He then states the method he had taken to "try the
mind of the people," by sending the "instrument," which
he had already given to Mr. Richards, by "two or three
discreet men" to almost every one of the brethren "that
were not then abroad at sea," and adds that the papers
came back with nearly unanimous approval, signed by the
members. Some sent their desire for immediate action.
Only four failed to sign the address, and of these, two
expressed assent. "Briefly, I have seventy-five hands
(whereof three are of their Majesties' council) and I suppose I could for asking, have when I will, ten more, solic-
iting me to go on."

Mr. Mather fully agreed with those who maintain that
no unregenerate adult is to be baptized; but adds: "I
also think that a person so qualified, as has been described,
and one so sensibly submitting to the laws of our Lord,
should not be pronounced unregenerate."

The question then comes up: Why do not such persons
come forward and commune at the Lord's table? The

first answer is that they are "under doubts and fears." The second is, "Because the Supper of the Lord, requiring not only grace, but some growth in grace, and being a sacrament of confirmation, for those who have heretofore in baptism had their initiation, we may justly expect more positive attainments for the one than the other; and so the primitive Christians practised."

Another passage in this letter suggests a caution to churches which needs perpetual recognition. There are ministers who have their pet notions and methods, and when they come to a church, whether for a term of years or as a brief supply, wish to bring in their own ways of administration. Some churches have so little character as to submit to these whims; whereas every church should have its own rules and methods, which are not to be altered or departed from, except by vote of the church. Mather writes: "It was in part for this cause, that I was willing to have this Instrument so circumstanced; namely, because if hereafter you should have a pastor who may not be so concerned for purity of administration as I hope you have always found, and may yet find me to be, you may have an everlasting clog upon all endeavors of any man, to prostitute an ordinance." He proceeds to say of this plan: "It is properly My Work; and I have therefore so cautiously stated the whole matter, that I avoid entangling any of our brethren who may be scrupulous in any Act which they may not see light for. And yet I resolve also, in all my admissions, to have the particular assistances of two or three or more of our understanding brethren; and particularly of some that have been most scrupulous of enlargements [most opposed to the "halfway plan"] until we have a consistory of elders more fully settled."

To make the matter more clear and remove any scruple

from the major's mind, the pastor becomes more explicit still in the following passage, which he puts in italics : —

I am even now and then visited, by well-disposed people, who, I believe, have the fear of God in them ; and these tell me : " Sir, your Ministry has broke our hearts for us ; we would willingly become the professed servants of Jesus Christ ; it is a trouble to us that we, or ours, are not by baptism dedicated unto him : will you baptize us ? Sʳ, if you can't, we must be forced to seek that blessing elsewhere, and so leave your Ministry, which we would not leave upon any other terms whatsoever. It is true, we should come to the Lord's table ; but such is our weakness, we dare not ; pray don't punish us for that weakness ; and when we are a little better confirmed in Christianity, we shall come."

He adds that it was his conviction that such persons should be baptized, but that scores of such had been banished from his ministry, because he had " been loth to go against the sense of but two very good men " whom he valued very highly, of which men, Major Richards was the chief. With an earnest plea for the major's consent, he urges: " Say then, ought I not to do what the church has in the most explicit manner called me to ? "

It is safe to infer that the major gave consent, either by word or by silence, as the plan was adopted and the harmony of the church was not broken. The first person who entered into covenant under this system was Mary Sunderland, and her son John was the first child baptized in accordance with it. It deserves notice, however, that Cotton Mather did not encourage any to form this engagement with the church, unless they gave evidence of spiritual renewal. In regard to such persons he believed it to be right and safe to take them under the watch and care of the church, on the "halfway plan," with the hope that they would be led along in the path of holiness, and gain courage to come to the table of their Lord and

Saviour. If administered in that spirit generally, it is probable that the system would not have caused the serious mischief which did grow out of it in many churches, and which, in the course of the next century, led to its abandonment.

The publications of Mr. Mather this year fill more than five hundred pages. The title of one was " Blessed Unions ; a union with the Son of God by faith ; and a union in the church of God by love, importunately pressed in a discourse which makes divers offers for those unions." This has a historic interest. The Presbyterian and the Congregational parties in England had been separate, and even hostile, for more than half a century. In the outbreak of what has been styled the Great Rebellion, the Presbyterian party in England became influential by its connection with the Church of Scotland, and thus came into great prominence. It gained a sort of establishment in London, Lancashire, and other parts, by act of parliament. At this date the Independents, or Congregationalists, were few. In the assembly of divines, notables, and statesmen, held for the purpose of discussing the great question of religious liberty, the number of Presbyterians was ten to one of the other party. But by degrees this relative difference was greatly changed. Cromwell and his special friends were Congregationalists, or Independents. Sir Harry Vane was of that way of thinking. Milton was a pronounced Independent. Through the Protector's ascendancy, this rising party had great power in the state. After the return of Charles II, Presbyterianism was disestablished and more than two thousand ministers, mostly under the Presbyterian régime, were driven from their pulpits. But some of these men were Independents in sentiment, and during the reigns of Charles II and James II the number increased. Common sufferings and persecutions, under those lustful tyrants, brought the two parties into mutual sympathy and respect. Early in the reign of William and Mary, efforts were made to bring about a union, in 1691–1692; and articles of union were adopted by representatives of the two bodies. Increase Mather was then in England, and, being held in high esteem by both sides, had great influence in effecting the happy union. The two parties, being thus united, took the name or title of the "United Brethren." The discourse of Mather was dedicated to the very reverend Matthew Mead, John Howe, and Increase Mather. Howe and Mead were among the foremost divines of Old England, and Mather fitly represented the churches of New England.

As an example of Mr. Mather's tireless efforts to do good, his "Midnight Cry" may be named. It was an "essay for our awakening out of sinful sleep," presented on a "day of prayer kept by the North Church." A small edition was printed, which led him to say of it, as a philosopher did of his book, "'T is published, but scarcely made public."

Rev. Samuel Lee, a very learned man who came from England and was settled for a few years at Bristol, R. I., and then returned to the old country, and whose daughter became Mr. Mather's third wife, issued a work on the "Great Judgment." To this Mather prefixed "Preparatory Meditations upon the Day of Judgment."

A volume of about one hundred pages was published this year, both in Boston and London, under the title of "Optanda: Good Men described, and good things propounded. A serious consideration of two very important cases; I. What should be our Spirits, and II. What should be our Studies, that so all things may go well among us?" The volume was addressed to Gov-

ernor Phips, who on this day met the general court for
the first time in his official capacity. A short time before
he had returned from England with the new charter,
obtained chiefly by the ability and persistency of Increase
Mather. The younger Mather greatly rejoiced in the
elevation of Phips, who was his personal friend and a
member of his church. In reference to the promotion of
Phips he writes in his diary, in May : " But the time for
favor is now come ; yea, the set time is come." This
refers to the deliverance from the personal malice of
Andros and Randolph, by the turn of affairs.

I am now to receive the answers of many prayers as have been
employed for my absent parent, and the deliverance and settlement of
my poor country. We have not the former Charter, but we have a
better in the room of it ; one which much better suits our circumstances. And instead of my being made a sacrifice to wicked rulers,
all the counsellors of the Province are of my father's nomination, and
my father-in-law, with several related to me, and several brethren of
my own church, are among them. The governor of the Province is
not my enemy, but one whom I baptised, and one of my flock, and one
of my dearest friends.

This harmless passage has been made the occasion of
reproach to the writer, as if he were too much elated, and
exhibited an unmanly triumph. If he had sent a paragraph of the sort to the press (as public men now often
do, and without reproach) or had uttered it in a popular
address (which is sometimes done without censure), it
might perhaps be open to objection. But he must be a
carping critic who would censure Mather for being glad,
and writing so in his diary, that the tyranny of Andros
and his master was at an end, and that the government
was in the hands of personal friends and patriotic citizens.
And that was the whole of it. Mr. Mather had nothing
to gain by the revolution except in common with the

whole province.   There was no promotion which he could receive from the new governor.   His position as pastor of the Second Church in Boston left him nothing to covet in his native land, and he seems never to have had the craving for the old country that impelled so many to seek employment and promotion there.   If he ever cared to be president of the college, it was not with the hope of distinction or emolument, for the pay was small, and the distinction of being the most learned and popular preacher in America could not have been enhanced by the presidency of the college as it then existed.   His throne was the pulpit, whether preaching to his own congregation or before the general court.   In either place he was not only a minister of the gospel, but, like an old prophet in the Hebrew commonwealth, he was the guardian of the people's rights, while maintaining the authority of the nation's God.

In the sermon above referred to he described, in the first place, "good men," taking his text from Proverbs 17: 27: "A man of understanding is of an excellent spirit."   He said: "By the spirit is meant the soul; by the excellency of the spirit some ornament upon the soul."   1. An excellent spirit is an extraordinary spirit; one of rare and various attainments.   2. Holiness is one of its traits.   3. It is an active and useful spirit.   4. It is excellent in speech.   5. Its natural humor is sanctified. 6. It communes with the unseen world.   7. It is given to self-reckoning.   8. It is a cool spirit.   Self-control is one reading of the text.

The second sermon in the "Optanda" volume was founded on the words: "Also in Judah things went well." He says: "It has been remarked that the Bible is unto the church, what the firmament is unto the world; the God of heaven has gloriously expanded these heavenly oracles over us, and in this expanse we have those things that are to give light upon the earth. The steersmen of this poor, shattered, sinking bark are in a general assembly this day convened ; and there is a bright star in the firmament of the Bible, which I would humbly recommend unto their observation ; 't is the text."

After referring to the benefits which come from having good magistrates and good ministers, he goes on to say that : " Things will not go well unless the people do their part. 1. When they improve their interest in legislation, in the making of good laws. 2. When education is liberally encouraged. [Here he puts in a plea for schools and the college.] 3. The people must stand by good men. 4. They must promote a spirit of union and love. 5. They must find remedies against poverty and idleness. 6. They will prosper when they remember the Sabbath day. 7. When people flock to and keep up well-constituted churches. 8. When regeneration is frequent and common. 9. When supplication is joined with reformation. On these conditions, things would go well with any people."

Every point in the discourse was intensely practical and bore directly on the wants of the time. Nor did he fail to take strong grounds against the persecution of " erroneous and conscientious dissenters by the civil magistrate." He censured the " zeal of former times," which had sent the " mad quakers unto the gallows instead of bedlam." He stood alone, as he supposed, among the ministry in *publicly* condemning the policy of suppressing heresy by persecution, and hoped for greater success in opposing error and upholding truth by " spiritual and evangelical endeavors."

This was a year of anxiety and labor to Mr. Mather while in feeble health. He began the year, so far as pastoral labors were concerned, with " handling of the

miracles of Christ, and reflections on the history thereof."
He also had his heart set on " Designs of Reformation ";
and he tried to secure a "union of churches to find out
evils," hoping thereby to raise the state of piety. The
response was not as cordial as he had hoped, but he
pursued the object in his own parish. All this while,
his health was miserable. He states that it had been
"broken for several years"; partly by "excessive toil in
public exercises of the ministry," and also because he
had "sinned against the God of his health." He often
preached when he should have been in bed, but had been
greatly assisted on such occasions. "Illness, and vapor,
and aguish indisposition" had caused him to live in
"exceeding misery," so that he could "see nothing but
approaching death." But he writes: "Blessed be God
that I can die."

Later in the year, and after the trials at Salem and the
execution of the supposed witches, he wrote a passage in
his diary, which has been printed and which will help us
to know the state of his mind in relation to that great
tragedy. As we are drawing near to the narrative of his
connection with it, this extract may prepare us to inter-
pret his course with candor : —

For my own part, I was always afraid of proceeding to convict or condemn any person as a confederate with the afflicting demons upon so
feeble an evidence as a spectral representation. Accordingly I ever
protested against it both publicly and privately; and in my letters to
the judges, I particularly besought them, that they would by no means
admit it; and when a considerable assembly of ministers gave in their
advice about the matter, I not only concurred with them, but it was I
who drew it up. Nevertheless, on the other side, I saw in most of the
judges a most charming instance of prudence and patience, and I
know the exemplary prayer and anguish of soul wherewith they had
sought the direction of heaven, above most other people; whom I generally saw enchanted into a raging, railing, scandalous and unreason-

able disposition, as the distress increased upon us. For this cause, though I could not allow the principles that some of the judges had espoused, yet I could not but speak honorably of their persons on all occasions; and my compassion upon the sight of their difficulties, raised by my journeys to Salem, the chief seat of those diabolical vexations, caused me yet more to do so. And merely, as far as I can learn, for this reason, the mad people through the country, under a fascination on their spirits, equal to that which *energumens* had on their bodies, reviled me as if I had been the doer of all the hard things that were done in the prosecutions of the witchcraft.

It is somewhat difficult to give the connection of Cotton Mather with the witchcraft visitation in the order of time, and perhaps impossible to fix the date of his various publications on the subject, as there were several editions of some of these works, and those editions received additions as they came out. But the first book, as given in the full catalogue of Dr. Sibley, was entitled 'Memorable Providences relating to Witchcrafts and Possessions; a faithful account of many wonderful and surprising things that have befallen several bewitched and possessed persons in New England; particularly a narrative of the marvelous trouble and relief experienced by a pious family in Boston, very lately and sadly molested with evil spirits." Two sermons followed, one of which related to the same subject. An appendix was added, vindicating a "chapter in a late book of 'Remarkable Providences' from the calumnies of a Quaker at Pennsylvania." This volume, the "Memorable Providences," was printed in 1689, and had several reprints in Boston, London, and Edinburgh. This then was Cotton Mather's first publication on witchcraft, so far as known to me, and the date could not have been 1685, as stated by Peabody, because the experiences of the Goodwin family, related in the book, took place in 1688. The author of the "Remarkable Providences" was Increase Mather.

As the motives of Mr. Mather in giving this volume to the press have been severely condemned, it is but fair to give his own statement of them. "None but the Father who sees in secret, knows the heart-breaking exercises wherewith I have composed what is now going to be exposed, lest I should in any one thing miss of doing my designed service for his glory, and his people." Yet it has been the habit of historians, biographers, and essayists to treat this claim as a piece of self-delusion, and perhaps of hypocrisy, and to accuse Mather of being moved by considerations entirely selfish in all his connections with the witchcraft troubles. By some his action was ascribed to youthful vanity. He was young, and it would serve to make him the theme of wonder through the countryside, if he could be seen to take the lead in suppressing the works of the devil. By others he has been accused of ambition, as being desirous of gaining influence and power early in life, by shaping the public mind and guiding the judges. And by others still he has been suspected, if not accused, of trying to uphold the "waning influence" of the clergy by fanning the flame of superstition and compelling the people, as it were, to call on the ministers to overcome the machinations of the demons; and to beseech the God of heaven to interpose for the deliverance of the bewitched. Other accusations as senseless as these have had their day.

Again, to overwhelm the memory of Mather with a flood of reproach, the influence of his book has been vastly overrated, as if the public mind had been so inflamed by it that the people in some sections ran wild with excitement. It would almost seem as if he created witchcraft itself, and set all the "powers of the air" in motion, to vex and curse the good people of Salem village and parts adjacent. It appears to be forgotten that something akin to witchcraft had been in the world, in all parts of it, for thousands of years before it broke out in New England. The fact is ignored that in the Christian nations of Europe, so called, witchcraft was tenfold more a delusion and curse in the sixteenth, seventeenth, and eighteenth centuries than ever in Massachusetts. Passing by the Catholic and Protestant countries of continental Europe, there was in England and Scotland a far direr state of things than in Essex County. Witchcraft had been treated as a heinous crime in England long before our fathers crossed the sea.

A statute passed in the thirty-third year of the reign of Henry VIII had regard to witchcraft. In 1588 Queen Elizabeth was alarmed by the suggestion that her own person might be put in peril by the great increase of witches and sorcerers. Soon after a law was enacted making enchantments and witchcraft felony; and upon this foundation, says the late Mr. Samuel T. Haven, "the English law relating to those declared crimes was built up, and established by repeated trials; by another statute in the reign of James I, and by the ruling of the most distinguished judges, till it acquired the explicit form and directory character set forth in 'Dalton's Justice,' which was the accepted legal guide of the Provinces." Under these laws, and the decisions of the English courts in accordance with them, it is stated on good authority that there was an average of one hundred and fifty executions for witchcraft per annum, for two hundred years, or thirty thousand in all. These facts were known in New England before Cotton Mather was born. Moreover the cases of alleged witchcraft which he collected and published in 1689, in connection with the experiences of the Goodwin children, were familiar to the general public throughout the colonies. Though there were but few newspapers in that day, and scarcely any public lines of travel, yet all strange, and especially all mysterious, events and those having a supernatural tinge were carried by letters and by travelers all over the country. They were the theme of talk in places of public resort, and the thrilling stories were told round thousands of firesides. The belief in witchcraft was as common as belief in the Bible. This belief was not created or increased by Mather's book. The most that can be said truly is that it brought the subject anew before the public mind, so far as its limited circulation extended.

In addition it should be remembered that the current superstition included much more than what was technically called witchcraft. The following extract will show that the minds of the people of Scotland in those days were saturated with superstitious notions. I quote from the Life of Burns a partial list of the denizens of the air, according to Scottish beliefs: " Devils, ghosts, fairies, brownies, witches, warlocks, spunkies, kelpies, elf candles, deadlights, wraiths, apparitions, cantraps, giants, enchanted towers, dragons, and other trumpery." If the northern portion of Great Britain was infested with such a numerous brood of superstitious imaginings, why should we wonder if the immigrants from England brought some of this "trumpery" with them? In fact they brought far too much of it, and the Mathers, father and son, with the clergy generally, exerted their influence to eliminate these superstitions from the public mind, because they believed that their prevalence was the work of the devil. And one great object of Cotton Mather's book was to make the practice of witchcraft, then prevalent, odious, and thus to cause its extermination. Another object was to exhibit a remedy for those afflicted by witchcraft.

The object of Mather in reciting previous cases of

witchcraft may have been to make the case of the Goodwin family seem more credible. Whatever his motive,
before proceeding to give the results of his own observation, he briefly referred to all the instances he could find
of witchcraft practices and trials in the northern colonies.
He gives the cases of Ann Cole, of Connecticut, of Elizabeth Knapp, of Groton, and of a Mr. Smith, of Hadley,
at some length. Passing by these and other like cases
(of no concern to us at present), and also stories of ghosts
and haunted houses, such as have not been wanting in
any generation, we come to the personal experience of
Mr. Mather in his own house.

This was in 1688, when the Goodwin family was supposed to be under diabolical inflictions. I shall abridge the
narrative as much as possible from Mather's statement.

He writes that John Goodwin lived in the south part of
Boston, by which he meant the part south of the north
end. The family did not belong to Mather's congregation, and he became interested in them, not by seeking
occasion to meddle with witchcraft, but by the strong
desire and even importunity of the father. Goodwin was
a "sober, pious man," a mason by trade, "whose wife
(to which a good report gives a share with him in all the
characters of virtue) made him the father of six (now —
1688) living children." The family, except the eldest son
and the baby, "labored under the direful effects of a (no
less palpable than) stupendous witchcraft." The eldest
son had also "some lighter touches of it in unaccountable
stabs and pains, now and then, upon him." Perhaps there
was some physical susceptibility in the family — "all
except the father and the sucking infant."

Four of these children (all except the eldest and youngest) were "handled in so sad and strange a manner as
has given matter of discourse and wonder to all the

country; and of history not unworthy to be considered by
more than all the serious and curious readers in this New
English world." The oldest of "the four" was about
fourteen, and the youngest some over four years of age.
"All enjoyed a religious education, and answered it with
a very towardly ingenuity; they had an observable affection unto divine and sacred things. Those of them that
were capable of it, seemed to have such a resentment of
their eternal concernments, as is not altogether usual."
They were industrious, and that kept them, as Mather
says, "from the temptations of idleness." He continues:
"Such was the whole temper and carriage of the children,
that there cannot easily be anything more unreasonable
than to imagine that a design to dissemble could cause
them to fall into any of their odd fits, though there
should not have happened as there did, a thousand things
wherein it was perfectly impossible for any dissimula-
tion of theirs to produce what scores of spectators were
amazed at."

About midsummer, 1688, the oldest daughter offended
a laundress whose "mother was an ignorant and scandalous old woman." The woman's husband sometimes complained of her, that "she was undoubtedly a witch."
This scandalous old woman "bestowed very bad language" upon the Goodwin girl, who immediately became
"indisposed in her health and visited with strange fits
beyond those that attend an epilepsie, or a catalepsie, or
on that they call the 'diseases of astonishment.'"

Soon after a sister and two of her brothers were seized
with "similar *affects*." Here follows a description of the
phenomena: — "All four were tortured everywhere in a
manner so very grievous that it would have broken a
heart of stone to have seen their agonies. Among skillful physicians who were consulted was the worthy and

prudent Dr. Thomas Oakes, who found himself so affected by the distemper of the children that he concluded nothing but a hellish witchcraft could be the original of these maladies." The narrative goes on : "For one good while the children were tormented just in the same part of their bodies, and all at the same time together ; and though they saw and heard not one another's complaints ; though likewise their pains and spasms were swift, like lightning, yet when (suppose) the head, or the neck, or the back of one was racked, so it was at that instant with tother too."

This would indicate that the children were in different rooms.

" About nine or ten at night, they always had a release from these miseries, and ate, and slept all night for the most part indifferently well. Yet in the daytime, they were handled with so many sorts of ails, that it would require of us almost as much time to relate them all, as it did of them to endure them. Sometimes they were deaf, dumb, blind, and often all this at once." Now "their tongues would be drawn down their throats," and then "would be pulled upon their chins to a prodigious length." Their mouths would be opened so wide that their "jaws went out of joint"; then they would "clap together again with a force like that of a strong spring lock. The same would happen to their shoulder blades, and their elbows, and hand-wrists, and several of their joints. They would at times lie in a benumbed condition, and be drawn together as those that are tied neck and heels ; and presently be stretched out, yea, drawn backwards to such a degree that it was feared the very skin of their bellies would have cracked. They would make most piteous outcries that they were cut with knives, and struck with blows that they could not bear. Their neck would be broken, so that their neck-bone would seem dissolved unto them that looked after it ; and yet, on the sudden, it would become again so stiff that there was no stirring of their heads ; yea, their heads would be twisted almost round, and if main force at any time obstructed a dangerous motion which they seemed to be upon, they would roar exceedingly." This continued several weeks. Once when Mr. Mather "went to prayer by one of them" who was very desirous to hear what he said, she utterly lost her hearing till the prayer was over.

The Goodwin family were religious, and though many superstitious proposals were made to them to get relief for their children, yet none but religious measures were resorted to by them. They resolved to "oppose devils with no other weapons but prayers and tears unto him that has the chaining of them."

The fate of the old woman was sad enough. Doctors visited her and heard her ravings, but reported that she was *compos mentis.* Her symptoms were strange and she was condemned to death as a witch, according to the law as it then existed, and the evidence as it was then interpreted, and in strict accordance with the practice of English courts. Mr. Mather visited her at different times and made strenuous efforts to prepare her for death, but had nothing to do with the proceedings that led to her condemnation and execution. When going to the gallows, she said that the children would not be "relieved by her death, as others had a hand in it as well as she." And so it proved. The boy next younger than the eldest girl seems to have been relieved, but "three of the children — that is, the girl, and the fourth and fifth children — continued in the furnace as before, and it grew rather seven times hotter than it was." Yet there are writers who would have us believe that not only the girl, fourteen years old, but the two other children, probably eight and six years old, went through all these experiences as cunning deceivers, making fools of Mr. Mather, the other ministers of Boston, the physicians, and their own parents, without any break in their concerted deception.

Much more is given, showing the deplorable condition of the children; but we must attend to remedies used. Mr. Mather took the oldest girl to his own home and regulated her diet, while employing moral and religious influences. The quietness of his home was also beneficial. He writes: "The young woman continued well at our house for divers days, and applied herself to such actions, not only of industry, but of piety, as she had been no stranger to. But on the 20th of November she cried out, 'Ah, — they — have found me out! I thought it would be so!' and immediately fell into her fits again." This was followed by another series of "bewitchments," as understood at the time, and by many unaccountable things in the girl's behavior, till the twenty-seventh of November, when Rev. Mr. Morton, of Charlestown, and Messrs. Allen, Moody, Willard, and Mather, of Boston, with some devout neighbors, kept a day of prayer at John Goodwin's house, and Mather says, "We had all the children with us there. The children were miserably tortured while we labored in our prayers; but our good God was nigh unto us in what we called upon him for. From this day the power of the enemy was broken, and the children, though assaults after this were made upon them, yet were not so cruelly handled as before. The liberty of the little children increased daily, more and more, and their vexation abated by degrees, till within a little while they arrived to perfect ease, and this they cheerfully enjoyed for some weeks or months."

But two days after the fast, the oldest girl had two remarkable attempts made upon her : one by dragging into the oven, then being heated ; and one by putting an unseen noose round her neck, by which she was choked till black in the face. This was, doubtless, a spasm of wild delirium, with such violent muscular contractions as physicians are too familiar with. She would now find her place in an insane asylum. But these things were less understood than at present, when there are mysteries still unexplored. Mr. Mather adds : " Marks of the rope, and of a finger and thumb were seen for a while afterwards." Possibly these were impressions made by the girl's own hands, but it requires a gullibility far exceeding the alleged credulity of Cotton Mather to believe that the girl went through all this for sport and deception !

After a lucid interval in the winter of 1688–1689, the oldest girl had another visitation, in which she displayed much of the wit which sometimes attends mental disease. This, in the time of it, was ascribed to the devil. In the first half of the present century, writers were wont to ascribe it all to the roguery of the patients or actors. Magnetism and spiritualism deal with similar phenomena in a more serious and not less rational way. Cases of the kind are now seen every day in scores of hospitals for the insane, and are classed under the general head of insanity. The Goodwin girl became flippant and impertinent. When directed to look to God, her eyes would be put out. When prayer was begun, "the devils would throw her on the floor at Mr. Mather's feet," and then she would try to strike and kick him. She would "whistle, and sing, and yell, to drown the voice of prayer. If she tried to strike or kick him, her fist or foot would recoil, when within an inch or two of him, as if rebounding against a wall." The girl, without doubt, had a natural sense of humor, which insanity stimulated, for when the minister had read to her a sentence of a discourse he was preparing in relation to some of the witchcraft cases, " she made of it the most ridiculous travesty in the world, with such a patness and excess of fancy to supply the sense she put upon it, as I was amazed at. And she particularly told me that I should quickly come to disgrace by that history." That history was indeed the occasion of much obloquy.

Towards the end of the second day he continues: " After prayer was made for her, she would revive for a minute or two, and continue as frolicksome as before, and this continued until Saturday, towards the evening, when, after this man had been at prayer, I charged all my family to admit of no diversion by her frolic from such exercises as it was proper to begin the Sabbath with. They took the counsel, and though she assayed with as witty, and as amiable, and as various an application to each of them successively as ever I saw, to make them laugh, yet they kept close to their good books, which then called for their attention. When she saw this, immediately she fell asleep, and in two or three hours she waked, perfectly *herself;* weeping bitterly to remember (for as one out of a dream, she could remember) what had befallen her."

None of the children were cured all at once, but they " first came to be always quiet unless upon provocations. Then they got liberty to work, but not to read ; then further on, to read, but not aloud. And at last they were wholly delivered, and for many weeks remained so." In no long time they were wholly cured.

The strange things which the oldest girl did would seem incredible if the testimony were not so positive. Besides her bodily contortions, she appeared to be moved by religious considerations. For example, when prayer

was made in the room, her hands were drawn by irresistible force to cover her ears; and when her hands were
drawn away by attendants, she claimed that she could not
hear a word. She was pulled by a chain out of her chair
towards the fire, and had to be held. She could read
a Quaker's book (which was then abominable to her
Christian neighbors) except the names of God and Christ.
These she could not utter. If asked to read the Bible or
the catechism, she was thrown into contortions. The
Book of Common Prayer, then objectionable to the common sentiment, she could read with ease and seem to
enjoy it, perhaps all the more because it was offensive to
her friends; but when she came to the Lord's Prayer her
eyes failed her. And what was very odd, she could read
passages of Scripture in the prayer book, but would sooner
die than read the same passages in the Bible itself.

These things may be accounted for in two ways : one
is that she was roguish; and the other, that she was
insane. The following specimen of her impertinence to
Mr. Mather may be explained on either theory. She
would knock at his study door, and tell him that some
one wished to see him downstairs. Going down he would
find that she had deceived him. When reproved for her
falsehood, she would pertly reply, "Mrs. Mather is always
glad to see you." But the contortions and bodily agonies
cannot be ascribed to a love of frolic.

The last fit of this girl was peculiar. The " demons
having once again seized her," they made her pretend to
be dying, and she " urged hard for some one to die with
her, seeming loth to die alone. She argued concerning
death in strains that quite amazed us, and concluded, that
though she was loth to die, yet if God said she must,
she must; adding something about the state of the country which we wondered at. Anon, the fit went over; and

as I guessed it would be, it was the last fit she had at
our house. But all my library never gave me any commentary on those paragraphs of the Gospels which speak
of demoniacs, equal to that which the passions of this
child have given me."

From a postscript we learn that the children (especially the brother) had some annoyance afterwards, but
with scarcely a trace of the former severity, and then were
left unmolested. The story would not be complete without adding that the oldest girl lived to be the mother of
a family and a respectable member of one of the churches
of Boston ; and that she always affirmed that the troubles
of her girlhood were real, and not the work of a cunning
and mischievous disposition.

Such is a fair statement, though brief, of the contents
and the spirit of the little book to which such dire consequences as the witchcraft and executions of 1692 have
been ascribed. But this was not the only utterance of
Cotton Mather on the subject. In 1693, according to
Sibley's list, there appeared a "little history of several
very astonishing witchcrafts and possessions, which partly
from my ocular observation, and partly my undoubted
information, hath enabled me to offer unto the public
notice of my neighbors" (pp. 75). To this were added
a "discourse on the power and malice of devils," and
a "discourse on witchcraft," and an appendix to his
father's "Remarkable Providences," issued in 1684.

A second impression of the "Memorable Providences"
came out in 1691, in London. This was recommended by
Rev. Richard Baxter and the ministers of Boston. The
preface by Baxter was dated "London, Sept. the 30th,
1690." With all its additions this edition contained 144
pages. Other publications on the general subject came
out in 1693 and later, which could have had no influence

in producing the calamity of 1692, and a notice of them belongs to a subsequent period. But before proceeding, it is important to notice the discourse of 1691, on the "Wonders of the Invisible World," contained in the "Memorable Providences."

Text, Revelation 12 : 12. The sermon was divided into five propositions : — I. There is a devil ; and many devils. Legion, 12,500. II. There is a devilish wrath against mankind. III. The devil, in the prosecution and execution of his wrath upon them, often gets a liberty to make a descent upon the children of men. IV. Most horrible woes come to be inflicted on mankind, when the devil does, in great wrath, make a descent upon them. V. Toward the end of his time, the descent of the devil in wrath upon the world, will produce more woful effects than what have been in former ages. These propositions are followed by five corollaries and three conjectures, and the sermon closed with a hortatory and necessary address to the country, alarmed by the wrath of the devil. Then follow eight answers to the inquiry, "What shall we do ?" There is much curious matter in this discourse, and it was doubtless quite alarming, but we have no facts to connect it closely with the delusion in Salem and vicinity, where nearly all the victims resided.

The direct action of Mr. Mather to deliver individual patients from the calamity — whatever was its cause — was wise and philanthropic, as will be seen when we come to read the story of Mercy Short and of Margaret Rule ; and his influence in discrediting the validity of "spectral evidence " in convicting those accused of using the diabolical arts of witchcraft will be made evident.

CHAPTER VII.

WE have seen the course of Mr. Mather in dealing with the children of the Goodwin family. This was narrated in the "Memorable Providences," and if it had been studied and imitated, it is possible, if not probable, that the whole awful tragedy of blood, in 1692, would have been averted. Whatever the trouble may have been with those children, they had been cured; or, if the reader prefers, they became sound in body and mind. If the devil was the instigating cause, working through human agents styled witches, it had been shown that the devil and his tools could be baffled. If bodily disease were the cause of the strange phenomena that amazed the good people of Essex County in the time of the witch epidemic, it was made plain that the bodily ailment could be overcome by gentle means. If the cause was insanity, pure and simple, it had been demonstrated that there was a man in the province who could minister to a mind diseased. If the phenomena, whether mesmeric or magnetic or spiritualistic, or what not, defied all understanding, still it was evident for all to see that there was "balm in Gilead, and a physician there." Though Mather shared the common ignorance in regard to the cause of the direful phenomena, he was more than one generation ahead of his coevals in relation to the proper treatment. Therefore his method was disregarded, and the horror ran its course.

It is aside from the scope of this biography to give an account of the trials of the so-called witches at Salem and of the execution of the condemned. That belongs to the history of the period or the annals of human delusion and misfortune. Full reports are to be found in the printed records and in such works as that of Mr. Upham. Our task is to consider the connection of Cotton Mather with the witchcraft tragedy.

I.   In doing this it is pertinent to inquire into several points, on the answers to which his blame or praise depends. One question relates to the law in regard to witchcraft which existed in England and in the colony at the time. In the old country and in Massachusetts Bay the penalty of the crime of witchcraft was capital. In the original "Body of Liberties" of the colony was this article: "If any man or woman be a witch (that is, hath, or consulteth with, a familiar spirit), they shall be put to death." Plymouth County had a similar law in 1636. Those laws were made before Cotton Mather was born ; before his father even saw the light of day.

II.   What was the usage of the courts and what the rules of evidence in England and in the colony or province, as it had now become? There was a special method of obtaining evidence in the English courts, which need not be specified here. It is enough to say that the confession of the accused party was one ground of condemnation. The fact that the accused party had shown a spirit of enmity toward a bewitched person was reason for violent suspicion, though not for conviction. The fact that uttered curses were followed by the sickness or bodily pain and injury of the party cursed was thought to be proof of the guilt of the curser, especially if the curses were repeated and followed by other pains and molestations. There were other criteria of guilt laid down in the books. But the evidence most relied on was what was styled "spectral evidence." This was considered next in force to the actual seeing a man commit a crime. It was a special kind of sight.

For example, a man is accused of being a wizard; or some strange old woman living alone in the skirts of the forest, of being a witch. Mr. Brown is suffering in some way; it may be by pains in different parts of the body, as if pinched or cut or pricked with pins, or with pining sickness, all of which cannot be accounted for until Mr. Brown has a sight or vision or specter of the wizard or the witch present at the time of suffering; or the sufferer may see the specter of a dog or cat when in his paroxysms of pain; and the spectral animal being struck or wounded, the accused wizard or witch will be found on examination to have a wound or mark on that part of the body where the animal was stricken. In one case the bewitcher was present in his spectral form; in the other he was present in the form of the animal. It was a case of sight on both occasions; in one, of the specter of a man or woman, in the other of a brute. And this was spectral evidence. But the point seems to have been overlooked that no one saw the bewitcher or the animal actually do anything to the sufferer; or if they did see anything done, they did not see the real presence of the devil, or the witch effecting the pinch, cut, or blow.

Now, this kind of evidence was valid in English judicial practice. It was held to be the strongest proof of guilt. Lord Chief Justice Hale convicted of witchcraft on this kind of evidence. It was the usage of the courts of England for several generations before and after the Salem horror. Such was "spectral evidence" as relied upon in the cases tried in the courts of the Bay.

III.   How was the court which tried the witchcraft
cases constituted?   It was "a special court of oyer and
terminer" for the specific purpose of trying those accused
of witchcraft, and for no other crimes.   There were seven
judges, most, if not all, of them already familiar with the
duties of a judge.   The chief justice was William Stoughton, a lawyer, and one of the most able and respectable men
in the province.   Another judge was afterwards Chief
Justice Sewall.   Though most of them were not bred
to the bar, they were all familiar with the law and usage
in regard to "spectral evidence" and all other admissible
testimony in regard to witchcraft.   It so happened that
the court had the help of an English lawyer as king's
attorney, a Mr. Newton, who came over in the spring,
attended the sessions at which the witchcraft trials were
held, and then went to New York.   The court thus constituted conducted the trials in accordance with the law
of England and of the colony on the subject, and by the
rules laid down in an English book which was an authority.   Says Mr. Haven, already quoted : —

The tests, the manner of examination, the nature of the evidence,
the process of trial, and the consequences of conviction, were laid
down with a clearness that admitted of no evasion or misrepresentation, in " Dalton's Justice," the accepted legal guide of the provinces.
. . . Since legislation explained and enforced by judicial decisions
of the highest authority, extending through several generations, had
clearly settled the English law and practice concerning witchcraft as
an acknowledged fact and felonious crime, how could our New England judges avoid condemning the alleged culprits, if they believed
them guilty?   And why should they not believe them guilty when the
evidence produced, the confessions, the incidents constituting the dis-
gusting phenomena of the offense conformed precisely to the signs,
symptoms, confessions, etc., detailed in the English precedents they
were constrained to follow?

IV.   What relation to the trials and their results had

Cotton Mather ? He tells us that he was in Salem at different times before the trials began, but for the purpose of finding out, if possible, just what was the affliction of the bewitched and of learning what was the best method of mitigating the curse. During the trials he was not in Salem on a single occasion. His health was poor in the summer so that his usual activities were restricted ; but there is no proof that he had any wish to be present. A story is told by Calef, that Mather was present once when one or more of the convicted was hanged, and that he rode around on a white horse, among the excited crowd, for the purpose of defending the judges, against whom a portion of the people cherished hostile feelings. It has been suggested that there was danger of a riot and of the rescue of the prisoners. The whole story is doubtful and stands on the unsupported word of Robert Calef, an apparently honest man, but one whose carelessness of statement renders him an unsafe reliance on any point where his prejudices were at work. But if Mather were present, the act may not have been deserving of censure. It was his right to be there if he chose to witness the scene. If he were there to uphold the authority of the government and the honor of the judiciary, his conduct may have deserved praise rather than blame. But we dismiss the story as of no significance. What is true is the fact that Cotton Mather would not have condemned a single defendant on the ground of spectral evidence alone ; and it is probable that he regarded all the other evidence as too weak to justify the taking of human life. He was assured by the judges, however, that they had other evidence than spectral and were convinced that the condemned were guilty. Resting on "Dalton's Justice" as a guide, they could not resist this conclusion. Mather, being a friend of the government and of the judges, and confiding in their ability and integrity, might well have felt it important to resist any display of mob violence on the occasion.

However this may be, nothing is clearer, in view of the facts now known, than that the clergy in general were opposed to the use of spectral evidence, except as sub-sidiary, and that of all the clergy Cotton Mather was the most strenuous and outspoken opposer of condemning the accused on such evidence. He wrote a letter to Judge Richards, taking strong ground against it, and warning him that it would be a serious thing in the end to take the life of an alleged worker of witchcraft because of spectral evidence. In this letter, of date May 31, 1692, he writes as one who fully believed in witchcraft, as a fact, as a sin, and as a crime which on proper conviction deserved condign punishment; but he was above all cau-tious about securing full proof of guilt before proceeding to condemn. The first paragraph shows the spirit of the writer and his relation to one of the judges : —

Honorable Sir, — I could not have asked you, as I now do, to excuse me from waiting upon you, with the utmost of my little skill and care to assist the noble service whereto you are called of God this week, the service of encountering the Wicked Spirits in the high places of our Air, and of detecting and confounding of their confederates, were it not that I am Languishing under such an overthrow of my health as makes it very dubious that my company may prove more troublesome than serviceable, the least Excesse of travell, or diet or anything that may discompose me, would at this time threaten perhaps my life itself, as my friends advise me ; and yet I hope before you can get far into that misterious affair which is now before you, I may with God's blessing recover so farr as to attend your desires, which to me always are com-mands. In the meane time, least I should be guilty of any sinfull omis-sion in declining what no good man amongst us can decline, even to do the best I can for the strengthening of your honorable hands in that worke of God, whereto (I thank him) he hath so well fitted you, as well as called you, I thought it my duty briefly to offer you my poor thoughts on this astonishing occasion.

Then, reminding the judge that good people had been "fasting and praying" for the direction of the court, and that such devotions in "Swedeland had been immediately followed with a remarkable smile of God upon the endeavors of the judges to discover and extirpate" the authors of witchcraft, he proceeds in the words following : —

And yet I must most humbly beg you that in the management of the affair in your most worthy hands, you do not lay more stress upon pure spectre testimony than it will bear. When you are satisfied or have good, plain, legal evidence that the dæmons which molest our poor neighbors, do indeed represent such and such people to the sufferers, though this be a presumption, yet I suppose you will not reckon it a conviction that the people so represented are witches to be immediately exterminated. It is very certain that the devils have sometimes represented the shapes of persons not only innocent, but also very vertuous. Though I believe that the just God then ordinarily provides a way for the speedy vindication of the persons thus abused. . . . I would say this : if upon the bare supposal of a poor creature being represented by a spectre, too great a progress be made by the Authority in ruining a poor neighbor so represented, it may be that a door may be thereby opened for the devils to obtain from the courts in the invisible world a license to proceed unto most hideous desolations upon the repute and repose of such as have yet been kept from the great transgression. If mankind have thus far once consented unto the credit of diabolical representations, the door is opened ! Perhaps there are wise and good men, that may be ready to style him that shall advance this caution, a witch advocate, but in the winding up, this caution will certainly be wished for.

In another letter addressed to a Mr. Sewall, of Salem, Mr. Mather took the same position. Another paper, signed by the ministers of Boston and vicinity, including President Increase Mather, while urging the judges to be firm in applying the law against offenders, also strongly urged that spectral evidence would not warrant conviction of the crime of witchcraft. That paper was not only signed by Cotton Mather, but was written by him. There is reason to believe that spectral evidence was influential in securing condemnation in all, or nearly all, the convicted cases. It is probable that if the judges had listened to the clergy instead of the English lawyer, if they had had the courage to break away from English law, usage, and precedent, but a few, if any, would have suffered death for the crime of witchcraft at the time. The odium which has clung to the name of Cotton Mather took its start from the publications of Robert Calef in later years, and the consideration of that writer's allegations will come up at the proper date. It is not necessary to do more in this place than to state that nothing in Calef's writings can shake the position above taken.

That Mather made a great mistake in relation to witchcraft, and that the consequences were deplorable, is not to be questioned; but his mistake was common to all ministers, judges, lawyers, physicians, and people of his age, with rare exceptions. He partly discovered his error near the close of his life. The explanation is reserved for the present. For the vindication of Mather, we are much indebted to Mr. William Poole, formerly of the Athenæum, and now of the Newberry Library at Chicago, and also to the late Delano Goddard, of Worcester and Boston.

We have now seen that Cotton Mather was not specially responsible for the outbreak of the witchcraft horror in Salem village in 1692, by the publication of his book in 1689; that he exerted no influence in causing the accused to be condemned, but rather sought to save life by interposing the plea that spectral evidence was not valid ground for conviction, and specially urging privately and publicly, orally and in writing and in print, the danger of evil consequences if such convictions were secured on such testimony, and that he strenuously insisted that the devil could personate good as well as bad men, and so fix charges on the innocent if spectral evidence were received. And since he took the lead in this action he merits praise rather than censure for his part in the matter. But this is not all; he deserves the peculiar honor of doing more than any other man, or any ten men, to heal the suffering and restore the deranged to soundness.

In line with his treatment of the Goodwin children, four years before, was his action in relation to two somewhat similar cases in 1692–1693. These patients were Mercy Short and Margaret Rule; of his treatment in the cases of these females, Mr. Mather wrote a brief narrative. That of Mercy Short is still in manuscript, and was not known to exist until within a few years, when it was found among the manuscripts in the Antiquarian Library at Worcester. Indeed the knowledge that there ever was such a manuscript was owing to the title of the Margaret Rule narrative, which was " Another Trophy Gathered." This last-mentioned pamphlet when in manuscript, in some way not known, got into the hands of Robert Calef, and by him was published without the consent of the author.

As the story of Mercy Short is still in manuscript, and under the restriction of the rules of the Antiquarian Society, only an extremely brief view of it can be given here. She had been captured by the eastern Indians, who butchered her father, mother, sister, and others of her kindred. She was then taken to Canada, with three brothers and two sisters, from Berwick, Maine. Having been redeemed, she was brought to Boston with others. It was in this year that Mr. Mather made this entry in the church records : " Our congregation gathered sixty-two pounds, odd shillings, for the redemption of our captives in the hands of the Indians." Mercy Short was bewitched by one Sarah Good, afterwards executed at

Salem. "A world of misery did she endure." Among other hardships, she "was made to fast twelve days together."

The remedy employed by Mr. Mather was "fasting with prayer." Every day a number of people came into her room and prayed with her. Singing was mingled with prayer. She had a blessed deliverance, except faint fits about New Year's.

We are told that the pious people in the north part of Boston — in Mather's parish — "did very much pray *with* the young woman, as *for* her." The young people in the vicinity, as we learn from Mather's diary, held several prayer meetings, statedly (the sexes apart), and these were sometimes held in the "haunted chamber." It is said that there was scarce a night for near a month which was not spent in devotion by those who watched. Finally, on the evening of March 16, 1693, the "*black man* and evil spirit, left her, and returned no more." She was still weak in body, but recovered strength by degrees. This is a very brief résumé of a long account of the patient's symptoms or torments; but in addition to the regulation of her diet, she was placed, as it were, in an atmosphere of loving sympathy and prayer. The means were blessed to the recovery of mental soundness and ultimately the restoration of physical health.

The story of Margaret Rule is another illustration of the fact that Cotton Mather was in advance of his age in his method of treating persons of disordered symptoms, whether in body or mind.

It is said of this girl that she was "born of sober and honest parents, and that she was careful to avoid the snares of evil company;" she had never seen the afflictions of Mercy Short; but half a year after the "deliverance of that poor damsel," she fell into a similar affliction.

On Lord's day, September 10, 1693, she was "disturbed in the public assembly, and fell into odd fits." In some way a "miserable woman in a house hard by had been provoked by Margaret, with no apparent ill-intention ; but in resentment, the woman threatened her with dire evils. Afflictions followed, such as were usual in cases of witchcraft. Friends prayed for her. She was assaulted by eight cruel specters. She imagined that she knew three or four of them, but they came with faces covered. She was cautioned not to mention their names ; but she privately named them to Mr. Mather." "They were," he says, "a sort of wretches, who for many years had gone under as violent presumptions of witchcraft, as perhaps any persons yet living upon earth ; though I am far from thinking that the visions of this young woman were evidence enough to prove them so."

But there is no need of detailing the phenomena in the case of Margaret Rule. It would be mostly a repetition of what occurred in the experience of many others. One incident will be noted, however, because it reveals the animus of Robert Calef towards Mr. Mather. It was as follows : —

Once the spectators thought they perceived something stir upon Margaret's pillow at a little distance from her, "whereupon one present, laying his hand there, he to his horror, apprehended that he felt, though none could see it, a living creature, not altogether unlike a rat, which nimbly escaped from him"; others were thrown into "great consternation" by the same thing. The above are the words of Dr. Mather. This is the scene in which Robert Calef represents Cotton Mather to have behaved himself with gross and unbecoming indecency, and it was the reading of his representation which first excited my suspicion that he was hostile to Mather, notwithstanding his protestations of respect and candor. This will be referred to again.

In view of the case of Margaret Rule, we need not stop to inquire how much of this mass of strange and diabolical facts or fancies would be left as solid truth if it had been subjected to the scrutiny of sharp-sighted and incredulous examiners at the time. On one point there need be little, if any, doubt. Something was the matter with her. She was either morally or physically "out of order." If she was a cunning impostor, or if the unhappy subject of a direful experience, as she claimed and the people believed, she needed judicious treatment.

And now the inquiry comes up and demands a candid answer: Could any treatment have been more wise and Christian than that pursued by Cotton Mather in his time? Prayer and regulation of the food are potent in their healing influence. They help nature mightly. If she was a rogue, a regimen of prayer and fasting would soon become irksome. If she was deluded, nothing would be more potent in restoring soundness of mind. If she was possessed of the devil, what could be more hateful to evil spirits than the frequent prayers of Cotton Mather and his father, and the other friends who were enlisted to pray for the victim of their malice? Settle this as we may, the girl was cured.

Turning from this episode, we proceed with the narrative.

The trials, convictions, and executions went on in that fateful summer, until sixty or seventy were accused as witches, and until nineteen were hanged. One, Giles Corey, was pressed to death. This case requires special mention, as the story has been so told as to lay undue blame on the judges, and at the same time withhold merited honor from Mr. Corey. He was condemned on the same evidence as governed the court in other cases, but as he refused to plead, he was sentenced to be pressed to death, according to English law and usage. In this the judges were not actuated by caprice or cruelty, but were guided either by the suggestions of an English lawyer present, or by their own knowledge of the English law in such case made and provided. But the refusal of Mr. Corey to plead was not the result of contumacy or contempt for the constituted authorities, but sprang from his desire to secure his property to his heirs, as by English law in such cases the property of the condemned was not confiscated. It was a noble act on his part, and it secures him a bright record in our history. Many others were accused and some were in jail, but the term of the special court had come to an end and no more trials could be had until the regular session of the Superior Court in September.

At the session of the Superior Court in December, the court cleared forty of those on trial, and condemned three at Boston. Graves were dug for these three and for five more who had been convicted at Salem : but these were all reprieved by Governor Phips. This interposition grew out of several causes. There was a revulsion of the public mind against capital convictions for witchcraft. There was a growing feeling that "spectral evidence" was a delusion. The ministers, seeing that persons were condemned on such evidence, were more than willing to have all judicial proceedings stayed. The governor had been away in Maine suppressing hostile Indians, but on his return, having time to examine the matter, appears to have made up his mind that executive interposition was demanded. He therefore reprieved those who were under sentence of death.

It has been surmised that he was moved to this course

because accusations had been made against his wife.
There is no proof that such was his governing motive.
It is easier to suppose from all we know of the man and
of the time, that he believed the executions were unjus-
tifiable. Some also think they see in his decision proof
that his confidence in the Mathers was shaken. This is
another of those surmises for which there is no proof
whatever. To the last, unshaken confidence existed between them. The better conclusion is that the Mathers,
father and son, grieved that the court had condemned
suspected persons without adequate proof, influenced the
governor to put a stop to the work of death. If they had
disapproved his action, they were not the men to keep
silence. If they advised him to stay execution, they were
not the men to publish the fact. The result was a
complete stoppage of the course of judicial proceedings.
Judge Stoughton, in February, 1693, declined attending
the sessions of the court any longer, on the ground that
the execution of justice was obstructed. Stoughton never
seems to have doubted that his course was according to
divine and human law, any more than Sir Matthew Hale
and other great judges of England ; but Judge Sewall,
and probably some others of the judges, not steeped in
English law or fettered by English usage, became convinced that these capital sentences were not justifiable, and
that in consequence innocent lives had been sacrificed.

The relation of Cotton Mather to the witchcraft horror
demands that distinct mention should be made of the
fact that while several prisoners were in jail he offered
to take six of the accused into his own family for the
purpose of testing the same regimen which he had successfully tried in the case of the Goodwin children, Mercy
Short, and Margaret Rule. He hoped that others would
follow his example, and that the results, in restoring the

afflicted to soundness, would be beneficial. The authorities declined the proposal for reasons not given. Perhaps
they perceived that the baleful epidemic had spent its
force. But here comes to view a specimen of injustice
in which the maligners of Cotton Mather are adepts. It
is more than hinted by writers of reputation that the design of Mather in his proposal was to get these bewitched
into his house and under his influence, that he might from
them elicit accusations against men obnoxious to himself,
and thus bring them under his power. In regard to this,
there is no proof that he ever used such power. He
warned the patients under his care not to make accusations against any. If they confided any names, they were
locked up with the secrets of his breast. As if to remove all fear, he expressly said that all the names mentioned to him were those of the lowest kind of wretches;
and in relation to them the evidence was not such as
entitled it to any weight. But aside from all this, the
suspicion that Cotton Mather would collect such information for the purpose of holding his enemies in dread is
monstrous. It can be accounted for only by the fact
stated by Mr. Drake (already quoted) that the odium
attached to Mather's name half a century ago was such
as to bring disgrace upon any one who ventured to speak
well of him.

CHAPTER VIII.

WE have referred to two matters under the date of 1692 which reached into 1693 (N. S.), but which were connected with the former year, as then was the usage when the year extended to the twenty-fifth of March. One was the adoption of the so-called "halfway" scheme; the other was a case of witchcraft healing. As Mr. Mather's birthday was February 12, and as he kept his diary by his birthdays, we are in danger of mixing up the dates of events in his life.

In the first place reference will be made to the records of the church in 1693. From this source we learn that thirty-one were received into the church by confession. In another place the pastor writes of a larger number of converts. Perhaps some joined later or united with one of the other churches in the town. One person was admitted on the "halfway" plan, as already stated. The record under date January 15 reads: "Received into covenant Mary Sunderland, and her son John baptized; this being the first so admitted in pursuance of the church's address unto me for that purpose and practice."

On the twenty-ninth of October he "baptized Richard, of a negro father, a member of the church in Cambridge, and of a negro mother, a member of the Church in Maldon." Perhaps the parents now lived together in Boston.

It is recorded, December 10, that "our congregation made a collection of about fifty-three pounds for the redemption of two persons that were in Turkish captivity."

Turning now to the diary for 1693, we find the following under date of February 12 : "This day, having finished the 30th year of my age, through the wonderful patience and goodness of God, I preached unto my congregation as agreeable things as I could, upon Psalm 102 : 24 : ' I said, O my God, take me not away in the midst of my days.' " By the word "agreeable," as often used by Mr. Mather, we are not to understand that he studied to preach pleasant things, but truths that were suited to meet the wants of his people.

At this time he "set himself to preach on the whole Epistle of Jude, as being a rich portion of Scripture, fit for our time and place." Other topics were to be intermingled, for he took special pains to give great variety to his pulpit services.

The case of one of the young women who were "horribly possessed of the devil," and had been "cast on his care," should be referred to here, because of two or three particulars not noticed heretofore. He called on some devout neighbors to unite in prayer for her, and they kept three successive days in this exercise. "When freed, they had a time of solemn thanksgiving." Her "torments returned," and he again resorted to prayer, with others, and she was restored. This person in due time was received into the church. He adds : "Many others, even four scores of young people, awakened by the picture of hell exhibited in her sufferings, were led to flee from the wrath to come." Doubtless these things had their influence upon the fifty-four persons who were received into the Second Church in the years 1693–1694.

In this season Mr. Mather had "many wonderful enter-

tainments from the spiritual world." He never failed, in
the stress of public duties, to take special care of his
interior spiritual life. He kept "many days of secret
humiliation before the Lord, not recorded "; but one day,
he writes that "his special errand before the Lord," was
to entreat the Lord to give him the assistance of the *Holy
Angels*. He wanted those kindnesses which the Scriptures said belonged to the heirs of salvation. But, he
says, " I requested that I might receive those kindnesses
in a manner and measure more transcendent than what
the great corruptions in the generality of good men permitted them to be made partakers of." He resolved that
he would not, on the "score of angelical communications,
forsake the written word," and he took pains to do what
would please the angels. His wisdom in receiving nothing
not in accordance with the "written word" kept him
from the baleful fanaticism of too many who have fancied
themselves to be favored with direct communications from
the spiritual world. He resolved to "conceal, with all
prudent secrecy, whatever extraordinary things" he might
perceive to be done for himself by the angels, who "love
secrecy in their administrations." At the same time he
expressed the belief that "some great things would be
done by the angels " in his behalf.

On the twenty-fifth of March a son was born to him of
a "most comely and hearty look." Friends made cordial
expressions of satisfaction, as this was the first boy after
three girls, the first of whom had been taken away. But
the child lived only five days, having a defect which was
fatal to life. At the funeral there was a "numerous and
honorable attendance." The child "died unbaptized," but
on the gravestone the father had these words written :
"Reserved for a glorious resurrection." It has been a
common slander that our fathers generally believed in the

damnation of infants, especially if not baptized. Mr. Mather's hopes at the decease of his children are expressed in the above epitaph.

There were suspicions of witchcraft in connection with this bereavement, as the mother supposed she had seen a *specter* a few days before the birth which strangely affected her, and a suspected woman had written to the father that something evil was to happen. In view of these tokens he wrote : " However I made little use of, and laid little stress on this conjecture, desiring to submit unto the will of my heavenly Father, without which not a sparrow falleth to the ground."

No minister felt more keenly the pressure of the times upon him, or more wisely improved occasions. There are some topics which cannot be usefully treated unless in connection with others in course, or when some event has fixed the public mind upon them. The seventh command- ment is an example. Mr. Mather felt the embarrassment but failed not to improve the occasion when one occurred. He wrote in his diary in June : " Many and many a weary hour did I spend in the prison to serve the souls of those miserable creatures." He referred to a young woman of Haverhill and a negro woman of Boston, under "sentence of death for the murdering of their bastard children." He preached the sermon preceding their execution, which was printed with the title : " Warnings from the Dead, or solemn admonitions unto all people, but especially unto young persons, to beware of such evils as would bring them to the dead." There were two sermons, in fact, with the last confession of one of the parties. One of the sermons had been preached before, but both were now printed and the pamphlet was "greedily bought up." It was afterwards printed in London. There was something singular in the manner of his having this opportunity to

preach. He writes : " I had often wished for an opportunity to bear my testimonies against ye sins of unclean-
ness, wherein so many of my generation do pollute
themselves."   While the unhappy women were in prison
he "had often opportunities in his own congregation to
speak to them, and from them, to vast multitudes of
others.   Their execution was ordered to have been upon
the lecture of another [minister] ; but by a very strange
providence, without any seeking of mine, or any respect
to me, (that I know of) the order for their execution was
altered, and it fell on my lecture day.   I did then, with
the special assistance of heaven, make and preach a sermon upon *Job* 36 : 14, whereat one of the greatest assemblies ever known in these parts of the world was come
together."   He had obtained from one of the condemned
a "pathetical instrument in writing, wherein she owned
her miscarriages, and warned the rising generation of
theirs."   Towards the end of the service, he read the confession to the congregation, and made what use of it he
thought proper, and then "accompanied the wretches to
the execution."   The impression on the community, parents and children, must have been something tremendous.

A fast day was kept on the day after commencement,
in the Old or First meetinghouse, on account of the
extreme drouth.   Mr. Mather preached both parts of the
day, and he says that "God inclined some of his people
to print the sermon."   The title was, " The Day and the
Work of the Day."   The amount of thought in the discourse may be inferred from the full title-page, as follows : "What fears we may have at this time to
awaken us ; what hopes there are for us at this time to
comfort us ; and what prayers would be likely to turn
our fears into hopes, with reflections upon the state now
come upon the church of God ; and collections of

certain prophecies relating to the present circumstances of New England."

Near this time the good people of Reading kept a day of prayer that the "rising generation of the place might be made a praying and pious generation." Mr. Mather was invited to preach, and a "vast assemblage" heard him with "extraordinary attention and affection," and he hoped with "successes very comfortable."

It was early in this year that he conceived the plan of writing the "Church History of New England; The Magnalia." The subject having been laid before the neighboring ministers, they encouraged him to proceed. He "cried mightily to God" that he might glorify God in the undertaking. This was the origin of the greatest literary enterprise in the first century of New England; a work which will carry the author's name and fame down through distant centuries.

In July a "most pestilential fever" was brought into Boston from the West Indies by the British fleet. It was the dreaded and fatal yellow fever. The sailors and soldiers had been in the "disastrous expedition to Martinico." King William's war with France, in its wide scope, involved not only Europe but the North American colonies and the West India Islands. The personal experience of Mr. Mather at this time will be read with interest. He became much exposed to the disease, and had what he considered a "merciful preservation." Some of the officers desired him to go down to an island in the harbor and preach to the sick. On the way he was suddenly taken ill, and was obliged to return. As soon as he reached home he was well, and preached in the afternoon to his people, when the admiral and principal commanders came to hear him. He records that, "knowing the horrid wickedness of those who were now come to be my hearers,

I preached unto them on *Ps.* 119: 59: 'I thought on my ways, and turned my feet unto thy testimonies'; and my God helped me in it." He records his belief that a "good angel struck him" with the sickness while on the water, and compelled him to return, thus saving him from fatal exposure.

The disease got into the town, and many fell under its power. Mr. Mather was indefatigable, both in the pulpit and in private visitations, improving the opportunity to promote sanitary measures and to lead dying men to God. His exposure was great, for he was not a man to shrink from danger; but he was preserved. He informs us that he had some "singular dispositions" in these dying times, and became more ready to die than ever before. He became also more desirous than ever before to visit the widow and the orphan — the "headless families" of the flock.

In the thick of all this toil and affliction, he tried to serve his "ungrateful country," as he styled it, by writing a "True and Brief Representation" of the country, with the posture of men and things in it. By the aid of the governor, Phips, he had it privately sent to England and put into the hands of King William, who "read it with much satisfaction." Probably this letter was never in print, as it is not noted in any catalogue which has come under my notice.

One of the publications of this year was entitled "Unum Necessarium, or awakenings for the unregenerate." It contains notes of two or three sermons upon regeneration preached seven years before, with two or three more delivered nearer the time of publication. The volume contained 165 pages, small octavo, and probably comprised the substance of his discourse at Reading, noted above. He was moved to this by the low state of religion in those years (1688–1693) and by the political and witchcraft troubles. Perhaps these calamities had diverted the public mind from those religious truths which most deeply concern the character and eternal welfare of men. The sermons are valuable now chiefly because they show the condition of society at the time, and the readiness of Mather to meet any exigency of the church.

In the introduction he says : —

There are three most undoing mischiefs which threaten my country with grievous confusions; yea, there are four evils that have a dire aspect upon us, boding like something of barbarism and extinction, unless the plentiful effusions of the good Spirit from on high relieve the inconveniences of our wilderness. The first is, the neglect and contempt of a well-formed education, appearing in a backwardness to encourage schools of learning; and a disposition unto a way of living so scattered as that it may be called a running wild into the woods. The second is the slothful, careless, quarrelsome delay of destitute churches to furnish themselves with officers appointed by the Lord Jesus Christ for their edification; by which omission, plantations quickly become full, either of sinners pining away in their iniquities, or of Christians plagued with leanness sent into their souls. The third is, the crime of ingratitude unto public servants, and the making of censure, slander and hatred the common pay of such as with most inviolate integrity seek the common good, which unthankfulness will, at last, make our times perilous, because it will render us friendless and helpless. But the fourth and worst of all is the lamentable want of *regeneration* in the rising generation. The God of heaven is with no less terrible, than evident blows from heaven rebuking of that generation; but alas, how few of them do seriously consider on the condition of their own souls ! How few of them do suitably reflect on the end for which God at first made them, or for which he now smites them ! How few of them do become experimentally acquainted with that faith, and repentance, and holiness, without which no man shall see the Lord ! It is indeed matter of exceeding joy that there are so many of our young ones that have their faces Zionward; but it is of all griefs the most bitter and pungent, that there are no more.

We have here a picture of New England near the

close of the seventeenth century. The people were straggling off into the wilderness to form new settlements. Such settlements always tend to barbarism, unless the settlers are peculiarly earnest in religion, or are followed up by the good people of the towns from which they have departed. Being few and scattered, they are unable to have good schools, and an ignorant generation grows up and propagates its kind. For the same reason the people find it hard to build meetinghouses and sustain ministers; especially so if they are divided on points of doctrine or modes of worship. Besides, a large part of the people in the same township live remote from the sanctuary and are unable to attend with regularity. As a natural result the state of vital religion is low, and few are induced to enter on a devout and Christian life. All these adverse circumstances the pious people of the time had to meet and, by the help of God, overcome. It needed all the zeal and energy of the Mathers and their worthy compeers to maintain the cause of good order, education, civilization, and religion. We hear it said quite often that the era of Home Missions began about a century later than the time of which we are writing; but the fact is that all during the first century of our history the work of home missions was done by colonization. The good people in the old towns sent not merely missionaries, as we do, but parted with their own godly men and women, to form new towns and churches in the wilderness.

Two other publications evince the wide scope of Mr. Mather's thoughts, and his strong desire to reach the minds of the people. One was called "Winter Meditations." In about eighty pages he treats of the way to "employ the leisure of the winter for the glory of God." It is addressed to the "Rt. Worshipful Sir John Hartop, knight and baronet." No abstract can be given of this work, so full of thought and illustration. The reader must search for himself on the title-page, which reads: "Directions how to employ the leisure of the winter for the glory of God, accompanied with reflections as well historical as theological, not only upon the circumstances of the winter, but also upon the notable works of God, both in creation and providence; especially those which more immediately concern every particular man in the whole course of his life; and upon the religious works wherewith every man should acknowledge God, in and from the accidents of the winter."

This was a year fruitful in great plans as well as of good works. Besides the *Magnalia*, Mr. Mather conceived the plan of what he always considered the greatest single work of his life. Toward the end of the summer he began to work on the "BIBLIA AMERICANA." The birth of this enterprise is thus recorded: —

With many cries unto the God of heaven, that he would by his good Spirit, assist me in my undertaking, and that he would employ his good angels to supply me from time to time, with materials for it, I set myself, every morning, to write upon a portion of Scripture, that should have in it something of curiosity. I considered that all the learning in the world might be made gloriously subservient unto the *illustration of Scripture*, and that no professed Commentary had hitherto given so much of illustration unto it as might be given. I considered that multitudes of particular texts had, especially of late years, been more notably illustrated in the scattered books of learned men, than in any of the ordinary commentators, and I considered that the treasures of illustrations for the Bible, dispersed in the volumes of this age, might be fetched all together by a laborious ingenuity.

Accordingly, resolving still to give the church of God such displays of his blessed Word as may be more entertaining for the *novelty* and *variety* of them, than any that have hitherto been seen together, in any exposition, and yet such as may be acceptable unto the most judicious for the demonstrative truth of them, and unto the most orthodox for the regard had to the *analogy of faith* in all, I now began my Great Work.

I thought that after the rate of one illustration in a day, I might, if the Lord would spare my life but seven years more, have without sensible hardship, gotten together a number of *golden keys* for his precious Word, and learned, charming and curious notes on his Word, far beyond any that had yet seen the light. Or, if I died in the midst of my work, yet my labor might not be in vain in the Lord. It would be worth the while, though I furnished none but myself with such accomplishments for a minister of the gospel.

The work was never published. A fuller notice of it the author would be glad to make, but space forbids. As we proceed, the reader will bear in mind that, amid all his multiplied labors and cares for nearly a score of years, the author was assiduously carrying forward this stupendous work, and in the doing of it enriching his own mind, while adding greatly to the variety, beauty, and solid worth of his own public ministrations.

Early in September he went to Salem to gather material for his Church History. Another object was to collect information about the "History of the Witchcrafts and Possessions." The result was the publication of "The Wonders of the Invisible World," which first came out this year in a volume of about 150 pages, but which was enlarged and reprinted. The second, third, and fourth editions were reprints in London. The fifth edition, London, with an addition by President Mather, bears date 1862, and fills about 300 pages. It contains a "narrative of a late outrage committed by a knot of witches in Swedeland," which resembled the cases of possession in New England. The work shows the undoubting faith of the people in those times in witchcraft, and gives counsel about the "methods to prevent the wrongs which those evil angels may intend against all sorts of people among us, especially in accusations of the innocent." As usual, none but base motives have been ascribed to the Mathers and others by their opposers for publishing this book, but the reason given by Cotton Mather would seem to be all-sufficient. It was not to "uphold the waning power of the clergy," but to suppress, so far as possible, by the force of public opinion, rather than by the penalties of law, the prevalence of witchcraft.

On the third of October the diary reads : " My daughter Mary was taken very dangerously sick of a fever, with a vomiting, and with worms. I was with a strange diversion on my spirit, hindered from importunate prayer for the life of the sick child, but at length, on 'October 5, in the evening, I had my heart wonderfully melted in prayer at my father Phillips, where the child lay sick." He resigned the child unto the "mercy of God in Jesus Christ, with such rapturous assurances of the Divine love unto me and mine, as would have made amends for the death of more children, if God had then called for them." He felt assured that this child should not only be happy forever, but that he should never have any child except what should be an everlasting temple to the Spirit of God. On Friday, the 6th, the child Mary died, "near a month short of two years old." This would fix the birth in the early part of November, 1691. The funeral, with an "honorable attendance," was next day, in Boston, and on one of the gravestones in Copp's Hill burying yard the father had chiseled, as expressing his hope, these words : " Gone, but not lost."

No child, out of four, was now left to him except his little Katharine, about four years of age, a bright and charming child. The next day was Sunday, the 8th, and he both preached and administered the Lord's Supper. Text, Genesis 22 : 12 : " Now I know that thou fearest God." I quote but this remark : " A man may, by many tokens, come to know that he has in him the fear of God ; but a right behavior under afflictions is the token that will more especially and eminently serve to make it known."

The Tuesday following was a day of military diversions to the whole town, but he spent the day in prayer with fasting in his study. He considered many of his "humbling circumstances," both as to his sins and his sorrows, especially in the breaches made upon his family. He was grieved also by the "reproaches with which the unworthy, ungodly, ungrateful people do load, not myself only, but both of my fathers too." A party at the time was dissatisfied with the charter obtained by President Mather, and both he and Colonel Phillips shared in the odium stirred up by the enemies of Governor Phips. It was a humor of the people, ever to be expected by men in public life.

About this time Mr. Mather prayed for a "young woman possessed with evil spirits," and desired the Lord to make it his business to engage his neighbors to pray for the girl. He adds : "In the close of this day a wonderful *spirit* in bright raiment, with a face unseen, appeared unto this young woman, and bade her count on me as her father, and regard me, and obey me as her father ; for, she said, the Lord had given her to me, and she should now, in a few days, be delivered. It proved so." This was one of those persons who about this time thought they saw "shining spirits," while others saw the specters of evil spirits. These were what Dr. Abercrombie styled "spectral illusions." They seem — "the shining spirits" — like those bright dreams which sometimes thrill us just before waking, and which, though appearing real, fade away like morning mist in the sunshine.

All classes of people, the unfortunate, the sorrowful, the nervous, prisoners, the despised, and the poor, seemed to resort to Mr. Mather as a friend and adviser. The negro servants in the town had few privileges, and though not in the abject condition of chattel slaves in the south, were yet at the bottom in the social scale, and were, for the most part, ignorant, and were treated with contempt. But the following citation proves that some of them had a desire to improve their state, and knew to whom they could apply. The diary reads: "Besides other praying and pious meetings which I have been continually serving in my neighborhood, a little after this time a company of poor negroes, of their own accord, addressed me for my countenance to a design which they had of erecting such a meeting for the welfare of their miserable nation that were servants among us. I allowed their design, and went one evening, and prayed, and preached with them, and gave them the following orders." These he inserted in his diary "for the curiosity of the occasion." The object of the association was to promote Christian character and good moral conduct; and the means to be used was expressed in the first article in the words following:

I. It shall be our endeavor to meet, the evening after the Sabbath, and pray together by turns, one to begin, and another to conclude the evening; and between the two prayers, a Psalm shall be sung, and a sermon repeated. This way we would spend the evening, which we observe too many of our condition to misspend unto the dishonor of God, and the prejudice of them to whom they belong.

The other "articles of agreement" respected the rights of their masters; the duty to avoid evil company; the purpose to obtain the presence of some good, wise men and officers of the church to attend their meetings and guide them; the resolve to avoid intemperance and other sinful habits; and their intention to punctually attend the meetings and help make them useful. Mr. Mather gave them his countenance and sympathy.

He also reviewed and revised the "Order of the Young

Men's Meetings," and preached to them to "prevent the snares of Satan which might threaten their welfare." This sermon was printed at the end of his book entitled "Early Religion."

As there was a "good number of *poor and old* people in the almshouse, who could not attend meetings, especially in the winter," Mr. Mather spent an afternoon with them, and prayed and preached on James 2 : 5 : "Hearken, my beloved brethren, Hath not God chosen the poor of this world rich in faith, and heirs of the kingdom which he hath promised to them that love him ? " This service was attended "with the comfortable assistance," and as he hoped, "the acceptance of heaven."

The next year (1694) opened with a grievous experience, though it terminated more happily than was feared. Mr. Mather records that "about the middle of January, my little and my only *Katharin* was taken so dangerously sick, that small hope of her life was left unto us." In his distress, when he saw the Lord was "quenching the coal that was left unto him, and rending out of his bosom one that had lived so long with him as to steal a room there, and a lamb that was indeed unto him as a daughter," he cast himself at the feet of God's holy sovereignty. When about to resign her to God in prayer, he looked first into the Bible, and his eye fell upon the account of the healing of the little daughter of the ruler of the synagogue ; and surprised and amazed, he read with tears ; and with more tears, turned it into a prayer. He resigned the child with the same assurance as to her, his children, and himself, as when the little Mary died, but, unlike that case, he begged for the life of this child, and promised to bring her up for God. He also promised to "essay some special service quickly for the rising generation in this land." She soon got well, and lived to be an accomplished, lovely, and very pious young lady.

In a memorandum he speaks of quite a part of his auditory who lived "on the other side of the water." They had to cross the water with considerable trouble for the purpose of attending divine service on the Lord's day. He suggested that they should have separate worship, and offered to help support the service, but they were not inclined to withdraw.

The diary failing for the remainder of this year, we turn to the records of the church, from which it appears that among those received into the church was Abigail Mather, probably a daughter of the senior pastor or teacher. She was now about seventeen years of age. I suppose the Abigail received a few years before was the wife of the junior minister.

It is a fact to be noted also that Margaret Rule was among the members admitted this year. The record in her case reads : "Received into covenant and baptized." This indicates that her parentage was not religious, and renders it probable that she was led into the new life by Mr. Mather's influence.

On the fourteenth of June, Abigail, the second daughter of that name, was born. This second one became the wife of Daniel Willard — descended from the famous Simon Willard — and had four children. She was the only child of Mr. Mather by his first wife who entered the married state.

Though he was daily adding to his great work on the Bible, and also putting the materials for his Church History into shape, he followed up his habit of giving occasional discourses to the public, to meet the present wants of his people and the community. One of the smaller works of this year was a book of 117 pages, entitled "Early Religion, urged in a sermon upon the duties wherein, and the reasons wherefore young people should become religious." To this were added extracts from papers written by several persons who, dying in their youth, left behind them admonitions for their survivors. It also contained brief memoirs, showing examples of youthful piety, as Nathaniel Mather and Nathaniel Shore. Several devoted young men had died in the Indian war, who had been bright examples of piety, as Nash, of Weymouth, and John Clap, of Scituate. Among examples of female excellence were Sarah Derby and Priscilla Wharton. This sermon was on a day of prayer kept by the congregation for the success of the gospel on the hearts of the young. It is a most searching discourse on the effects of sin and the cure of sin. He informs us that "it was usual in several towns of the country, for the pious young men to associate themselves in pious meetings for their mutual assistance in the affairs of religion." The articles of agreement of such an association are in the volume, but need not be given. They were adapted to make the meetings helpful to the religious life of the members. This kind of Young Men's Christian Association was continued in parts of New England far into the next century.

The "Short History of New England" was really a sermon from Ezekiel 22: 30: "I sought for a man among them, that should make up the hedge, and stand in the gap before me for the land, that I should not destroy it." It was spoken at a lecture, in the audience of the general assembly, on the seventh of June. It began with a recapitulation of wonderful passages which had occurred, first, in the protections, and then in the afflictions of New England, with a representation of several matters calling for the singular attention of that country. The discourse was the outcome of a most solicitous spirit, yearning for the good of the country. He showed the errors, mistakes, and sins of the people, and called for reform.

I. He referred to the "day of temptation," when a "flood of antinomian and familistical opinions, cast out by the dragon, had like to have swallowed up the church, fled into this desert, in its infancy," when a factious distinction was made between "men under a covenant of works, and men under a covenant of grace." Secondly, he referred to the controversy about the "extent of baptism, and the church-watch on the halfway plan," which had been waged with great severity. Next, he spoke of the day of temptation, when evil angels were let loose to annoy with tormenting afflictions and unheard-of delusions. Fourthly, he called to mind the "controversies about the negative;" that is, the veto of the elders upon the acts of the churches. Also, he spoke about "compliance with demands made on the other side of the water." He referred to unsettlements since the revolution in 1688, in renewing a rebuilding of meetinghouses, and in parish disturbances. He then pointed out the gaps, and sought for means to close them up. He concludes with three queries. "One man may do very much towards the restoration of our impaired hedge. What may not be done for our impaired hedge by one governor?" He expected much from Governor Phips, and doubtless would have seen his wishes in some measure gratified, but alas! about this time Governor Phips was pursued by his enemies, by whose instigation he was obliged to sail for England to defend himself, where he died the next year. 2. "What may not be done by one magistrate?" Here he refers to Phinehas (Num. 25 : 11), who says God "turned my wrath away from the children of Israel, while he was zealous for my sake among them." 3. "What may be done by one minister?" Aaron was but one man, yet he stood between the living and the dead, and the plague was stayed.

A volume came out in London in 1695 which may properly be connected with this year, because it evidently had been written, in part at least, in 1693 or before. It is printed with an address from Rev. Nathaniel Mather, then of London, to his "worthy nephew, Cotton Mather," under date December 15, 1693. It was probably sent over to London in 1693, kept through the year 1694, and given to the press a year later. I have not seen the book, which was in Mr. Brinley's library, but its present location is unknown to me. The titles of the several pieces, filling 192 pages, are given for their curiosity. "Batteries upon the kingdom of the devil. Seasonable discourses upon some common but woful instances wherein men gratify the grand enemy of their salvation." "Sacred Exorcisms; or, the care and cure of persons possessed by the devil" ("giving cases of bodily molestations by evil spirits" which the author had seen). "The dumb devil cast out." "The stage player unmasked." "The door of hope." "Honey at the end of the rod." "The golden club." Appendix: "The great ambition of a good Christian."

A discourse preached in 1694, and printed in London the next year, may be noticed here, inasmuch as it is a presentation of the ideas relating to divine providence cherished by our forefathers. It is entitled "Brontologia Sacra — the voice of the glorious God in the thunder, explained and applied." On the twelfth of September he expected to give a lecture on a selected topic, but a severe thunder-shower coming on at the time of worship, he changed his subject, and made the shower the theme of the occasion. While he was preaching the lightning struck his own house and set it on fire. The fire was put out before serious damage was done, but the preacher seems to have been annoyed by the fact that the incident became the town talk. On the next Lord's day he added in his discourse, "Some reflections formed by the voices of thunders upon the great things which the great God is now doing in the world ; a discourse useful for all men at all times, but especially intended for an entertainment in the hours of thunder." The sermon, extemporized while the storm was raging without, was a wonderful thing in its way. One can almost see and hear the changes of the tempest as the preacher went on in his discourse — the flashes of lightning, the deep rolling of the thunder, and the rush of downpouring rain. The matter of the sermon was ingenious, apt, and weighty ; the quotations, mostly from Latin writers, came in at the right point, and the spirit of it, evincing calmness of soul and readiness to meet his Lord at any moment, was admirable. His doctrine of universal providence was the same that is accepted at the present day, but then it was held in its fullness. The plan of God was an unbroken warp, into which all the acts and events of life were woven as into a perfect web, with which no chance interfered. Even the wrath of man was made to praise God, and the remainder of it that could not be utilized was restrained.

For the year 1695 we have no diary, but there is proof enough that he worked as hard and prayed as devoutly as in other years before and after.

It is a question in our churches whether deacons should be ordained, or indeed whether their election should be marked by any kind of observance. The records of the Second Church, date of April 25, show the usage in early times. Three deacons were "ordained by solemn imposition of hands" by Increase and Cotton Mather, on a public fast day.

The death of Sir William Phips, on the eighteenth of February, was a grievous blow to his pastor, Mr. Mather, as well as a serious loss to the province and to all New

England. He had been acquitted of the charges brought against him by his enemies, and still enjoyed the confidence of the king, who, like Cromwell, "knew and appreciated a man." But his work was done. While suffering under a sudden attack of a distemper then prevailing in London, he "received the honor of a visit from a very eminent person at Whitehall, who bade him get well as fast as he could, for in one month's time he should be again dispatched away to his government of New England." The "malignant fever" was fatal, and his "sudden death was an extreme surprise to his friends, who honorably interred him in the church of St. Mary Woolnoth, and with him how much of New England happiness!"

Mr. Mather bore all the families of his parish on his heart. In all their afflictions he was afflicted. In April he gave to the press "Help for distressed parents." Text, Proverbs 10 : 1. Subject : "What is to be said for the counsel and comfort of godly parents afflicted with ungodly children ?"

"Durable Riches" belongs to this year's work. In two brief sermons, Mr. Mather, impressed by the "impoverishing blasts of heaven which the undertakings of men, both by land and sea," had met withal, considered (1) The true "cause of losing ;" and (2) the "true cause of thriving." This was reprinted in 1717. The "cause of losing" was "the displeasure of God because of sin." Haggai 1 : 7–11. The second sermon (text, Ecclesiastes 11 : 1, 2) was on the "true way of thriving." First, "Trust in the Lord," "Cast thy bread upon the waters." Secondly, By "generosity." Ecclesiastes 11 : 2 : "Give a portion to seven, and also to eight."

"Johannes in Eremo," or John in the wilderness, contains brief sketches of several distinguished Johns ; as, Cotton, Wilson, Davenport, and Norton, which later went into the *Magnalia*. At this time, with a memoir of the renowned Thomas Hooker, of Hartford, they made a volume of about three hundred pages. Admirable fairness and generous appreciation characterize all these compact and comprehensive sketches.

"Observanda, or, Observable Turns of Providence" in the life and death of the late Queen Mary, was one of the timely productions of the year. It is prefaced with "some observations upon the turns of Divine Providence, now bringing of mighty changes upon the world." The strikingly appropriate text was Ezekiel 10 : 13 : "As for the wheels, it was cried unto them in my hearing, O wheel!"

The world, with all its persons, and all the concerns of it, is liable to a continual revolution ; or the state of the world is fitly compared unto a wheel. "Whenever you look upon any part of this world, you may hear the Son of God crying, 'O wheel' unto it ; 'World, I will have thee to wheel about.'" He proceeds : "A wheel is a very moveable and voluble thing ; and oh ! believe it, oh, expect it. So is the state of this world." Great and little men are wheels turning down and turning up. A wheel turns apace when once it begins to turn. A wheel sometimes makes a noise in the turning of it.

"II. It is the glorious Lord Jesus Christ upon the throne by whom all the changes of the world are ordered and managed. 'T is the God-man who turns, who checks, who holds all the wheels of Providence. III. The angels are employed in turning the wheels of Providence. IV. All the quarters and all the ages of the world have all their changes governed by the Lord whose kingdom ruleth over all. V. A most surprising harmony in the dispensations of God, whereby the changes of the world are brought about. All the wheels move together. VI. They have a various aspect ; look more ways than one.

Collateral designs of Providence. VII. Changes are irresistible when the providential time has come. Nothing human can stop the wheel. VIII. All the changes of the world have the infinite wisdom of heaven to give method, guidance, effect unto them. Wheels full of eyes round about. IX. Changes both formidable and extraordinary. The wheels run high."

He then specifies intricacies of Providence : — Ex. 1. Men when going on their own errands do the will of God. Ex. 2. Enemies of God are confounded by the very means which they took to be preserved by. Ex. 3. A mischief shall become a kindness when the Lord will have it so.

"Christians ! while the Lord Jesus Christ is crying to the wheels of providence, O wheel ! he cries unto us also to behold the turns of those wheels. Behold them with wonder ; behold them with patience ; behold them with profit, and behold them with profound submission of soul." He then turns to the great and solemn event, the death of Queen Mary. The wonderful changes of her life are noticed, and then he gives one of the best sketches of Mary's character ever written. One is inclined to think that he must have received information from his father, who had known her while in England.

CHAPTER IX.

THE records of the North Church in 1696 contained two items showing the benevolence of the congregation. The churches were in the habit of assisting their own indigent members. "April 22. This day being a *Fast* through the Province, our congregation made a collection for the relief of the poor, fifty five pounds, and all money." And on the "4th day, 12 m., this day being a day of Public Thanksgiving through the Province, our congregation made a collection of near sixty pounds, to assist the propagation of the gospel unto places that want it." This entry really belongs to the second month of the next year (1697), but being recorded according to Old Style, I have copied it with the date.

A notable book which came out in 1695 has already been mentioned, but as it had a singular history and a unique table of contents, the reader will be willing to know more about it. The title is "Seven Select Lectures," etc. The manuscript was sent to England in a ship which was captured by the French, but the lectures, we are told, were "by a singular providence of God, preserved from the hands of the French, whereinto they were fallen, and now published by an English gentleman, who providentially lit upon them." It appears that the captain of the French cruiser, setting no value on the writings, disposed of them to an English gentleman who returned home, and found a publisher in Nathaniel Hiller, London.

The heads already given are repeated here, more at length.   I.   " Sacred Exorcisms ; the care and cure of persons possessed by the devil.   *Acts* 5 : 3.   Prop. I.   There is a devil whose employment is to tempt the poor children of men.   *Eph.* 6: 12 ; *Jude* 6; *Luke* 8: 30; *Matt.* 12.   Prop. II.   The temptations of the devil sometimes prevail so far as to *fill* the hearts of the men whom they are used upon. Full of the devil.   2 *Cor.* 4: 4.   Blinds the heart ; gains the heart.   Prop. III.   When once the temptations of the devil have prevailed so far as to fill the hearts of men, they go on to all wickedness and misery.   *Matt.* 17 : 15, 18.   When Satan fills the hearts of men, he keeps them from all good impressions by means of grace upon them. Directions.   1. Fly from the devil.   2. Fight the devil. *Jas.* 4: 7.   3. Keep your hearts.   *Prov.* 4: 23.   4. Prayer."

Second lecture.   " The Dumb Devil Cast Out, or the horrible sin of a prayerless life discovered.   *Ps.* 53 : 4." An incitement to prayer.   " III.   The Stage Player unmasked ; or the signs and woes of a wretched, hypocrite. *Matt.* 24: 51."   It has no reference to the theater, but to hypocrisy in everyday life, and in a thousand forms.   " IV. The Door of Hope.   An antidote against the sin of despair, in them that have been most guilty of other sins. *Ezek.* 37 : 2."   He gives the reasons or causes of despair and the answers to them, with directions, which made the treatise very valuable to desponding Christians at that time and at all times.   The fifth lecture was titled " Honey at the end of the rod.   *Heb.* 12 : 5.   How to bear afflictions ; 1. With a submissive contention of soul. 2. With a believing expectation of soul.   3. With a generous resolution of soul."

The sixth lecture was the " Golden Curb, or some checks given to rash passions."   (2 Sam. 19 : 29.)   After an ingenious introduction in which he explains and clears up the conduct of David in regard to Mephibosheth, he said : " The hasty passions do sometimes put even good men upon those rash things which they should always be ready to retract. Inferences. 1. Beware of rash jealousies. 2. Beware of rash promises. 3. Beware of rash prejudices. 4. Beware of rash conjectures. 5. Beware of rash enterprises. 6. Beware of rash dissatisfactions. 7. Beware of rash zeal. Appendix. The great ambition of a good Christian. *Eph.* 3 : 19. Filled with the fulness of God. What is that fulness of God we are to labor for ?"

This abstract has taken space, but it vindicates its right to it. Several printed discourses of this year have escaped my search. Some of them are noticed in Samuel Mather's list of his father's productions, or have a place in Mr. Brinley's catalogue. One was " The Christian Thank-Offering "; another, " A Cry against oppression"; a third, " A good Master Well Served," giving the necessary properties and practices of a good servant, and showing the methods that should be taken by the heads of a family to obtain such a servant. A timely topic for the present day.

The decease of good Queen Mary occasioned a memorable discourse in 1695. The condition of affairs in the province prompted another in the present year, entitled " Things for a Distressed People to Think Upon." It was a time of distress. The Indian war still raged in the eastern settlements, entailing loss of life and immense expense for the poor people. The sermon was before the General Court, May 27, wherein the " condition of the future as well as the former times" was considered. To this was added a narrative of the late wonderful deliverance of the king and the three kingdoms and all the English dominions. This refers to a great plot between the king of France and the English and Scotch malcontents to invade the kingdom, kill King William, and set up again King James with the Roman Catholic religion. The plot was exposed and the ringleaders were executed, amid the execrations of a loyal people. To the narrative of these events was annexed "a relation of no less than seven miracles, within this little while, wrought by the Almighty Lord Jesus Christ, for the confirmation of our hopes, that some glorious hopes for the welfare of his church, are quickly to be done." The contents of the sermon may be given in some detail, because they picture the times in which the author lived.

It is styled "An Artillery election sermon." Perhaps the General Court attended. Some of the things to be thought upon are thus specified : —

1. The horrid sins committed in the land. There is not one of all the ten commandments in the law which our God has given us, but the people are notoriously violating of it, from one end of the land unto another. [The land was perfectly defiled by the impurities of the Indians.] Now, is it not a wonderful and a horrible thing for so many English that have succeeded them, to *Indianize*, and by the Indian vices of lying, and idleness, and sorcery, and a notorious want of all family discipline, to become obnoxious unto the old score and store of wrath due unto the land? Is it not a wonderful and a horrible thing that the sins of Sodom should so much prevail in a land which was once a land of uprightness?

2. The call to "bewail the visible degeneracy in all orders of men throughout the land." He admitted that New England was still " blessed with very worthy men in all orders ; but alas ! we have not such a choice of them as once we had. I suppose 't were easy to single out, it may be, less then twenty men, upon whose removal from us, all our affairs would be palsy-struck with an incurable feebleness, and the country would almost fall for want of pillars to support it." There was some foundation for this statement ; but the removal of leading men upon

whom public affairs seem to depend is generally followed
by a display of abilities from unexpected quarters. He
proceeds as follows : "There are very many families of
everlasting renown throughout New England, wherein
some or other of the grandchildren are become either
foolish or wicked, and it may be, notoriously children of
the devil."

3. Next he specifies the "ill-conduct of many professors." 4. "Evident blows from an angry God in a long
train of disasters upon all our affairs"; grains blasted,
fires, shipwrecks. 5. They had been "deprived of charter
liberties, and English liberties," though a happy revolution had restored them. The remedy was "supplication,
repentance, reformation, and seeking the conversion of
the young."

Two items from the records of the church in 1697
shed some light on the workings of Congregationalism
about two hundred years ago. "4 d. 2 m. [or April 4].
This day our church voted a letter of admonition to the
church of Charlestown, for betraying the liberties of the
churches, in their late putting into the hands of the whole
inhabitants the choice of a minister." In pure Congregationalism the church existed without a parish, and did all
its own business. After the towns were made parishes
by the General Court, and later in "poll parishes," the
church took the initiative in the choice of a minister, and
called on the parish to concur. If the latter body, which
raised the money for the support of the ministry and the
building of church edifices and parsonages, non-concurred,
the church made a new choice and again called for approval. It appeared that the church in Charlestown had
departed from the primitive usage. The Brattle Street
Church, when formed a few years later, was put upon this
basis ; but the orthodox churches, as a general rule, have

always followed the way defended by the Second Church. Church power and regulations are kept under Christ, the Head, in the hands of the church. The parish is simply a legal body, to assist the church in maintaining the public worship of God in its purity.

The second item is dated "26 d. 7 m., and reads: "Baptized Vynes Elicut, a youth about twelve years of age, presented by a woman of the Old Church, (one *Cable*) who had brought him up in the knowledge, and for the service of Christ, and promised still to do so." This boy was presented by one who was not his mother, and probably not a relative, and by one who was not a member of the church of Mr. Mather. A good woman, taking the place of a mother, sought Christian baptism for a boy whom she had brought up, but not in the church of which she was a member. This was not according to the usual custom, but who could deny the request of a Christian man or woman presenting a child in this way?

The diary of this year furnishes copious material for the study of the inner life of the writer. We shall make a few citations, beginning with the date of February 22 : —

Being this day thirty-four years old, I set apart this day for a Thanksgiving to be offered unto God, from a sense of the great obligations unto thankfulness which my life hath now for thirty-four years together been filled withal.

Though interrupted by company he "paraphrased, improved and applied the whole 103d Psalm, on his knees before the Lord." He then deliberately read over a "*catalogue* of the Divine dispensations" towards him from the beginning, "particularly blessing of God on each article." He read over the record or diary of the year, saving such things as were suitable. Towards night he "acknowledged more special instances of divine favor." This whole day's employment is a lesson to those

Christians who do not know how to spend the hours in a protracted season of private devotion. Therefore the closing lines of the diary for the day are subjoined. In the evening of this day he had a most wonderful time. He was so spent with the preceding exercises that he seemed to have no strength to proceed further. He laid himself prostrate on the floor before the Lord, as was his wont, and he thus narrates what followed : —

Then did the Spirit of the Lord Jesus Christ, after a wonderful manner, irradiate my mind, and quicken me, and rejoice me with wondrous assurances that he would possess me, and employ me, and grant me to glorify my Lord Jesus Christ exceedingly. Yea, the good angels of that Holy Spirit were so near unto me, in my rapturous praises of my Lord-Redeemer, that the præ-libations of heaven which I enjoyed in this matter, *are not fit here to be uttered.*

He then, with wonderful assurance of being heard, "prayed mightily that God would cause the Spirit of reformation to come down on the nations of Europe, and that a mighty revolution upon France, and upon Great Britain might accompany it. It will be so. This poor man cried, and the Lord heard his cry." There was no special spiritual renovation in France or Great Britain in these years, but events took a strong turn against the French and the partisans of James in their attempts to subvert the throne of King William ; and no believer in sacred Scripture need doubt that God inspired praying hearts to beat in sympathy with his grand designs.

This praying for a mighty revolution in France and Great Britain was a frequent exercise. On the twentieth of February he prayed much, with fasting, in preparation for the Lord's Supper. His petitions were, first, "for his family, his ministry, and for the whole nation." He cried "importunately to God for the Reformation to be revived, and perfected, not only in Great Britain, but in France,

with a *mighty revolution.*" England became solidly established in Protestantism, and began slowly to rise from
the base immorality of the restoration, in the time of
Charles II, to a purer style of living ; but the mighty
revolution in France waited nearly a hundred years, and
then came in fire and slaughter. "The mills of the gods
grind slowly," but with effect.

On the Sabbath at communion he had a "powerful
persuasion that he would ere long be with the innumerable company of the holy angels," and that his "departure would be easy and joyful." His honesty in leaving
the above and similar "persuasions " on record, when he
might have omitted them, will be noted. A part of his
record this day was his "faith that his offspring, left in
this evil world, would be the servants of the Lord Jesus
Christ, who would, as a Father, take care of them." He
lived about twenty years, and before his death, nearly all
his children had been gathered into the garner of God.

His "little Mehitable " died on the twenty-eighth of
February, being about a year old. There was a singular
fact connected with her death, the substance of which was
as follows : It was Mr. Mather's habit to pray for all his
children by name, when he rose in the morning. Soon
after his prayer, this morning, it occurred to him that he
had omitted the name of Mehitable. He was surprised
and grieved at this, and chided himself for the omission.
An hour or more later, he was told that the child was
dead, and that she died before he offered the prayer.
His first surmise was that death was caused by sudden
colic pains, but inquiry proved that the nurse had overlaid
the child. The inference was that the Inspirer of prayer
did not move the father to pray for the child who was
beyond the need of a mortal's supplications. He had
now Katharine and the second Abigail. Hannah was born
in the course of the year.

About this time, to render his pastoral visits the more significant, he published his sermon on Proverbs 5 : 11 : "And thou mourn at the last, when thy flesh and thy body are consumed." This is in Brinley's list, but I have been unable to find it. The title is, " The Thoughts of a dying man," and the preacher with " cogency and fervency" set before his people what they would "think and choose at the last, when they came to die"; and he urged them to make that choice at once. He made visits every week, as a rule, and left his little book. This volume contained a report of matters uttered by many in the last moments of their lives.

His heart expanded in many prayers for several objects. One was that the " distempers of his soul might be removed by the Spirit of God." Another was the breached condition of some of the churches in the wilderness; and a third was the " divided condition of the church in Watertown." He was also in prayer because of the " danger of a French invasion in the ensuing summer, and because of the decease of considerable persons in his congregation." He resolved every day, "like Daniel, the man of desire," to pray for the " captivity of the church to be hastened to a period."

Looking for the great reformation at hand, he invited a select number of Christians whose " appetites were strong to be informed about the *characters* and *approaches* of *those* events, to meet in his study, to inquire and discourse, at set times, about those things which the angels desire to look into. Concluded with a prayer for the hasting of the glorious things that are spoken about the city of God." The plan was carried out with an " unspeakable consolation."

The seasons of Mather in high communion were not a few, and it is needful, if one would get a right idea of his

character, to view him in more than a few of his "irradiations." What happens but once in a lifetime to some
good Christians was almost habitual with him. For
example : —

"20 d. 3 m. [or Friday, May 30]. Day set apart for secret or private
thanksgiving." When on his knees, confessing the glories of God,
and full of praises, he "requested and obtained the irradiations of the
Spirit, and received heart-melting assurances that as my heart was become desirous to please him, he would never send me down to that
miserable world where they do not praise him, but hate him, and curse
him, and blaspheme him for ever. No, but grant me a state of eternal
blessedness." He bewailed his "own horrible sinfulness" and gave
thanks for the operations of the Spirit upon him; for the privilege
of preaching the unspeakable riches of Christ; for upholding him in
seventeen years of ministry, and in so eminent a place, and so large
a congregation, though one of the most "inconsiderable wretches"
in the land; for enabling him to preach in other places, and on public occasions, and making his performances profitable unto the souls
of multitudes; for liberty of the press, and his numerous publications more than those of any young man — read also in Europe as
well as in America; for the respect shown him among the churches;
for comforts and supports ; " especially my *life*, my *health*, my *speech*,
my *library*, my *dwelling house*, my *salary*. And my *consort* with my
children; and my *unblemished reputation*." Also "such deliverances
granted unto my *country*, that my opportunities to be serviceable have
not been overwhelmed in the ruins of it."

These lines were not flaunted abroad in the world, as
would be done by a vain boaster in these days, but were
hidden in the secrecy of a diary intended for the eyes of
loving children to see; written too in the time of King
William's war, when the power of France was joined with
that of the eastern and Canadian Indians, to ruin the
province and "overwhelm" all New England. In the
evening he went into the empty church, and alone in the
pulpit, prostrate on the floor, with "great elevation of
soul," gave himself up unto the Spirit of the Lord Jesus
Christ. He praised Christ for his good angels, and, as he

writes, "for my good Angel." He closed with special
thanks for "divine assistances and singular fervor" in enabling him to finish his Church History, as he styled the
"Magnalia Christi Americana." This was not published
until 1702, and then in England, because no native publisher could undertake to bring out such an extensive
work.

On Friday, August 27, he writes about an "allotted
journey" to Salem and Ipswich. This seems to have
been an annual tour. All the earlier part of the week
before he started, he was under "sickly disorders." There
was a violent storm in the afternoon before he left home,
which was probably upon Tuesday. He resigned the
matter to the Lord, as he "was going on the Lord's business." The weather cleared up and his health returned.
He had a comfortable journey, made more so by the
company of some "young gentlemen, who by dutifully
waiting" on him, gave him an "opportunity of studying"
how he might "effectually recommend the service of
Christ unto them." He preached on Wednesday at
Salem, and on Friday at Ipswich. At the latter place his
subject was "Glorifying God by Bringing forth Much
Fruit." He records that he was "everywhere received
with undeserved respect and honor." He had private
interviews, and "preached to vast assemblies." At
Salem, on Lord's day, he preached twice on "Christ seen
by Angels, and Preached unto the Gentiles." After an
absence of about ten days, he reached home on Friday,
September 3, but too weary to devote as much time on
Saturday as usual for preparation for the Eucharist ; but
yet "made some effort at devotion." At the Lord's table,
Sunday, he enjoyed "rapturous communications from
heaven."

A week later he was in prayer for the "spread of

the knowledge of Christ more in England, Scotland, and Ireland," and that the "angels of the Lord Jesus Christ may bring a wondrous convulsion on the French empire." He records that he "received a wonderful assurance from the Lord that it should be so." Possibly the Hearer of prayer had a wider field of vision than his petitioner, and saw in the wars under the leadership of William and Marlborough, and the corruptions and wastings under Louis XV, the causes of a "wondrous convulsion" in France.

On the eighth of September, Mr. Mather was much in his closet. He "exceedingly abhorred himself before the Lord for the incredible vileness of his life." He admired the grace that had not utterly rejected his service, and "had not permitted Satan to precipitate him" into scandalous miscarriages. By "vileness of life" we now mean a life of grossly immoral conduct. He meant nothing of the sort, but simply a life defective in the degree of its fidelity. Judging himself by a perfect law, he saw how far he came short of full and constant obedience. On this occasion he prayed for his family and flock, the country, the college, and for several miserably disordered churches. At the close of the day, prostrate on the floor, in the deepest humility of spirit, he "received from heaven, in a manner that he *might not utter*, a wonderful assurance that his sins were pardoned by the wonderful grace of God, imparting to him the righteousness of the Lord Jesus Christ."

The next day being the Sabbath, he writes : —

The Spirit of the Lord came near unto me. Doubtless the Angel of the Lord made me sensible of his approaches. I was wonderfully irradiated. My Lord Jesus Christ shall yet be more known in the vast regions of America; and by the means of poor, vile, sinful me, he shall be so. Great Britain shall undergo strange revolution and reformation, and sinful I shall be concerned in it. France shall quickly feel mighty impressions from the Almighty hands of my Lord Jesus Christ, and I shall on the occasion, sing his glorious praises. Nor was this all that was then told me from heaven; but I forbear the rest.

Mr. Mather, in common with many others in his age and the preceding, regarded the great Reformation as a work suddenly arrested, and they prayed that it might be made complete. Besides, he and many of his coevals lived in expectation of the speedy coming of Christ, to work mighty changes in the world. These views and expectations gave a tone to his prayers and meditations and entered into his language as he recorded his experiences.

Another phase of his many-sided mind is revealed in a note dated September 24. No man but Cotton Mather would have conversed in the manner which he records in the words following : " I was discoursing this day with a worthy minister, dangerously sick, and said to him, that to *praise* Christ in the midst of myriads of angels in heaven, may in some respects be as good as to *preach* Christ in the midst of hundreds of mortals on earth." The minister assented. Mather then inquired (for he says, " the discourse was managed with a certain serious and sacred hilarity ") if his friend " had prepared a song, and meditated what to say when he arrived among the blessed angels." He replied : " Why, pray, what do you intend to say ? " Mather answered : " I 'll say, Behold, O ye holy spirits, the most wretched and loathsome sinner that ever arrived among you ; that was the most abominable sinner that ever was in the world, and yet I have as good a righteousness as any of you ! I 'll say : O ye illustrious angels ! if you don't wondrously glorify the grace of the Lord Jesus Christ, in fetching so vile a sinner into these mansions, you 'll never do it."

A " singular errand unto heaven," on the ninth of October, was to be " informed if he should glorify Christ by writing a treatise. 'The Great Mystery of Godliness in the several articles of it.' I *Tim.* 3 : 16. Yes." The work was not given to the press till 1701.

An entry in the diary on the ninth of October gives an inkling of Mather's anxieties, labors, and sympathies, almost perpetually recurring. " With other ministers praying for a brother minister," who was sick. He attended a council at Watertown, where a long and complicated difficulty had divided the church, and was active and successful in bringing about a happy result.

His belief in the ministry of angels comes out in the record of October 13. In a journey to Dedham on horseback, which was his usual mode of journeying, he had the "sensible protection of angels," in several particulars. His headstrong horse broke the clasp of his bridle. His horse fell down with him so as to be lamed. The gentleman in company, mistaking the way, a person unknown, just then in sight, informed them of their mistake, and thus saved them from extra travel. Many would call this "providential"; Mather considered it the same, but by angelic agency.

Under date of the eighth of October, he mentions an event and a publication, not noticed in any life, or list of his books. The general assembly was holding its autumnal session, and he had an opportunity to address that body in common with a large congregation. " Considering that Jesus Christ, as the great Sacrifice for the great congregation, had never been enough preached, and praised, and magnified in this land," he took for his text Lev. 4: 21. The topic was : "A Sin-Offering for the Congregation," and he showed the people how to "glorify the Lord Jesus Christ, by acting faith in him as a sin-offering for our public atonement and salvation." He concluded by telling the *elders of the land* that they ought not to stir out of the place till the exhortation was put in execution. He called on the assembly to stand in prayer, and pledge, as it were, to carry out the " sacrifice for deliverances." The sermon was published with a letter from a Frenchman full of " divine rarities," Mr. Neau, a pious confessor who once lived in his neighborhood, but was now a prisoner in a French dungeon. To this Mather added a discourse in the French tongue, addressed to the French Church in Boston, advising them, as prudently as he was able, to " reform things that were amiss among them."

Among the publications of the year, besides those mentioned, were : " Ecclesiastes ; the Life of the reverend and excellent Jonathan Mitchell, Pastor of the church, and glory of the college ;" "Faith at Work, or, the nature, the order, and the necessity of the good works by which the faith of the Christian is to be evidenced ;" "Gospel for the Poor ;" " Narrative of wonderful passages relating to the captivity and deliverance of Hannah Swanton," annexed to a sermon, and also printed in the *Magnalia;* " The Way to Excel," in a notice of Rev. Joshua Mody, an " eminent person " ; " Thoughts of a dying man," giving things uttered by many in the last minutes of their lives ; " Terribilia Dei, or Remarkable Judgments of God, on several sorts of offenders," in two sermons ; "Songs of the Redeemed, a book of Hymns," referred to by his son Samuel ; " Pietas in Patriam, the Life of his excellency Sir William Phips." There was a second edition of this last in 1699, and it has appeared in every edition of the *Magnalia.* Calef in his carping way says that Cotton Mather published this book anonymously, in order to praise himself. Mather could not disguise his style by withholding his name. If that were possible, he made no effort to disguise it in this remarkable production. Moreover, the author was well known at the time. A note prefixed to the volume, signed by Nathaniel Mather, John Howe, and Matthew Mead, reads : " The author of the following narrative is a person of such well-known integrity, prudence, and veracity, that there is not any cause to question the truth of what he here relates. And moreover, this writing of his is adorned with a very grateful variety of learning, and doth contain such surprising workings of Providence as do well deserve due notice and observation." So far from praising himself, his name and deeds are kept out of sight. In reciting the events connected with the revolution in Boston in 1689, he mentions the declaration that was from his own pen, but does not hint at the authorship ; in referring to the paper, signed by the ministers of Boston, cautioning the judges against giving credence to "spectral evidence," he merely mentions that it was written by the author of this " Life of Phips," thus veiling his name. But enough of this, which has been dwelt upon solely to show the untrustworthiness of all Robert Calef's animadversions upon Cotton Mather.

The volumes and pamphlets of this year from Mather's prolific pen filled about four hundred and fifty pages. In December he heard that the Life of Phips was published in London, as well as a small book on the " Gospel for the Poor." The last was written on the supposition that the long war now closed in England would be followed by hard times, as is often the case, for a while, by the change of values. In reference to the Life of Phips, the author writes that "our base tories are in much anguish at this book, but it will certainly prove a great service unto the Lord Jesus Christ." It is one of Mather's best productions, and is indispensable to the student of a very interesting period of New England history.

It appears from the diary that Mr. Mather had an impression about this time of approaching death, for on the seventh of November he records that he took his little daughter Katy, "then not far from eight years old," into his study, and there, as he writes: "I told my child that I am to die shortly, and she must, when I am dead, remember everything that I now said to her." He then spoke, (1) of her sinfulness by nature, and charged her to pray every day in secret places, that God for the sake of Christ would give her a new heart. (2) He told her that after his death she would have to meet with "more humbling afflictions than now, when she had a careful and tender father to provide for her; but if she would pray continually, God would be a Father to her, and make all afflictions work together for her good." (3) That the people of God would much observe her, and that he had put forth a book about ungodly children, in which he had written that the book would be a terrible witness against his own children, if any of them should not be godly. Both shed many tears, and then he told her that God from heaven had assured him that "she should be brought home unto the Lord Jesus Christ, and be one of his forever." He says: "I bid her use this as an encouragement unto her supplications unto the Lord for his grace." They then knelt down, and he prayed that God would bless her, and save her, and make her a *temple* of his glory." This was the second, but now eldest living child of the family, the bright, witty, and lovely Katy, who was her father's delight and comfort for nearly nineteen years longer, until her lamented death.

On the tenth of November was a "day of public Thanksgiving for deliverances." In connection with this we find the following *memoranda* : — (1) A great salvation had come into the land : a plentiful harvest came when scarcity was feared. (2) A great body of Indians and French, on their way to our frontiers, were met and beaten, and the lives of hundreds of our people were saved. (3) A squadron of about fifteen French men-of-war was coming, and no doubt would have made the place desolate, but "when a little way off, the Angel of the Lord went forth and smote them with such a wasting sickness" that they gave up the enterprise.

But the year did not close before a discovery of sin among his people filled him with grief. On the fourth of December he records as follows : "Horrible crimes are, by strange dispensations of heaven, discovered in some communicants of my church; especially, one very criminal adulteress." He prayed for pardon if the sin had come by his neglect. He also prayed for "speedy and wondrous rebukes upon the eastern Indians," and writes : "The Lord heard me." I do not suppose that he regarded his own prayers as the only prayers that concurred in moving the Hearer of prayer to subvert the pagan power in the eastern settlement. The last record of the year, on the twenty-sixth of December, states that he had a young gentleman who was going to England, in his study, for "conversation and prayer."

The peace of Ryswick, which marked the close of a war of several years' duration between England and her allies and the king of France, had been signed on the eleventh of September at one in the morning. On the fourteenth the poet Prior, secretary of the British embassy, presented himself with a copy of the document before the Lords Justices at Whitehall. It was an occasion of boundless joy in England, because the king of France had acknowledged William as the sovereign of

England, besides making other stipulations gratifying to both English and Dutch. Macaulay describes the general gladness in the following words :—

In every part of the kingdom where the peace was proclaimed, the general sentiment was manifested by banquets, pageants, loyal healths, salutes, beating of drums, blowing of trumpets, breaking up of hogsheads. At some places the whole population, of its own accord, repaired to the churches to give thanks. At others, processions of girls clad all in white, and crowned with laurels, carried banners inscribed with "God bless King William." At every county town, a long cavalcade of the principal gentlemen, from a circle of many miles, escorted the mayor to the market cross. Nor was one holiday enough for the expression of so much joy. On the fourth of November, the anniversary of the king's birth, and on the fifth, the anniversary of his landing at Torbay, the bell-ringing, the shouting, and the illuminations were renewed both in London and all over the country.

When the news reached Boston and extended over New England in December, the rejoicing was scarcely less general and ardent than in the old country, and no man more felt the full significance of the event or rejoiced in it more sincerely than Cotton Mather.

The record of this year should not be closed without noting the death of Simon Bradstreet, one of the most eminent and venerable men who came to New England in the first generation. He was born in 1603, came hither in 1630, and died at the age of ninety-four. His father was "son of a Suffolk gentleman of fine estate." He became a Nonconformist, and preached in England, and afterwards in Holland. He was a man of ability and possessed a temper of mingled firmness and gentleness. Being neither a radical nor a conservative of marked type, his convictions and sympathies generally allied him to the former in every crisis in the public affairs. Though evidently willing that the regicides Goffe and

Whalley should be discovered and sent to England, yet when the news came of the overthrow of James II, he, though an old man of eighty-six years, took the leading position in setting up the provisional government and in proclaiming William and Mary. He was sincerely religious, upright in all his transactions, a man of public spirit, an ornament of society, and a pillar of the state. He married Anne, daughter of Governor Thomas Dudley, and became the father of numerous and respectable descendants.

CHAPTER X.

FROM the church records it appears that discipline was administered with mingled fidelity and Christian kindness. Every step was taken in accordance with the spirit of Matthew xviii, and none were excluded until proved unworthy and every practicable means used to reclaim and to restore. The following were disciplinable offenses: adultery, drunkenness, lying, gambling, theft, evil speaking, slander, idleness, keeping bad company, neglect of family worship, and profane swearing. Offenses against the seventh commandment were oftenest charged upon female members, simply because the proof of guilt was more apparent.

The winter of 1697–1698 was the "severest that ever was in the memory of man," says Cotton Mather. Clough's Almanac, as quoted by Drake, says that "from the middle of January to the first or second of March, it held cold with very little or no intermission. All the Bay was frozen over quite out to sea, so as it was common to go horse and man over all the ferries, for two months together. It snowed between twenty and thirty times that year. Slays and loaded sleds passed a great part of the time upon the ice from Boston as far as Nantasket." Grain was high and trade had never suffered more than at this period.

On the eighth of January, Mr. Mather offered "special prayer for the direction of heaven" in reference to the publication of his "Magnalia Christi Americana." The manuscript had been sent to London and the author was naturally solicitous about the matter until the work was in print.

The remainder of the month, he informs us, proved to be a "time of much calamity to him, as well as others. Epidemical and pestilential *colds* afflicted many; proved *mortal* to many and grievous to more." A sore cough lacerated his throat; headache and fever confined him almost a month. In the prospect of death he "tasted the consolations of God." He writes of a "sweet contradiction in Christianity," namely, the desire to go to heaven and be with the blessed angels, and the desire to live and serve Christ. "I resolved, out of respect unto the service which I desire to do for the name of my Lord Jesus Christ, that I would keep out of those blessed hands yet for a while, if I could, by using the best means for my recovery." He notes these lessons as the result: — "1. That this present *evil* world is not my home. 2. Inquire after sin as the cause of sickness. 3. Ascribe to Christ the glory of deliverance."

He records a "very particular experiment" on the sixth of February. He was so very ill at noon, the first Lord's day of his going abroad, that he thought it impossible for him to do any public service. He could hardly rise from his chair. He took his Bible and read Daniel 10: 8, 10–19. He says: "I was left alone — and there remained no strength in me. . . . Then there came and touched me one like the appearance of a man, and he strengthened me. And said, O man, greatly beloved, fear not; peace be unto thee; be strong, yea, be strong." Then he prayed the Lord to send his angels ("and my angel") to touch him. When the time came for meeting he received new strength, and the longer he continued in the public service the more his strength seemed to return. He prayed and preached and baptized and managed other church matters for the space of three hours together. His text was Psalm 103 : 3, and his subject, "Christ the Healer of all the Diseases of His People."

He was so anxious to make up for lost time, and "managed with so indiscreet an intemperance," as to bring on a fit of the colic; but recovering, he preached on Lecture day to a great assembly ; and as almost all the town had been sick, he "set himself to direct the best improvement of it, on Isaiah 33 : 24 : 'The inhabitant shall not say, I am sick.' "

During the twelve months preceding this date, February 12, 1698, he had preached twenty-four sermons on the fifty-third of Isaiah on alternate Sabbaths, besides over thirty others. On this day he wrote: "Through the forbearance of God, I am thirty-five years old, and astonished that the Lord has spared me so long as a barren fig tree." He was too feeble to spend the day as usual in devotions and fasting, but did engage in thanksgiving for mercies.

Nothing but death could stay the voice or pen of Cotton Mather. On the twenty-second of February we find that he had been writing a book during the winter, being "Essays for the Illustrations and Demonstrations of the Christian Religion." It was finished this day, and entitled "The Confirmed Christian, Beholding the Triumphs of Christianity over all its Adversaries." He had enjoyed a "wonderful assistance of heaven in the writing of it," and says : "Although I have been full of other employments, and have lost more than a little time through *sickness;* and *sloth,* and *sleep* do shamefully prevail upon me, yet in a few weeks' time I have now composed this treatise of about twenty-four sheets." This appears to have been given to the press in 1700.

On the same day he wrote : "Some of my neighbors, and some from whom I little expect any such respect, call for the discourse lately spoken at the Boston Lecture on Sickness." It was published under the motto, *Mens Sana in Corpore Sano*, and with the title, "A Discourse on recovery from sickness." He exclaims: "O my Lord Jesus Christ! I am astonished, I am astonished at thy favors in thus employing the most unworthy sinner in the world."

The fourth of March was kept as a secret fast before the Lord. He was in "tearful agonies" about his sins, but laid hold on the offered righteousness of the Lord Jesus Christ. "The Spirit and the Angel of Jehovah came nigh unto me, and so as I cannot utter, assured me that I should serve my Lord Jesus Christ yet exceedingly. And more particularly, that I am soon to do a *special* service of great consequence for the name of the Lord Jesus Christ, which as yet, I know not what it is."

A wonderful thought came into his mind March 20 with a heavenly force, that God *loved* my Lord Jesus Christ infinitely, and had given worlds unto him, and made him the Lord of all. "I was assured that the angels of my Lord Jesus Christ had wondrous offices of good-will to do for me, and that they would, on the score of my Lord Jesus Christ, *love* me, *help* me, *teach* me, be *nigh* unto me, be *with* me, fetch me to be with them forever."

Memorandum. I was a little comforted with a word spoken to me by a gentleman, a lawyer, who came a few months ago out of England, and who, since he came, had set himself a little to observe the people of New England. Said he, "Mr. Mather, I can tell you this. All the men that have any virtue, or any reason in them, I find love you, and value you, and honor you; but all the base people, who are scandalous for vice and wickedness, hate you, and can't give you a good word.

In the following entry of the diary, April 1, the "scandalous peace" referred to was the Peace of Ryswick, mentioned above. Mather thought France had been let off too easily, which may have been the case, for King William had a hard task in trying to keep the allied powers together against the arms and the intrigues of Louis XIV. In his devotions this day, the diarist prayed for "pardon of sins; support of his ministry; welfare of his family; deliverance of his countrymen from invasion of salvages; and for the whole Protestant religion and interest from the threatening circumstances whereunto the *scandalous peace*, lately concluded, has involved it." As several Catholic powers were allied with England in checking the encroachments of France, King William could not wage the war openly in the Protestant interest. Mather knew this and did not censure the king, whom he admired, but he prayed that the Protestant religion might be saved from threatening perils. The war was soon renewed, and was not definitely closed until Marlborough, in several hitherto unparalleled victories, had driven the French king to the wall. The interest that we Americans of the present day take in great European contests is faint in comparison with the intense anxiety felt by our fathers in the wars waged two hundred years ago. Their own welfare, secular and religious, was bound up in that of the mother country. If France triumphed, the Catholic interest would prevail in all North America.

On this day, April 1, Mr. Mather made special request for the gracious presence of Christ in his design at the Lecture in the following week, to relate and improve the History of the Divine Dispensations towards the town of which he was a native. This leads us to the masterly discourse spoken on the seventh of April to a "vast assembly." It was entitled "The Boston Ebenezer," and was "much desired for publication." It was printed with another sermon entitled "Household Religion," in eighty-two pages. The first was republished in the *Magnalia*, first volume, where it may now be read, and from which may be learned much of the history and character of Boston. It will well repay the reading. Of this effort he writes : —

The Lord having helped me, beyond my expectations, in preparing a discourse for the Lecture, he yet more gloriously helped me in uttering it unto a vast assembly of his people. I first laid my sinful mouth in the dust, on my study floor, before the Lord, where I cast myself, in my supplications, for his assistance as utterly unworthy thereof. But the Lord made my sinful mouth to become this day, the trumpet of his glory, and the hearts of the inhabitants of the town were strangely moved by what was delivered among them.

His " little daughter Hannah," a month or two over a year old, was taken very dangerously sick of a fever, with convulsions to such a degree that there was little hope of her life. He writes : " I cried unto heaven for the child and cheerfully resigned her unto the Lord. Now, behold the result : resigned enjoyments will be still enjoyed. Had something of a particular faith for her being restored unto me. And to my amazement, it came to pass accordingly."

A work written two years before came out in London this year. Its title was " ELEUTHERIA, or the Idea of the Reformation in England : and a History of Non-comformity in and since the Reformation ; with predictions of a more glorious reformation and revolution at hand." This hope of a " reformation at hand " was probably suggested by the fact that a " Convocation " was about to be held in England, in which it was hoped by many in and out of the national church that measures would be taken to secure a general " comprehension " of orthodox Protestants in the national church by mutual concessions. Such expectations met with total failure, as the high church party opposed the plan with violence. The work of Mather was designed to show, from writers of authority in the national church, that the position held by the Nonconformists was sound and scriptural, and that there was no good reason for excluding them from the Church of England.

In the diary (" 5d. 3m.") the author refers to this work as having been "written with exceeding pains," and of his having recently sent it by a brother-in-law to a bookseller in London. He says : "If it be possible, I have a secret hope that it will much affect the church in the changes that are approaching. In this treatise, because I distinguish the friends of the reformation by the name of *Eleutherians,* (while I call its foes Idumæans) for the causes there assigned, I therefore entitled the book ELEUTHERIA." Later in the year he wrote : "There comes to my hand my Eleutheria . . . with circumstances which give me to see a special care of the holy angels concerning it . . . and I believe it will have some notable effect on the English nation." But the plan of King William and many of the wisest and most liberal churchmen, including Archbishop Tillotson, was, as said above, defeated. The hard-and-fast churchmen were afraid of the effect that would follow the inclusion of such a mass of evangelical and non-prelatical members as composed the dissenting body. On the other hand, it is more than probable that the hopes of the dissenters, that their inclusion would reform the Church of England, would have been disappointed.

One of the best sermons of our author was occasioned by the decease of Rev. John Bailey. It is given in the *Magnalia,* with the title, "A Good Man making a Good End." It was preached at the funeral, December 16, 1697, but printed in pamphlet form in the year under review.   An extract from the preface is inserted here, because it intimates the merits of Mr. Bailey and gives the author's reasons for preparing biographies.

> We are not so *wise* as the miserable Papists !   Among them a person of merit, shall at his death, be celebrated and canonized, by all men agreeing in it as in their common interest for to applaud his life. Among us, let these dues be paid unto the memories of the most meritorious person, after his decease, many of the survivors are offended, I had almost said, enraged at it.   They seem to take it as a reproach unto themselves, (and, it may be, *so it is*) that so much good should be told of any man, and that all the little frailties and errors of that man, (and wherein no mere man was ever free,) be not also told, with all the unjust aggravations that envy might put upon them.   This folly is as inexpressible an injury to us all, as it cannot but be an advantage unto mankind in general for *interred* virtue to be rewarded by a *statue*.
>
> If ever I deserved well of my country, it has been when I have given to the world the histories and characters of eminent persons which have adorned it.   Malice will call some of these things romances, but that *malice* itself may never hiss with the least color of reason any more, I do here declare, let any man living evince any one *material mistake*, in any one of these composures, it shall have the most public recantation that can be desired.   In the meantime, while some impotent cavils, nibbling at the statues which have been erected for our *worthies*, take pains to prove themselves the enemies of New England and of religion, the statues will outlive all their idle nibbles ; "the righteous will be had in everlasting remembrance," when the "wicked who see it and are grieved shall gnash with their teeth, and melt away."

In the latter part of May, Mr. Mather was deeply concerned about the condition of " many poor friends, prisoners among the Turks and Moors, and in horrible slavery at Sallee."   That he might comfort them, he wrote a letter to strengthen them in the Christian faith.   He took "some care to print many copies of this large letter, that so it might be, by diverse opportunities, the more certainly conveyed unto them."   He styled it a " Pastoral Letter."   He begins : —

We are distressed for you, O our brethren ; we are distressed for you.
Our neighborhood, with bitter anguish, pouring out the lamentations
that were of old heard among the people of God, in *Lam.* 1 : 38 :
" Hear, I pray you, all people, and behold my sorrow ; my virgins and
my young men are gone into captivity." And when we consider what
a dreadful, and what a doleful, and how inexpressibly a miserable captivity is that you are gone into, the lamentations of our sorrow do indeed become inexpressible. But though we cannot express the anguish
of mind that seizes us, when we do, at our full tables, and in our soft
lodgings, with all our friends about us, call to mind, as we often do,
how 't is with you, yet we would express a little of that effection that
we bear you, by letting you know that we remember you. Our remembrance causes us, without ceasing, to make mention of you in our
prayers, and in our ardent and constant cries unto the God of all
grace, that you may have grace to help you in your time of need.

He therefore wrote them what might help to interest
and strengthen and comfort them in their captivity.
Hoping that they might continue faithful unto death in
the Christian faith, and that they might experience the
practice and power of it, he urged them to repentance for
all sin and to prayer without ceasing. The letter closes
with many promises from the Scriptures. To prayers and
promises Mr. Mather and his people added liberal gifts of
money to aid in securing the ransom of the captives. He
states in his diary that he afterwards heard that the letter
"was blessed wonderfully to the captives ; yea, it proved
the preparation and introduction unto their deliverances."

The twenty-ninth of May was the Lord's day, on which
he recalled the fact that he had privately and publicly
given out his convictions of a great reformation in England,
Scotland, and France. On this subject he had exercised
particular faith. Now for the fulfillment.

Well, in Scotland, the last year, the reformation of the church is
accomplished unto the satisfaction of them that breathed after it. In
England, upon the unanimous vote of the parliament, the king has
emitted an excellent proclamation, for the suppression of all profane-

ness; and the effect of that, and other things, has appeared in a sudden and wondrous alteration upon the whole face of the kingdom : — a notable reformation ! Also, for punishing those who publish doctrines derogatory to the person, and office, and glory of Christ. As to France, behold the whole Principality of Orange, which is in the bowels of France, has had an astonishing work of grace done upon it. Its pastors being restored, the holy religion of Christ is restored with them ; and the poor Protestants who had been dragooned into apostacy, are all, with transports of joy, recovered.

The recovery of Orange from France was an object on which the tenacious heart of King William was set, both as a point of honor, as it gave the title to his family, and as the recovery was the reinstitution of the Protestant religion in the principality. In Scotland, besides the religious changes which Mather refers to, it should be noted that the great scheme of universal education for the children and youth of the nation was put in action at this time. The act for the settling of schools was passed in 1696. I quote from Macaulay : —

The effect before one generation had passed away began to be felt. It was evident that the common people of Scotland were superior in intelligence to the common people of any other country in Europe. To whatever land the Scotchman might wander, to whatever calling he might betake himself, in America or in India, in trade or in war, the advantage which he derived from his early training raised him above his competitors. If he were taken into a warehouse as a porter, he soon became foreman. If he enlisted in the army, he soon became a sergeant. Scotland, meanwhile, in spite of the barrenness of her soil and the severity of her climate, made such progress in agriculture, in manufactures, in commerce, in letters, in science, in all that constitutes civilization, as the Old World had never seen equaled, and as even the New World has scarcely seen surpassed.

The changes above spoken of were great things for Mr. Mather to rejoice over ; still his heart was sad because Jerusalem was yet in ruins ; the French Protestant churches were dissipated ; the Hungarian churches were

desolated ; and the Piedmontese churches were in affliction.

"Interviews with Heaven," he writes, June 10, had left
a savor on his spirit. He puts in Latin his expectation
that before his death an angel would exhibit himself
visibly to him, and lay open certain signs concerning the
church, and new things, and then adds : " I pray thee, my
dear Redeemer, free and protect me, thy most unworthy
servant, from devilish illusions." This was a prayer very
needful to be made, but it should be said that whether or
not the writer was ever misled by "devilish illusions," he
kept them to himself, for there is no instance on record
wherein he based public utterance or action on his private
experience with angels.

The proclamation of King William against profane
swearing and other forms of wickedness was echoed by
Lieutenant-Governor Taylor, which led Mr. Mather to
resolve that at his next lecture he would give to the
country a sermon upon the " zeal with which we should
all endeavor to do what is thus called for." It was done
with the " special assistance of heaven."

He had trials during the summer, caused by the misconduct of some members of his own church and by
the " contentious and apostatising state" of some other
churches. In August he attended a council in Sudbury
to rectify the *male*-administration there." He drew up
the " Result," and addressed the people.

The many *miserables* in prison excited his sympathy,
so after the services of the day, September 4, were over,
he visited the prison, " prayed with the poor creatures "
and preached to them on Psalm 142 : 7 : " Bring my soul
out of prison, that I may praise thy name." They heard
him with " floods of tears." He adds : " Who can tell but
that I have, this day, found one Onesimus ? Who can tell

but some wretches, by running into prison, may run into the arms of Christ, and his victorious grace ? "

The next day he went to Salem, and on Tuesday "traveled with a council of five churches" to Chebacco, now Essex, where, on the next day, he was helpful in bringing a difficult case to a "good issue." On Thursday he gave the lecture at Ipswich. The next day he came back to Salem, where on Sunday he preached both parts of the day, and " God's presence was mightily " with him.

One touching incident while at Salem excites our interest. His brother Nathaniel, next to him in age and scarcely second in genius and learning, was buried at Salem. So he writes : "While I was in Salem, I retired unto the burying place, and at the grave of my dear younger brother there, I could not but fall down on my knees before the Lord, with praises to his name, for granting the life of my dead brother to be writ, and spread, and read among his people, and be very serviceable ; and for sparing me, a barren wretch, to survive these many years, upon the earth, to serve his people in several parts of the world." He proceeds, saying, " I then considered, what if I were speedily to be called away by death, after my younger brother. I found my spirit gloriously triumphing in the thought of going by death to be with the Lord Jesus Christ, and among the angels. But when I further thought of staying to glorify him in the world of many temptations among his people here, I did at present, because of my *age*, prefer this, and request it of the Lord."

The eleventh of December was observed as a secret thanksgiving in the usual way, but with more than usual enjoyment. " The holy Lord dealt familiarly " with him. "I have this day gone into the suburbs of heaven. The Spirit of my Lord God has carried me thither, and has told me glorious things, yea, heaven has come near unto

me, and filled me, with joy unspeakable and full of glory.
I cannot utter, I may not utter, the communications of
heaven, but this I will say, I have tasted that the Lord is
gracious."

He baptized four negroes on Lord's day, the 13th, and
the Lord helped him to "make the action a special occasion of glorifying him."

About this time it was feared that a vessel at sea, of
which a brother-in-law was captain, was lost. Mather was
"assured from heaven" that the vessel was safe and
would soon arrive. Another vessel soon came in ; but
the next week the vessel of his relative sailed into port
bringing a printed copy of his Eleutheria.

The fifteenth of December was Thanksgiving Day, and
he was grateful for the many mercies of the year ; and
was specially interested that God might be glorified in his
own family and in the families of his immediate friends.
It was his belief that the God of heaven vouchsafes,
especially to some of his faithful saints, a more singular
conduct of his providence, with the managements and
ministry of his holy angels.

The next year (1699) was a busy one, but the diary
being closed against use, the record will be brief. Besides
all his parish duties and pulpit exercises, Mr. Mather put
to press nearly seven hundred pages ; though part of this
matter was written in the year preceding.

A few items are culled from the records.

On the sixth of February the church voted that "the
salary of the present pastor should be three pounds per
week, and that the deacons, out of the church treasury,
furnish the families of both teacher and pastor, with fuel,
as there is occasion."

During the year Mr. Mather preached at home and
abroad about seventy times.

In this year he was "brought low." A grievous, painful, wasting headache seized him. "Fears, and temptations, and despondency" were the consequence.

The sermon preached on the seventeenth of the preceding November was published with the title, "Pillars of Salt." It was a lecture in which he gave a "History of some criminals executed in this land, for capital crimes, with some of their dying speeches." A brief discourse about the "dreadful justice of God in punishing of sin with sin," was added. About a month before delivering the sermon he wrote : "Because I foresaw that before my next lecture, the whole country would be entertained with a tragical instance of a young woman who was to come upon her trial the next week, for murdering her baseborn child, I now began to discourse on *Rom.* 1 : 28, handling the case of God's punishing of some sins by leaving them to worse. Intending in a monthly lecture, if the Lord pleased, to finish what I now began, to make the sad examples before the country, subservient to my design."

The General Court, then in session, "ordered the public services to be in a larger and a stronger house " than the one usually occupied on such occasions. On the day appointed, Mr. Mather was "weak, and faint, and spent," but humbly gave himself up to the Spirit of his heavenly Lord, and was "assured of help by a good angel, to strengthen him." The greatest assembly ever preached to in the country came together ; "it may be four or five thousand souls." He writes, as given by Sibley :—

I could not get into the pulpit, but by climbing over pews and heads ; and the Spirit of my dearest Lord came upon me. I preached with a more than ordinary assistance and enlargement, and uttered the most awakening things, for near two hours together. My strength and voice failed not ; but when it was near failing, a silent look to heaven strangely renewed it. In the whole, I found prayer answered and hope exceeded, and faith encouraged; and the Lord using me, the vilest in all that great assembly, to glorify him. Oh! what shall I render to the Lord!

Another work, written in the preceding year but now given to the press, was entitled "Decennium Luctuosum." With a sermon added, it filled 254 pages. It is in all the editions of the *Magnalia*, and was joined in a volume with Increase Mather's History, edited by Samuel G. Drake, in 1862. It should be read by all students of the period from 1688 to 1698. It was as "agreeable a history of the Indian war" as he could compose, and he "incorporated into it as charming and useful entertainments for the country" as he could. He closes with the words: "O my God, I exceedingly give thanks to thy name, for the help thou hast given me in despatching this work."

Mr. Mather was specially interested this year (1699) in Jews and Spaniards. For the former he prepared "The Faith of the Fathers." He presented the "Articles of the true religion in the express words of the Old Testament."

To benefit the Spaniards, he learned their language, and wrote an essay (pp. 16) called "La Fé del Christiano, en vente-quarta Articles." A part of this pamphlet had the title, "La Religion Pura," in a few articles, with Scripture references. Communications with the Spanish Indies had recently become more frequent, and Mather seized the occasion to scatter words of truth among that people. His progress in learning the language would seem impossible to any one but himself. "In two or three weeks, by using a few leisure minutes in the evening of every day, he could write very good Spanish." His "Little Body of the Protestant Religion" was sent in "all possible ways, to the several parts of Spanish America."

"A well-ordered Family," a book of eighty pages, came

out this year. The design was to "render parents and children happy in each other." The design and execution were most excellent. It would seem as if such preaching must have been irresistible.

The churches were infested at this time and for more than a hundred years longer by unworthy ministers, native or foreign born. Mather exposed those of his day in a "History of Some Impostors." It required courage to do this work, for by it he incurred the enmity of the impostors and of their dupes.

"The Serious Christian," a book of 116 pages, was one of the last productions of this fruitful year. It is well to reflect that the man who endured such pain, toil, and strain upon his whole nervous system was one of the happiest of men, joying in the work that was given him to do.

CHAPTER XI.

THE last year of the seventeenth century was full of
work, anxiety, perplexities, and buffetings to Mr.
Mather; but he toiled on under a divine impulse to bear
meekly what was trying and to do steadily what was in
the way of duty.

Among the additions to the church was Jerusha
Mather, later the wife of Peter Oliver, supposed to have
been the youngest sister of the pastor, born in 1684.
The following items are from the church records: —

March 3. Elizabeth Ryal desiring to join unto the new church in
this town, — the "Manifesto" or Brattle street church — this church
declared themselves discharged from the obligations of the covenant
unto her.

July 11, 1700. The brethren of the church, being assembled at the
desire of the governor and the general assembly, and messengers from
both houses in the assembly, coming to them with a motion that they
would consent unto the removal of their teacher's residence to the
college in Cambridge, the ensuing vote was passed. "Being under the
sense of the great benefit we have long enjoyed by the labors of our
revered pastor, Mr. Increase Mather, among us, it must needs be
unreasonable and impossible for us to consent that his relation to us,
and our enjoyment of him and them, should cease. Nevertheless,
the respect we have to the desire and welfare of the publick, does
compel us to consent that our said pastor may so remove his personal
residence to the college at Cambridge, as may be consistent with the
continuance of his relation to us, and his visits of us with his public
administrations, as often as his health and strength may allow it."

"A Cloud of Witnesses against balls and dances," a
book ascribed to Mr. Mather, came out near this time.

Also a "Defence of Evangelical Churches" is noted in the list of his son Samuel.

On his birthday, February 12, he writes of an old author, Geilemus, who styled his birthdays as *dies calamitatis,* but Mather would not so style his natal days. He addressed the Lord with *praises* for the favors of the year, and with *prayer* for the pardon of his sins. He visited a meeting of the faithful, and preached a sermon on the words, "Lord, let it alone this year also."

He writes that he " had been fearing afflictions of late, and behold, my fear comes to pass, for on Friday of this week, my only and lovely son [Increase, born July 9, 1699] — a son given me in answer to many prayers among the people of God, and a son of much observation and expectation, was taken with convulsion fits." He was helped to resign the child to God. " Nevertheless, that I might more effectually conform to the dispensations of heaven, when I saw an angel of death, with a drawn sword thus over my family, I thought it my duty to betake myself unto more than ordinary supplications." The father prayed often, " If it may be, let the cup, (the human cup for this my son,) pass from me; yet not my will, but thine be done." Towards evening the convulsions left the child. On the twenty-third of February, being Lord's day, he "addressed heaven with prayer, no less than ten times." This of course included private and public prayer.

" The Everlasting Gospel," as held and preached in the churches of New England, was printed this year, to meet the wants of the time. It was attested by " several reverend and eminent persons, now most considerable in those churches." This was reissued in 1767 in Philadelphia, and also in Wilmington.

He writes of the "venoms of that malignant company

who have lately built a new church in Boston," who "added unto the storm of the present persecution." At the same time he "bewailed his own sins and imperfections," while glad that charges against him had no foundation. He forgave all that reproached him, and "prayed God to forgive them." Doubtless Mr. Mather was too sensitive to opposition, and sometimes took aggravated views of the spirit of his opponents.

From this time, for several weeks, his mind alternated between hope and fear, in regard to little Increase, who had successive fits and relief, besides being nearly choked to death by a pin in his throat. In prayer he was, as all his life long, struggling for "particular faith," and was often in doubt in relation thereto. If he had cultivated more *permanent* faith, perhaps it would have conduced to his comfort. The child survived to manhood and was the source of much hope, and anxiety and anguish of soul.

One trial was peculiar to him, and specially mortifying. There were people who complained that he published too much. Who they were we are not told; probably those who did not relish his works. There was a class in Boston who disliked his activity in many lines of work, and took every means in their power to discourage him and hinder the carrying out of his desires. His success in the pulpit and by the press was a continual irritation to them, and he felt their hostility too keenly for his own comfort. In regard to publishing he had no reason to heed the sneers of enemies or the doubts of friends, so long as there was a demand for the fruits of his mind; and this continued through his life, and has not ceased to this day. He considered the "press a great agency for good," and he was "assured from heaven that he should have greater opportunities than ever to serve the Lord by publications." But he was of too sensitive a spirit, and felt too readily the deed of unkindness and the word of disparagement. We find him in March in "black dejections and sore discouragements." In this state, he prayed that "before he broke off," he might have some token of divine acceptance. And as he believed, it was "again assured his weeping soul from heaven, that it should not be denied to him to be employed in eminent services for Christ."

Three young men in the neighborhood were drowned about this time. It seems that many young men had fallen by various casualties in the months before, and these accidents he regarded as "judgments of God on the young men of New England." This induced him to preach on the subject. The sermon was published with the title, "Things which Young People Should Think upon." It had a good circulation. It contained "Consolations to the bereaved parents of such young people, as are by an early and perhaps a sudden death, taken from them."

Two letters require notice because of their timeliness and their adaptation to promote the end in view. One had relation to the Noncomformists in the English nation; and the other to the men who debauched the Indians by selling intoxicating liquors to them. In the "Letter of advice to the churches of the Non-conformists in the English nation," he endeavors to satisfy them on one point — that "they are the true Church of England." He claims that the Dissenters are "members of the Church of England." The reasons are, because, (1) They hold the Articles of Faith held by the National Church. (2) Many of the great leaders of that church have scrupled many of the ceremonies, and also some of the expressions in the ritual, in which they agree with the

Nonconformists ; and (3) Because, in the words of Dr. Stillingfleet, the bishop of Worcester, "God will, one day, convince men that the unity of the church lies more in the unity of faith and affection than in the uniformity of doubtful rites and ceremonies." The letter was anonymous, but signed *Philalethes.*

A gentleman desired him to write a sheet upon the "horrid evil of debauching the Indians by selling drink unto them ; a crime committed by too many in our country, and a crime fruitful in wickedness and confusion." Therefore he wrote a "Monitory and hortatory letter" to those English who were engaged in supplying the natives with strong drink. The letter effected "more good than he had imagined." Intoxicants have been the bane of Indians wherever they have not been Christianized.

On the third of April Mr. Mather "engaged in the duties of secret thanksgiving." The service was peculiar in this, that he gave special attention to the "various and marvellous answers to prayer." He records particular answers, as follows : — "1. In being preserved from sin, and advanced in grace ; 2. continued life ; 3. health ; 4. in being a minister ; 5. miraculous freedom of speech ; 6. vast congregations ; 7. remarkable assistances ; 8. publications ; 9. library, extraordinary in size and quality ; several thousands of books ; 10. desirable consort, given and spared to him ; 11. three daughters, and now at last, a son, all of them wonderfully recovered from the jaws of death ; 12. for a great salary, and a comfortable habitation ; 13. being preserved from wicked men, and embalmed with good men ; 14. for mercies obtained for others — the sick, captives, and salvations to the public."

The families of the great congregation were arranged in groups, and held meetings in each other's houses. The family meeting of the gentlemen in the neighborhood

came to his house in course this evening. He composed
a discourse for the occasion on Psalm 138 : 3 : "In the
day when I cried thou answeredst me, and strengthenedst
with strength in my soul." The topic was in the line of
his thanksgivings during the day, namely, "How a Christian should make a profitable observation of the answers
wherewith his prayers are answered."

The following lines, exhibiting the personal influence
of Mr. Mather over the inmates of his family and occasional callers, are significant of a remarkable character :
"April 21. My barber admitted to the church. He gave
the church this account, in that his attending for me,
and my continual dropping of counsels, and warnings,
and lessons upon him, was the great means of his conversion to God." "This day my servant was offered to
the examination of the church. In the account of her
conversion, she told the church that the living in my
family was the means of it ; that she should forever bless
God for bringing her under my roof." And he adds
that the same result had been true of other servants and
of almost all who had ever lived with him.

While fearing that his opportunities to be serviceable
would be brought to an end, a gentleman called on him
with a desire that he would "write a pastoral letter to
the Indians, comprising the sum of the glorious things
revealed unto them in the gospel," and offered to be at the
expense of translating and printing. In accordance he
wrote "An Epistle to the Christian Indians," giving them
a short account of what the English desire them to know
and to do, in order to their happiness. The right-hand
pages are in English, and the left-hand pages in Indian.

Our author had prepared a discourse for the Lecture
on evil speaking, but the evening before he preached it a
letter came from some one in the Bermudas, desiring him

to publish on the subject of evil speaking, and sent money to pay for the impression. He gave his sermon to the publisher, adding another with this title, "A Good Linguist."

The Earl of Bellamont, the new royal governor, was now in Boston, and was present, with all branches of the government, to hear the discourse usual at the opening of the General Court in May. Mr. Mather was the preacher, and made this record of the event : " After my prayers and my tears, in raised faith, I preached unto his excellency, the council, and the representatives." The subject was " A Pillar of Gratitude, or a brief recapitulation of the matchless favors with which the God of heaven hath obliged the hearty praises of his New English Israel." The house of representatives voted thanks for the sermon and the "publication thereof found encouragement among them."

The condition of Harvard College lay near his heart. In behalf of neighboring ministers he had presented to the General Court a paper in relation to the settlement of the college ; and on the eighth of June the assembly took up the matter, upon which he writes, "will turn or fall my father's voyage to England." This voyage had been a "point of particular faith, marvellously circumstanced," both to his father and himself. On the 16th he wrote in his diary, "I am going to relate one, of the most astonishing things that has befel me in all the time of my pilgrimage." This refers to the special act of "particular faith" which he had exercised in reference to a voyage to the old country by his father in relation to the interests of the college. The institution had no charter. When the elder Mather was in England (1688–1692) he made strenuous efforts to obtain a charter, but was not successful. The object had never been abandoned, and overtures had been made to him to go over in person. He was encouraged by the college authorities and by public men to undertake the service. Moreover he had come, as had his son, to cherish a "particular faith" that the way would be opened for him to go. He was satisfied that he had assurances from heaven that he was "angelically" informed on this point. Not a doubt seems to have crossed his mind but that the voyage would be taken. He made his calculations upon going, and his son Cotton was as full of faith as himself. The church consented. One branch of the General Court approved. It was expected that the government, in all branches, would concur ; but after all, the plan miscarried. The particulars of the story belong to the life of President Mather, but the feelings and opinions of Cotton Mather on the subject belong to this passage of our work. He writes from bitter disappointment, but with chastened wisdom, in "Parentator" (pp. 94, 95) : —

If I may be thought worthy to offer my advice, upon the whole, I would humbly say : Christians, reproach not a *particular faith* as if there never were a gracious work of heaven in it. But yet be cautioned against laying too much stress upon it, lest you find yourselves incautiously plunged into a hope that will make ashamed. A particular faith may be a work of God ; but the counterfeits of this jewel are so very fine, that it will require a judgment almost more than human to discover them. It is best not being too fond of enthusiasms that may carry us beyond the dispensation of the day. It is best that you should be content with the ordinary satisfaction of praying, and so waiting for the blessings of God, in such pious resignations to his will, and annihilations of your own, as an uncertainty about issues would most properly lead you to.

In this connection it is pertinent to say that Cotton Mather was not used to parading his *particular faiths* before the public. Were it not for his private diary, we should know little of his opinion or his practice in relation to the matter.

The founding of Brattle Street Church, in Boston, was an event which excited great interest and aroused vigorous conflict at the time, and it is often referred to as working a revolution in our church history. It has been much misunderstood and greatly overrated as to its intrinsic importance and its positive influence. Doubtless some of the movers in the enterprise had in mind quite a modification of the existing custom in founding churches and took preliminary measures with that end in view. Young Mr. Colman, a man of a good family and fine education, being in England, was ordained there, in the Presbyterian way, lest there might be some difficulty in procuring his ordination here, when the designs of the founders became known. This excited distrust. Then on the part of some there was free talk about liberality, and breaking away from some of the methods in use in choosing ministers and admitting members to the church. Quite naturally the churches already existing, and their ministers, were solicitous on the subject, and were anxious that the new church should be put on such a foundation as to keep it in harmony with themselves and in conformity to ancient usage. When the steps were beginning to be taken in the new enterprise, Cotton Mather, in common with his father, exerted himself to prevent a breach of charity and harmonious working; and the results were both good and lasting. One of his efforts is recorded under date "4 d. 5 m. Thursday," in the following terms : —

This day, in a very great assembly of ministers, the Lord helped me, in a long speech, to bear my testimony against the attempts, now afoot in the country, to unhinge our churches, and subvert and confound the order of the gospel in them. On this occasion, I saw, to my sorrow, that there was hardly any but my father and myself, to appear with any strength of argument or fortitude, in defence of our invaded churches. Therefore I thought I must cry mightily unto the

Lord, that he would mercifully direct me, and protect me, in all my feeble, but faithful endeavors to serve him; and that he would particularly furnish me with *patience* to undergo all the obloquy whereto my fidelity to his interests may expose me in an evil generation, and preserve me from all the devices of Satan ever to blast me with reproaches that may at all incapacitate me for eminent serviceableness. I also thought that if it be the purpose of heaven that the apostacy shall go on, they that will vigorously and significantly stand in the way of that apostacy, may be in danger of a stroke from the angel of death, that so a way may be made for the anger of God; but that I resolved, that I would not, from this consideration, abate any of my opposition to the sinful degeneracy. No, I will oppose it, tho' it cost me my life.

The result of these efforts by the Mathers, and especially the younger, was that the plan of the new society was modified, so that they and others could heartily join in the services of installation. And here the matter might rest, as a substantial victory of the faithful men who stood stedfastly for the ancient faith and polity of the Puritan churches of New England; but the falsification of the history of this event is so gross and persistent and oftrepeated that the true state of facts needs to be told.

In the diary for the year 1699, now in the library of the American Antiquarian Society, is an entry, as quoted by President Quincy (vol. i, History of Harvard College), in the words following, written by Cotton Mather : —

I see another day of temptation begun upon the town and land. A company of headstrong men in the town, the chief of whom are full of malignity to the holy ways of our churches, have built in the town another meeting house. To delude many better meaning men in their own company, and the churches in the neighborhood, they passed a vote in the foundation of their proceedings, that they would not vary from the practice of these churches, except in one little particular. But . . . these fallacious people desert their vote, and without the advice or knowledge of the ministers in the vicinity, they have published, under the title of a *manifesto*, certain articles that utterly subvert our churches, and invite an ill party through all the country, to throw all into confusion on the first opportunitie.

The date of this extract was "1699, 7 d. 10 m.," or December 7.

In this state of things, the Mathers — father and son — "with many prayers and studies" prepared for the press an "Antidote against the Infection of the Example." Instead of issuing this, after the first sheet was in the hands of the compositors, they "stopped it with a desire to make one attempt more for the bringing of this people to reason." Says Cotton Mather : —

I drew up a proposal, and with another minister, carried it unto them, who at first rejected it, but afterwards so far embraced it, as to promise that they will, the next week, publicly recognize their covenant and one another, and therewithal declare their adherence to the Heads of Agreement of the United Brethren in England, and request the communion of our churches in that foundation. A wonderful joy filled the hearts of our good people far and near, that we had obtained this much from them. Our strife seemed now at an end; there was much relenting in some of their spirits, when they saw our condescension, our charity, our compassion. We overlooked all past offences. We kept the public fast with them, (on 31st. 11 month, Wednesday, that is, January 31, 1700) and my father preached with them, on following peace with holiness, and I concluded with prayer.

With this record, drawn from Cotton Mather's diary, before him, President Quincy (vol. i, page 115) writes : "This account is singularly illustrative of his [Cotton Mather's] disposition to wrest every occurrence into a subject of eulogy on himself or his father." Proceeding, he says that contemporaneous documents compel the belief that the above statement of Cotton Mather, that he "drew up a proposal," etc., was "wholly without foundation ; that he neither drew up the paper, nor had any material agency in producing it. In this, as in many instances in his voluminous writings, the conviction is forced on the mind that he was not quite so scrupulous as might be wished, in his relation of facts, particularly in cases where his own or his father's reputation was likely to be affected."

This is an indirect way of stating that the record of Cotton Mather, so plain and unequivocal, is false. And then the venerable president attempts to prove this by quotations from the records of Brattle Street Church, written by Rev. Mr. Colman, the first pastor, and also from the diary of Judge Samuel Sewall. Quotations to prove Cotton Mather a circumstantial falsifier, for the sake of eulogizing himself or his father, should be clear and strong, or the attempt must fail. What does Mr. Colman write? Does he record that Mr. Mather did not draw up a "proposal," and with "another minister" take it to some of the members of the new church? Not a word of this. He records: "I omit on purpose the differences and troubles we had with any neighbors about our proceedings. I am only obliged to leave this acknowledgment of our great obligations to the Hon. William Stoughton, the Rev. Mr. William Brattle, the Rev. Mr. Clark, of Chelmsford, and Mr. Danforth, of Dorchester, for their good and kind endeavors for our peaceable settlement." Now because Mr. Colman did not insert the names of the Mathers in this record of gratitude, the president draws the positive conclusion that the statement of Cotton Mather is false! Why should he record the fact that the strenuous efforts of Increase and Cotton Mather had constrained the new church to make reasonable concessions?

But this is not all the foundation of the president's insinuation of falsehood. He says (page 136), "Judge Sewall's statement is apparently irreconcilable with that of Cotton Mather." The following is from the diary of Judge Sewall: —

1699–1700, January 24th. Lieutenant Governor [Stoughton] calls me, with him, to Mr. Willard's, where, out of two papers, Mr. William Brattle drew up a third, for an accommodation, to bring on an agreement between the new church and our ministers. Mr. Colman got his brethren to subscribe to it.

January 25th. Mr. I. Mather, Mr. C. Mather, Mr. Willard, (Old South), Mr. Wadsworth, (First church), and S. Sewall, wait on the Lieutenant Governor, at Mr. Cooper's to confer about the writing drawn up the evening before. There was some heat, but grew calmer, and, after lecture, agreed to be present at the fast, which was to be observed, January 31st.

This is the statement of Sewall, and this the proof relied on to sustain the charge that Cotton Mather obtrusively claimed credit for himself, and made a false record of preparing a "proposal," and taking it to a member of the other party, in company with another minister. Does the statement in Sewall's diary disprove the statement in Mather's diary? No; it does not suggest a doubt on the point to a dispassionate reader. It expressly states that "out of *two* papers," Mr. Brattle drew up a third. Cotton Mather's proposal was made on the twenty-first of January. Mr. Brattle's paper was written on the 24th, in presence of Stoughton, Willard, and Sewall, and on the 25th the same persons, with the Mathers and Mr. Wadsworth, met at Mr. Cooper's, where they conferred upon the paper drawn up the evening before by Brattle. "There was some heat," writes Sewall, "but grew calmer, and after lecture, agreed to be present at the fast, which was to be observed January 31st."

With these records before us, what is the conclusion? 1. Neither Mr. Colman nor Judge Sewall disproves the statement of Mather, that he drew up and presented a proposal to the Brattle Street party. 2. Neither contradicts the assertion that the proposal was, after some delay, approved by the other party. The delay, according to

Mather, was from the twenty-first to the twenty-fourth
of January.   3. Judge Sewall states that *two* papers were
before Mr. Brattle on the 24th, from which he prepared
a third, in the presence of Sewall himself and others.
4. Sewall states that at a meeting the next day, the
writing (that is, of Brattle) was before a party of gentlemen, and that the party agreed to be present at the fast on
the coming thirty-first of January, when all parties united
in public service.   Here follows the record which the
judge made of the fast (vol. ii, pp. 2, 3, diary) : —

1700, January 31st.   Fast at the new church.
A.M.   Mr. Colman reads the writing agreed on.   Mr. Allin prays.
Mr. Colman preaches, prays and blesses.
P.M.   Mr. Willard prays, Mr. I. Mather preaches.   Mr. Cotton
Mather prays.   Sing the 67 Ps. without reading.   Mr. Brattle sets
Oxford time.   Mr. Mather gives the blessing.
His text was, " Follow peace with all men, and holiness."   His
doctrine, — must follow peace so far as it consists with holiness.
Hebrews 12 : 14.   Mr. Colman's text was *Rom.* 15 : 29.   " And I am
sure that, when I come unto you, I shall come in the fulness of the
blessing of the gospel of Christ."
Mr. Willard prayed God to pardon all the frailties and follies of
ministers and people ; that they might give that respect to the other
churches due them, though were not just of their constitution.
Mr. Mather in 's sermon, and Mr. Cotton [Mather] in prayer, to
the same purpose.   Mr. W. and C. M. prayed excellently and pathetically for Mr. Colman and his flock.

In passing, it may be well to notice a discrepancy between one word as given in the above quotation from
Sewall, and the same word as quoted by President
Quincy.   According to the judge (as printed in the Historical Collections), Mr. Willard prayed that " *they* might
give that respect to the other '*churches*' due them."
According to Quincy, who probably copied from the
manuscript, the word " church " was used instead of

"churches." The reader will note the difference in the
meaning. I have not cared to ascertain whether the
editor of Sewall or President Quincy was correct, by
examining the manuscript. Though the difference is
significant, it was of course not designed.

Another paragraph may be interposed here, not as
bearing upon the veracity of Cotton Mather, but as re-
vealing the fact that one of the most prominent and
estimable laymen of the time was in full sympathy with
those ministers who labored to bring the Brattle Street
Church into harmony with the other churches; and in
this he was a representative man. The following lines
are from the first volume of Judge Sewall's diary
(pp. 516, 517) :—

Decr 9 [1699]. Mr. Colman visits me: I expostulat with him
about the 3d Article in the Manifesto, that had shew'd no more
respect to N. E. Churches. I told him Christ was a Bride-Groom,
and He loved to have his Bride commended. . . . He satisfied me as
to Baptisme and said the word [*adopted*] was left out. I told him
he was the more in danger, and had need to be more upon his Guard;
lest any hard sharp words he had met with should tempt him to do
what he intended not. Warn'd him of the Cross in Baptisme, &c.
Said he was of our mind, Because I told him merely saying *Conform*, did not express such an Aprobation of the N. E. way as I
desired. Many in England conform'd to things they professedly disliked. At his going away, I told him, if God should please by him
to hold forth any Light that had not been seen or entertain'd before;
I should be so far from envying it, that I should rejoice in it; which
he was much affected with.

No one questions the fact that Mr. Brattle, " out *of two
·papers*," prepared a third, and that this was accepted by
both parties. Is there now any room for doubt that
one of these *two* papers was written by Cotton Mather ?
Can there be any rational doubt that the "proposal " of
Cotton Mather was the main thing — the uniting element

— in Brattle's paper? Bear in mind that the Mathers and
their coadjutors were contending against what they considered a dangerous innovation; that they were seeking
for a concession which would bring the new church into
line with the existing churches, and that they were satisfied with the final draft which Mr. Colman read to the
assembly on the day of the fast, and that they united cordially in the services of that day, Cotton Mather praying "excellently and pathetically for Mr. Colman and his
flock." As the Mathers knew what they wanted, and as
they were men not to be trifled with or deceived, is it not
the only reasonable conclusion that Mr. Brattle's paper
had in it the substance of Cotton Mather's "proposal"?

The vindication of Cotton Mather's veracity being thus
accomplished, the affairs of Brattle Street Church might
be left at this point, were it not that the truth of history
needs to be vindicated. Since President Quincy, in his
History of Harvard College, gave currency to the notion
that the founding of Brattle Street Church was a departure from the ancient ways of the New England churches,
and that, both in doctrine and some points of polity, it was
a "new departure," and the beginning of a great revolution, many orators, preachers, and writers have spoken of
this event as a long step in the way of broadening and
liberalizing the churches in the province. The truth is
that this claim is pure fiction in whole, and in all its parts.
There is not a line in Dr. Lothrop's History of Brattle
Street Church to sustain the claim. Before the Messrs.
Mather, Mr. Willard, and the other ministers of Boston,
and their churches, received the new church into their
fellowship, the members of it had adopted the "Heads of
Agreement," by which the Presbyterians and Congregationalists of England were brought into harmonious relations: they avowed their acceptance of the Westminster

Catechism, and expressed their desire to be in fellowship with the surrounding churches. From the Articles of the Church I condense the following statements : —

I. Approve and subscribe the Confession of the Faith put forth by the Assembly of Divines at Westminster.

II. Suitable that some part of the Scriptures be read by the minister, in public worship, as was done in many churches in England, styled United Brethren. Conform in all other respects to the ordinary practice of the churches.

III. Hold Communion with the Churches here as true Churches.

IIII. Such Orders and Rules of Discipline as may preserve Evangelical Purity and Holiness.

V. Allow baptism to those only who profess their faith in Christ, and obedience to him ; and to the children of such ; yet we dare not to refuse it to any child offered to us by any professed Christian, upon his engagement to see it educated in the Christian religion.

VI. Sacrament to persons of visible sanctity.

VII. The Pastor to examine and recommend for admission, and require the renewal of the baptismal covenant.

VIII. Impose no public relation of their religious experience. Pastor to publicly declare his satisfaction, and to seasonably propound candidates.

IX. The members to inquire into the life and conversation of those propounded ; and if finding objections, to make them known.

X. No objections being made, that will be a sufficient consent and concurrence, and the person may be received into communion.

XII. In suspending or excluding members, the consent of the church was necessary.

XVI. In choosing a minister, "every baptized adult person, who contributes to the Maintenance," should have a voice in the election.

The intelligent reader will see that the new church was planted solidly on the doctrinal platform of the New England churches.

The reading of the Scriptures as a distinct exercise in public worship was adopted gradually, till it became universal in the Congregational, and later in all evangelical, churches.

The only change of importance was in giving the choice of a minister to all the members of the congregation who were baptized adults and who contributed to the maintenance of public worship. This took the initiative from the church, but doctrinal soundness was secured by the Article respecting the Westminster Catechism. This innovation made little, if any, headway among the churches which continued evangelical, and as an historical fact Brattle Street Church remained in full fellowship with the other churches of Boston and Massachusetts on the ancient basis and in the spirit of the early fathers during the whole eighteenth century. Dr. Colman lived and worked in harmony with the elder and the younger Mather while they lived, and with the other ministers and churches until his decease in 1747. He was a man of breeding, ability, culture, and sincere piety, and a fragrant memory of him remains to this day. And it may be added that among the many eulogies of Cotton Mather no immortelle cast upon his grave was sweeter or brighter than that of Benjamin Colman.

Another word needs to be said before taking leave of this episode in our church history. It has been stated already that the Mathers stopped the printing of their book in relation to the new church, in the hope of effecting a harmonious settlement of the difficulty. This hope was followed with the pleasant results already recited; but now comes another charge against the authors of the book, as guilty of bad faith, in that they afterwards gave the work to the public. It is said that they renewed the conflict after peace had been established. This is the charge. The fact was this : in the time of the trouble, it became evident that there were, through the country, even as far as Hartford, scattered sympathizers with the radical party in the Brattle Street Society, and the book

was published to counteract their plans. As the Mathers
had succeeded in placing the new church on a sound
foundation, according to their views of truth, so they endeavored to prevent the spread of error and its organization in other places. A reply came out, written by
several men, some of whom held caustic pens. But their
efforts came to nothing visible. Many new churches were
formed in New England in after years, but all of them
were on the old-time basis. Cotton Mather, writing of
this answer, says that the writers "were left to a strange
infatuation, for the pamphlet not only violates the third,
the ninth and the fifth commandment, but also bur-
lesques the holy churches of God with silly scoffs and
flouts. It makes them loathsome, and will bring them to
shame." It is common to associate Dr. Colman with the
writers of the book, but I see nothing in its style, argument, or spirit to induce the belief that the elegant pen
of the gentlemanly pastor of Brattle Street Church had
any part in the writing of it.

CHAPTER XII.

THE desire of the general assembly that President
Mather should reside at Cambridge, and the vote
of the church in relation thereto, caused great anxiety in
the son through sympathy with his father. From the
diary (July 6, 1700) it is evident that Cotton was of the
opinion that the president should reside at the college,
yet preach as he could in the city; but to this the president was invincibly opposed. The full account of the
struggle in his mind belongs to President Mather's Life.
One extract from the son's diary comes in here, who says
of his father: "But he was in a strangely melancholy, and
disconsolate condition of mind, as he must move to Cambridge, (the place which of all under heaven, was most
abominable to him)." It was this which filled the son
with fear as to the result. "If he would be cheerful, all
would be easy, but his spirit is prodigiously infirmed,
unhinged and broken, and if the Lord be not very merciful to him, the name of the Lord Jesus will suffer more
dishonor from his uneasiness, than I am willing to see."

So far as the son felt a personal interest in the matter,
he expressed in the statement that he himself " would be
left alone with the care of a vast congregation, the largest
in all these parts of the world." He was feeble, and in
the town had many enemies; "indeed all the enemies of
the evangelical interest are mine."

It is evident that Cotton Mather was of the opinion
that his father should yield to the general desire, and

remove to the college. If this had been done, the college would have been under the tuition and influence of the senior Mather all his life, in all probability, and the solicitude of both father and son about the institution in the years following would have been avoided. The reason why the father declined to reside in Cambridge, as given above, was his invincible repugnance to live in a "place, which of all under heaven was most abominable to him." In President Mather's writings I find no reason of this kind mentioned, but the feeling in relation to it was doubtless well known to his son.

Besides two anonymous letters, near the middle of the year, one of them about the "Maintenance of Ministers," and the other on "The Old Principles of New England," Mr. Mather "printed a small book to be distributed among his families as he made pastoral visits," with the title, "Reasonable Religion," in seventy-two pages. He set forth the "wisdom of its precepts," and the "folly of sinning against" them. This, with additions, was reprinted in London in 1713.

It is a mistake to suppose, as is quite common, that interest in the conversion of the young is of recent growth. In the time of President Edwards there were special efforts for bringing the children and youth into the active duties of a Christian life; and the ministry of Mr. Mather was an example of fidelity in this line of labor which ministers in any age might safely follow. Besides training his own children in ways of piety, and bringing his young people into religious associations, he reached after the young through the press. At this time the "Token for Children," by Janeway, was reprinted in Boston, and Mather added "Some Examples of children in whom the fear of God was remarkably budding before they died, in several parts of New England."

It is not uncommon to hear Christians affirm that their prayers for this or that blessing were answered, as if they alone were concerned in moving the "Hearer of prayer." Mr. Mather was guarded against this form of egotism, as appears in the record of August 9 : "A dry time ; fears of *terrible* famine.   Moved for a *fast*, but an old minister opposed."   Mather pleaded that God, through Christ, would accept him as an "intercessor for his churches." So he prayed for rain, confessing his sins, and those of the country, in the forenoon.   "Now behold the issue. At noon the clouds gathered, and the afternoon was all spent in sweet, gentle, refreshing showers, which brought a plentiful relief to our languishing and perishing fields." He then adds : "What use now should I make of this experience ?   For *better* and more holy, fruitful, useful and prayerful Christians than I, were elsewhere praying this day, before the Lord, as well as I.   And yet it is not amiss for me, humbly to receive the consolations of God."

Later in the season, the drought returning, the Lecture day was turned into a fast, and the preacher whose turn it was requested Mr. Mather to occupy the pulpit.   He had a "great audience, and an opportunity to say some things that otherwise would not have been heard by so many."

He went to Salem in September, "attended by two young gentlemen, who kindly offered, as sons," to wait upon him.   He went next day to Ipswich, "and had opportunity to do several services to a company of ministers."   This day he "preached to a great assembly, with great assistance."   Friday he returned to Salem, and on Sunday "preached, both parts of the day to extraordinary auditories."   He concludes with the remark : "Remember to pray over a journey before starting."

About this time he gave a course of sermons on the eleventh chapter of Hebrews, and the one on the grace displayed to Rahab, being desired for publication by the hearers, was printed with the title "Grace Triumphant."

Noting a tendency to apostasy and innovations upon the churches, as appeared in the stir in connection with the formation of the Brattle Street Church, though that body itself had taken right ground, assented to the Westminster Catechism, and, with its excellent minister, coöperated in defending the ancient faith and ways; and seeing that a "minister of some note for his piety had published a book entitled 'Novelties,'" which was "offensive to good men, but pleased a carnal, giddy and rising generation," Mr. Mather wrote a "Defence of Evangelical Churches," which was published with the sanction of his father's name.

He writes in the diary: "One notion advanced by the 'New Modellers' of the churches, who, without right, call themselves Presbyterians, was that persons who 'know themselves ungodly,' yet may and should come to the Lord's table." Mather added to the "Defence," just mentioned, a "savory little discourse of Mr. Quick, a Presbyterian, entitled 'A Claim to the Sacrament,' which opposed the notion. This was given to the press with the approbation of ministers in Essex." It may be said that Mr. Warham came to this country with the same "notion," and that Dr. Stoddard, of Northampton, advocated it. Opposition to this baleful error by Jonathan Edwards was one cause of the trouble he experienced in Northampton about thirty years later.

Mather's mind was continually interested in the state of religion in England and on the continent. In this respect he felt as a native-born English Christian. We find entries in his diary wherein he expresses his expectation of great changes for the better. On the fifteenth of September we find this specimen: "Irradiation from heaven in public prayer. Though the religion of Christ was in extreme hazard in Europe from the power and malice of its enemies, and the evil dispositions of its professors, yet the Lord was to do an amazing thing for its preservation." He then adds: "After I had this written, on the following day came tidings which astonished me," announcing then, as he believed, the accomplishment of all his faith could have expected. This was the death of the Duke of Gloucester. This boy was the son of Queen Anne, and the last one of several children. His death secured the accession of the house of Hanover. But, as the child was brought up a Protestant, the reason of Mather's rejoicing is not evident to us.

Dark days were coming on in the province. Mr. Mather speaks of sickness in his family, in the town, and in the country, as prevalent in various forms. "Funerals daily from fevers and fluxes." Visiting the sick engrossed his time and threatened his health. He preached a sermon on the question, "What should be the carriage of a Christian at a funeral?" But before he slept, had cause to fear it might prove his own funeral sermon. His blood, he found, had received a contagion from visiting the sick, and he was cast into a fever. A tumor on his right cheek broke on Friday. In this condition he composed a sermon on Matthew 9: 12: "They that be whole need not a Physician, but they that are sick." Though too weak to keep "prayer with fasting," he had "illapses from heaven." His soul was filled with lively resolutions to glorify the Lord Jesus Christ more than ever heretofore. He preached this sermon the next Sabbath forenoon, and it proved so awakening and acceptable to some of his neighbors that they asked for a copy. It was given to the printer with the title of " The Great Physician."

The eighth of October was "spent with the South [now

Old South] Church, praying and fasting for the life of their sick minister," Mr. Willard. Such facts as these enable us to realize the intimate connection and tender love of the ancient ministers and churches towards one another.

On the sixteenth he notes an "odd experience." In his pastoral visits, in which he had the "special presence and conduct of heaven," though, as ministers do, he found, from the expenditure of nervous force, that the labor was "very spending," he was thinking how many books he had given away, and was "chiding himself" that he had done so. No other minister did so, and perhaps he "overdid the matter." Then he had an "impulse on his mind that he should quickly see something to encourage his practice." Well, a "sudden inclination took him to call on a gentlewoman who had long been in a state of disconsolate widowhood." He thought it would be "pure religion" to visit her. He did so; and she told him that she had a parcel of books which once "belonged to the library of our famous old Mr. Chauncey," who died in 1672. She added that, "if I would please to take them, she would count herself highly gratified in their being so well-bestowed. I selected out about forty books, and some of them large ones." He had already between two and three thousand volumes in his library, but several of these were greatly useful in his design of writing, the "Illustrations of the Divine Oracles," the great work he was laboring upon at every spare moment. He exclaims, "Behold how the Lord smiles upon me!"

In October he wrote that "about this time one of the judges desired him to write an historical account of the Greek churches." He had a design and was at the cost of publishing the work. Mather prepared a volume, entitled "American Tears upon the Ruins of the Greek

Churches : a compendious but entertaining history of the darkness come upon the Greek churches in Europe and Asia ; and published partly to bespeak a more frequent remembrance of those once famous churches in the prayers of the faithful afar off; and partly to suggest unto other churches the advice and warning to be there taken, that their candlestick may not be removed out of its place." To this was added an Appendix relating the conversion of a Jew, Shalome Ben Shalomah. The book, of eighty pages, was anonymous, except the preface ; but the work was Mather's, as proved, if proof were needed, by the citation from his diary.

From the same source it appears that another sermon, preached this season, was published. In Sibley's list it is called anonymous, but the following record reveals the author. " Having preached a sermon to one of the young men's meetings, on the evening after the other services of the Lord's day, against the *Evil of Apostacy from Good Beginnings in* Religion, the young men desired a copy of it. Text, *Heb.* 10: 39. 'But we are not of them who draw back unto perdition; but of them that believe to the saving of the soul.'"

The following entry may contain a useful hint to some in regard tc the matter of their praying. It is possible that there is more craving for blessings than giving of thanks. "21 d., 9 m. Resolution that in future, my evening prayers in family and private, should partake more of thanksgiving." He thought that perhaps this might be "singularly acceptable to heaven, and profitable to himself."

And near this time he records a singular experience in a pastor's life. There was an old man named Ferdinand Turze, with whom Mr. Mather had but little acquaintance. Saturday night, December 28, he " was strangely accosted in his sleep." It was said to him in a dream: "*Take notice of this old man; speak to him; do for him.*" The next day he saw the old man at meeting, very *attentive.* He had rarely attended before. Mr. Mather met him next day in the street and said to him, "How d' ye do, old man? I am glad to see you still in this world. I pray God prepare you for another. I suppose it won't be long before you are called away. Can I do you no service?" Next day the old man called at his house. Mr. Mather begged him to prepare for death, and gave him a little book, "Grace Triumphant," adding a piece of money. He called several times, but in seven weeks the man suddenly died. Going to the funeral the minister learned from people who knew him, that he "had been a poor, carnal, sorry old man, until nearly seven weeks, when a wonderful change came over him. He spent the whole time in reading and praying, and the little book was his continual companion day and night. They never saw a man so altered, and believed he died a regenerate man."

At this time Robert Calef's name begins to appear in the diary in connection with the matter of witchcraft. As this annoyance lasted several years, the subject will be treated as a whole when the proper place is reached.

In the diary, of same date as above, we read that "all the rage of Satan against the holy churches of the Lord" had fallen on his father and himself. There was a "mighty ferment among the people"; but Mather writes that the "Lord filled his soul with consolation," and he closed the day with these words: "Much in prayer in this critical time for patience, courage and watchfulness. A day of devotion much carried on with singing agreeable psalms." As he opened the book, the most agreeable psalms to his situation arrested his eye. He adds the discreet remark: "This observation may easily be abused to superstition ; but yet sometimes there is an angelical agency in these occurrences."

The year's record will be closed with a brief reference to trying scenes in Mr. Mather's domestic life. It has already been noted that the little boy, Increase, had been "shaken with convulsive fits" in February. These returned again and again, till the child's life would have been despaired of if the father had not been comforted with "assurances from heaven" that the sickness was not unto death, as on the thirteenth of April: "In family prayer, heart strangely melted with assurances that the Lord had great blessings in store for the family."

On the first of October his "charming little daughter Nancy — Hannah — was taken with a violent and threatening fever, beginning with a terrible convulsion." Some feared she would not recover. "Seeing the angel of death with a drawn sword standing there," he kept a day of fasting and prayer. While resigning the child to God, and professing that, if she might not live to God and be a servant of the Lord Jesus Christ, he did not ask for her life, he received "astonishing assurance from heaven that the child should recover." He records also that his son *Creasy* was not only delivered from his fits, but had become a "healthy and a hearty child."

On the twenty-fourth of October he was specially concerned for his wife. Her health was failing. She had in some former years suffered from "sore throat, and such tremor, and such dolor, and such danger of choking, and such exhaustion of strength, as was not common." She was now "languishing under the malady, and it was very near too hard for her." He set himself to "cry unto the Lord in her behalf, saying : 'Behold, I serve a good Lord who will deny me nothing.'" And then he adds the fact that on this day the "tide of her distemper turned, and she immediately recovered."

Four days later we find this record : "Extraordinary deliverance." His little daughter Nabby, six years old, was alone, and the candle somehow set her headgear on fire. The child was not able to help herself or cry for help. "The flame consumed all before it, and was just come as far as her head. In one quarter of a minute more, the child would have been destroyed." A person passing the window just in the nick of time saw an unusual blaze and ran. Happily, not only was the child's life saved, but she got "no manner of hurt. What shall I render?"

In the middle of November I find note of an "epidemic of colds and coughs." It reached his own family. His eldest child, "Katy, had a very violent fever." As usual he prayed. The Lord sent "healing mercies" to all the family.

On the fifteenth of December, being Lord's day, he baptized his son, born on the preceding Friday, and "called him Samuel, and gave him unto the Lord as long as he lived." He was a "lovely and lusty infant."

Little Nancy was very ill again on the 20th. The next day the physician gave up hope, but on the 22d (Lord's day) he writes: "This child, little else to me me than a subject whereupon faith and prayer have been procured and answered, all the forenoon was diverting herself, and running and laughing about the house, and at noon sat at the table with her father." It was the custom in the early days of New England to baptize children soon after birth. Franklin was taken to church for this purpose on the day he was born. Perhaps the reader, if brought up to believe the erroneous notions so common about the austerity of a Puritan family on the Sabbath, will be surprised to learn how a child in an ancient minister's family behaved on a Sunday. Nancy, in her fourth year, was "diverting herself, and running and laughing about the house all the forenoon." Doubtless the happy father enjoyed the cheerfulness of the child.

At the opening of the eighteenth century Plymouth had been settled eighty years and Boston seventy years. Both colonies were united now under one government as a province. Notwithstanding the stoppage of immigration from England at the outbreak of the "great rebellion" in 1640, and the frequent French and Indian wars, population had increased steadily, and new towns had been formed until the whole number in the province was not far from ninety. As early as 1653 they extended westward as far as the Nashua valley. Passing over the wilderness between the Nashua and the Connecticut, a number of towns had been settled between Springfield and Northfield. South and southwest of the Wachusett were Worcester, Leicester, and Brookfield. In 1700 Worcester County was not organized, but its scattered towns were Lancaster, Mendon, Brookfield, and a few others which had secured a permanent settlement, though subject to savage invasions. Eastward of the line formed by the Nashua running north and the Blackstone running south, the territory to the sea was nearly covered by organized society. But few of the aborigines remained. By the new charter, Plymouth was merged in the Bay, and the large province of Maine was put under its authority. The province of Massachusetts Bay was one of the most populous and wealthy of the British colonies. It made war and peace with Indian tribes and their allies, and it became accustomed to a self-consciousness of future greatness.

The governor was the Earl of Bellamont, a British nobleman of excellent character. Though connected with the Established Church, he was an Episcopalian of the stamp which respected the convictions and religion of the Dissenters. In this respect his conduct was acceptable to the people of New England. His death occurred in New York, March 5, 1701.

The number of churches in the province was about ninety. Dr. Clark numbers eighty-eight, but he probably did not include all the Indian churches. The towns, with rare exceptions, had at least one church, and the municipality with which it was connected was under legal obligation to sustain public worship where this was not provided for by voluntary gifts. The churches in Boston, Plymouth, and some others, took up a contribution every Sunday for this purpose. If the voluntary system had prevailed throughout the province, many future difficulties and much reproach would have been avoided; but the new settlements were sparsely settled and poor. Some of the settlers were indifferent about religious worship, and not appreciative of the benefits of every kind which come to a community through the preaching of the gospel; therefore the General Court required every town, as a condition of its incorporation, to build a meetinghouse and support a minister. All land was bought under this liability to taxation, and thus the formation of homogeneous towns with an educated ministry was secured. To this was united the common school system, giving to every child the elements of education. To these two provisions the people of the province were indebted for their general intelligence, high morality, and their freedom from division. The system was invaluable to the state in all generations, though differences in religion, in the course of time, made it necessary that the support of religious institutions should depend on voluntary gifts.

At the beginning of the eighteenth century the town of Boston had four large congregations, including the

new Brattle Street enterprise. The custom of having two
ministers to each church, teacher and pastor, was still in
vogue, and the ministers of Boston were men of a high
order of character and learning. In Ipswich, as it then
existed, there were two churches. In Newbury there
were two, and in Plymouth, before its division, were two
or more. In some towns public worship was sustained
by the town, before a church was formed, and thus it
happened that the whole number of churches was about
equal to the number of towns.

In doctrine, polity, administration, and order of worship
there had been no essential change from the beginning.
The plan of having an eldership, consisting of teacher,
pastor, and ruling elder, was beginning to go into disuse,
some of the churches ceasing to elect the elder, and
many of the churches had but one minister. Out of this
change a conflict sprang up later, when the single minister
claimed the whole power and influence of the eldership;
but this was settled, when the time came, on the basis
of pure Congregationalism, the " negative " of the minister
to church action being abandoned.

In the remainder of this chapter we shall note some
facts in the personal and family history of Mr. Mather,
and refer to his public labors and his publications. He
writes, January 2 : —

" Little daughter Nancy is again taken very ill. Her
illness this day grew upon her into a heart-breaking
extremity. Prayed and obtained mercy for the child."
Five days later he records : " The Lord restored my dearest consort, and put my family again into many circumstances of comfort." He then refers to a season of
thanksgiving in his study. " Many things to be thankful
for," but specially that, though he was reproached and
stigmatized for the defense of the churches, he was

thereby enabled to glorify his Master. "The reproaches
of them that reproached him are fallen upon me." Had
"assurance from heaven that as I now suffer with the
Lord Jesus Christ, and for him, I shall one day reign
with him."

On the 17th he exclaims : "What cause to be thankful
to God, in view of slanders by the Satanic party!" He
wrote a letter to a gentleman, desiring him to expose it,
which was done. Copies of it were taken. In the letter
to him he made two propositions : — 1. "If all they that
have used so much liberty to express their unkindness
to me, will please to produce, with evidence, any one
instance wherein I have wronged or harmed any one of
them all, or done any one thing unbecoming a man whose
business it is to do good unto all, I'll submit unto the
hardest censure my worst enemy can impose upon me.
2. If they that report what they please concerning me,
will please, first of all, to satisfy themselves, as every
Christian or gentlemen would, before they take up a
defamatory report, and they don't find that I have acted,
not only blamelessly, but also suitably, I will again submit
unto censure. Thus do I challenge all the world."

On the 18th he refers to his little son Samuel, born in
the previous December, and states that he had "often
and often made essays to raise his heart to a *particular
faith* for that child, for the service of the churches,"
but that he never could obtain to it. "A man cannot
believe *what and when he will.*" This made him continually apprehensive that the child, though hearty and
healthy, would die in infancy. He mentioned this to his
wife and his father. His fears were fulfilled. February 7
he writes : "The evil that I feared is come upon me."
On the preceding Tuesday his child was "taken with
many sad convulsions." These continued all the next

day while the family awaited the sad result. The next day he had more than a hundred terrible fits. The father, however, was comforted in spirit, and preached the Lecture in his turn, on the text, " I know that my Redeemer liveth," which he says is a "satisfaction to us at the sight of our dying friends." About midnight the child, after a fit, " most unaccountably fell a-laughing ; yea, into a very great laughter for several minutes, to the amazement of all, who could hardly keep from swooning." He had no return of the fits, but lingered till the hour of death on Friday morning.

The father kept a secret fast on Saturday, in view of "rebukes of Providence, buffetings of wicked men, and deaths, and griefs in his family." He needed help from God ; desired to bear all patiently, and be more serviceable, especially to the children of his flock. The next day was Sunday, and he preached to the great congregation on Job 35 : 10 : "But none saith, Where is God my Maker, who giveth songs in the night." Topic: "The Songs which the triumphant faith of the saints has to utter in the darkest night of affliction." On Monday the burial took place, with more "attendance and respect than was usual with children," and on the gravestone the hopeful father caused this motto to be inscribed : " Not as they that have no hope."

His observance of his birthday (February 12) was saddened because of his great concern about his little Nancy, who had an unknown distemper which the ablest physicians in the town did not understand. Mr. Mather had *particular faith* about her case several times, but she was still a sufferer. It may be stated here that Nancy outlived her father. Not long after the above entry he inserted this : "*Mem.* Faith is not a fancy. Little daughter Nancy is wonderfully recovered."

A general fast was held on the eighteenth of September, when a singular incident relating to prayer occurred. Mr. Mather called on a young gentlewoman who was in affliction, having heard that her husband had been killed in a fight with a Sallee man-of-war. He called to console the widow and offer prayer. There was present a sister of the woman, who was also supposed to be a widow, and had been for many months. In his prayer he was, as it were, compelled to pray for this last one. All his expressions applied to the condition of the sister, and he wondered at his frame in this matter. "But the spirit of the Lord knew what I did not know." In two days came news that the husband of the supposed widow whom he visited was yet living.

The third of October was a "day of thanksgiving for many blessings," specified thus :— 1. Special answers to prayer. 2. Wonderful defeats of those who had labored to blast his efforts in the defense of evangelical interests. 3. The success of his Church History and other works. 4. Opportunities to preach and print. Then comes this beautiful tribute to his wife : —

There was another signal article of *my praises* to the Lord on this day, and this was the confluence of blessings which I enjoy in my dearest consort, who bore me company in some of the duties of the day. Her piety; the agreeable charms of her person; her obliging deportment to me; her *discretion* in ordering her and my affairs, and avoiding everything that might be dishonorable to either of us; and the *lovely* offspring that I have received by her; and her being spared to me for now more than fourteen years; these are things that I should thankfully acknowledge before the Lord.

At this time favorable news came across the water in regard to the *Magnalia*, or Church History, about the publication of which the author had been very solicitous. Assurances also came from on high; yet his mind had no settled repose until a copy was actually in his hands. He often made it the burden of his prayers. Though he waited on the Lord submissively and even with acquiescence, yet he was long in learning to wait patiently.

The public labors of Mr. Mather during this year (1701) were mostly connected with his publications; but his preparation for the ordinary services of the pulpit were incessant, and his pastoral duties were attended to with his usual fidelity. He preached, at home and in other places, his usual quota of sermons. The annual journey to Salem and Ipswich was taken, in which he was called upon to preach three or four times. Sometimes he gave the Lecture in Salem, then went to Ipswich and lectured; returning to Salem he occupied the pulpit in both parts of the day. This visit of a week or ten days seems to have been his *vacation*. His interest in the affairs at home and abroad, and in the political changes in Europe, so far as those of his own beloved country were concerned, was evinced in his publications, to which we will now attend.

On the ninth of January he writes: "The Lord blessed me exceedingly to glorify, and edify and satisfy his people, who much approve my conduct and spirit under the *Satanic assaults* now made upon me." Preached to a vast assembly on Genesis 50: 20. "As for you, ye thought evil against me; but God meant it unto good." By some good people "the sermon was put to press with the title, *Triumphs over Troubles*."

In this winter season he seems to have meditated much before the fire, out of which exercise grew a book containing "Forty Meditations on the Fire," selected from over forty, which he "dressed up so as they might afford both pleasure and profit unto a serious reader." The title was "Christianus per Ignem, or, a disciple warming of himself, and owning of his Lord, with meditations fetched out of

the fire, by a Christian, in a cold season, sitting before it."
John 18 : 18. He says that the " Work, though never
out of season, was yet more particularly designed for the
seasonable and profitable entertainment of them that
would well employ their leisure by the fireside." As
he knew not how to get it published, he laid the matter
before the Lord, when a gentleman, of whom he had little
reason to expect it, came in, " saw the manuscript lying
on the table, and offered to be at half the expense of the
publication." It came out in 1702 (pp. 198), with a " Prefatory Poem " by Nicholas Noyes. The following note is
as characteristic of the author as the title-page. " I gave
it unto the bookseller, with resolutions, when it is published, I will take off two or three, every week, and
scatter them in the families, when I make my visits in the
neighborhood."

In the early part of this year Mr. Mather, at the
desire of a general convention of the ministers of the
province, prepared " A Testimony unto the Order of
the Gospel in the important point of the Consociation of
Churches." Two aged ministers had signed a " Testi
mony," approving of the " Testimony." Opponents gave
out that Mather had signed their names, and the " speaker
of the deputies " abused him for so doing. Whereupon
the aged Mr. Higginson came out with the avowal that he
" signed the piece freely with his own hand." This matter
of church order, or " Consociation of the Churches," has
reappeared from time to time, and every time the movers
for a change have met with little favor. The question in
another form has been before the National Council three
times (in 1880, 1883, and 1886), and has resulted in no
material change. What will come in the future, time
only can reveal ; but it is probable that the more the
primitive order is studied, the more will it be approved.

Some of the fathers who studied deeply the subject of Church Order before and after their coming from England, as Thomas Hooker, Richard Mather, and others of their stamp, seem to have searched to the deepest foundations, and those who essay to improve upon their work need to look well unto their ways. Certainly no true Congregationalist will seek to displace or dishonor the *pro re nata council.*

Another "composure" bears this date. It was a "discourse to a private meeting," of which the "master of the family" desired a copy. "Lessons to be learned in the school of affliction" was the subject. Another sermon was added, and the whole was entitled "A Companion for the Afflicted." It was "accommodated unto the condition that all at some times, and some at all times, do encounter withal."

At the public fast, on the fourth of April, Mr. Mather let drop the remark, "There is much reason to suspect that a war is breaking out in Europe. In the late peace of *Ryswick*, at the close of King William's war, the wind came not about in the right way. There must be another storm of war before all clears up according to our desires. If so, the French will probably fall on us, so that he may possess all America. The record proceeds: "Three days later came news that all Europe was in a flame because of the union of France and Spain, by a family marriage." The old question of *balance of power* in Europe was the irritating cause. France aimed at supremacy. William combined half Europe against Louis, to preserve the liberties of each and all. But the real occasion of the war which was on the eve of explosion was the recognition of the Pretender by Louis on the death of James II in the autumn of 1701. King William at once broke with France, and all the kingdom sprang to his side. But his death ensued in a few months, and it was left to Marlborough, with the splendid aid of the great Prince Eugene, to lead the allies, humble the pride of Louis, and achieve immortal fame for himself. In this condition of things, Mather made extracts from books relating to the affairs of Europe and the American plantations, that "might excite the prayers of all men, and the cares of *all* good men." He showed the compilation to a member of the council, who caused it to be published.

Early in May "most astonishing accounts came of the sufferings of Protestants in the French king's galleys, and of the Lord's wonderful works in supporting them under sufferings, and the converting of some at the sight." Mr. Mather showed an *Abstract* of these accounts to the ministers at their weekly meeting, and caused it to be published under the title, "A Letter concerning the Sufferings of our Protestant Brethren."

He preached May 23 to a numerous assembly, with a "great assistance," about shunning bad company. In the evening he attended the young men's meeting, when near one hundred serious, devout young men met, to whom he preached further on "The Danger and Folly of bad company." They asked for a copy, which was printed with the title of "The Young Man's Preservative," to which he added "A remarkable history of a young gentleman converted to a heavenly life, and rescued from the snares of evil company."

The Church History had been the occasion of great discouragements, by reason of the delay in its publication in England. Reference is often made to this in the diary. I have refrained from quoting these entries, but an occasional sentence is needed to show the various workings of the author's mind and the continual anxieties of his intense life. No bookseller could hazard the work

here, and even the English houses were "cold about it."
It would cost £600 sterling, a great sum to risk on a
book in those days. But on the twenty-fourth of June
the cloud seems to have lifted. Mr. Bromfield had written from London that Mr. Robert Hawksham would put
the work to press at his own charges, "with no expectation for himself, but for the glory of God," and give the
author as many copies as he desired. "And did you
know him as well as I do," he continued, "you would
believe him." This news was "wonderful" to the author.

In July he preached on the "Glorious Wonders that
shine in the Lord Jesus Christ. He is the Wonder of
Angels!" This was printed with the title of *"Thauma-
tographia Christiana,* or the Wonders of Christianity."
He writes of "many wonderful mysteries in our Lord
Jesus Christ, which are admired by angels in heaven, and
should be the contemplation and admiration of Christians
on earth." This was printed in two sizes: one of fifty-
five and the other of seventy-four pages.

We find this entry July 5, which must have been very
gratifying. A letter was received from a gentleman in
London, saying, "Your *Spanish Faith* is gone farther,
it may be, than you thought of. Mr. Chamberlain, an
acquaintance of mine, a secretary of religious societies,
has a correspondence with the Dutch and French Ministry in Holland. They have now at the Hague a considerable Spanish or Portuguese *proselyte,* who desired such
a thing as that was, and said he could make great use of
it." This proselyte was of a very good family, and was
in orders there. "He declared that Portugal was very
ripe for a reformation. The good ministers of Holland
sent the book to Portugal, and received abundance of
thanks."

The following curious item belongs to the same month.

A bookseller, going from Boston to London, took certain of Mr. Mather's manuscripts with him, intending to publish them there. He carelessly left them in the hands of Mr. Cockeril, a bookseller, who died some time after. All trace of the manuscript was lost, but "a friend who went to London last summer, did, in the last winter, inquire for the missing package, and found it." He carried the papers to another bookseller, who published them, and copies of the book had now come over to Boston. "The book which had such a happy resurrection from the dead, has this title, 'Death Made Easy and Happy.'"

Two discourses, one on the general calling and the other on the personal calling of a Christian, were given to the bookseller, with the title, "A Christian at his Calling."

Thinking it "might glorify his Lord Jesus Christ" if he should exhibit his *example* to his neighbors, he prepared two discourses on "Christianity in the Life." This came out in the next year.

In October he prepared a work which also saw the light in 1702. His neighbors with a "mighty zeal favored the publication of it." The title was "Maschil; or, The Faithful Instructor." It contained the New English Catechism of his grandfather Cotton, with twenty-six exercises upon it, with "questions so familiar and intelligible, that only an answer of *yes* or *no* was needed." The book contained several additions, as "The Assembly's Catechism; Memorials of Christianity; the Ten Commandments; the Lord's Prayer; a Paraphrase of the Creed, and a Confession of Faith, directed by some eminent ministers"; all in 192 pages.

The record of Mr. Mather's publications for the year closes with a "Poem of Consolations under blindness, unto an aged and pious gentlewoman, visited with total blindness," which was published by her son-in-law.

The strain upon body, mind, and heart caused by all the work, sympathy, anxiety, and grief of the year now closed was enough, one would think, to make life a burden ; but we are relieved from over sympathy by the thought that this life was so full of good works, so sustained by an ennobling faith, and so happy in its union with God that it is quite credible that Cotton Mather was the happiest man in the province or in all the British dominions.

CHAPTER XIII.

ROBERT CALEF AND THE WITCHCRAFT CONTROVERSY :
1698–1703.

THE most violent assault upon the reputation of
Cotton Mather was made by Robert Calef, or
Calfe, as the name was sometimes spelled by himself as
well as others. The connection of Mather with the
witchcraft horror was the occasion. This attack was
followed up persistently by Calef during several years,
and his allegations against Mather, though unproved and
incapable of proof, have gone into many histories as veri-
table facts. This makes it necessary to enter upon a
thorough investigation of the whole subject, because the
charges against the great divine include not only superstition, credulity, rashness, hypocrisy, and clerical ambition,
but also falsehood, in accusing others and justifying himself ; and cruelty, in creating a public opinion and wield-
ing a personal influence which led judges and juries to
condemn innocent persons to an ignominious death.

It is well to remember that Robert Calef's writings
gained but little credit in their day. The impression
sought to be made against Cotton Mather was transitory.
It is even doubtful if any adverse impression was made
upon any, unless upon a few minds predisposed to believe
evil of both the Mathers. In the early part of this century it became fashionable in a certain quarter to belittle
the younger Mather, and to impute to him motives which
are incompatible with religion, or even ordinary morality.
If any excuse were sought for him, it was only by imput-
ing to him silly superstition or narrow bigotry. He was

either a consciously bad man or a credulous dupe. His vast learning was only a mass of undigested information, picked up in miscellaneous reading, and his immortal *Magnalia* was only a collection of materials for history. This is not an overstatement, as every one will admit who reads noted and even celebrated works that came out half a century ago. So far had this gone, that he was habitually spoken and written about in the language of contempt. The Life of Cotton Mather, by Rev. Dr. Peabody, of Springfield, is an illustration — a work which incurred the mild but severe censure of Hawthorne, who was far from being a champion of Mather. So far had this spirit of depreciation gone that Mr. Drake, in the brief " Memoir " published as late as 1855, remarks as follows : " So far as it is now remembered, Dr. Douglass seems to have been the author of the fashion or practice, so much in vogue of late years, of reviling Cotton Mather. It has been carried to such an extreme in some quarters that whoever presumes to mention his name does it at the peril of coming in for a share of obloquy and abuse himself." These words were printed only a generation ago, but since then a reaction has come. The words of Mr. Drake, who was far from sharing many of the opinions of Mr. Mather, have had an influence in turning the current in his favor. He says : " There need be no concern for the reputation of Cotton Mather, even in the hands of his enemies. . . . All his biographer needs to do is to caution those a little who want caution, and save them, if he may, from having the windows in their own houses broken by the very missiles they themselves have thrown."

The first notice of Calef's attack upon Cotton Mather which I find in Mather's diary is under the date of " 10 d. 4 m., 1698," where he says : " Moreover the Lord is furnishing of me with one special opportunity for the exercise of his graces, under a trial of a very particular importance." The whole bears weightily on an event in his life for which his reputation suffers to this day, and therefore the record is copied here : —

There is a sort of a Sadducee in this town, a man who makes little conscience of lying, and one whom no reason will divert from his malicious purpose. This man, out of enmity to me for my public asserting of such truths as the Scripture has taught us about the [power][1] and influence of the invisible world, has often abused me with the most venomous reproaches, and most palpable injuries. I have hitherto taken little notice of his libels and slanders, but this contempt enrages him. I understand that he apprehends the shortest way to deliver people from the belief of the doctrines which not I only, but all the ministers of Christ in the world have hitherto maintained, will be to show the world what an *ill-man* I am. To this end, I understand, he hath written a volume of invented and notorious lies ; and also searched a large part of my books, which I have published, and with false quotations of little scraps, here and there, endeavored for to cavil at them. This volume he is, as I understand, sending to England, that it may be perused there. And now I thought it high time for me to look about me. Wherefore, in my supplications, I first of all declared unto the Lord, that I freely forgave this miserable man all the wrongs which he did unto me ; and I prayed the Lord also to forgive him, and to do him good, even as to my own soul. But then, I pleaded with the Lord, that the design of this man was to hurt my precious opportunities of glorifying my glorious Lord Jesus Christ ; and I could not but cry unto the Lord, that he would rescue my opportunities of serving my Lord Jesus Christ, from the attempts of this man to damnify them. I submitted my name unto the disposal of the Lord, owning my deserts to have it vilified, and begging his help to bear it prudently and patiently, if it must be vilified. But yet, I earnestly besought the Lord, that for the sake of the calumnies which my Lord Jesus Christ once did suffer for me, I might be delivered from such calumnies as might unfit me to serve him. So I put over my calumnious adversary into the hands of the righteous God, unto whom I make my appeal against him. In those hands I left my adversary,

[1] Word illegible.

as not having any other to appeal to. And I now believe that the holy angels of my Lord Jesus Christ, whose operations this impious man denies, (which is one great cause of his enmity against me,) will do a wonderful thing on this occasion.

This passage, the reader will remember, was written in a diary. It was as secret as the thoughts locked up in a man's inmost heart. The writer never published it. There is no proof that he intended or wished to have it ever come before the eye of the public. It has been kept in a mass of manuscripts to this day, all unprinted except as the custodians of them have permitted extracts to be made. They were, therefore, not written and given to the world for the purpose of injuring Robert Calef. They only show the writer's sense of injury, his forgiving spirit and his desire for vindication lest his power of doing good might be hindered.

Passing over the year 1699, about the middle of November, 1700, there is another reference to this matter: " A very wicked sort of Sadducee had raked together libels," written at several times, relating to "The Wonders of the Invisible World." In this collection Mather, as he alleges, was made the "butt of the author's malice, (though many other better servants of the Lord were most maliciously abused)." The author had "sent the vile volume to London " to be published. Mr. Mather records that he laid the matter before the Lord ; he states that the books he had sent over to London did not get published ; but the books which vilified him were published, and hindered his doing good. He humbled himself before God to obtain pardon for sins, and besought the Lord to assist him with his grace to " carry it prudently and patiently, and not give way to any distemper." He closes thus : " I would imitate and represent the gentleness of my Saviour."

It was a rule of Cotton Mather to avoid all personal controversies, and in this matter with Calef he adhered to the rule so far, at least, as not to print anything in his defense. He had friends, however, who were aggrieved by the attack on the character of their pastor and friend, and who published a small volume in his vindication. This is referred to in the following citation from the diary, under date of February 12, 1701, his birthday : —

I happen to begin this new year of my life with a very agreeable employment. The six friends who published my vindication from the abuses of our calumnious and malicious adversary, (the first of the seven is gone to a better world,) being willing to commit their good cause into the hands of the Lord, I sent for them, and spent the day with them in my study, where we fasted, and prayed, and sung psalms ; and we also put over our adversary into the hands of our Almighty Lord, with supplications that he would send his angel to stop that ill-man from going on any further in his wicked enterprise.

All the various letters and writings of Mr. Calef, which had appeared from time to time for several years, had now, it appears, been collected into a volume, and published in London as well as in Boston. It was this book which the seven friends of Mather answered. The curious reader, if he is hungry for hard work, or craving for sleep, can devote himself to the perusal of these obsolete volumes. The purport of them will appear as we proceed.

In considering the relation of Robert Calef to Cotton Mather, the first question that arises is, Who was Robert Calef ? Was he a philosopher who saw the absurdity of prevailing superstitions and errors, far in advance of the times in which he lived, and so was a benefactor of humankind ? Or was he simply a pamphleteer who possessed no more than ordinary sense and knowledge, and who was utterly unable to treat the subject of demoniacal possessions with candor and sound judgment ? It is certain that he made no impression of greatness on the community in which his life was passed. A few contemporary writers mention him with respect, but none as a man of talent or learning. The reputation he has acquired is of comparatively modern growth. It has been said that from the time when Calef's writings appeared the reputation and influence of Mather steadily decreased to the time of his decease. Nothing could be further from the fact, as the course of this memoir will prove.

There is some perplexity about the identity of Calef, the author. Was he Robert, the father, or Robert Calef, Jr.? This question has been in doubt, but the settlement of it is of no immediate concern in this connection. Dr. Belknap quotes a note which says that he was "a young man of good sense, and free from superstition." Leaving the genealogists to settle the question, we will proceed.

There is nearly as much doubt about Robert Calef's business and his standing in the community as about his age. Some would seem to be desirous of making him a "merchant prince of Boston," while others are accused of a desire to sink him to a lower plane of life as a "clothier." It is of little consequence, for all agree that he was a respectable man, and the town records show that he held offices which, though not indicative of distinction, yet prove that he was a man of reputable character. He was at various times overseer of the poor, hayward and fence viewer, clerk of the market, and assessor. It is supposable that he was both a mechanic and a trader, or merchant; that is, a man who kept both shop and store, and sold in one the products of the other. A clothier is one "who makes cloth," and one "who sells clothing." His will disposes of between two and three hundred pounds in money. Nothing in his life has secured to him a place in our annals, except his writings on the subject of witchcraft, and especially his persistent attacks upon Cotton Mather. Probably his writings would have been entirely forgotten long since if their continued remembrance depended on their merits, for they evince neither ability nor learning above mediocrity. They have been floated down to posterity because of their connection with the most remarkable man of his time in the colonies.

Secondly, when did Robert Calef begin to resist the witchcraft delusion? This is a pertinent inquiry, since all his reputation rests upon his allegations against Cotton Mather as aiding and abetting that delusion. Mr. Mather saw the evil as early as 1688, manifesting itself in sporadic cases, and there seems to have been something "in the air," so to speak, which was of evil portent. Believing in diabolical possessions, and knowing also that there were those in almost every town, if not neighborhood, who made pretenses to tell fortunes and to dabble in some form of the "black art," he bestirred himself to hinder and counteract the evil. He would restrain the witch-workers by the penalties of law and by appeals to conscience and by Scripture; he would deter all good people from giving countenance to the sin. But what was Robert Calef doing all this time to enlighten the public mind, and thus ward off delusion? What was he doing to prevent the awful prevalence of what he considered superstition and fanaticism? Nothing, so far as is known. His voice was not heard. His pen was idle. If he was mature enough in 1693 to write the letters of that date attributed to him, he must have been able a few years earlier to make some show of his righteous indignation. Did he take any of the afflicted into his house and succeed, by judicious treatment, in recovering them from the affliction or delusion or disease which made them the objects of care? Did he, at the time of the trials, write to the judges, warning them to be wary about condemning men and women on insufficient proof of guilt? There is no evidence that he took any measures to correct public sentiment, or to hinder the trial and execution of the accused. Why did he not unite with others in forming a party to arrest the great horror when the trials were in progress? No answer comes to these inquiries. But in 1693, after the trials were all over, and the condemned were reprieved by the governor and the remaining accused were discharged and the special court dissolved, and the very thought of judicial proceedings was odious, he begins to write nagging letters to Cotton Mather; and these he follows up with others to him and other gentlemen, notwithstanding their contemptuous neglect to take notice of his arguments or speculations. And for this he is held up as a benefactor to his species, and as wiser than the wise men of the age in which he lived.

In this connection it is proper to inquire, What was the *animus* of Calef in reference to Mather? because it will help us, if we know it, to estimate the value of his testimony against the latter. Had he the disposition to misrepresent, and by assertions or insinuations to blacken the memory of the greatest divine and the most laborious pastor of the time in New England? Nothing is needed in this quest but the writings of Calef himself. The reader shall judge. Calef asserts in several places that he held Mather in respect, and denies that he had ever been discourteous to him or had written anything to give him a bad name. His words of civility, at times, are so emphatic as to give the impression that they are merely conventional phrases. But these, if sincere, are overbalanced by such epithets as "bigoted," "very bigoted," "superstitious," and such like.

His temper towards Mather comes out in his reference to the "Life of Governor Phips" (a superior piece of biography), in which Calef insinuates that the book was written to glorify Cotton Mather and his father. As Mr. Sibley interprets Calef, "Mather wrote this book anonymously, in order to praise himself." In reference to this statement, it may be remarked that nothing short of omniscience would authorize a man to make it, for the author never avowed such a motive, and nowhere betrays it. None but an enemy would have made the accusation, even if true, because it gives a most despicable character to the biographer, which there was need of exposing. Again, though no name was given as author, the book was not, in any strict sense, anonymous, because it is one of the most characteristic of the author's works, in language, illustration, construction — in a word, in everything. No one familiar with his "composures" could mistake its parentage. Several papers and letters have been ascribed to Mather which have little resemblance to his in style or matter; but this book could have been written by no one else. The earmarks are on every page — in almost every line. Besides, the volume is replete with the most generous praise of its subject and hero. It has been the fashion to depreciate Phips by making prominent a few acts of rudeness and roughness in castigating insulting enemies, and by ignoring his vast energy, his earnest patriotism, his large views, his noble magnanimity, and his brilliant successes. But Mather delights to show how the poor boy, without the advantages of family or education or friends, rose by sheer dint of native qualities to honorable distinction.

Again, Calef, in "More Wonders of the Invisible World" (p. 151), states that Mather, "in manuscript and anonymously handed about a paper of fables, wherein his father, under the name of *Mercurius*, and himself under the name of *Orpheus*, are extolled, and the great actions of Mercurius magnified ; the present charter exalted by trampling on the former, as being very defective, and all those unreasonable that did not readily agree with the new one; and indeed the whole country are compared to no better than beasts, except *Mercurius* and *Orpheus ;* the governor himself must not escape being termed an elephant, though as good as he was great ; and the inferiors told by Orpheus that the quiet enjoyment of their lands, etc., they were beholden to Mercurius for. Though this paper was judged not convenient for publication, yet some copies were taken, the author having shown variety of heathen learning in it." From these extracts it can be seen how much reliance can be placed on Calef's expressions of respect for Mather.

We are now led to ask, What was the real belief of Robert Calef in regard to witchcraft ? Was, he, in fact, in advance of the age on this subject ? Was he a philosopher, who demonstrated the impossibility of demoniacal possessions? Did he understand the teachings of the Bible in relation to this matter? Did he, in a word, throw any light on a series of phenomena which horrified the people in his age? We should infer from the laudations he has received from a class of writers that he was a man of peculiar enlightenment, vainly striving to make a benighted age and generation listen to the words of sober wisdom.

The truth is that Robert Calef had no intelligent, consistent notion or view of witchcraft ; that he was opposed to the management of the cases which occurred in the province in 1688–1693 is beyond a doubt. That he condemned the action of the special court in the trial and sentence of the poor victims, in the summer of 1692, is to his credit. But that he understood the matter of witchcraft, or the peculiar phenomena of those years of supposed Satanic visitation is not made evident from his writings. Sometimes he goes so far in his statements as almost, if not quite, to justify Mather in styling him a "Sadducee," or one who believed in neither angel nor devil. But when pressed with this allegation he took ground by which he gave his whole case and contention away. Thus, in his second letter to Mather, November 24, 1693, he writes: "That there are witches is not the doubt; the Scriptures else were vain, which assign their punishment to be by death."[1] "Not but there are witches, such as the law of God describes."[2] "But what this witchcraft is, or wherein it doth consist, seems to be the whole difficulty."[3]

Mr. Mather had not only the special care of the Goodwin children in the time of their affliction, but also of Mercy Short and Margaret Rule. The story of Mercy Short is still in manuscript, in the library of the American Antiquarian Society. That of Margaret Rule was written by Cotton Mather, and the manuscript was read by a few. It came into the hands of Calef, who, without the knowledge or consent of the author, published it. This is an exhibition of the man's sense of honor. He then began to write letters to Mather in relation to points in the work, and to tell what he saw of Margaret Rule, and here are disclosed his notions concerning witchcraft:[4] "As the Scriptures are full that there is witchcraft, so 't is as plain that there are possessions, and that the bodies of the possest have hence been, not only afflicted, but strangely agitated, if not their tongues improved to

[1] Drake, vol. ii, pp. 5, 6.   [2] Ibid. p. 8.   [3] Ibid. p. 56.   Consult also Samuel A. Flower's "Salem Witchcraft," Part II, p. 54, *et al.*
[4] Drake, vol. ii, pp. 58, 59.

foretell futurities ; and why not to accuse the innocent as
bewitching them ? "

The position he seems to hold consists in "believing
that the devil's bounds are set, which he cannot pass ;
that the devils are so full of malice, that it cannot be
added to by mankind ; that where he hath power, he
neither can nor will omit exercising it ; that it 's only the
Almighty that sets bounds to his rage, and that only can
commissionate him to hurt or destroy any." [1]

Further, he defines his views in regard to prevalent
erroneous notions, in these words : " And consequently
to detest as erroneous and dangerous, the belief that a
witch can commissionate devils to afflict mortals ; that he
can at his, or the witch's pleasure, assume our shape ; that
hanging or chaining of witches, can lessen his power of
afflicting, and restore those that were, at a distance,
tormented by him." And he seems to doubt whether
witchcraft ought in modern times to be understood as
the same thing it was when the divine oracles were given
forth.

To be more definite, he states, in the words of another,
that the witchcraft as exhibited in the Scriptures "is a
maligning and oppugning the Word, Works and Worship
of God," and by "an extraordinary sign, seeking to se-
duce any from it." And he refers in proof to Deut. 13 :
1, 2 ; Matt. 24 : 24 ; Acts 13 : 8–10 ; 2 Tim. 3 : 8. The
first citation will indicate the tenor of all the passages.
"If there arise among you a prophet, or a dreamer of
dreams, and giveth thee a sign or a wonder, and the
sign or the wonder come to pass, whereof he spake unto
thee, saying, Let us go after other gods, which thou hast
not known, and let us serve them ; thou shalt not
hearken unto the words of that prophet, or that dreamer

[1] Drake, vol. ii, p. 76.

of dreams. . . . And that prophet, or that dreamer of dreams shall be put to death." Here Calef seems to have caught a glimpse of the crime of witchcraft as a case of *læsæ majestatis,* but not a clear view of it in its essential character.

Finally, in 1694, he was led to state more fully his position on this subject, in a letter to a naval officer in Boston harbor. His conclusions were as follows : —

1. That the glorious angels have their mission and commission from the Most High.

2. That without this they cannot appear to mankind.

3. That if the glorious angels have not that power to go till commissioned, or to appear to mortals, then not the fallen angels who are held in chains of darkness to the judgment of the great day.

4. That when the Almighty free agent has a work to bring about for his own glory, or man's good, he can employ not only the blessed angels, but evil ones in it.

5. That when the Divine Being will employ the agency of evil spirits for any service, 't is with him the manner how they shall exhibit themselves, whether to the bodily eye, or intellect only; or whether it shall be more or less formidable.

To deny these three last, were to make the devil an independent power, and consequently a God. The bare recital of these is sufficient to vindicate me from that reiterated charge of denying all appearance of angels or devils.

This statement is explicit enough. It suggests the query whether it was not one of those places where Calef received help from the Brattles, as his abettors allege was the fact, in some parts of his letters. But the statement leaves us to wonder in what respect it differs from the general view held by Cotton Mather and the divines, lawyers, and physicians of that day. If God employs "evil angels" as well as "good angels," to bring about any "work for his own glory and man's good," and if it is with him to determine the "manner how they shall exhibit themselves, whether to the bodily eye, or intellect only; or whether it shall be more or less formidable," then the way is open for all the infernal manifestations that were alleged to have occurred. Like any other forces, whether of voluntary agents or mere agencies of nature, if they worked by God's permission and were overruled for good, they would work according to their nature; and thus devils might enter into partnership with men, to work out their ends, or might inspire mortals to do their bidding. The postulate is, that all was overruled for the glory of God. Who can tell, unless he can see the end from the beginning, that any infernal phenomenon may not be for the glory of God? The door is open for all sorts of pretended miracles. For aught Calef could show, the phenomena of the Salem witchcraft were genuine, and divinely permitted, and in that sense, authorized. Thus it appears that Calef, instead of being the enlightened philosopher, whose writings prove him to be superior not only to the clergy of his age, but to such men as Lord Bacon, Sir Thomas Brown, and Sir Matthew Hale, actually held to a scheme which justified the belief of those whom he opposed and abused. In fact, neither party had reached a true conception of the scriptural doctrine of evil angels in conjunction with wicked mortals, working out their malign designs; but the misfortune of Calef was that his views were an inconsistent jumble.

We are thus led along to notice the actual treatment which Cotton Mather received from Robert Calef. Was the latter fair and truthful in his representations of the conduct of Mr. Mather? In 1693, Margaret Rule, as said above, came under the care of Mr. Mather, and he used the means which had been successful in the cases of the Goodwins and of Mercy Short. Mather, in his pamphlet, which Calef published without warrant, thus describes a scene in the room of Margaret Rule : —

We once thought we perceived something stir upon her pillow at a little distance from her, whereupon one present, laying his hand there, he to his horror, apprehended that he felt, though none could see it, a living creature, not altogether unlike a rat, which nimbly escaped from him; and there were divers other persons who were thrown into a great consternation, by feeling as they judged, at other times, the same invisible animal.

Surely there is nothing improper or indelicate in this report. Whatever one may think of witchcraft in general, or of this supposed rat in particular, the deportment of the actor and the terms of the report suggest nothing derogatory to a saint. But it was Calef's report of this scene which first led me to suspect his unfairness, and also the tendency of his mind to what is low and disreputable. In his " More Wonders " he refers to the case of Margaret Rule, and reports the scene above described in his own words. A part of Calef's report is so foolish and ridiculous as to be incredible ; and if credible, it is too indelicate and indecent to find a place in these pages.

I have read the letters of Calef with care, as well as the replies of Cotton Mather, and am convinced that in nearly all the details into which Calef enters he has misrepresented the Mathers, and that the replies prove that his letters were the production of either a very careless, or else a malicious and dishonest, man. In addition, the tone and air with which he hints and insinuates vile actions of Mather convict him of possessing a vile mind. His statements are inaccurate in nearly every particular, but those about the " moving thing " are gross and palpably absurd. In replying to him, Mr. Mather says : " There are divers other downright mistakes which you have permitted yourself, I would hope, not knowingly, and with a malicious design, to be receiver and compiler of, which I shall now forbear to animadvert upon ;" and concludes in these words : "I beg of God that he would bestow as many blessings on you as ever on myself."

To this Calef replied, but his reply is not a justification of his conduct, and it is surprising that his editor, Mr. Drake, or any one else, could think it anything but a disgrace to the writer. He does not seem to have had any sense of honor, or to know that his report had put the Mathers — reputable ministers — in a disgraceful position ; and that if what he stated were true, Cotton Mather was a ruined man. And his catch to clear himself about the touching of Margaret Rule is enough to turn him out of court as a witness.

Calef's offense may be illustrated in this way : a reputable physician describes a female clinique in a harmless and delicate way ; but a bohemian reporter present describes the scene in terms that convey a shameful meaning, and one fitted to cloud the doctor's reputation with disgrace. And it appears that such an impression was made by Calef's narrative, at the time, and that Mather was accused of doing a " smutty thing." When we remember that an insinuation of the sort, though it may not seriously injure other men, is utterly ruinous to the reputation of a clergyman, we see the heinousness of Calef's offense, and we cease to wonder that Mather would have no more to do with his slanderer.

Calef, unabashed, had written to Mather, asking for an interview, which was promised, and he makes great ado over the fact that the promise was not kept. How could a person with any self-respect have an interview with such an enemy ? But on the ground of Calef's plea that he wanted light on the subject of witchcraft, Mather offered him the use of all the books in his library bearing on the subject ; but Calef did not seek light from that

source. However, he wrote letters to several other ministers, inviting answers to his writings, and as he received none, he ga᷈ e out that he understood from their
silence they admitted his letters to be unanswerable.
Mr. Mather intimates that they disdained to reply to one
so ignorant and so unfair. The anecdote which he gives
respecting Mr. Willard, pastor of the South Church, and
afterwards president of Harvard College, seems to confirm the supposition. When Mr. Willard was informed
that Calef demanded and expected an answer from him,
he only replied: "Go, tell him that the answer to him
and his letter is in the twenty-sixth of Proverbs, and the
fourth," which reads: "Answer not a fool according to
his folly, lest thou also be like unto him."

This seems to be the place in which to make a final
disposal of the witchcraft question, so far as this biography is concerned.

1. As is well known, the belief in witchcraft, in one or
another form, was universal in the seventeenth century,
as it had been in all preceding periods of known history.
In heathen, savage, barbarous, half-civilized, and Moham-
medan, as in Christian, nations there were dealers in the
black art, and the people were in thraldom to the diabolical horror. The same is true to this day, except where,
in Christian communities, the influence of the Bible has
partially dissipated the darkness and broken the power
of superstition. And even now there are vast multitudes,
sometimes estimated at millions, in our own country and
in Europe, who believe in manifestations as strange and
unaccountable as many of those which attended the
horrid epidemic in the colony or province of Massachusetts Bay in 1685–1695. There were individuals at the
time who denied the reality of any occult powers or
spirits causing the phenomena, and ascribed the whole

to trickery on the part of the performers and gullibility
on the part of the believers.   There were others, probably, as there are now, who believe that the appearances
sprang from unseen and unknown powers or forces, who
yet did not believe in the presence of invisible, intelligent
agents.   But as a general fact, the belief in witchcraft
was universal.

2. This belief, stated generally, was, that men and
women — wizards and witches — by compact with the
devil, or under his inspiration or that of his hellish confederates, could do wonders, and that their intentions and
deeds were mischievous.   There were some who believed
that the devils could act upon good people without the
assistance of human partners.   Some of the phenomena
in the period under review were the following : —

(*a*) There were many persons, generally singular people, living apart from others, sometimes in the edge of
woodland, who claimed the power of finding lost things
without search ; of designating the place where drowned
bodies might be found ; of working mischief upon others
by charms and incantations ; of foretelling future events,
particularly of fortunes ; and of doing various other things
beyond the power of unaided mortals.   Some of these
admitted, and even claimed, that they were in league with
the devil.   This increased their power over the credulous ; but when danger was incurred, they disclaimed the
aid of diabolical agency.

(*b*) Some persons, not claiming to be witches or wizards,
were accused of bewitching others who were suffering
under peculiar maladies.   The sufferers, for some reason,
accused certain individuals of being the authors of their
troubles.   It might be because they had incurred the
enmity of their supposed tormentors ; or because the sufferers took that mode of injuring an enemy whom they

wished to be revenged upon ; or it might be mere wanton mischief. Sometimes the suffe:ers alleged that they saw the specters of the witches by whom they were bewitched ; and they detected the witches by inflicting some blow or making some mark on the specter, which was, by examination, found on the person of the accused. For example, A. was suffering from some strange malady ; he suspected B. of being the cause. While suffering, he saw something which he supposed was a specter. He inflicted a blow on the specter. On examination, B. was found to have a wound or mark on the very part of his body where the specter was stricken. Therefore, B. was a witch and was the guilty cause of the suffering of A. This was bewitched logic.

(*c*) Many asserted that they suffered from being pinched, bitten, burned, pricked with pins, and made sick in various forms ; and in some of these cases the phenomena were entirely unaccountable at the time, if the riper knowledge of two hundred years has found a solution. Persons lying flat rose from the table to the ceiling and came down gently, without any visible support. In some cases, we are told, the attendants could not hold down the patient when this strange fit of levitation was at work. That is, such were the reported phenomena. Modern spiritualism makes the same report.

(*d*) Some of these phenomena were, and are still, inexplainable, unless all are to be ascribed to deceit and trickery.

(*e*) In many cases, without doubt, the phenomena were the result of mischievous cunning. There is no end to the sly deceit of old and young, when they find a state of mind on which they can operate with safety. It sometimes seems as if this mischievous cunning were stimulated by partial insanity.

3. The ancient belief was that all these phenomena which were not ascribable to natural causes were the direct effects of the devil and his legions ; but that those evil spirits could only act as they were permitted by the Almighty. Their malign power was overruled for good, as in the case of sinful men. "Surely the wrath of man shall praise thee : the remainder of wrath shalt thou restrain."

4. It was held that the Bible warranted the belief that wizards and witches, by the help of evil spirits, wielded superhuman power, and possessed knowledge above the ken of ordinary mortals ; and

5. That the commands in the Bible, enjoining that wizards and witches should be put to death, were of perpetual force in countries whither they should come and be known. Some of the passages denouncing capital punishment on this class of offenders read as follows : —

" A man also or a woman that hath a familiar spirit, or that is a wizard, shall surely be put to death." Lev. 20 : 27. " The soul that turneth . . . after wizards, I . . . will cut him off." Lev. 20 : 6. " Thou shalt not suffer a witch to live." Ex. 22 : 18. " There shall not be found among you any one that maketh his son or his daughter to pass through the fire, or that useth divination, or an observer of times, or an enchanter, or a witch, or a charmer, or a consulter with familiar spirits, or a wizard, or a necromancer. For all that do these things are an abomination unto the Lord." Deut. 18 : 10–12.

We are now able, as it seems to me, to see in just what the error of good men lay. It was first, in believing that witches and the whole crew of dabblers in the black art had any supernatural power. The Bible does indeed prove that such pretenders existed in great numbers ; but it treats them as liars, deceivers, pretenders, cheats, and, in a word, impostors. The necromancers of Egypt, the astrologers and magicians of Babylon, the wizards and witches of Canaan, the diviners amongst the Jews, as the witch of Endor and Simon Magus, were one and all false pretenders to occult power, and willing confederates and slaves of the devil, or of false gods. That is the biblical teaching throughout. The belief in these pretenders — these unabashed liars — was well-nigh universal among all the nations with whom the Jews came in contact; they partook of the belief; but the enlightened among them, especially such great leaders and teachers and chosen servants of God as Moses, David, Elijah, and Daniel, were employed to confute and detect and expose and to put to shame the false claims of the whole brood of dealers with familiar spirits. The first great mistake of our fathers was in not recognizing this fact.

The second mistake which led to the shedding of torrents of blood in Christian lands was this : that the sentence of death upon wizards and witches, necromancers, magicians, and astrologers was of universal and perpetual force; whereas it had validity only under the Hebrew régime. According to the Jewish constitution of government, witchcraft, under whatever name, was rebellion. The crime was treason. "For rebellion is as the sin of witchcraft," or divination. 1 Sam. 15 : 23. Witchcraft was acknowledging another god besides or instead of Jehovah, the God of Israel. In this respect the sin of a Jew was peculiar. It is a sin for any one to resort to a creature, whether diabolic or in human shape, as to a god, or one having divine power; but to the Jew the sin was treasonable. This grew out of the fact that the Jewish government was a strict theocracy, and in it God was the national king. He was just as truly and just as much the king of the Jewish nation as if he had a room in the capital city, Jerusalem, and in the capitol, or temple, and thence had issued his laws and sent forth his edicts. For a Jew, therefore, to resort to a dealer with familiar spirits was as treasonable as it would have been to acknowledge another king — the king of Moab, of Egypt, or of Babylon. In either case it was treason. An overt act in such allegiance was rebellion. The New England governments were never theocracies in any strict or legal sense. The fathers aimed to be governed by the laws of God in public as well as in private life; but that is entirely different from having God take the place of governor of the state, and rule from the State House in Boston or in Hartford.

While, therefore, it was legal and constitutional and necessary that a Hebrew who resorted to a confederate of the devil for aid and counsel should be treated as a rebel, — a traitor to his national sovereign, — there was no biblical authority for the sentence of death upon a wizard or witch in New England, or any other part of the Christian world. Doubtless the dabbling with witches and fortune tellers and necromancers is a grave offense now under the divine law; but the sin of witchcraft, pure and simple, was a capital offense only in the Hebrew commonwealth. The error on this point was well-nigh universal. The Brattles and Robert Calef, as well as Cotton Mather, and the clergy, and the whole mass of the people, were alike under the delusion. And to this day, writers on this subject take it for granted that the Bible sanctioned, and still sanctions, the taking of life in all countries for the sin and crime of witchcraft. This mistake of the fathers brought reproach upon the Bible — a reproach which is slowly lifting, but it rested like a pall of blackness in the time of our fathers. Hence the horror of the witchcraft delusion in Essex County; and the still greater horror in England, Scotland, Ireland, France, and in all Christian countries, that denounced death upon the offenders. Cotton Mather, as usual in advance of the times, seems to have caught a glimpse of this vital distinction in his old age, but, alas! too late to save the province from the stain of innocent blood.

Mr. Longfellow, in his New England Tragedies, rose above the poisoned air about him, and in the serene light of truth saw Cotton Mather as he was, perplexed indeed with " unintelligible circumstances," but honestly seeking to be true to God and merciful to unhappy men. In the following passage we see his reliance on prayer : —

> The Unclean Spirit said, " My name is Legion."
> Multitudes in the Valley of Destruction!
> But when our fervent, well-directed prayers,
> Which are the great artillery of heaven,
> Are brought into the field, I see them scattered
> And driven like Autumn leaves before the wind.

Next he shows Mather's distrust of "spectral evidence":

> We must inquire . . .
> But not receive the testimony borne
> By specters as conclusive proof of guilt
> In the accused.

Mather's zeal for the honor of New England is finely expressed in the lines following : —

> God give us wisdom
> In the directing of this thorny business,
> And guide us, lest New England should become
> Of an unsavory and sulphurous odor
> In the opinion of the world abroad!

> Ah, poor New England! He who hurricanoed
> The house of Job is making now on thee
> One last assault, more deadly and more snarled . . .
> Than any thou hast hitherto encountered!

Again Mather cautions the judge : —

> . . . . Yet one thing troubles me.
> May not the Devil take the outward shape
> Of innocent persons?   Are we not in danger,
> Perhaps, of punishing some who are not guilty?
>   The Scripture sayeth it,
> But *speaketh to the Jews* ; and we are Christians.

The following supposed words of Cotton Mather in the potter's field express the real sorrow of his heart : —

> O sight most horrible !   In a land like this,
> Spangled with Churches Evangelical,
> Inwrapped in our salvations, must we seek
> In moldering statute-books of English Courts,
> Some old forgotten Law, to do such deeds?
> Those who lie buried in the Potter's Field
> Will rise again, as surely as ourselves
> That sleep in honored graves with epitaphs ;
> And this poor man,[1] whom we have made a victim,
> Hereafter shall be counted as a martyr !

[1] Giles Corey.

CHAPTER XIV.

A YEAR OF GRIEF. — SICKNESS OF THE CHILDREN AND DEATH OF MRS. MATHER: 1702.

THE year 1702 was an eventful one in the life of Mr. Mather. He styles it a year of grief. His personal history is merged to a great extent in that of his church and family, but some things were peculiar to himself and will warrant separate notice.

He had great and, we cannot help the feeling, undue anxiety about his books and manuscripts, for one who cherished uncommon trust in providence; but he kept this to himself. He was not in the habit of conversing on this topic even with his most intimate friends. If we had no record from his own pen, it would never occur to us that one whose publications followed each other in such quick succession could have so much solicitude concerning them. But such was the fact. Whether the work were large or small, whether put to press in this country or in London, he was often in a state of anxiety about its appearance. Sometimes his desires were gratified by the offer of a friend to bear the whole or part, of the expense of publication. At other times a public expression of desire that the manuscript might be printed gave him a gleam of encouragement. When manuscripts were sent to England he was distressed about the delay of publication. This was specially true in relation to his great work, the *Magnalia*, and he often refers to it in his diary. It was the subject of frequent prayer, and nothing would compose his mind but an *assurance* from heaven; and he wanted these assurances to be renewed.

This was a year of *vigils* in comparison with other periods of Mr. Mather's life. He kept them more frequently, and had unwonted enjoyment in them. On the fourteenth of March, being Saturday, he made preparation for the Eucharist on the following day, by "watching unto prayer." He remembered that primitive Christians, in obedience to the command about *watching* unto prayer, "sometimes had their vigils which were of great use to them." He kept vigil that night, of which he writes in these words : —

Dismissed my good consort unto her repose, and in the dead of night returned unto my study and cast myself into the dust on the study floor. Was rewarded from heaven with communications that cannot be uttered. Wrestled with the Lord, and received some strange intimations about the time and the day of my death ; and about matters intended for my family. Lord, what is man that thou shouldest 'thus visit him !

He was aware that such vigils endangered his health, as appears from the following note: "If these be vigils, I must (as far as the sixth commandment will allow), have some more of them." Things that were of trifling importance to some, who would smile at his anxieties about them, were serious troubles to him. Thus he observed that when he had received some "near, and sweet, and intimate communion with heaven," he "immediately encountered vexations, as bodily illness, or popular clamor, or Satanic buffets." He expected something of the kind on this occasion. And what does the reader suppose was the price he deemed he had to pay for his previous exaltation? The next day his chimney took fire, and his own house and some of his neighbors' were endangered while he was preaching, and the great congregation ran out of the meetinghouse, while he calmly kept his place. He "was thus marked out for talk all over town"! Not the fire, but the talk was the trouble. Doubtless the talk was an annoyance, as some could not appreciate the faith nor the philosophy which enabled him to continue the public service while his house was in danger of being consumed by fire. But he soon found that this gossip was but a mere trifle in comparison with what was to come.

On the second of April he kept another vigil, and the next day enjoyed a " mighty presence of the Lord in ministering to a vast congregation of his people." Another vigil was kept on the twelfth of April in which he was "irradiated with celestial and angelical influences," assuring him that his Church History should be of "great service in the work of cleansing the temple," for which the Lord would speedily pour out a spirit from on high. Under the influence of this exercise he "became as a weaned child," resolving to be satisfied with whatever might be ordered. In another vigil, on the twenty-third of May, he prayed with his "whole heart" that the "*virtue of Love to Souls*, might, by the Holy Spirit, be mightily working" in him.

In the line of personal experience and influence is the following, which exhibits his singular power in enlightening and comforting persons in distress of mind. It was an interview with a "very religious young minister (and one doubtless of much more grace than myself), desiring advice about his distressed case, being convinced that he was, to this day, an unconverted and unregenerate creature." The record is very interesting, and scarcely admits of abridgment. "Lord," said I, "what cause have I to examine seriously and thoroughly, my own state, if one so much better than I, hath such thoughts of his? But setting myself to comfort him, I found a wonderful comfort conveyed unto my own soul, with a dialogue of this importance."

I pray, Syr, what is that stands on the shelf before you? Answer. A repeating clock, and a very curious one. What use do you think I will put it to? Syr, you 'll assign it to a convenient and an honorable place in your house, and put it to the noble use of measuring your time. How do you know that I shall not make it a stool to sit upon? a block to read upon? a backlog to be thrown into my fire? A. Syr, the workmanship of it makes it appear to be intended for no such miserable use. Well, then, have not you, upon your soul, a divine workmanship far more excellent than the most cunning *clock work* in the world? A work of grace is a work of God, even of him who does nothing in vain. You find in yourself a disposition, — a strong disposition and inclination to glorify God, and serve the interests of the Lord Jesus Christ, and slay all sin, as being most contrary unto him. This is a work of grace. You know no delight comparable to that of serving the Lord Jesus Christ. God has wrought you for this self-same thing of being to the praise of his glory for ever. What use can you think he will now put you to but that of serving the Lord Jesus Christ in his heavenly world? Such a piece of workmanship, (created unto good works,) as what is wrought in you, was never intended to be thrown into the *fire of hell*. No: there is no use of it there. God intends you for a heavenly use, undoubtedly.

Mr. Mather's labors for his church were, as usual, incessant. His record of sermons this year contains the titles of about seventy, the far larger part of which were delivered to his own congregation, though his services were often in request on Lecture day and in other churches.

In laboring for the welfare of all his parishioners, Mr. Mather appears to have anticipated all the judicious methods used in more recent times. The following passage from his diary, February 10, throws light on this point : —

One thing that hath cost me more than a little time and care in the [preceding months] has been to set up a number of religious private meetings among the Christians in my neighborhood, besides those that are already maintained. I considered with myself that the spirit of religion was mightily preserved and promoted by private meetings well managed among the people of God. The Lord has now so marvelously prospered my labors for and with such private meetings, that I shall have at least thirteen or fourteen of these, (besides my vast congregation) under my charge. These unavoidably demand of me a deal of time, and care, and expensive industry; nor do I know another minister on earth, at this day, that has the like number to look after. Lord, assist me to value and improve my precious opportunities.

Whether these neighborhood private meetings included the meetings of young people — male and female separate — is uncertain, but probably those were distinct and on the evening of the Sabbath. At the same time he formed a " Society for the propagation of the Christian religion." "A number of the more significant gentlemen," he says, "have combined with me to set up a conversation at each other's houses, upon the point, 'What is the present state of the Christian religion at home and abroad?'"

At the same time his interest in the town, the province, and the world generally did not abate. He originated a " Society for the Suppression of Disorders." A dozen or fourteen good men, "whereof some are justices, agree to meet for consultation on the point, *What* and where disorders do arise in the town, and how such disorders may be prevented?" He drew up the orders, or regulations. The members hoped for a reformation, and, by combined effort, effected good results.

In the month of March (diary, 14th), he made his influence felt in several ways; for example : —

1. Incited the justices and selectmen to put the Bridewell into good condition, for the cure of much idleness and wickedness. 2. Procured that the town appoint a committee to consider on methods for setting the poor to work, and set forward a town vote for rectifying gross abuses in the choice of jurymen. 3. Procured a clause to be put in the Order for a general fast, exciting the churches through the Province

unto successive days of prayer to be kept in particular congregations.
4. Wrote many letters to forward the designs of prayer for the distressed churches of God.   5. Prosecuting a design of obtaining able
and faithful Indians to undertake the work of evangelizing the salvages
in the eastern part of the country.

He closes with a characteristic touch of humility thus :
"And several other things, worth as much as these; that
is to say, worth none at all.   But it may be, the Lord has
them in the book of his remembrance."

About the middle of April he took into consideration
the fact that there were in the "skirts of the colonies,
diverse plantations that lived destitute of any evangelical
ministry."   He drew up an address as "pungent" as he
could, to those "*ungospelized* and paganizing plantations,
to urge on the necessity of having the means of grace,
and to look out for having an evangelical ministry among
them."   This was styled "A Letter to Ungospelized
Plantations."   As the law then was, no town could
receive municipal powers which did not support an evangelical minister.   A grant of land was made to the town
for the use of the minister; and to the first minister a
direct gift was made of a parcel of land to be his private property.   There were, however, on the frontiers, or
"skirts," of the colony, thin settlements, or plantations,
among which religious privileges were almost unknown.
Mr. Mather's effort in their behalf was most praiseworthy,
and his method was wise: that is, to excite in them a
desire to better their condition by maintaining the worship of God.

The death of King William (on the eighth of March),
whom Mr. Mather greatly admired, and the accession of
Queen Anne were events of great interest in the households of father and son, as the elder Mather had been
admitted to the closet of the king more than once, when

in England, and he, as well as his son, regarded William as, under God, the restorer of English liberties.

Changes in the government of the province, about the same time, were matters of solicitude. The Earl of Bellamont had been absent, and the lieutenant-governor, William Stoughton, had been for some time acting governor. He was a good and capable man, belonging to the old régime. But now by the death of Bellamont and the coming of Joseph Dudley with the commission of governor, a new face was put upon affairs. Dudley was a man of capacity and of fair morals, and, as son of Governor Thomas Dudley, a prominent founder of the Puritan commonwealth, might have been expected to walk in the steps of his excellent father. We shall hear of him again.

Mr. Mather made more use than usual of the press during this year. Among other things he took great interest in sending the gospel to Spanish America. In February, considering the troubles of the churches, he "digested into a single sheet of paper, as exact, and perfect, and curious account as he could, of the deplorable condition in which the church in this time was languishing;" and with as "many charms" as possible, directed and entreated the prayers of good men for distressed Zion, with the title, "Advice to the Churches of the Faithful." His "dear friend," Mr. Bromfield, paid the expense of publishing and gave two copies to each delegate in the General Court, one of them for the minister of the town where he lived. Many ministers had it read in their congregations, and Mr. Bromfield sent a like number of copies to the general assembly of Connecticut.

Mr. Mather's interest in the spiritual welfare of children was evinced in many ways. In February he took his last two lectures, and with the title "Cares about the Nurseries" gave them to the printer with the purpose of scattering two or three a week in his pastoral visits.

In March he made a complete abridgment of the Assembly's Catechism, and "composed brief systems of the Christian religion," all in one single sheet of paper. These were published with the title, " Sound Words to be held fast in Faith and Love."

The month of May found him engaged in two small publications. Knowing that many in town and country neglected public worship, he sent abroad an " Admonitory Letter to them who needlessly and frequently absent themselves from the public worship of God." Like most of his works, this met a practical want in a practical way. It had three editions.

The other volume or tract was " A Seasonable Testimony to the glorious doctrines of grace, now many ways undermined in the world." This was intended as an antidote to Arminian books, many of which were coming over from England. The author considered them " proper cautions against Antinomian abuses of the doctrines of grace."

Though to his public labors were added the cares of a sick family, Mr. Mather neglected no duty to the Christian public. In June he read to a convention of ministers "Proposals for the preservation of religion in the churches, by a due trial of them that stand candidates for the ministry," which was given to the printer.

In the next month came out " The Portraiture of a good man, drawn with the pencils of the sanctuary, in such colors as the oracles of the Sacred Scriptures have given him." This was preached in the hearing of the general assembly and then printed. It has an historical significance. Probably the new governor, Joseph Dudley, was present, and the discourse was intended to set before him, among others, the elements of a good character. In a letter to Dudley, in January, 1708, after the two had become alienated, Mather wrote : " I flattered myself with a belief that you would know no interests but those of a glorious Christ, and of his people and his kingdom, and study what you should render to him for his wonderful dispensations towards you, in restoring you to your family, with the government of a people with whom you had been in such evil circumstances. The whole country were witnesses to some of my poor and plain endeavors to do the part of a faithful monitor unto you in the portraiture of a good man, at your arrival." It is possible that Dudley was not pleased at having such a standard set up for his imitation.

His " Necessary Admonitions " had a singular origin. It was his turn to give the Thursday lecture, and he had prepared for it ; but a few minutes before the time of delivery he resolved upon giving this lecture, which " proved so acceptable to some of the hearers that they were desirous to publish it." It contains " just thoughts upon some sins too little thought of " ; that is, " Sins of Omission." In the preface he observed " that the things and ways from which any service to the church of God is least of all expected, are they that sometimes prove the most serviceable." And he proceeds to say : " I have found it so. . . . Little did I amagine that this poor discourse would ever have had this improvement made of it."

" *Arma virosq: cano ;* or, The Troubles which the churches of New England have undergone in the wars which the people of that country have had with the Indian Salvages." This is in the *Magnalia*, and was republished in 1862 in an edition of the " History of King Philip's War," edited by Samuel G. Drake, with notes.

In the autumn, when the smallpox was in his family and raging in the neighborhood, it was impossible for him to visit much among the sick, whereupon he sent out in print, "Wholesome Words ; or, A Visit of Advice to Families visited with sickness."

The "*Maschil,* or the Faithful Instructor," already mentioned, came out this season, with many additions of Catechism, Creed, and Ten Commandments, in a volume of 192 pages.

We have already given a few of the many entries in the diary, in which the anxiety of the author was expressed in reference to his Church History. Again, on the fourth of April, in his inexpressible solicitude, he rose in the dead of night and sang psalms and prayed and resigned that book and other writings into the hands of the Lord, and, as he assures us, received answer that the "Lord was his Father, and that the Lord took delight in him, and would smile upon his endeavors to serve him ; and that his Church History should be accepted and prospered." Yet later entries show that his anxiety was scarcely abated.

But on the first of May came news that the work would be out in March. This shows how long news was in coming from England. A letter written before March was received on the first of May. However, the glad author could rejoice in the belief that his prized History had already been before the public two months in the mother country. Still he had to wait five weary months before his eyes saw the coveted volume, when, on the thirtieth of October, a copy, which had been bought in Newcastle, came to hand. It was a large folio in double columns. The author's feelings at sight of this fruit of his labors, studies, and prayers shall be given in his own words : —

30 d. 8 m. Friday. Yesterday I first saw my CHURCH HISTORY since the publication of it. A gentleman arrived here from Newcastle,

in England, that had bought it there. Therefore, I set apart this day for a solemn THANKSGIVING unto God for his watchful and gracious providence over that work, and for the harvest of so many prayers, and cares, and tears, and resignations as I have employed upon it. My religious friend, Mr. Bromfield, who had been singularly helpful to the publication of that Great Book, (of twenty shillings price at London) came to me at the close of the day, to join with me in some of my praises to God.

In turning to the family life of Mr. Mather this year, we find it truly described by him as a year of grief, loss, bereavement, sorrow. His custom had been, as he wrote in March, "in evening prayer in his family to preface the devotions with some meditation upon a text of Scripture." He now concluded to read a passage from the Scotch Commentators, and read a portion in his family. He began with Hutchinson on Job, and many times after he had begun had it darted into his mind that he might expect some trials (perhaps of long sickness) to come soon upon his family, and that the lessons fetched from Job were to prepare him for those trials. However this may have been, the trials soon came.

In the latter part of May his wife, whom he calls his "dear consort," had the misfortune of a premature birth. From this time (May 25), during six or seven months, he was in the deepest anxiety about her. She was apparently often on the brink of the grave, and as often somewhat relieved. He fasted and prayed and often had assurances of faith that she would be healed and be strong again ; and as often his hopes were fallacious. At last it seemed to come to him, as a half conviction, that the faith was only in reference to the prolongation of her life, rather than her restoration, and that all was to prepare him gradually for the sad event that was surely coming. But the noteworthy fact is that he never dictated to God in the matter, and never found fault with God, or lost confiding trust in him, on account of disappointment. The fluctuations of this long illness, which are often mentioned in the diary, need not be given. During the whole he showed the most warm and gratifying affection for his wife, and did all that was possible for her comfort, both bodily and spiritual. Many times she was thought to be dying. Once she was much better and began herself to hope for recovery. At one time she came out of her room into the study.

In August he wrote a passage which will help us to an insight into his theory of a *particular faith*. He records :

> I suspect I have been too inattentive unto the meaning of the Holy Spirit, and his Angels, in the particular faith I have had about my consort being restored to me.
>
> First, when she has been, several times in apparently the last agonies of death, unto the apprehension of all about her, I cry unto the Lord, that he will yet spare me. He tells me that he will do it. Accordingly, to our astonishment, she gets over that ill turn. She stays yet longer with us to employ our prayer, and faith, and patience, and resignation. But it may be, after all, the Lord has given me admirable demonstrations of his being loth to deny me anything that I importunately ask of him, and therefore does, one month after another, delay the thing which I fear; yet I must at last encounter the death which I have so deprecated, when both my wife and myself shall be better prepared for it.

Elizabeth Barrett Browning seems to have a similar idea about our prayers, in some cases, keeping our friends from going to their felicity. The following lines are full of beauty and may perhaps express a truth. A sick child exclaims : —

> O mother, mother, loose thy prayer!
>   Christ's name hath made it strong!
> It bindeth me, it holdeth me
> With its most loving cruelty
>   From floating my new soul along
> The happy heavenly air!

It bindeth me, it holdeth me
  In all this dark, upon this dull,
Low earth, by only weepers trod.
It bindeth me, it holdeth me!
  Mine angel looketh sorrowful
Upon the face of God.

Mr. Mather proceeds with the suggestion that when he prays the Lord to pity him and his poor family, in "reference to the taking away of his dear consort," the Lord may have "wondrous blessings" in store for him and his children, beyond what he can imagine; and so his faith, mistaken as to an individual thing, may be well founded as to what he most needs.

And in regard to another matter wherein many Christians may have erred, he shows that he observed caution. He had a way of opening his Bible and noticing what verse first caught his eye, and was often astonished at its pertinency. He does not state how many times it had no pertinency whatever, but says that "it is an action which I would not encourage ever to be used in a *Divinatory Way*." The wonder about this matter is that almost every page of the Bible has something that is so pertinent to our experience, or so suggestive of rich and germinant thought.

While Mrs. Mather's life was lingering to the end, all his living children in succession, except the eldest, Katy, were nigh unto death. On the thirtieth of October his little daughter Nabby, eight years old, began to fall sick of the smallpox, which was raging in the neighborhood. It continued with scarlet fever through the year 1702. On the twenty-first of November his "godly maid" became sick. His study was turned into a hospital, because his large house was full. His wife, his daughter Nibby, or Nabby, and now his maid, were very sick at the same time. The latter had the smallpox. Three days later, on the 24th, his daughter Nancy, five years old, was taken with the horrible disease, and on the 27th, his little boy Increase, three years of age, came down with the same loathsome malady, "full, and blind, and sore." Four were sick in the house besides the mother, who was anxious to help, yet was slowly dying. Writes the father: "The little creatures kept calling me so often to pray with them, that I can scarce do it less than ten or a dozen times a day, besides what I do with my neighbors." He adds: "But the most exquisite of my trials was the condition of my lovely consort. It now began to be hopeless."

But this was not all. The poor servant, who "knew and loved the family," and would have been a tender nurse to the children, became so "distracted" that they were obliged to part with her. And now another cup was pressed to his lips, for in the next month his "pretty little Nancy had a violent and malignant fever." She was in violent convulsions. Her agonies were so great that he "would have been glad if she had been released by death." On the sixth of January, 1703, he "fasted and prayed that the child might obtain a speedy and easy death, and everlasting bliss, rather than a continuation of life." She lay speechless and he lost all hope of her recovery. After lying in that condition all day, she surprised all about her by saying: "I heard my father give me away to-day, but I shall not die, this time, for all that." She became speechless again, and remained so two days; but after all got well, and survived her father.

Mrs. Mather's sickness continued from the latter part of May till the fifth of December, and the progress of it is copiously recorded in the diary; but though exceedingly interesting, all but a few entries must be omitted. In one of the conversations between husband and wife, near the end, she was speaking of the trouble caused by her protracted illness, and expressed fear lest all her friends would be weary; but she added with thoughtful tenderness: "I don't mean you, Mr. Mather." He had been with her night and day, more than any one in the house, though attentive to all other duties, and busy at intervals in his studies.

Passing by intervening dates, we come to the twenty-fourth of November, when he wrote: —

> I spent much time with my lovely consort. I prayed with her as agreeably as I could; I endeavored her most consummate preparations for the heavenly world, by suitable questions and proposals. I comforted her with as lively discourses upon the glories of heaven, whereto she was going, as I could make unto her. I disposed her and myself, all that I could, unto a glorious resignation.

On Tuesday, the fifth of December, we find this record: —

> At last the black day arrives. I had never yet seen such a black day in all the time of my pilgrimage. The *desire of my eyes* is this day to be taken from me. Her death is lingering and painful. All the forenoon she was in the pangs of death; sensible until the last minute or two before her final expiration. I cannot remember the discourses that passed between us, only her devout soul was full of satisfaction about her going to a state of blessedness, with the Lord Jesus Christ. And as fast as my distress would permit me, I studied how to confirm her satisfaction and consolation.
>
> I remember that a little before she died, I asked her to tell me faithfully, what fault she had seen in my conversation, that she would advise me to rectify. She replied, (which I wonder at) that she knew of none, but that God had made what she had observed in my conversation, exceeding serviceable unto her, to bring her much nearer to himself.
>
> When I saw to what a point of resignation I was now called of the Lord, I resolved with his help therein, to glorify him. So two hours before my lovely consort expired, I took into my two hands a dear hand — the dearest in the world. With her thus in my hands, I solemnly

and sincerely gave her up unto the Lord; and, in token of my real
RESIGNATION, I gently put her out of my hands, and laid away a most
lovely hand, resolving that I would never touch it any more. This
was the hardest, and perhaps the bravest action that ever I did. She
afterwards told me that *she signed and sealed my Act of Resignation.*
And though before that, she called for me continually, she, after this,
never asked for me any more. She continued until near two o'clock
in the afternoon, and the last sensible words she spoke, were to her
weeping father, " Heaven, heaven will make amends for all."

The closing scene was followed by prayer with " her
father, and the other weeping people in the chamber," in
which the bereaved husband prayed for grace to " carry
it well under the present calamity"; and, to use his own
words : " I did consummate my resignation in terms as
full of glory to the wisdom, and goodness, and all-suffi-
ciency of the Lord as I could utter." They had lived
together just as long as she had lived in the world before
her marriage, with the exception of the last seven months,
" in which her dying languishments," he writes, " were
preparing me to part with her."

The interment took place three days later, on the
8th, when she had a " very honorable funeral." " No
gentlewoman who had died in the land for many years
was more generally esteemed and lamented. This was
every one's observation."

Everything that occurred to Cotton Mather must be
made the occasion of good to others. He writes : " The
long sickness of my wife, and the late sicknesses of my
family, caused me to employ, first and last, near one hundred watchers. At the funeral I presented each of these
with a book, either that entitled, ' Ornaments for the
Daughters of Zion,' or that entitled, ' Death made happy
and easy,' " with a paper pasted in at the beginning,
which contained at whose funeral it was given, and had
this epigram added : —

Go thou my Dove, but now no longer *mine*;
Leave earth, and now in heavenly glory shine.
Bright for wisdom, goodness, beauty here,
And brighter in a more angelic sphere.
Jesus, with whom thy soul did long to be,
Into his ark and arms hath taken thee.
Dear friends with whom thou didst so dearly live,
Feel thy *one* death to them a *thousand* give.
Thy prayers are done; thy alms are spent; thy pains
Are ended now in endless joys and gains.
I faint till thy last words to mind I call:
Rich words: Heaven, heaven will make amends for all.

The day after the funeral was set apart for fasting with prayer for pardon of all sins for which he " had been chastised," and with a keen forecast of the future for "grace and help from heaven to glorify the Lord with a nice behavior under the temptations of the new condition " he was now in by reason of his bereavement.

Ezekiel's wife (Ezek. 24: 15–18) was the theme on the Sunday following, and Mr. Mather studied that the sorrow in his family might prove an occasion of benefit to others. In this exercise he was " greatly assisted of the Lord."

It has been stated in publications that the "Mather tomb," so called, in Copp's Hill burying ground, was built by Cotton Mather. The facts are given in the following citation from the diary: "The Lord gave me to see wondrous demonstrations of the love his and my people had for me. One was their building a costly tomb for the ashes of my lovely consort, and of my children, whereof there were five buried, with no more than common gravestones." In this tomb were laid the remains of his children, his father, and several other relatives. It is still to be found in the ancient cemetery, towards the northeast corner.

The children who were sick at the time of their mother's decease "came alive out of the fiery furnace of the smallpox, which almost consumed them." Mr. Mather spent much of his time in "venomous, contagious, and loathsome chambers," but was preserved and was thankful. In the "black month of December, more than eighty persons " of Boston were carried to their long home.

In review he could but acknowledge "much of the divine compassion and faithfulness" in the removal of his wife. And he presents various reasons which convinced him that it was better for all that she had been taken. If continued in life, the probability was that it would be a life of prolonged weakness, in which case his own health would have been sacrificed, and his children would have "suffered miserably in their education." Her temperament was naturally melancholy, and events came on soon which would have aggravated that susceptibility. Her youngest brother, and some hundreds of pounds of her husband's, had recently fallen into the hands of the French enemy. Her eldest brother, by misconduct, became a grief to his friends. She did not live to see the condition of these brothers, though seen by all the rest of the family before she died. The second brother seems to have been her favorite — her " idol — whom she doted upon," and, if she had lived, he would have been the innocent cause of heartbreaking grief. He went in poor health to London, with the hope that the voyage would be a benefit. At his going she said with a " more than ordinary passion and agony, that she desired God would never let her live to hear of the death of that young man." Though the news of his death came three months before her own, she was not informed of it. "About three hours after she expired, a letter came directed to her from the gentlewoman in whose house her brother had died, giving an account of him, and the manner of his hopeful death."

And now, that one great lesson learned by the chief sufferer may not be lost, we make room for one passage more. A fortnight after the death of his wife, Mr. Mather preached on John 4: 47. His subject was: "Though faith be no folly, yet faith may be mixed with folly, and particularly with the folly of limiting the wisdom of God unto our own way of answering it." His good sense appears in the following extract : —

I can mention to you a mystery of practical Christianity, relating to a *particular faith*. Sometimes we ask for temporal blessings, or for such as are not particularly promised in the covenant of grace. The Holy Spirit of God favors with so much of a particular faith as to say, "The Lord hath heard the voice of my weeping; the Lord hath heard my supplications; the Lord will hear my prayer." We may be too ready to *limit* the sense of the Holy Spirit by our own strong affections to the *temporal blessings*, and conclude : the thing must be done in just such or such a manner. No: the sense of the Holy Spirit is more than this : "I may do something towards those temporal blessings, which may show how able and how willing I am to gratify thee; but then, I 'll carry the matter into another channel, wherein thou shalt have thy desires more than answered." The bravest effort of a true and strong faith, is to leave all entirely unto the Lord, and be satisfied with the infinite wisdom of his conduct. It may be, the Lord will ere long, enable me to see further into the nature, meaning, and mystery of a particular faith. However, I have met with enough to awaken in me a more exquisite caution than ever I had in my life concerning it.

The death of Mrs. Mather closed an era in the life of her husband and family, and suggests the propriety of gathering up the experience of the family to this point of time. And fortunately a volume, published in 1703, but made up of discourses previously printed, gives us the materials. The book was entitled, "Meat out of the Eater, or, Funeral Discourses occasioned by the death of several relatives : a work accommodated unto the service of all that are in any affliction, but very particularly such as are afflicted with the loss of their consorts or children." The titles of all the discourses are given in Sibley's list, but I have collated what answers my purpose from the volume itself, which is in the Athenæum. In the preface Mr. Mather says : —

One of the most sensible calamities afflicting him — the author — has been the death of sundry children, which was at length followed with the more grievous death of his lovely consort, the mother of them. When these afflictions befell him, though sometimes they fell out very near the Lord's day, he still judged it might somewhat glorify the Lord, if he should never, for the sake of grief himself, omit any of the usual offerings of the Lord, on the Lord's day, in the assemblies of his people, to whom he has been a servant. And having his thoughts, after some sort, compelled and confined unto the subjects of meditation which were most likely to rescue him from the distempers that flesh and blood often indulge on such afflictive occasions, he still apprehended that it might not be unedifying unto his flock to be edified and armed with the same things that had counseled or comforted him in the multitude of his thoughts within him.

The title or subject of the first sermon was " Abraham's offering of Isaac. A tried faith offering an only son," and his text was Heb. 11 : 17. It was "preached 2 d. 2 m. 1693, April, A.M., my only son having died in the night before." This was Joseph. After speaking of Abraham and his offering, he gave the "doctrine" in these words : " A true and a great faith will make a man readily, easily, cheerfully part with the dearest enjoyments in the world, when God shall put him on such a trial of his faith." The motto on the gravestone was: " Reserved for a Glorious Resurrection." The child had an organic defect which was fatal on the fifth day of his life.

The subject of the second sermon was " The Fear of God under trials from the hand of God," preached on the eighth of October, 1693, "the day after the funeral of my daughter Mary, and the day of my administering the sacrament." Genesis 22 : 12. Topic, "A man may, by many tokens, know that he hath in him the fear of God ; but a right behavior under afflictive trials, is a token that will more especially and eminently serve to make it known." An inspection of the text will show how beautifully the theme is drawn from it. The words on the headstone were : "Gone, but not Lost." The discourse is followed by six verses, the first and last of which are copied here, to show the piety, rather than the poetry, of the sufferer :

> The dearest Lord of heaven gave
> Himself an offering once for me :
> The dearest thing on earth I have,
> Now Lord, I'll offer unto thee.

> Now my believing soul does hear
> This among the glad angels told,
> I know thou dost thy Maker fear,
> From whom thou nothing dost withhold.

The third sermon was founded on Luke 2 : 15, and the subject derived was : "Good News from a far country, for the solace of them whose friends have gone thither." This was on the twenty-ninth of February, 1695, "the day after the funeral of my daughter Mehitable." Mr. Mather was preaching a course of sermons on the "Angelical Descent," and took the subject for his obituary discourse, "Gone away from them into heaven." That is, the angels had done their errand, and returned unto heaven ; and so he believed that the angels had taken his child thither. He exclaims : —

Heaven ! what a grateful subject for our meditations, are we now fallen upon ! Heaven ! 't is the state and sum of our perfect blessedness, and the only home of every godly man on earth. Heaven ! 't is the strong tower whereinto our devout friends do retire for the eternal harvest and reward of all their devotions, when mortality takes them off. Heaven! 'tis the rendezvous of the bright angels attending on the throne of God, and beholding his face continually. Yes, a better and a brighter thing than all of this. Heaven! 'tis the place where our most glorious Lord Jesus Christ is to be seen in all his glory. That we may hear and know anything about heaven, 'tis the wonderful mercy of our God unto us. But then, what a wonder of mercy is it, that an offer of this heaven may be made unto us, who are as miserable sinners as any that are out of hell, and as unworthy ones as any that are in it.

His doctrine was: "There is a glorious heaven, where heavenly spirits do go alway when they leave this earth." He makes two inquiries: "1. What is the glorious heaven whereunto glorious spirits go away? 2. Who are the spirits that go away to this heaven?" The application has this remark: —

Our desirable relatives are gone away to a glorious heaven when they go from us. The pale horse only came to fetch them away unto the heavenly Father's house. Oh, why don't we rejoice when they say unto us; Let us go up to the house of the Lord? But may this consolation be applied unto the death of our infants? Yes; why not? Is it not expressly said of our infants, that they have their angels in heaven? No doubt there are more spirits of infants in heaven, than saints of any other age.

His faith in the salvation of infants was expressed in the text on the gravestone: "Your bones shall flourish like an herb" (Is. 66: 14). In some lines of acquiescence and hope, he recognizes that God gave the child, and in mercy took her away, and closes with this verse: —

> The name of my great God, I will
> For ever then adore;
> He's wise, and just, and sovereign still
> And good for evermore.

The fourth sermon is on "Light arising in darkness," preached on the ninth of February, 1701, "my son Samuel then lying dead in the house, and carried, the day following, to the house appointed for all living." He took for his text Job 35 : 10: "God my Maker, who giveth songs in the night." The teaching he derived from it was this : "In the darkest night of their affliction, the children of God are furnished by him with glorious matters of satisfaction and consolation." One remark was : "Our Lord loves us too well to hurt us in the worst that he shall do unto us." And the sentiment on the stone at the child's grave was : "Not as they that have no hope."

Another sermon was spoken when this same infant son Samuel "lay a-dying, and within a few hours actually did die." The topic was from Job 19 : 25. "The living Redeemer in the balance against a dying relation." He added Sir Richard Blackmore's "Paraphrase upon Job's confession of faith." The father wrote a hymn, of which the last verse follows : —

> I know when I or mine shall die,
>   We shall to heaven go;
> For our forerunner lives on high,
>   Concerned for us below.

I find no printed sermon in relation to the firstborn child, Abigail, who died in infancy ; but the last discourse in the book before me was occasioned by the decease of these five children : namely, Abigail, Joseph, Mary, Mehitable, and Samuel. In the preface to this are these words : "The sudden death of his *first-born* produced a discourse about fourteen years ago, printed in London, under the title of 'Right Thoughts in Sad Hours.'" This has been already referred to under date 1688–1689. The preface continues : "Four more of his *Olive Plants* have been since withered ; the Fruits yet produced by those occasions, are collected and exposed in the book now before the reader." Then follows a pathetic statement which is introductory to the funeral sermon on the death of his wife :

A more trying death by far than all the former, is at length in-flicted on him. Their lovely mother must be at last laid in a *tomb*, where they must now sleep together with her. A sermon uttered just after the saddest funeral that ever he saw, and composed under the most grievous desolations of his mind, as well as of his house, that ever were upon him, is now added to the rest.

The title of the sermon was "*The House of Mourning;* the death of desirable relatives lamented and improved, occasioned by the death of Mrs. Abigail Mather." A consolatory poem by Nicholas Noyes, dedicated to the husband, follows, in which he speaks of the "excellent and virtuous wife, that well-accomplished gentlewoman."

The text was from Proverbs 31 : 28. Prayer: "Aspice, Domine, viduitatis et orbitatis meae lacrymas." He ex-claims: "Behold how his calamities grew upon him! Lord, how are the things increased which trouble me! But God, in his free and rich grace, makes the calamities of the sinful man who is now writing, to be subservient unto the interests of religion among those to whom what he writeth may be in any way acceptable." The above is a sort of introduction, and is followed by another text, as was his way at times — taken from Ezekiel 24 : 16, in reference to the prophet's wife. The lesson he drew from it was this : "When the desire of our eyes, or a relative that was very desirable in our eyes, is taken away from us, 't is God that has taken it, and stricken us by taking it." A brace of paragraphs is subjoined, because in showing the worth of the wife they reveal the character of her husband : —

The God of love sometimes disposes them whom he has made con-sorts in the conjugal relation, greatly to love and prize one another. The consorts are to each other as the desire of their eyes, and they so love each other, that they love to be as much as may be in the sight of each other. About the one of these relatives 't is said, "he that findeth it, findeth a good thing, and obtaineth favor of the Lord."

And that is the opinion which both of them have of each other. "This is a great gift of God to me! Highly favored of God was I in the giving of it." It may be, before they were first acquainted, they humbly cried unto God that he would choose for them what consorts they should live withal, and God so answers those prayers and cries, that every day afterwards, as long as they live together, they give thanks unto God for giving them to live together. . . . They live together in such harmony and happiness that they could freely die for one another, and when either of them does die, it gives a thousand deaths to the survivor. They set a mighty value upon one another; the satisfaction which they take in one another is inexpressible. The husband is in great esteem in the eyes of his wife. She loves to see him, and much more, loves to please him. Such a covering to the eyes is he to her, that all the men on earth are nothing in her eyes in comparison of him. And she will no more look upon another, than the wife of Tigranes, who, after the wedding of Cyrus, whom every one did commend as the person rarest in the company, being asked by her husband, what she thought of him, answered, "In truth, I looked at nobody but you, my husband." But her esteem for him is like that in the life of Phocion, who, when a lady had shown her treasures and jewels unto her, by way of requital, only showed her Phocion, saying "all my treasures and jewels are in him."

The wife is of as great esteem in the eyes of her husband. He loves her, and her love; and rejoices in his loving hind, and his pleasant roe. He had rather lose all his possessions, than suffer the loss of one whom God hath thus enriched him withal. He can scarce relish anything, if his eyes have her not also before him. If by death she leave him, he can, it may be, say as one once of his lady *Crescentia*, "She never grieved me but once, and that was by her death." And he is ready to write upon all his other entertainments, the motto written upon one of his by a worthy man among ourselves, when he became a widower, "In lugenda compare vitae spatium compleat orbus."

CHAPTER XV.

THE available materials for 1703 are meager, compared with those of the year preceding. The diary
began on the twelfth of February, 1702, and extended to
the same day in this year. For the remainder of this year,
nearly ten months, the diary being in the Antiquarian
Library, we must look elsewhere for the events which
mark the year, except a few extracts which are in print.
For the year 1704 there is no diary extant.

The history of the church during the life of the
Mathers, and before and after, for a time was a record
of harmonious action as well as of general prosperity.
Since he had an invincible repugnance to residence in
Cambridge, the father was now released from all care of
the college and could devote his whole time to pastoral
duties, except as he wrote for the press or was called to
services abroad in the churches. His presence was in
great request at councils, and especially at ordinations,
where a principal part was always assigned to him.

The junior minister had some special embarrassments
this year, growing out of his widowhood, though he seems
to have conducted himself with great discretion. His
labors in the pulpit were abundant, as about seventy
sermons, with text and topic, are recorded in his list.
Fourteen of the sermons were lectures preached in Boston and elsewhere. On Thursday, June 25, his text was
Proverbs 12: 2: "A good man obtaineth favour of the
Lord." On that occasion, as already said, his motive was,

as he himself says, "to let my whole country see, that if the governor did not prove such a one — 'a Good Man' — it should be none of my fault." The governor, it will be remembered, was Joseph Dudley, concerning whom the following note is made in the diary, June 16: "*Mem.* Visit from Gov. Dudley." In conversation Mather suggested this advice: "By no means let any people have cause to say that you take all your measures from the two Mr. Mathers. By the same rule I may say, without offence, by no means let any people say that you go by no measures in your conduct, but by Mr. Byfield, and Mr. Leverett. This I speak not from any personal prejudice against the gentlemen, but from a due consideration of the disposition of the people." It is not easy to imagine what better advice could be given, if any were thought proper. There were two parties in the province. The leading men of one party, which had been in power more than a decade, had a high esteem for the Mathers. They had been firm in their opposition to Governor Andros, zealous for the revolution of 1688–1689, and great admirers of William and Mary. Joseph Dudley belonged to the other party. Twelve years before he had been a supporter of Andros; had been thrown into prison, and had been sent to England. There he became a courtier and obtained preferment. He came back with the commission of governor, obtained, partly at least, through the Mather influence. Cotton Mather, forgiving and hopeful, had written in his behalf. The letter was read at court, but was supposed to be from President Mather, who was held in high honor. But Dudley returned unchanged in temper. Burning with revenge, he vetoed the choice of every councilor who had been opposed to him ten years before. If he had followed the friendly and fair suggestion of Cotton Mather, and governed with an even, impar-

tial hand, he would have had a more pleasant and useful
term of office and secured a brighter page in history.
But the governor had not the discretion or the magnanimity to take this course, as the following passage
reveals : " The wretch went to these men and told them
that I had advised him to be no ways advised by them,
and inflamed them into an implacable rage, against me."
The relations of these two men to each other will appear
again in the record of a future year.

An incident in the preceding year, not being noticed at
the time, was referred to in the diary in the early part of
the present year.   It helps us to an insight into the character of Mr. Mather and his mode of dealing with hard
cases.   While he was attending the bed of his dying wife,
the keeper of the prison called his attention to the condition of a young Indian, under twenty, sentenced to
death for the murdering of his friend.   He did not know
that he had a soul.   He never had heard that there was
a God.   It was an incredible task to convey a notion of
religion into a mind so ignorant, so desolate, so barbarous.
Mr. Mather took a "deal of pains to illuminate him," and
God prospered his efforts.   "The young Indian learned
much of religion.   He expressed his believing in Christ,
and repenting of sin, in an agreeable manner."   The only
sermon he ever heard was preached, at his request, by Mr.
Mather, on the Lord's day before he died.   He advised
the man to live and die with these words in his heart :
"*Jesus Christ came into the world to save the chief of sinners.*"   He was executed, and made a "hopeful end."
The minister prayed with him.   His last words were :
" Jesus Christ came into the world to save the chief of
sinners ; O Lord Jesus Christ, save me, I pray thee."

Several small books appeared without a name in the
early part of this year, which are ascribed to Mr. Mather.

One of twenty-eight pages bore the title, "Sound Words to be held in faith and love." It was in three essays. One was "Our Saviour's Creed"; the second was "The Body of Divinity Versified"; and the third was an "Abridgment of the Assembly's Catechism." This was appended to the "Cares about Nurseries." Another volume, of forty-eight pages, was "Agreeable Admonitions for old and young." A third related to the observance of the Sabbath, entitled "The Day the Lord hath made." This was reprinted four years later, and translated into Indian, and "inserted for the more special meditation of the Indian readers." The reader will notice how applicable are all these topics to the wants of various classes.

A sermon preached in May, on a day of "prayer with fasting, for the rising generation," was printed with the title, "The Duty of Children whose parents have prayed for them; or, Early and real godliness urged especially upon such as are descended from godly ancestors." Reprinted.

"A virtuous Woman found," suggested by the death of Mrs. Mary Brown, and "A Family Sacrifice to direct and excite family religion," were well adapted to promote religion in his parish and at large. A second edition was called for in 1707. The "Glory of Goodness" is hard to find, but is still in request, as it contains his "Remarks on the redemption of captives from the cruelties of Barbary." It contains fifty pages. Four or five other small works or pamphlets saw the light before the close of the year. One gave "Methods and Motives for society to suppress disorder," and another indicated the "Duty of secret prayer." All the while the author, with unflagging zeal, was piling up the material for his great "Biblia Americana."

Turning now to the domestic side of Mr. Mather's life,

we find the following entry in the early part of the year:
"One day, considering how frequently and foolishly widowers miscarry, and by their miscarriage, dishonor God,
I earnestly, with tears, besought the Lord, that he would
please to favor me so far as to kill me, rather than to
leave me unto anything that might bring any remarkable dishonor unto his Holy Name." He was heard, but
he was sorely tried in this matter.

Mr. Mather was (February 12) forty years old and was
growing still in fame and influence. The intimations
of some writers that his reputation and power had begun
to wane since the witchcraft distress, and that they
went on declining to the close of his life, have no basis in
recorded facts. Enemies rose up against him, and they
have had successors; but the evidence seems to show
that his reputation and influence went on increasing till
his dying day. The truth of this will be disclosed as we
proceed. At the time of his wife's death he was one of
the most celebrated, as he was the most learned, man in
America. His popularity in the pulpit was unabated, and
his position in his parish, in Boston, and through the
province was enviable.

It is not strange, therefore, that he was considered an
eligible party in marriage; but in this connection a very
strange experience befell him. In affairs of the heart,
especially where widowers are concerned, it is often the
case that amusing things occur, and sportive people find
occasion to smile. Some have made merry over certain
passages in the affair to which allusion has been made;
but a candid judgment of Mr. Mather's deportment will
decide that he bore himself with rare delicacy and wisdom
in a very embarrassing situation.

In February, about two months after the loss of his
wife, he refers to a "very astonishing trial." This was in

the shape of a very accomplished young lady, who was so
enamored of him as to make proposals of marriage. He
describes her as abounding in wit and sense, lovely in
person, and winning in conversation, so that no one in
the land surpassed her. She began her wooing by writing a letter or two, and followed them up by a visit. She
had long been deeply interested in him as a minister, and
his present condition had given her liberty to think of
him in another relation. He reports of her: "She had
become charmed with my person to such a degree, that
she could not but break in upon me with her most importunate request that I would make her mine." With all
this she averred that her desire for a more intimate relation to him was prompted by religious considerations, as
she hoped association with him would make her salvation
sure.

Thus he was assailed in two most vulnerable points.
He was not insensible to approbation, and the admiration
of a beautiful and accomplished young lady was pleasing.
But perhaps stronger than this was the appeal to him as
one who had what has been styled a " passion for souls."
To bring a sinner into the joys of the Christian covenant,
he would make any sacrifice. He would visit jails and
hovels and pesthouses to search out beggars, Indians,
negroes, thieves, prostitutes, murderers, and pirates, in
order to bring them to repentance and make them to be
"sons and daughters of the Lord Almighty." But here
was an inquirer who came from the ranks of fashion, in
all the attractions of female loveliness, and craved his
assistance in her effort to live a saintly life. Doubtless
the appeal came with force. How many men would
have resisted it, coming from fascinating lips? Nay;
why should he resist it at all? There were reasons,
and he felt the force of them. He saw that she was

not the one for him in his laborious calling and with four young children needing a discreet mother. Thereupon his mind was soon made up, probably, but it was hard to give the lady a blunt negative. He therefore wrote her, informing her of his manner of life, full of self-denial, much taken up in study, visitings, authorship, fasts, and vigils, expecting that this representation would enable her to see the folly of joining such a man in wedlock. Her reply must have astonished him, as she declared that all these things had been considered by her, and in fact that it was because of these that she desired his intimate companionship.

In this exigency he writes : "I was in a great strait how to treat so polite a gentlewoman, thus applying herself unto me. I plainly told her I feared whether her proposal would not meet with insurmountable objections from those who had an interest in disposing of me. However, I desired that there might be time taken to see what would be the wisest and fittest resolution. If in the meantime, I could not make her my own, I should be glad to be any way instrumental in making her the Lord's." Here seems to have been a mistake, growing out of an unwillingness to give his fair admirer pain. A decided No would probably have ended the suit. But this delay doubtless encouraged the lady and only added to his perplexities, which pursued him till he wrote as follows : —

My sore distresses and temptations I this day carried before the Lord. The chief of them lies in this. The most accomplished gentlewoman mentioned, though not by name — in a former passage of the Diary, one whom everybody sees with admiration, confessed to be for her charming accomplishments, an incomparable person, addressing me to make her mine, and professing a disposition unto the most holy flights of religion, to lie at the bottom of her addresses, I am in the greatest straits imaginable what course to steer. Nature itself causes in me a mighty tenderness towards a person so amiable. Breeding requires me to treat her with honor and respect, and very much of deference; but religion, above all, obliges me, instead of a rash rejection of her conversation, to contrive rather how I may imitate the goodness of the Lord Jesus Christ, in the dealing with such as are upon a conversion to him.

The lady was persistent, and he was still certain that the union must not be formed. He records again: "I did, some days ago, under my hand, beg as for my life, that it might be desisted from, and that I might not be killed by hearing any more about it." The lady had the "gift of continuance," and pleaded her desire for her spiritual welfare. Fear of losing hold of her as an inquiring soul seems to have kept him for weeks from ending the quest.

But his troubles were aggravated on another side. His friends, — father, parishioners, and others, — fearing there might be an engagement, made him wretched by their complainings. The strain upon his feelings is indicated in his diary: —

My grievous distresses, occasioned especially by the late addresses made unto me by the person formerly mentioned, cause me to fall down before the Lord with prayers and tears continually. And because my heart is sore pained within me, what shall I do, or what shall be the issue of this distressing affair?

One reason why the all-accomplished and charming young lady and her mother desired the union may be found, perhaps, in the following passage of the diary, and it is quite possible that Mather perceived it in time. On the sixth of March he wrote: —

That young gentlewoman, of so fine accomplishments, that there is none in this land comparable unto her, who has with such repeated importunity, pressed my respects unto her, that I have had much ado to keep clear of great inconveniences, hath by the disadvantage of the company which commonly resorted to her father's house, got but a bad name among the generality of people. There appears no possibility of a speedy recovery from it, be her carriage never so virtuous. By an unhappy coincidence of some circumstances, there is a noise, and a mighty noise it is, made about the town, that I am engaged in courtship to that young gentlewoman; and though I am so very prudent, and have aimed so much at a conformity with our Lord Jesus Christ, yet it is not easy prudently to confute the rumor.

He resolved, however, that the time had come for decision, and to make it known, and he did so in the following way : —

The design of Satan to entangle me in a match that might have proved ruinous to my family or my ministry, is deferred by my resolution totally to reject the addresses of the young gentlewoman. I struck the knife into the heart of my sacrifice, by a letter unto her mother.

There was a happy sequel to this singular suit. Mortified vanity at first led the disappointed ladies to threaten dire things to the invincible minister, but their better nature conquered, and they accorded to him the testimony of their high esteem. He was reproached by some and ridiculed by others it relation to the affair, but he had one great consolation. He writes : —

God strangely appears for me in this point, by disposing the young gentlewoman, with her mother, to furnish me with their assertions, that I have never done any unworthy thing; yea, they have proceeded so far beyond all bounds in my vindication, as to say that they will look on Mr. Mather, to be as great a saint as any upon earth. Nevertheless, the devil owes me a spite, and he inspires his people in this town, to whisper impertinent stories.

Here we might leave one of these satanic stories, if one of the most impertinent of them had not been repeated in print by the editors of Sewall's Diary (vol. ii). We will not honor it with reprint, for the charge of a "lie with circumstance" against Cotton Mather carries on the face of it all the marks of an invented falsehood.

The affair was rightly settled, but the strain upon Mr.

Mather's nervous system had been great, and he suffered severely in his health. He was moody in mind, and subject to depressions and temptations which he ascribed to the assaults of Satan. He was tempted to sin, and even to suicide; but he fell down into the dust on his study floor "with tears, before the Lord; and then they quickly vanish, and it is fair weather again. Lord, what wilt thou do with me?" "It is a scriptural truth that Satan takes advantage of bodily weakness and mental trouble to tempt people to despair of divine mercy."

The circumstances of Mr. Mather and his family of young children — four of them between three and fourteen years old — rendered another marriage almost imperative. His friends also urged him to marry again. He was as wise in his choice as when he sought the hand of the young and "well-accomplished" Abigail Phillips. In this affair he prayed for divine guidance and had his reward. His son Samuel wrote many years after on this wise : —

He looked to heaven to heal the breach that had been made in his household, and his petitions were abundantly answered. God showed him a gentlewoman, a near neighbor, whose character I give as I had it from those who intimately knew her.[1] She was one of finished piety and probity, and of unspotted reputation; one of good sense, and blessed with a complete discretion in ordering a household; one of singular good humor and incomparable sweetness of temper; one with a very handsome and engaging countenance, and honorably descended and related. She was the daughter of Dr. John Clark and had been the widow Elizabeth Hubbard four years when married to Mr. Mather, August 18, 1703. He rejoiced in her as having found great spoil.

Coming to the year 1704, the diary is missing except up to the twelfth of February. From this part only a sentence or two is drawn. Mr. Mather wrote that he was forty-two years old on that date. The day was spent in his

---

[1] She died when he was a little boy, only seven years old.

study with thanksgiving to God for sparing his life, and
for the astonishing mercies with which his life had been
filled.   The records of the church give nothing of special
interest.   Every occasion on which members were received was the cause of joy to ministers and people; but
such occasions make no history, while the trouble made
in excluding a single member will fill more pages than the
enrollment of a thousand who prove faithful unto the end.
As there is no record of sickness during the year, it may
be concluded that Mr. Mather preached as often as usual
at home and in other churches, and filled his place in
whatever councils were called.   His great work was growing on his hands, and his correspondence was extensive.

Queen Anne's war was still raging, and Marlborough
was beginning to exhibit his transcendent genius as a
general and diplomatist.   The contest between England
and France drew the American colonies into the fray,
and the enemy in Maine and Canada broke out in savage
hostilities on our frontiers.   In the preceding year Governor Dudley made an ineffective expedition against the
eastern Indians, and in this year the famous Colonel
Benjamin Church was in command.   Reference to this
war with the savages and their Catholic allies will be
made in a future page, when reviewing the censure by the
Mathers of the conduct of the governor.   The interest of
Cotton Mather in the welfare of the scattered plantations
at the eastward caused every incident in this war to be a
matter of thought and prayer.

On the twenty-eighth of April the initial number of
The Boston News-Letter, the first newspaper ever published in America, was issued.   The little sheet looks now
very insignificant, but its issue was the beginning of a
mighty force which has grown to titanic proportions.

One of Mr. Mather's first publications this year was

"The Armor of Christianity." In an anonymous volume of 234 small pages, he first detects the plots of the devil against the happiness of mankind ; then declares the many wiles by which he manages those plots ; after which he shows how those wiles may be defeated. The text is from Numbers 25 : 17, 18 : "Vex the Midianites and smite them : for they vex you with their wiles." Topic : "The armor of Christianity is needed to ward off the wiles of the devil." He writes : "I am entering into a contest with a very formidable adversary ; horror walks in state before him ; when he raises up himself, the mighty are afraid, and by reason of terrors, they run out of the way." Therefore he prays : "Remember me, O Lord God, I pray thee, and strengthen me, I pray thee, O God." He continues : "We must not imagine that one devil alone is able to vex all mankind with continual wiles ; a Manichean imagination ! Having read of the devil, we immediately read of wicked spirits in high places." As a specimen of thinking and writing nearly two centuries ago the following may be quoted : —

The first matter of observation that now lies before us is, that the great intention of the devil is, to plunge the sinful children of men into the same lamentable circumstances of yet greater sinfulness and wretchedness.

He inquires why the Satanic host entice men into sin and speaks of their many subtle wiles, and then suggests a guard against their plots : —

Good armor will do your business. First, for a *belt*, we must get acquainted with the truths of our holy religion. They will be to us as the girdle of our loins. For a breastplate, we must put on a righteousness that will preserve the vitals of our inner man. . . . For our shoes, the gospel of peace between God and us, must be so studied by us as to prepare us for all the difficulties of the rough, cragged and thorny way we have to go through.

He went on till all the arts of the "evil one" are exposed, all his lies detected, and all the ways to resist and overcome are made plain.

"A Comforter for the Mourners" came out in the early part of this year in thirty-four pages. The explanatory part of the title was : "An Essay for the undoing of heavy burdens, in an offer of such good words as have a tendency to cause glad hearts in those who are stooping under various matters of heaviness."

Then we have another issue which gives a glimpse of the times. The whole title is given with the exception of names and dates. It was "A Faithful Monitor, offering an abstract of the laws in the Province against the disorders, the suppression whereof is desired and pursued by them that wish well to the worthy designs of reformation, with some directions and encouragements to dispense due rebukes and censures unto all censurable actions. *Sic agitur censura.*" Also, "An Abstract of the laws," and "The Reprover doing his duty, uttered at Boston Lecture," and an "Abstract of the directions for a general reformation given in the Declaration of the great and general assembly, lately published." The work reveals to us the disorders prevalent at the time, with the laws against them ; the declaration of the government in aid of their enforcement, and the action of the pulpit in maintaining law and order.

The "Nets of Salvation" was published in New London, perhaps because it was the home of one branch of the Winthrop family, from members of which Mr. Mather often received aid in printing and circulating religious works. This was an essay in fifty-six pages, upon the "Glorious Ways and Methods of winning the minds of men into serious religion." This, like others of his works about this period of the author's life, was anonymous ;

perhaps because disparaging remarks were made by some in regard to his appearing so often in print.

The Baptists were making efforts in various places to lay permanent foundations, and the result in some cases was to divide Christian communities where they were scarcely able to maintain worship in one society. The Mathers, father and son, though firmly holding to infant baptism, yet were liberal and fraternal towards all Christian churches. They felt the importance of guarding their own folds from inroads of proselyters, while respecting the legitimate rights of all sects. Both of these divines united in the public services by which a Baptist minister was settled in Boston. But desiring that all should enjoy the privilege of dedicating their children to God, in accordance with nearly the whole of Christendom, in all preceding ages, they advocated the baptism of infants. This led to the publication of "Baptistes: A Conference about the subject and manner of Baptism, between C. M. and R. D." A second edition came out in 1724 with this remark: "The mischief which the Anabaptists are doing in the neighborhood, puts me upon abetting and assisting the design of some to reprint my Baptistes, and scatter where there may be occasion for it." In the dialogue, which is a fine specimen of logical argument, Mather holds that if the infants of the faithful were in the covenant of grace under the old dispensation, then they are still in the covenant; otherwise infants now are destitute of a great blessing enjoyed by those who lived under the Jewish economy. R. D. admits that the blessings for children in the old covenant were desirable. Mather then says: "Mind how I prove that the infants of the faithful, which were once under a dispensation that allowed them an interest in the covenant of grace, are not now under a dispensation that cuts them off."

He proceeds to show that infants now would be worse off than under the old dispensation, unless they are in the covenant, and then calls on the other party to show him a Scripture that gives such an intimation. This staggers R. D., as he could find no such passage in the Bible. Mather proceeds then to show that baptism is the seal of the new covenant, as circumcision was of the old. Nor does he fail to consider the mode of baptism.

In this connection may be placed a little volume of sixty-nine pages, called "A Tree planted by the rivers of water; or, An Essay upon the godly and glorious improvements which baptized Christians are to make of their sacred baptism."

"Faithful Warnings to prevent fearful judgments," "A Servant of the Lord not ashamed of his Lord," and "Le Vrai Patron des Saintes Paroles, designed for the instruction of our French captives," were thrown off by his rapid pen. The heart of Cotton Mather went out after all sorts and conditions of men. The French captives taken in the war must be taught the way of salvation.

Another title was the "Weaned Christian," with a suggestion of its purpose on the title-page, in these words: "Some things by which a serious Christian may be made easy when great things are denied unto him." His design was to make the "language of heaven in multiplied judgments upon the earth articulate." Every trial has a meaning, a voice, and our wisdom is seen in learning that message. Jeremiah 45 : 5 is full of instruction : "Seekest thou great things for thyself," etc. He tells us that a Christian, hoping for good things in another world, has reason to be content without the great things of this world. He then refers to things that are esteemed great by the worldly mind, as riches, honors, etc., and shows how these things are really small, and not satisfying,

compared with the things which make for our greatness
and peace; with many illustrations from history. Finally,
is not the glory of heaven a great thing? Yes. There is
the greatness of a kingdom in it. "Oh! when we come
to heaven, our God will do great things for us. O our
God, our God, how great is the goodness which thou hast
there laid up for us!"

In November, Mr. Mather preached a sermon, the general assembly being present, on the "Just Rules of Commerce." This was not published till the next year. "Lex
Mercatoria" is the title. In this he noted the "offences
against the rules of justice" in the dealings between man
and man, and bore testimony against all dishonest gain.
The spirit of the sermon may be inferred from the text,
which was (Ezek. 22: 13): "Behold, therefore I have
smitten my hand at thy dishonest gain which thou hast
made." All forms of dishonesty in private and public life
are fearlessly exposed. With characteristic courage, he
arraigns those who cheat the government as well as those
who take advantage of their neighbors.

Three of his rules of dealing are as follows: — 1. "I
am to deal with every other man as I would have another
man to so deal with me. 2. I am to deal with another
man, that the man with whom I deal, may be benefitted
as well as myself. 3. Let my dealings be such that I
should not he ashamed of their coming to the knowledge
of other men able to judge of the honesty of my dealings." He adds: "These rules are not only Christian,
but are applauded in the pages of the sober pagans.
Our little sons at the schools fill their themes with
them." One quotation from Ovid is given: —

Reddite depositum. Pietas sua fœdera servet.
Fraus absit; vacuos cædis habete manus.[1]

[1] Roughly rendered: "Restore what is entrusted to you; keep your engagements
with sacred fidelity; spurn fraud; let not your hands be stained with bloodshed."

He closes with these impressive words : —

They that work deceit, shall be no dwellers in that city of our Great King. I have read that an eagle violently struck his talons into a heavy fish, but the mighty fish plunged with the eagle to the bottom, who not being able to pull out his talons, was drowned there; and the fish, swimming to and fro in the lake, with his enemy fastened unto him, gave no little surprise to the adjacent monastery. Methought the story was a notable emblem of what befalls many nefarious dealers in the world. These birds of prey go to fasten their talons upon dishonest gain; but verily it plunges them down into that lake, from whence we read, the smoke of the torment ascends forever. Ah! worst of all fools! Wilt thou sell a soul, perhaps for a shilling?

The year 1705 seems to have been a season of great prosperity to the church. There were no cases of scandal that called for discipline, and the number of members received into communion was large.

The services of the junior minister outside of his special field of labor were in frequent request, while he was ever busy among his own people in all the modes of welldoing. Perhaps it will be well to follow him through the year, and note how he was employed from week to week, without classifying his work as pastoral or reformatory or literary, but all in succession, mixed daily with family interests and private devotions. The diary is in the library of the Massachusetts Historical Society. The publications not referred to in the diary are found by title in the list of Sibley.

The first sermon of this year, probably, was on the fourth of January, at the funeral of Mrs. Sarah Leverett, widow, or, in the words of the author, "once the honorable consort of John Leverett, Esq., who changed earth for heaven" on the second day of the month. Its title was "Monica Americana." It was followed by an "Elegy upon her Memory." She was an exemplar of female piety.

On the first of March, at that time the first month of

the year, Mr. Mather remarks : " The year begins well, and though a dispensation be ever so bitter, if it embitters sin unto me, and recovers me from the hazard of sin, blessed be God for it."

He had his customary days of " prayer with fasting " this year, and the record fills several pages, with the usual results ; but a few citations will answer our purpose.

March 9. His soul, this day, was full of contrition and abasement, because he took part with the holiness of God against himself. " But then, I cannot express the assurances with which the Lord irradiated me, that he would bring me nearer unto himself."

Sixteenth day. He cried unto God that his " opportunities to do good might be still rescued and preserved from all that might threaten damage to them." This was one of his anxieties, that injury to his good name might lessen his power to do good. Though his whole time, all the day long, was " spent in contrivances to do good," yet he was " cloggd by the indignity of evil people." He resolved, however, that he " would not abate his endeavors to be universally serviceable."

About this time he got out a book for Christianized Indians, to give them a better knowledge of the laws of the province. He made an " Abstract of the Laws," and had it " turned into the Indian language," and printed with the title, " Hatchets to hew down the tree of sin, which brings forth the fruits of death." The Indians were not citizens, and all the laws did not apply to them, but this abstract contained those by which the " magistrates were to punish offences among the Indians as well as among the English." There are twenty of these laws, each of which is followed by an English translation.

His interest in the well-being of the Indians led to two other publications in their language at this time. The

title of one was "Family religion excited and assisted."
It was prepared for Christian people, and had many editions down to the year 1740.   In one of the early editions
the Commandments were inserted, and the Lord's Prayer,
and a translation was carried forward on the opposite
pages.   This was substantially the "Family Sacrifice," of
1703.   The author says of one of the editions : "I printed
a thousand copies of them ; these I bound up in bundles
that had convenient parcels in them, and printed a short
letter to be added unto each of the bundles ; entreating
the person whose name I inserted with my pen to find
out what *prayerless families* there may be in the town
where he lives, and to lodge these essays of piety in
them.   So I concerted with some of my friends, a way
to convey a bundle to every town in all the colonies, and
some other places."   It was reprinted in Newport and in
London.

The third paper, of fifteen pages, relating to the Indians, was written to encourage effort for their benefit,
by stating the results of Christian labor among them.   It
was "A Letter about the present state of Christianity
among the Christianized Indians of New England."   It
was addressed to Sir William Ashurst, "governor of the
corporation for propagating the gospel among the Indians
in New England and parts adjacent."   It ought to be
reprinted to correct the false impressions still current on
the subject.   A few citations are given to vindicate the
truth of history.   After referring to the facts given in
the *Magnalia*, he says : —

There were in the southern parts of this Province, about four or
five years ago, — 1700 — no less than thirty several congregations of
Indians, who commonly assembled every Lord's day, and a great part
of them to Lectures on other days also, for the worship of the great
God, and our Lord Jesus Christ.

The number of Indians is not comparable to what it was fifty years ago. They were wasted in the war of 1675–6. Almost all that remain under the influence of the English in Massachusetts Province are so far Christianized, as they believe there is a God, and but one God, and that Jesus Christ is the Son of God, and the Saviour of the world.

Mr. Mayhew stated that "there are about one hundred and eighty families on his vineyard, and only two or three remain in their paganism." There were thirty-seven Indians who were the constant preachers of the gospel to them. Besides there were seven or eight English ministers who had learned the Indian tongues, and visited the Indian assemblies, and prayed and preached to them. Some new churches had recently been formed. In regard to the eastern Indians in Maine, Mather says that they were *Frenchified.* Measures had been taken to send them a preacher, but the design had been hindered.

A public thanksgiving was observed on the twelfth of April, for successes against the common enemy, thanks for success at the East, against the French and Indians, and also for the triumph of the English arms in Europe.

"May 4. Dear little Nancy — Hannah, about eight years old, — was again visited with a violent fever, and seemed near her end." He writes: "God sanctified the condition of that pretty and lovely child unto me." To the surprise of all, she recovered.

He records that a "glorious work of God" had been enjoyed in the "populous and vicious town of Taunton." A sermon by the minister of the town, relating to the event, was prefaced by Mather.

His help was desired at Sudbury, where, on the twenty-fifth of May, a "council met prejudices and prepossessions," and with little hope of settlement or union. He prayed and received light; upon which he made a suggestion to the council, which met their approval, and at their request he put it in writing. It was adopted. The fault was in the minister, who was censured and suspended.

Another trouble concerned himself more directly. "A very wicked fellow in the church at Woburn, applied to him to consider his case, with hope of relief." Mather advised repentance. The man then wrote a letter of lies to parties and churches to obtain a council. This was irregular, but it was held, and the man used it as a means of maligning, far and wide, the minister who had advised him to repent of his misdeeds. Mr. Mather hoped God would overrule the matter so that he could do some service far and wide, not in a few congregations, but in all the country.

He writes in June that much of his time was taken up with the affairs of "discomposed places." Not a day passed without employment and services. He was also a member of several societies; more than one or two whose business was to "devise good." But as he was "never easy unless he found himself bringing forth some fruit unto God," he had a reward in his labor.

One of the societies of which he was an efficient member was for the "suppression of disorders." It was composed of members from different churches. It was already large enough, but there "were many who would be glad to engage in the same design"; therefore he started two more such societies, one for the north, and one for the south, end of the town.

The Rev. Michael Wigglesworth died in June, and Mr. Mather preached a sermon at Maldon (now Malden), on the 24th. The title was "A Faithful Man described and rewarded." It contained "observable and serviceable passages in the life and death" of his friend; also "Memorials of piety left behind him among his written experiences." It had a second edition in 1849.

A sermon to a meeting of young men on the evening of the Lord's day, respecting "Parental wishes and charges," was published, and of these he gave away half a dozen or more every day, when making pastoral visits. The subject is expressed more fully in these words : " The enjoyments of a glorious Christ, proposed as the great blessedness which Christian parents desire for themselves and their children."

Here are some of his entries in the diary : —

> 8 d. 5 m.   With persons merciful that are,
> Thou merciful thyself wilt show.

He resolved to be merciful to all and to be sure to be kind to those who were unkind to him.

> 25 d. 5 m.   A thunder storm, and the lightnings were very fierce and quick. *Ps.* 18 : 13. " The Lord also thundered in the heavens, and the Highest gave his voice."

He asked himself for whom he should pray, for their preservation, for himself, or the two or three people in the town who persecuted him with malignity ? His heart immediately prompted him to pray for them.

> 27 d. 5 m.   Conceived the idea of preaching a course of sermons, and gather them into a Body of Divinity. The fulness of Christ, and the glory of Christ, to be the burden of it.

In the early part of September he attended a meeting of ministers, delegates from the several associations in the province, to " make Proposals in relation to Councils." In Dr. Clark's " Congregational Churches " it is stated that at a " meeting of the Boston Association, held November 5, 1705, sixteen ' proposals ' were drawn up and put forth for the consideration of the several associated ministers in the several parts of the country. Though couched in plausible terms, and embodying some useful hints, they were nevertheless repugnant in their general spirit to the Cambridge platform and the popular usage, or, as Rev. John Wise describes them : 'They seem a conjunction of all the church governments in the world, and the least part is Congregational' — the 'specter or ghost, of Presbyterianism — something considerable of prelacy '—'something which smells very strong of the infallible chair.'" Mr. Wise probably magnified the evils of the proposed changes, yet his work was needed, and its wholesome influence was great. Mr. Clark briefly summarizes the "leading ideas" contained in the sixteen "proposals" under three heads.

First, to give the ministerial meetings, which were then coming into vogue, an ecclesiastical character, by the introduction of business pertinent only to the churches.

Second, to combine these associations of ministers, thus ecclesiasticized, and enlarged, by a lay delegation, into standing councils, whose decisions in ordinary cases should be " final and decisive."

Third, to allow " no particular pastor or congregation to employ any one in occasional preachings, who has not been recommended by a testimonial under the hands of some association."

This last proposal is practically the usage of Congregational churches. If a church departs from it, by that act it becomes an independent church. Neither the first nor second proposal was ever adopted by our churches, in any convention or meeting ; but old records tell us that some associations, as late as the end of the last century, did " consider business matters which pertained only to the churches." It is not singular, perhaps, that endeavors have been made within a few years, and are still continued, to enlarge the functions of ministerial associations, and to bring in standing instead of *pro re nata* councils. Both movements are hostile to the spirit of true Congregationalism.

At the desire of the people, the author published
"*Mare Pacificum,*" a short essay upon those "Noble
Principles of Christianity, which may always compose
and rejoice the mind of the afflicted Christian."

Being desired in September to write on the topic of
"Christian Visits" and how to make them serviceable,
he prepared the "*Rules of a Visit.*" As the sermon was
preached by request, and as it met the desire of the
hearers, they united in sending it abroad. The author
states that he delivered the sermon after he had "exceedingly humbled himself before the Lord." He adds: "The
Lord was mightily with me." A "considerable number of
good men," who heard the discourse, proposed giving it to
the press. Of it he says: —

That the mercy of the Lord unto me, in this matter, may be the more
signalized, it was put into the hearts of the reforming societies, in this
town, to divide all the colonies of New England between them, and to
provide that at least a couple of the books be put into every town in
the country; one directed unto the minister of the place; the other
having upon it this subscription, *To be lent*. Thus I shall have another
glorious opportunity to glorify the Lord in every town throughout New
England. I shall serve the Lord in all his congregations, from one
end of the country to the other.

He also, about this time, "composed a scheme of erecting and supporting charity schools, and moved well-disposed people thereunto." These were to be "schools ·for
the education of poor children."

On the tenth of December a council was held at Watertown Farms, their "miserable condition requiring it."
On his way his calash was overturned and he was thrown
out, but received no injury. It was a complicated case,
and affairs were under a "woful entanglement." He
prayed to God and his "mind was irradiated." His suggestions to the council were agreeable, and his proposal

was approved.   A word may be said here in relation to
the frequent cases when Mr. Mather "prayed and was
guided or irradiated," as he reports.   There is a class of
persons who look upon this as fanaticism.   They regard
all believers in divine suggestion as narrow-minded and
enthusiastical.   There are others who believe that the
Scriptures give a full warrant to the conviction that
prayer for divine guidance will be answered.   Eitner the
sobriety and concentration of mind produced by prayer
directly leads to the best conclusions, or the direct influence of the promised spirit enlightens the mind in
regard to the given subject ; or both causes combine to
lead the mind to a right decision.   But whether the matter can be explained or not, those who are accustomed
to pray and to observe the results will continue to pray
on, in spite of all the philosophizing of worldly minded
men.

"26 d. 10 m.   Very cold season."   In the midst of his
comforts he thought of those not so well provided for.
His "soul was grieved for the poor."   He helped as he
could by the "hand of his wife."   This is the first mention of her in the diary after the marriage, and surely it
is one to her honor.   His own means were not enough,
and a young gentleman supplied him liberally for the help
and comfort of the poor.   This closes the record of the
year 1705.

But in the following curious speculation, under date of
November 9, Mr. Mather expresses his "idea of man in
his totality."   He doubtless had in mind 1 Thessalonians
5 : 23, "Your whole spirit and soul and body," and Hebrews 4 : 12, "Dividing asunder of soul and spirit," and
also the contest described in Romans 7 : 5.

The Oracles of God make a distribution of man into three parts:
The *Spirit*, The *Soul*, and The *Body*.

The Anatomy is admirable; the consideration of the distribution would be of no little consequence.

The *Spirit* is the notional mind, created and infused by an immediate operation of God.

The *Soul* is a vital flame, conveyed from our parents; the next seat of the passions; of so fine a temper, that it can strike the spirit, and yet of so gross a temper, that it can also move the body. 'T is the soul by which mere animals are actuated.

The *Body* is the obvious receptacle and habitation of those wonderful agents.

A man bitten with a *mad-dog*, has not only his body, but his very soul also poisoned. The poison seizes and pervades the nervous fluid. The ARCHEUS is all enraged. The sensitive soul has a canine fury now sensibly enraging it. The Spirit of such a man will cause him to say to his friend: " I would not hurt you; but half an hour hence my fit will come upon me; I shall then bite you, if you are in my way. I advise you to bind me fast, or keep out of my way." Notwithstanding this knowledge of the man, and this advice, yet when his fit arrives the Spirit must knock under, or lie fettered. The man will grin, and snarl, and bite like a dog, and his *dog-bitten* soul will show him the face of a dog in a looking-glass. He has drunk water in his thirst, but the water put his parched and poisoned glands to horrible torment. The poor *Spirit* of the man commends water to him again. He goes to drink, but the horror which his dog-bitten soul conceived at the exquisite pain which the water had given him, will by no means permit him to touch it. He perishes in his *Hydrophobia*.

There are numberless instances wherein the *affections* and the *aversions* of the Soul have the perfect mastery of the Spirit.

Well, the soul of every man is dog-bitten; or, what is as bad, serpent-bitten; or, devil-bitten. Original sin has depraved it; the venom of original sin has overrun it.

A regenerate Spirit; a sanctified Spirit chooses above all things, to glorify God and his Christ, and has gotten an empire over the Soul in doing of it.

Briefly, the Spirit of an ungodly man may refuse to gratify the criminal desires of his carnal Soul in many instances; but then, 't is always upon considerations that rise not above the level of carnality. 'T is either because the things will hurt his health, or blast his name, or sap his estate, or disoblige the friends on whom he has dependence; or, perhaps, as among the Catholics, he may purpose unto himself to work himself a righteousness. But if it once comes to this, — that

I may gratify the criminal desires of my Soul, and these also become violent and impetuous, and I may do it without any prejudices in the world, unto any of my secular pursuits : — But now, my Spirit abhors, rejects, denies these criminal gratifications of my Soul, only upon these [following] considerations : — " No ; the great God will see it, and be offended ; I shall ungratefully abuse the blood of my Redeemer ; the Holy Spirit that would seal me for the day of redemption, will be grieved ; I shall render myself unmeet for the inheritance of the saints in light." If by these pure considerations, (as also without proposing to make myself thereby a Righteousness) my Spirit has the force to go quite another way than my Soul would have it ; then I have, most certainly, a regenerate Spirit. The discovery of a regenerate spirit is not altogether so difficult as many may imagine it. This our Trial will plainly and surely discover it. If my *Spirit* will fly Godward and Christward, (as I find it will,) when my *Soul* raves to be going *sinward*, and they are not considerations fetched from *flesh*, but from God and Christ, that gave my *Spirit* the victory over my *Soul*, I have then a *Spirit* that is most certainly renewed by the Spirit of God. And though there may be particular instances in which the ferment of sin in my Soul, inflamed by furious temptations of Satan, may overthrow the choice and voice of my *Spirit*, yet the Spirit of God will never loosen the hold he has taken of me. This hypothesis a little solves the phenomena of the *dog-tricks* often found in some whom we still own for godly men.

CHAPTER XVI.

CHILDREN. — CHURCH. — PATRIOTISM. — PUBLICATIONS ON VARIOUS SUBJECTS : 1706–1707.

ONE author of a Life of Cotton Mather informs us that, though he sought for information from every available source, very little could be found about his life and doings outside of his diary. What more could he ask? The diary shows the reader the spirit of the man and his employment, nearly every day of his active life. From other sources, and in Sewall's diary, we find frequent mention of him, and in his scores of volumes we have not only the fact of his writing them, but occasional biographical items which enable us to trace his busy life of toil from boyhood to the end of his days.

The year 1706 was marked by his usual activity in all lines of authorship and of pastoral work. As he advanced in life he did not slacken his efforts to associate others with himself in care for the neglected and the criminal classes. For example, take the record of February 6 : "The several societies for the *suppression of disorders* with the society for the *propagation of religion*" met at his house, — about forty men, — where they spent the day in a religious fast, that they might obtain the blessing of heaven on their *essays to do good.*

Domestic trials were mingled in his cup. His little daughter Nancy was again brought nigh to death by a violent fever.

He notes "many great accessions to his library" of late years ; but now he had a great addition of many books from the libraries of the three Shepherds, all ministers; but their manuscripts, which also came into his possession, he esteemed more valuable than the books.

The "dispositions of his mind" relating to "having a great reputation in the world" are curious, and no doubt sincere. The record must be abbreviated. Instead of being desirable, such a reputation is to be deprecated. If one is proud of his reputation, he is guilty of idolatry, not giving glory to God. But if people could say, "The God of all grace has disposed that servant of his to do virtuously"; or, "The power and wisdom of God have carried that servant of his well through trials, labors, and sufferings," all would be right. He gives what he esteems "an encouragement" in these terms: "If a man often thinks 'What good may I do in this world?' God will bless the efforts of even very little men."

Some special points in relation to the education of his children will come before us in another connection. His eldest daughter, Katharine, was in her eighteenth year; Abigail was twelve; Hannah, nine; and Increase, seven; Elizabeth, first child by his second wife, was less than two years old. It was a critical period in the life of them all, and their education engaged the heart of the father.

At the same time "some special points" in relation to his flock weighed upon his mind. These will find a place when we come to consider his work as a pastor.

The forty-fourth year of his life began on the twelfth of February, and he credits himself with seventy-two sermons and lectures during the preceding year. He begins his new year with a statement of his daily occupations, for the use of his sons who might survive him, in thirty-one particulars. They show him unceasingly engaged in useful ways, though he bewails his slothfulness.

He also refers to his correspondence, which required

much attention. Correspondents in Europe, the West Indies, and America, besides family letters, demanded a ready pen. Some of his letters were long, and took considerable time in their composition.

His birthday this year was set apart in his study to praise the Lord for his favors, and to confess and bewail his sins. He was full of employments, and it was a satisfaction to him that God employed him in so many ways of usefulness.

In regard to his children, he writes that, at night, the last thing, he goes into his study, and on his knees confesses the mercies of the day with wonders and praises. He prays for any who have been instrumental in doing good. He prays for pardon to himself, and anew gives himself to God, so that if he should die he would be prepared. The consolation from this was "unspeakable and full of glory." He concludes: "Children do this, and you shall find it so." He states that he had not leisure to write a thousandth part of his thoughts relating to God and the spiritual and heavenly world.

One of his reflections was this: —

I see all creatures, everywhere, full of their delights. The birds are singing; the fish are sporting; the four-footed are glad of what they meet withal; the very insects have their satisfactions. 'T is a marvelous display of infinite goodness. He accommodates them with continual delights. Their delights are the delicious entertainments of his infinite goodness. His goodness takes pleasure, and is delighted with the delights of his creatures. Well, is there no way for me to resemble and imitate this incomparable goodness of God? Yes; I see my neighbors all accommodated with their various delights. *All* have *some*, and some have *many*. Now, I may humbly make their delights my own, and may rejoice in the delights which I see the goodness of God bestowing upon them. I may make their prosperity not my *envy*, but my *pleasure*. I may be glad at all the good I see done unto them. Oh! the glory; oh the glorious joy of his goodness! Lord, imprint this thy image upon me.

He resolved not to judge other people wrongfully, but rather pray, " Lord, preserve me from ever falling into such miscarriages."

On the eighth of March he "prayed with fasting " for a blessing on his ministry, his family, on the churches, and especially some very discomposed ones in the country; and also in referen̂ce to changes expected in the country. He adds this *Mem.:* " Prayed for the captives among the French and Indians.   Had some faith, — some assurance, that some would be gloriously delivered "; but his disappointment in one "famous case of particular faith " made him "shy of it."   Yet it (faith) made "illapses upon him," at times.

Sending Increase, his little boy, to school in the spring of this year, he wrote, every morning during several months, a lesson for him in verse, to learn, in addition to learning to read.   He took pains to write in a plain hand. After a while he thought it might be good for other children to have them, and so gathered them into a little book, entitled " Good Lessons for children ; or, Instructions provided for a little son to learn at school when learning to read."   A second edition was soon in demand. The original design of the verses was to have the " child improve in goodness, at the same time that he improved in reading."   A thousand copies of the first impression were sold in a week.

The young people to whom he preached a sermon about this time desired it for publication.   He gave it to them, with the title, " A Young Follower of a Great Saviour."

Observing that many " turned the doctrines of grace intʊ wantonness," he was led to preach and publish his " Free Grace maintained and improved ; or, a general offer of the gospel."   He designed to rescue from abuses the " illustrious doctrines of divine predestination and human impotency; and to render those doctrines highly useful to the designs of practical piety." His text was John 6: 37: "All that the Father giveth me shall come to me; and him that cometh to me I will in no wise cast out." After explaining the "doctrine of predestination," which, he says, is "free grace at work," he refers to the matter of "reprobation," to reply to objections, thus: —

Multitudes accuse the predestination of God as the cause of their impenitent unbelief. None but the elect shall be saved; I don't know that I am elected; if I am not elected, unto what purpose is it for me to seek to be saved? Idle words. It would be a very great sin, in the greatest sinner among us all, to conclude himself a reprobate. Reprobation is a secret thing. You have no direction to meddle with it. I am sure it is recorded, that every one of us ought to come to the Lord Jesus Christ with as much alacrity as if we were already assured that the Father had given us to him. Again, should a man be ever so wicked, it would be a further wickedness in him to desire himself a reprobate. . . . Let the chief of sinners among us be quickened in seeking and pressing after conversion to God. . . . I pray you; I charge you, let no one of you all, pronounce yourself a reprobate. But let every one of you fly away to God in the Lord Jesus Christ; accept his mercy; resolve his service; do it as cheerfully as if it were from heaven revealed unto you: "Thy name, O man, thy very name, is written in heaven." . . .

Men do not urge the decrees of God so injudiciously, so impertinently, so irreverently, in any inferior matters, as they often do in the matter of their salvation [as in seeking health, getting money, etc.]. There is no such decree as this, that the elect shall be saved, whether they work about their own salvation or not. Or that the elect may continue unconverted and unconcerned about eternal blessedness, and yet get safe into it at last. . . . Damnation overtakes no man but because he is a sinner. Reprobation by God enforces no man to be a sinner.

Although the theology of that day was fettered by the fatalistic dogma of the slavery of the will, yet the earnest ministers believed and preached the duty of sinners to repent and believe; and that salvation was offered to

all such.   Says Mather : "Salvation by the Lord Jesus
Christ is tendered unto every one of us all, and none of
us will miss salvation by that blood, but such as wilfully
refuse it."   Such is the tenor of the first discourse.

In the second, " Free Grace is exhibited in the gracious
offers of the gospel," a full and free and unlimited offer of
salvation is presented; and in the words of Christ, " Go
ye into all the world, and preach the gospel to every
creature," there is a universal invitation.   The author
inserts the following note : —

My dear friend, Mr. Bromfield, must be mentioned by me in these
memorials, as the great instrument to the printing and publication of
this book ; and unto him, and unto his family, all the service which he
has this way, or any other, done unto his people.

On the seventh of May Mr. Mather aided in settling
a church trouble at Malden, and on the twenty-third a fast
was kept by the North Church (the other good people of
the town joining) on account of the " distressed condition
of the American Islands ; our own danger; the captives,
and the excessive cold and rains of the season."   We
must not forget that the great war between France and
the allies, headed by England, involved the colonies in
distracting fears and distressing calamities.   Two years
before Marlborough had defeated the French at Blen-
heim, and this year, 1706, was marked by one of the
greatest battles in history, when the French at Ramillies
were again put to disastrous rout; but the time for peace
had not yet come, and our fathers still had to fear the
midnight raid of a savage foe, and contend with French
and Indian combined.

A poor state of health is not conducive to hard study,
but in some cases it is an incentive.   We find Mr. Mather
writing on the twenty-eighth of May : " Health poor " ;

and it caused him to "despatch at a great rate " his *Biblia Americana,* lest it would never be done. It was already a vast accumulation of illustrations, which would make two volumes in folio, or double the matter of the *Magnalia.* He solemnly gave thanks to God for his smiles on the undertaking.

"The Negro Christianized" was written in the early part of June. It was an essay to "excite and assist that good work, the instruction of negro servants in Christianity." He writes : " It is a golden sentence that has been some-times quoted from Chrysostom, ' that for a man to know the art of alms, it was more than for a man to be crowned with the diadem of kings ; but to convert one soul unto God, is more than to pour out ten thousand talents into the baskets of the poor.' Surely, to raise a soul from a dark state of ignorance and wickedness, to the knowledge of God, and the belief of Christ, and the practice of our holy and lovely religion, this is the noblest work that ever was undertaken among the children of men." This is the keynote to the little book of forty-six pages, which is an earnest plea for the Christianization of the negroes in families and in the community ; that is, bond and free. There is no escaping the grip and clinch of the reasons given. Assistance is suggested as to the mode of in-structing this class, and a plain Catechism is added. The Lord's Prayer, in sentences, is accompanied with a peti-tion. For example : —

Our Father which art in heaven.	Heavenly Father, thou art my Maker; help me to own thee as my Father; pity me, relieve me, as one of thy children.
Give us this day our daily bread.	Thou knowest what is best for me; Lord, let me want nothing that shall be good for me.

A few sentences may be quoted, as they show the design and spirit of the author : —

A work which my heart was greatly set upon; a work which may prove of everlasting benefit unto many of the elect of God; a work which is calculated for the honor and interest of a glorious Christ; and a work which will enrage the devil at such a rate, that I must expect he will immediately fall upon me with a storm of more than ordinary temptations. I must immediately be buffeted in some singular manner by that revengeful adversary. And the late calamities on the American Islands, I thought had a word in them to quicken my doing of this work. . . . My design is not only to lodge one of the books in every family in New England which has a negro in it, but also to send numbers of them into the Indies, and write such letters unto the principal inhabitants of the islands as may be proper to accompany them.

A noble trait of character comes out in the record of June 29. The diarist states that he was "much distressed because of the criminal action of some who unlawfully traded with the French and Indian enemies." It was war time, and the charge was that certain men of Boston and vicinity supplied the enemy with contraband articles, whereby the war was prolonged. Some of his relatives by marriage were suspected. Mather denounced this conduct severely, and what added to his grief, his good father-in-law, Colonel Phillips, justified his sons in the matter. No ties of relationship could induce Cotton Mather to excuse wrongdoing.

Near the end of June he went to Andover, "at the often request of the people, and preached to them a lecture." What was not an uncommon occurrence on such occasions, several young gentlemen very kindly accompanied him, which "added more than a little to the consolations of the journey." He notes a singular providence in the timing of this journey. It seems that a party of Indians from Canada made a raid on this section, so that he would not have dared to go if he had delayed a short time. When going, being desirous of doing some good on the road in the woods, he called some children to him whom he met there, gave them instructions and a little book. He heard afterwards that no little impression was made on the minds of the children and of the family. This family in a few days was visited by the Indians, who murdered the mother and some of the children.

Mr. Mather highly valued private meetings of Christians, and had several, of various kinds, carried on in his parish. He desired to have them "revived about the country." It appears from this and the following sentences that this had been a former usage. He wrote a "sheet" for this purpose, and it was printed with the title, "Private meetings animated and regulated; a short essay to preserve and revive the ancient practice of lesser services, formed among religious people, to promote the great interests of religion." This was "written at the desire of some who ask to be furnished with such instruments of piety." Ecclesiastes 4: 9: "Two are better than one." A Latin motto from Seneca follows, the idea of which is that the best and strongest societies are those in which good men, similar in morals, are joined together in close intimacy. This was printed in book form, though filling but a few pages. Mr. Brinley had a copy, but I could not find it in any public library. From a copy lent me by a friend I quote the following lines. They concur with many other things in the life of Cotton Mather, to show that most modern plans of doing good, that are judicious, were tried by our fathers and mothers long ago.

The little treatise begins with "remarks for animating and regulating private meetings." The writer says that "where such private meetings, under a good conduct, have been kept alive, the Christians which composed them,

have, like so many coals of the altar, kept one another
alive, and kept up a lively Christianity in the neighborhood."

Mr. Mather then gives scriptural warrant for such
meetings, and quotes "holy and famous Mr. Rutherford,"
who in a letter to certain good people gave advice and the
following suggestions : —

" 1. Conference and prayer meetings.   See *Isaiah* 2 : 3 ;
Jer. 50 : 4 ; *Mal.* 3 : 16 ; *Luke* 24 : 14, 15 ; *John* 20 : 19 ;
Acts 12 : 12."

It is then stated that " near seventy years ago, that is,
in 1636, private meetings of the faithful were held in a
renowned nation of Protestants"; probably referring to
Scotland.

This kind of private meetings, sometimes called "family meetings," were made up and conducted as follows : —

I.   About a dozen families, in the vicinity, meet, men and their
wives, at each other's houses ; once a fortnight or month, as agreed
upon.   Spend a convenient quantity of time in exercises of religion.

II.   Brethren begin and conclude with prayers, in their turns.   Sing
psalms.   Repeat sermons.

III.   Ministers now and then, be present.   Pray, instruct and
exhort.

IV.   Candidates for the ministry perform first service here.

V.   United prayer to ask blessings from Heaven on the family
where met, as well as the rest.

VI.   All bound in one bundle of love.   Mutually take and give
advice.

It is stated further that it had been "usual in many
parts of the land, for holy women, both elder and younger
ones, to have their holy meetings.   They prayed, and then
read things that the minister had furnished them.   All
was done with discretion and modesty ; and domestic
affairs were not to be neglected."

Sometimes whole days were spent together. Not too many were to be in any one meeting.

Young men's meetings had been "incomparable nurscries unto the churches." Great numbers of them had been "lately erected in London."

This little book is instinct with undecaying life and interest. The author had made full proof of these meetings in his own large parish, with happy results.

Under date of July 5 the diary says: "About this time, I preached a sermon to the great congregation, with the intention of promoting early piety. Then to a great meeting of young people on the Sabbath day evening." The young people desired it in print. The theme is thus stated: "The Joy of Heaven over them that answer the call of heaven; or, powerful and wonderful motives to repentance and early piety, fetched from the joy of heaven over every repenting sinner on earth."

"Lord's day, 11d. 6m. The Lord lately brought home to us between forty and fifty captives, though many were left behind." Mr. Mather was visited by many of them daily, and he improved his opportunity to give them books, and do good to them otherwise. They agreed to come to meeting on this day, and the Lord having "annihilated" him by an ill turn upon his health, assisted to glorify Him on the occasion. "We gave thanks together in the great congregation, and I preached unto them a sermon on the great things done by the Lord for them." The next day he wrote a collection of *memorials* relating to the captives; the marvelous displays of the divine Providence towards many of them, especially in deliverances; the means of their constancy under temptations to popery; and edifying poems written by some of them to confirm their children; and a copy of a Pastoral Letter written by a worthy minister (the Rev. Mr. Williams, of

Deerfield), "who is now a captive, (that so he may be doing service even when confined from serviceableness)." "Good fetched out of Evil" was the title, and the sale within a week was a thousand copies.

The failure of his *particular faith*, especially in one memorable instance, made such an impression on his mind that he often referred to it as a great disappointment. For example, he wrote in this connection : " I had a strong persuasion ; I would say, a 'particular faith ' (but having been once buffeted in that experience, I hardly durst any more countenance it), that I should yet see more captives returned." The probability was, from past experience and from the Indians' love of ransom money, that some would be returned.

His service on Sunday, August 22, was exhaustive, but perhaps not much more prolonged than usual. " I was engaged in almost continual speech from two to nine o'clock ; three hours in a vast assembly ; two hours with the young men in the evening." The intervening two hours were occupied in more private labors.

Mr. Mather was thankful that the Lord gave him a very great auditory on the Sabbath, and on the thirtieth of August he resolved, first, as he records it, that "I will mightily study to serve and feed such a vast congregation ; which indeed has none in all the land, comparable unto it ; few in the world. Secondly, that I will proceed upon the notable intention of exhibiting a glorious *Christ* unto the congregation, with discourses that shall rescue and ascribe unto him all the glory which belongs unto him, in all the Articles of our holy religion." We find here none of that decay of power and influence which some writers would have us believe came upon him after the witchcraft tempest. Certainly there was no slacking of activity for the good of others, and no loss of hearers and no narrowing of his field of labor. He writes that the Lord enabled him to glorify Him in many services : in *alms*, by *books*, by *letters*, and by *watchful discourse ;* and then to lose all remembrance of them, and press after more, as if he had done just nothing at all. *Nil credens actum, quicunquid superesset agendum.*

Near the end of August he rode to Reading, as he seems to have done at different times, and preached the Thursday lecture. And about the middle of September he made his annual visit to Salem, staying several days. His journey on the eleventh was " exceedingly accommodated both with a Christ, and company." He preached that day, and spent the days till Sunday in conversation with many friends, who " obliged him with very kind entertainments." On the Sabbath he addressed a great assembly.

In the latter part of this month, and the early part of October, he was busy in many ways. He announced in print his " *Biblia Americana*, an American Offering to serve the interests of learning and religion." He also wrote letters to gentlemen in Scotland and England, to " procure settlements of good Scotch colonies to the northward of us." Also, to most eminent men to promote a design of Christianizing the negroes. Also, to Sir William Ashurst, and by him to the parliament, to procure an Act for that intention.

Prophecy was a favorite study with him. He took up the *Millennial Question* at this time, and sent a book to a London publisher, with the title, " *Problema Theologicum ;* an Essay to develope a truth of great importance in the scope and life of Christianity, but hitherto too little received and understood by the Christian world." He gives what he conceives to be an " unanswerable demonstration that the second coming of our Saviour

will be at the *beginning* of the happy state which we are
to expect for the church on earth;" and then he explains the "true doctrine of the *Chiliad*" so as to
"answer and remove the prejudices which have usually
encumbered it."

"New Remarkable Discoveries of the Spirit of Quakerism" next occupied his teeming mind.   He writes,
September 6 : "The *wretched Quakers* have made their
addresses, and complaints, and clamors at home in England
against the country, which the ministers in London had
written about as if we had persecuting laws." Mr. Mather,
in reply, wrote to vindicate his injured country, and also
to "expose more and more the wicked spirit of Quakerism, and to demonstrate that their *light within* is a *dark,
feeble, sinful creature;* and that to set it up for Christ,
and God, (which is done in Quakerism) is a very horrible
idolatry." He sent the manuscript to London, but I have
not found the work, and Sibley remarks that perhaps it
was not printed. Those who judge the Quakers of New
England in the time of the Mathers by their peaceful
successors of the present day make a great mistake.

"The Man of God Furnished," published at this time,
seems to have been a new edition of "Supplies from the
Tower of David," with additions to meet new and pressing wants. Some of our captives had been seduced into
popery, and the design was, in part, to fortify those taken
captive by Frenchmen and Indians against apostasy.
The book comprised seven essays about seven dangerous
errors.

The seventeenth of October was a day of thanksgiving,
and his special action was to have his children — four
of them — successively come to his study, and observe
and mention to him the special mercies they had received
of God ; and he charged them in succession, to "retire

and give thanks unto the Lord, and beg to be possessed by the Lord."

Mr. Mather found that in his appeals to people of all sorts to set upon the practice of serious religion, they fearfully abused the doctrine of man's inability to turn to God and abide with him, until supernatural grace enabled them to do it. He wrote a treatise and had it printed immediately, with the title, "A Conquest over the grand excuse of sinfulness and, slothfulness; or, The Cause of God and religion pleaded against those who make their inability to do good, their plea for their continuance in the way of evil-doing."

On Wednesday evening, October 30, his first son by his second wife was born. He was named Samuel, the same name that the last son of his first wife bore. Samuel was the most frequent name in the Mather family. The boy lived to great age, and in scholarship sustained the honor of the name. On the Sunday next after birth he was baptized, and, says the father, was "lent to the Lord as long as he might live."

The next week he preached the Lecture, and the general assembly was present. The subject presented was the "horrid paganism and atheism in many of the plantations within the Province," and he hoped to awaken general interest in that great matter.

We have the following, dated the twenty-third of November: "In the course of this week the Lord granted (a harvest of many prayers) the safe and quick return of more than sixty captives, and among them, Rev. Mr. Williams of Deerfield, after nearly three years in captivity." He had married Eunice Mather, daughter of Cotton's brother Eleazar. Her sad fate was the cause of general mourning all through New England in the early years of the last century. Mr. Williams and

Cotton Mather now "counselled and contrived together how the Lord might have revenues of glory from his experiences." Mr. Williams preached the Lecture and the General Court attended.

Mr. Mather gave to the press a discourse, at the request of his young people, with the title, "The Best Ornaments of Youth ; An Essay on the good things that are found in some, and should be found in all good people, and which wherever they are found, Heaven will take a favorable notice of them." It was preached on the third of November, and published by a society of young people early in the next year. The text was 1 Kings 14 : 13, and the outline is as follows : —

I. What are the good things in some? II. What shall be done for them? About the "good things" of the king's son, the Jews tell us that Jeroboam set guards of soldiers to hinder the more devout Israelites from repairing to the worship of God at his temple. But this young man hindered the soldiers from doing that violence.

The sermon closes with a powerful appeal to young people.

Some of Mr. Mather's relatives were the causes of great trial and grief. About this time two brothers-in-law were the occasion of trouble. One was the brother of his wife, and the other was the husband of his sister Hannah. The first was a Phillips, and we have a hint of his enmity. The latter was John Oliver, who married Hannah Mather when she was seventeen years of age. For some cause, we are told, they treated their brother-in-law most wickedly. He asserts that he never wronged them, but only sought to do them good. It is quite probable that they hated him for his religious strictness. His sister, Mrs. Oliver, "was a most ingenious, sweet-natured and good-carriaged child." He calls her "child" because she was about eighteen years his junior. She loved him dearly, and it was a grief to her that he was badly treated by her husband. She had languished several years under an incurable malady, and at last, on the first of December, the "pangs of death came upon her. In her dying distresses, she kept calling on her brother Cotton, 'My brother! my brother!!' He prayed with her on this day six times." The bereaved husband, who had been unkind, then "with anguish, bore a most honorable testimony for her, as the best wife in the world, and a great example of piety. And from a convicted conscience, now spoke of her brother with no little pretence of honor and acknowledgment."

The fifteenth day of December was a day of thanksgiving. In the forenoon he raised the question, as a subject for preaching, and perhaps printing, "Unto what special flights of piety should the pious be awakened, by their being left to stumble in any points of iniquity?" In the afternoon he visited a society of devout women, keeping the day as a solemn thanksgiving. He prayed and preached with them, saying of this service that he was "perhaps the only man in the world who had preached to such an auditory."

A company of gentlemen, without any application from him, learning that he wanted a good servant, bought a negro, a very likely slave, for forty to fifty pounds. He named him Onesimus, and his first resolve was, "with the help of the Lord, to use his best endeavors to make him a servant of Christ."

A discourse delivered late in the preceding year was given to the public in the latter part of this year, and is worthy of notice, both for its subject and its treatment. It is called " *Vigilantius;* or, a servant of the Lord found ready for the coming of the Lord," from Matthew 24: 44. Seven young ministers had died within a few months.

These were all settled, and all appear to have been men
of a superior stamp. Some were of great promise. All
were godly and faithful. One of them was Rev. Andrew
Gardner, of Lancaster. The circumstances of his death
are alluded to in the following touching lines : —

God called him to work in a field of blood. The repeated incursions
of a barbarous enemy, in one of which their former minister, Rev.
John Whiting, was murdered, made it so. It [the field] began to
flourish under Mr. Gardner's cultivation. It began to think that it
might wither if he did not cultivate it. He acquitted himself most
literally as well as figuratively, a watchman to the garrison. One most
unhappy discharge of a musket kills him, and almost kills a whole
plantation with him. With his dying breath, he calls to the survivors,
" be ye also ready."

Passing into the year 1707, the diary will aid us to the
birthday of its author, February 12. Besides, there is a
fragment of a diary covering about three months — July
to September — of the new year. Supplies from other
sources will eke out the record of a busy, anxious, and
useful year.

The war was still in progress in the old world, and our
own frontiers were invaded by the French and Indians,
whose united skill and savage cunning caused the death of
many, while others were carried into captivity. No man in
the country felt a deeper interest in the grand cause which
was at stake in Europe, and no one had a keener solicitude
than Mr. Mather for the welfare of the men, women, and
children who were exposed to the midnight attacks of savages, more cruel and deadly than prowling wolves. For
these he prayed and preached and printed and raised money
for the ransom of the captives. Every sufferer looked
upon him as a friend. The prisoners in Canada and their
mourning friends at home turned to him for sympathy,
counsel, and help, and his fruitful compassion never failed.

In the records of the church it is written that ten were received as members on confession of faith, and an entry dated October 19 presents a notable case of discipline. "Mr. John Barnard, having given scandal, by the liberty he took of using the scandalous game of *cards*, when he was lately a chaplain abroad in the army, he this day made his public acknowledgment, which gave satisfaction to the people of God."

The diary, January 4, incidentally reveals his motive in keeping it. "To excite his sons to kindness and benevolence" he left a "brief reference to his *Alms-deeds*" this week. He had been in the habit of taking care of some of God's poor as the winter came on; but now thought he would help the "poor that had not the character of godliness." He found ten or a dozen persons, and gave them "some money, and the best advice he could, and left a little book to excite to serious religion."

Two days later he writes that one way of doing good was this: he wrapped up seven little distinct parcels of money with seven little books about repentance, and seven of the "Monitory Letter against profane absence from the public worship of God." He sent these things with an unsigned letter to a minister in Salem, where there was much laxity in Sabbath keeping, desiring the minister to disperse the charity in his own name, hoping thereby to ingratiate him more with his people. His reflection was this: "Who can tell how far the good angels of heaven may coöperate in these proceedings? And how far the Holy Spirit of God may make them serviceable for the best of purposes?"

He records on the tenth that his "father-in-law was in a very froward and stout frame." The reference is to the fact stated in last year's record, about illicit trading with the enemy. One of his sons had been detected, in

company with others.   It was thought by some that the
governor was indulgent to the culprits.   They escaped
prosecution before the courts, but the great and general
court took up the case and imposed a fine upon those
found guilty.   The circumstances filled the country with
a "mighty inflammation."   The fact that one of the de-
linquents was a relative made no difference with Cotton
Mather, unless to make him more strict to secure merited
penalty.   He felt it to be his duty with other ministers
to bear his testimony.   He did it as mildly and modestly,
though as faithfully, as possible, but the "humorsome old
man was enraged" at him.   He had fears that the matter
would injuriously affect the affairs of his first wife's children, who were heirs.   He had but one remedy, as there
was no speaking to the irascible old gentleman; so he
went to God in prayer, as Jacob did when his father-in-
law had done him wrong.   He prayed for divine direction,
that he might behave wisely, and for a blessing on each
of his abusive relatives.

After spending part of the seventh day of February in
private supplications, at the close of the day he went and
preached and prayed with a number of devout families,
who had spent a part of this day together in worship.

Mr. Mather closed the forty-fourth year of his life with
the mention of an unhappy experience.   "Many poor
servants of God have been strangely distressed with
temptations to *atheism* and *blasphemy*.   In this was an
evident energy of Satan"; but he had temptations of
another importance, with a "wonderful impetuosity."
He was not plied by Satan with any "grosser pollutions."
It was an "Idea" raised in his soul.   Possibly, it was
something in relation to the mode of God's being, the
trinity in unity, or something of that kind; but he gives
no hint of the great thing or "idea."   He was greatly

troubled, and prayed much for relief. "*Mem.* At the table of the Lord, flying to the Lord Jesus Christ for salvation from the guilt, and the power, and the presence of sin, I have been comforted with hopes that I shall yet see the favor of God." In the year preceding his birthday he had preached and lectured over seventy times.

Coming to the fragment of the diary, the first entry that I cull shows the writer "full of a variety of employ-ments." In a meeting of Christians he spoke of the unhappy condition of the frontier plantations, so irre-ligious and destitute of religious privileges. Some pres-ent offered to be at the expense to send and lodge in all their families a little book (if he would write it), agree-able to their condition. With the "singular assistance of heaven" he composed the book entitled "Frontiers well-defended; or, an essay to direct the frontiers of a coun-try exposed unto the incursions of a barbarous enemy, how to behave themselves in their uneasy station." He added a "Catechism to inform and fortify captives against the delusions of popery." He sent some hundreds of the Catechism by itself to Maryland, where there were many of that religion. The whole volume was over fifty pages. He sent out the little work with the modest hope that "it may be, the Lord will bless this essay for much good unto many poor people in a land of unwalled villages." The part relating to popery had for its title "The Fall of Babylon." The whole was addressed "Ad Fratres in Eremo," to "Brethren in the Wilderness," and was full of sympathy with the dwellers on the frontiers in the time of war and exposed to a savage enemy. He refers to their "notable deliverances, notable difficulties, and nota-ble dangers," and exhorts them to maintain religion and secure religious training to their children.

The matter of "particular faith" was continually coming

up anew in Mather's experience. His trouble appears
to have risen from his inability to discriminate between a
real intimation from heaven and a hope growing out of
his own strong wishes. It is too much for any believer
in Scripture to say that impressions are never made on
human minds by divine influence, in respect to coming
events; and on the other hand, no student of religious
biography can doubt that good people often believe that
divine or angelic impressions are made upon them, when
their expectations grow out of their desires. The inquiry
may then arise, What is the good of "particular faith,"
if it is not reliable? It may be replied that, perhaps,
whenever the Spirit of God inspires such faith, the result
will be answerable; and that in other cases, the disappointed party would do well to imitate the example of
Cotton Mather, and on this question "observe a most
exquisite caution." The above remark was suggested by
the following passage in the diary : " 13 d. 5 m." He did
not "know what to say of an *experiment*," under this date,
because of one certain case of *particular faith*, wherein
he was disappointed ; yet feared he might be losing something in distrusting *particular faith*. The case was this :
a brother-in-law (Phillips), master of a vessel, bound from
Barbadoes to Virginia, was supposed to be lost, and hope
of the safety of the vessel was about given up. But this
day, in pouring out his prayers before the Lord, he had
an "afflatus" that the man was safe and well. He "told
his consort " that was his belief, and "behold, on the seventh day after this, news came that the man had safely
arrived in Virginia."

July 24, Mr. Mather set his children to find what points
in themselves needed amendment, and resolve to amend
themselves accordingly. They were to report in the
evening "what resolutions they had taken up."

Being Fast day in the province, in reference to the miserable condition of the expedition to Port Royal, or Annapolis, and with the design of conquering Acadia, he offered to set himself to do something for glorifying God as the Hearer of prayer, or for the encouraging of prayer among his people, if God would grant a good issue to the expedition.

About this time frequent calls came to Mr. Mather for services away from home. On the eighth of August the Lord gave him a "comfortable journey to Salem, in company with his friend Mr. Mahew," one of the Mayhews of Martha's Vineyard. He preached in Salem on the Lord's day, and returned on Monday. On the second of September he attended a council at Hull "for the composing of difficulties. The troubles were most happily healed"; and his "poor tongue and pen were particularly employed in this work." On the tenth a new church was gathered in the south part of Braintree — the present First Church in Braintree. "The action was carried on with sensible effects, and affecting tokens of the gracious presence of the Lord." Mr. Mather "preached, and enjoyed a marvelous presence of the Lord." The people desired a copy of the discourse. Title: "The Temple Opening." It was not published till 1707. His topic was: "The Church as a Temple of the Lord" (Eph. 2: 22). "Every particular church of the Lord Jesus Christ is to be together built in the glorious Lord as a temple of God." On the sixteenth of this same month he "made a comfortable journey to Salem," that he might lecture at Beverly the next day. He was "much broken, and spent, and ill," but the Lord gloriously carried him through the work, so that he "preached with great flame and force," and his sickness left him.

In this month he fitted for the press his discourse on

"Manly Christianity." This was one of the "composures" which he sent to England, "commending his whole
work unto the conduct of heaven." It was not published
till 1711, but a brief note of it may find a place here. It
was a "brief essay on the signs of good growth and
strength in the most lovely Christianity; or, the marks
of a Christian become strong in the grace that makes him
one." Text: "My son, be strong." He writes: —

It is a conjecture which our Brightman, and after him, our Burroughs,
has upon the four living creatures, that four successive states of the
church were thereby denoted and predicted. First, the church was like
a LION, for the courage of encountering the persecutions of the Roman
and pagan emperors. Then the church grew to be like an Ox, for submitting to the heavy impositions of Anti-Christ. As the Reformation
came on, the church became like a MAN, and would no longer submit
to the yoke, nor take anything but what it sees reason for. Anon, the
church becomes an EAGLE, for high flights of Christianity. Churches
must now be more heavenly-minded, and soar up like the eagle towards
heaven in their dispositions.

"*Doctrine.* It is the concern of true Christians to
become strong in the grace that makes them Christians."
And the author shows at some length what are the marks
of a Christian strong in the grace of the Lord Jesus
Christ. Near the close he mentions three things to be
desirable in becoming a manly Christian: — 1. To be swallowed up in God, in Christ; 2. To be full of benevolence
and beneficence toward men; and 3. To have humility.

The closing passage in the fragment for 170⁷⁄ was probably written in the latter part of the year, as it appears to
be a general summing up of duty, and a believer's "covenant with a glorious Christ, in all things at the close of
the year." It is exceedingly rich, but too long to be
quoted in full. All his blessings, all his afflictions, all his
duties, all his joys and griefs; all his bereavements and
allotments and favors; all his relations to friends and to

enemies, to his wife, to his children, to the church; and all his hopes are to be considered in their relation to his glorious Christ.

In Mr. Sibley's list we find "Another Tongue brought in to confess the great Saviour of the world; or, some communications of Christianity put into a tongue used among the Iroquois Indians in America; and put into the hands of the English and Dutch traders, to accommodate the great intention of communicating the Christian religion among the salvages, among whom they find anything of this language to be intelligible." Sabin says: "Sentences in relation to God, Jesus Christ, and the Trinity, in the Iroquois, Latin, English, and Dutch languages."

"The Greatest Concern in the World" came out this year in a pamphlet of twenty-two pages. The design was to answer in a brief and plain way the question, "What must I do to be saved?" There was a second edition in 1718, printed at New London.

"Ornamental Piety," and "The Soldier taught what he shall do," met the wants of a class. The latter was reprinted.

An awakening discourse, of forty pages, was entitled "The Spirit of Life entering into the spiritually dead; an essay to bring a dead soul into the way wherein the quickening Spirit of God and of grace is to be hoped and waited for; and to prophesy over the dry bones in the valley of death such Words of the Lord as used to be the vehicles of Life unto them. *Ezek.* 37 : 2, 7." "In the conversion of a sinner, a dead soul has life conveyed unto it, and a dead sinner comes to live unto God." The dry bones, (1) can *hear* the words of the Lord; (2) can *meditate* upon them; (3) can *pray.* It was a tremendous and melting appeal to the unconverted.

"A very Needful Caution" was an essay against a "sin that slays its ten thousands," that is, *Covetousness;* with Antidotes (pp. 60). It presents the "character and condition of the covetous." Remark : "From a tang of covetousness, how are many children educated? The great concern of parents is, how to make the children rich? They are not concerned so much how to make them good and kind unto salvation. How are many matches prosecuted? The question is not, whether the parties are gracious and virtuous, but are they rich? This turns the scale upon all other qualifications. O sinful covetousness! Bare-faced covetousness! There can be no hiding of thee."

We close with a singular title : "A Treacle fetched out of a Viper." It is evidence of the unfailing ingenuity of the author in deriving instruction from every source. It is a "brief essay upon falls into sin ; directing how a recovery out of such falls may be attended with a revenue of special service and glory to God from the fallen sinner."

CHAPTER XVII.

NO diary of the year 1708 is known to exist. Mr.
Mather states at a later date that some volumes
were destroyed by his third wife, but those are supposed
to have been of years in which her life was blended with
his. Possibly his children or grandchildren may have lost
or suppressed some of them, but this supposition seems
improbable, as they would have been more likely to omit
parts than to have destroyed the records of a year.
Possibly some fragments are still in secluded existence.
The records of the church contain no items of importance, except the very welcome fact that the church was
enlarged by the addition of twenty members.

There is, however, enough matter to prove that 1708
was a busy and productive year of Mr. Mather's life.
The publications were as numerous and as well adapted
to the wants of the public as usual, and one or more
letters of his will show his relations to public men.

The *Justa Winthropi* was a sermon at the funeral of
Fitz John Winthrop, the governor of Connecticut, who
died when on a visit at Boston in November, 1707. The
following is a letter to John Winthrop, of New London,
a nephew of the foregoing. A notice of the sermon will
fitly follow extracts from the letter. The letter is dated,
"16 d. 10 m. 1707," or December 27.

SIR, If there be a family in the world which I have endeavored
always to treat with all possible service and honor, 't is the Winthropian.

If there be a person in that family, for whose welfare I have even travailed in agony, 't is you; whereof the walls of a certain *Bibliothe-cula* in the world, are but some of the many witnesses.

As I continue to wish all happiness to you, so I must now do it unto the vertuous lady whom you are making your consort.[1]

And, as from the beginning, you know you had all possible encouragements and commendations from me, to the match wherein I am now wishing you joy, so the late calamity I have suffered, by a cruel incivility offered me in England, cannot hinder me from all the dispositions of personal good will unto the family unto which you are becoming related.

But shall I not rather chuse to put my wishes into the terms the excellent Philip Henry would use to his new married friends: " *Others wish you much happiness; I wish you much holiness; that will make you sure of happiness.*" I am glad the duty I have done to the character and memory of your honorable uncle — late governor of Conn. — finds any acceptance with you. I confess freely to you that, contrary to my usual conduct on such occasions, (which is to stay till such a thing be desired by others,) I have myself desired, and I do again request, the publication of it.

I do it for a hundred reasons, needless to be mentioned. I will only mention one that comes after the ninety-ninth. Our paltry News Letter, when it reports the death of that meritorious gentleman, takes care that not so much as one honorable word shall be spoken of him, an omission like to which it was never guilty of, no, not when such a blockhead as old *White*,[2] of *Marshfield*, was to be spoken of. . . . I remember when *Johannes Brevis* mightily desired to be turned into an Angel, he met with a rebuke, and returned with this temper. *Homo sum, alienum nil hominis a me puto.* My desire to have you here, and to do what spirits do not, forbids me to wish your being turned into an Angel, (any further than the Angelical disposition of serviceableness to a glorious CHRIST will make you one,) but I heartily desire, (what I do indeed with pleasure see daily accomplishing) that you may be

---

[1] He was married on the day this letter was written, to Ann, daughter of Governor Joseph Dudley.

[2] This Peregrine White, who was born on board the Mayflower before the landing, has always been a kind of pet child to New Englanders, from the fact that he was the firstborn of the Pilgrims on these shores; but it appears that he was a man of little account, and his conversion in old age was a matter of wonder, his life had been so frivolous. It is pleasant to think that he worshiped the God of his fathers at last.

turned into your uncle; be a lover of your country, and inherit the *true spirit of a gentleman*. . . .

With my hearty service to the Major-General,[1] and his lady, I take leave to subscribe, Syr,

Your true Friend and Serv't, COTTON MATHER.

We turn now to the sermon at the funeral of the late governor, the third Winthrop who had borne that title. As he died in Boston, his funeral was attended there, and he was buried in the Winthrop tomb, in King's Chapel burying yard. He was in his sixty-ninth year. He does not seem to have been such a favorite with historians as were his father and grandfather, though nothing is recorded to his disparagement. I have heard a Winthrop of the last generation say that he had the name in the family of not being generous, but that may have arisen from the fact that he had no children, and that his heirs, perhaps, did not receive so much as they desired of his estate. But this is merely conjecture. Mather extols certain excellent traits, but is silent as to his religious character. He was certainly a man of ability, and probably he was the best military man in New England in his maturity. His training in the art of war, when a young man, was under the famous General Monk, in Scotland, under whom he marched as a subordinate officer when Charles II was restored.

The text of the sermon was Genesis 5 : 5 : "And he died." The subject was "Mortality considered," under which the preacher drew out the obvious considerations from such a subject. All must die; officers of all grades must die; ministers, magistrates, governors must yield to the common lot and die like the meanest of the children of men. In regard to his character and services the preacher said that General Winthrop was a "governor greatly and

1 Wait Still Winthrop.

justly beloved among his people." He was "buried with wondrous lamentations." Moreover, he had the "spirit of a true gentleman," and was "highly esteemed for his courteous way of treating all men, but especially good men, and old men, on all occasions; and for his patience, and patient and generous administration of the public affairs."

The sermon was printed in Boston in 1708; it had a reprint in Boston and London in 1709; and again in Boston in 1710.

Biographical and personal matters will fill a large part of the record of this year. On the eighth of August, "when mortality took him off," in the ninety-fourth year of his age, died a man as eminent in the sphere of scholarship and education as was Fitz John Winthrop in statesmanship. Indeed, but few men lived in New England in the first two generations whose memory is so green and bright as that of Mr. Ezekiel Cheever. Cotton Mather was one of his pupils, and he paid him the tribute of a learned and admiring scholar. He says : —

Out of the school he was *antiqua fide, priscis moribus*. A Christian of old fashion. An old New England Christian. And I may tell you, he was as venerable a sight as the world, since the days of primitive Christianity, has ever looked upon. He was well-studied in the Body of divinity, and an able defender of the faith and order of the gospel ; notably conversant and acquainted with the Scriptural prophecies, and by consequence, a sober chiliast.

Mr. Cheever taught first at New Haven and Salem, and then from 1671 to 1708 at Boston. Among his writings was an essay on the Millennium, and also a Latin grammar which went through twenty editions. Many fine scholars came out of his schools. Unto the end he continued "an unusual instance of liveliness, and his intellectual force was as little abated as his natural." Several editions of this funeral discourse were called for. It had a "poetical essay on the memory of my venerable Master." Among the editions, one is dated 1731, another 1774, and another 1828. It is common to this day in meetings of educators in Boston and other places of New England to hear the name of Ezekiel Cheever mentioned with peculiar honor.

"A Good Evening for the Best of Days" is a plea for the proper observance of the Lord's day evening, and contains information about the ancient custom as to the keeping of Saturday evening as part of the Sabbath. The quaint title is : "An Essay to manage an action of trespass against those who mis-spend the Lord's day evening, in such things as have a tendency to defeat the good of the day." The general assembly heard the sermon and the house voted to publish it. The question is raised, When does the Sabbath begin ? and the following is quoted as giving a view of ancient opinion not generally understood.

An aged person, more than forty years since, — 1668 — assured me, that he was once present at a very great convention of ministers, who were old Puritans and Non-conformists, and that they all declared themselves to be of that which is the common persuasion, excepting two or three of them ; and these were, (as I remember) those famous men of God, Mr. Dod, Mr. Hildersham and Mr. Cotton, who pleaded for the beginning of the Sabbath in the evening before it. Among the first pastors of these American churches, the venerable Mr. Allen, (as I have heard) Mr. George Phillips, of Watertown, and his worthy son, Mr. Samuel Phillips, of Rowley, were of the same opinion with the most of the Christians in other lands. But the rest of ours generally fell in with Mr. Cotton's argument, which was thought not easy to be answered.

This extract is from a prefatory address to the reader by Dr. Increase Mather. In the sermon (on John 20: 19) the preacher gives strong reasons for keeping Sun-

day evening, even if Saturday evening were holy time.
Mr. Mather utilized the evening of the Lord's day by
the "religious societies, especially of younger persons,"
who spent the evening in "repeating sermons, and in
praying, and singing of psalms."

The Indian wars, which had been draining the province
of life and treasure much of the time since the accession
of William and Mary, were attended and followed by a
low state of morals, as is always the case in time of war.
Drinking prevails in the army, and the soldiers bring
home the habit of indulgence. This has been the result
in all our wars from the beginning, with the exception of
the war of the rebellion, in which, with exceptions, the
soldiery maintained a degree of abstinence uncommon in
armies. In 1708 the evil of intemperance had become
alarming, and it was in reference to this that Mr. Mather
preached one of the first temperance sermons ever delivered in the country. Perhaps it was the first ever published. Its title was : " Sober Considerations on a growing
flood of iniquity ; or an essay to dry up a fountain of
confusion and every evil work ; and to warn people particularly of the woful consequences of the prevailing abuse
of rum."

Before closing the annals of this year, it is in order to
refer to the correspondence between the Mathers, father
and son, and Governor Joseph Dudley. This episode in
our minister's life might have been passed over by a mere
reference in a brief paragraph, had it not been made the
occasion of severe and unjust criticisms. Though on
all points referred to in Cotton Mather's letter he is
sustained by nearly all the New England historians, and
Joseph Dudley is held up as obnoxious to the charges
brought against him, yet in some biographies, which are
not rash enough to justify the governor, occasion is taken

to condemn the minister, as if it were a piece of daring presumption in him to arraign the chief magistrate. The proper place for the treatment of this matter is in the Life of Increase Mather, and therefore the reference to it here must be brief. The letter of the senior Mather was a compact, solid, terse, and terrible presentation of the unprincipled course of an able, politic, scheming man, who, though a son of one of the foremost Puritans, had joined the enemies of the old order of things in Church and State, set up by the fathers, had become a courtier, and made himself familiar with the corrupt practices of public men in the times of Charles II and Queen Anne, which even the strong arm of King William could not wholly control. Referring the reader to the Life of President Mather, I will give in this place a concise abstract of Cotton Mather's letter.

He begins by reminding the governor that he had written several letters to him in friendly style for the purpose of inciting him to favor measures such as the public good required. In these letters he had acknowledged all the laudable things in his excellency's administration, but his letters had been treated with contempt; shown to other people, yet unheeded by the governor. He now proposed to speak more plainly, and inform the governor of his misdeeds, and of the estimation in which he was held by the good people of the land. In doing this he would return good for evil.

He then reminds the governor that his appointment had been obtained partly by the influence of a letter which he (Mather) had written, which letter had been read to the king, who had the idea that it was from President Mather, who was much valued by his majesty. When that letter was written, the writer was under the impression that Dudley had repented of his complicity with

Randolph and Andros before the "righteous Revolution,"
and of his concurrence in the judicial murder of Leister
in New York.   It was his hope at that time that Dudley
would return to his country with the purpose of promoting
its true welfare.   On the contrary, he had come back with
a spirit of selfish revenge, and had so comported himself
as to deserve and receive the censure of those very near
to him in friendship and of those most eminent in the
province.   By a wise course he might have escaped a
troubled experience in office, and when his government
ended his epitaph might have been: "Them that honor
me, I will honor."

Mather attributes much of the maladministration of
the governor to covetousness.   This led him to sell offices
and commissions of the peace and wink at illicit trading
with the enemy and mismanage the war, so as to promote
private interests and personal ends.

> The main channel of that covetousness has been the reign of bribery
> which you, Syr, have set up in the land, where it was hardly known
> till you brought it into fashion.   When you were going over to ex-
> hibit articles against Sir William Phips, . . . you said you could put
> him in a way to make the perquisites of his government worth £1,200
> a year.   He did not understand that way, and said he was sure he
> must not be an honest man if he did so.   But you, Syr, have made
> the way now to be understood.   In the matter of trading with the
> enemy, the house of representatives did by their vote, several times
> over, generally declare that they could not clear you from that unlawful
> trade.

He then refers to the loose way in which the governor
— still a member of the Congregational Church — spent
his Sunday afternoons with his Episcopal friends, after
attending their service in the morning; and then speaks
of his hostile ways against "this poor people of God" who
adhered to the primitive order of worship.

Before the war broke out against Port Royal, men had volunteered to take the place and save the government from all charge; but their offer had not been accepted and the result had been great expense and loss.

Among other charges were the governor's abuse of the council; his frequent changes of opinion and plan, to the disgust of the councilors, and his violation of the public faith. He concludes with assurances of his desire to do all the good he could to the governor. " Finally, I can forgive and forget injuries; and I hope I am somewhat ready for *sunset;* the more for having discharged the duty of this letter."

The reply of Governor Dudley showed a spirit of resentment and disdain, as if the minister had forgotten his place to arraign a governor; asserted that some of the charges were about things his accusers did not understand; that other accusations could be explained, if they would come to him in a proper spirit, etc. This loftiness becomes ridiculous when we consider the birth, the education, the abilities, the reputation, and the character of the respective parties. A Puritan minister, like a prophet in the Hebrew commonwealth, was both a prophet of the Most High and a defender of the rights of the people, and it was his office to rebuke wicked rulers and espouse the cause of the poor and the oppressed.

The year 1709, which now comes under review, was a time of attempts and disappointments to the province and the neighboring colonies. As the Indians and their French allies kept up their system of raiding, it was felt as an ever-pressing necessity that their power should be broken by the capture of Quebec and the conquest of Canada. An address was sent to the queen by the General Court praying for aid to an expedition, the object of which should be the conquest of both Canada and Nova

Scotia. The address was favorably received. Ships and men were sent from England, forces were raised in New England, a fleet lay in Boston harbor several weeks taking in supplies; but nothing was really done, and the season passed away, leaving the people exposed to the incursions of the enemy, while smarting under the feeling that all they had done in getting ready for giving the enemy a telling blow was wasted. In all the agony of disappointment, they had to confront a heavy debt, incurred in getting ready for action, while the mourning for their dead fathers, husbands, sons, and brothers was a legacy of woe.

The diary for this year is more than usually full of "Good Devisings," as well as interior experiences. These are not available, but this is not so much to be regretted, since we are soon coming to a work which seems to comprise almost all possible methods and schemes of doing good, while the experiences of the closet were only a continuation of such as we have already enjoyed. After a few names, dates, and personal facts have been gleaned, we must look elsewhere for the life of our subject during this period.

The spiritual work went forward in the church whatever might be the distractions of the public mind and the personal involvements of the minister.

There was a case of discipline growing out of Quakerism. The record reads: "A man whose name was Miller, had been seduced into something of Quakerism. The circumstances had peculiar temptations in them." The matter was taken into consideration, but no conclusion was recorded, if it was ever reached.

An account of Boston, dated this year, states that it was "near two miles in length, and about three quarters of a mile wide in some places." There were four thousand houses, most of them brick, and about eighteen thousand people. The state of the population must have fluctuated about this period, for we read that the number in different years, not far apart, differed five or six thousand. Probably the census was not taken accurately. On one occasion the number was taken when many were out of town — a thousand or more — on account of uncommon sickness. This was one of those years. Between March, 1709, and March, 1710, there were 377 deaths; whites, 295; negroes, 80; Indians, 2; an increase of 88 over the preceding year.

It is noticeable that in all the "devisings for good" with which Mr. Mather's mind was ever teeming, there is no alloy of selfishness, nor does it appear that he ever conceived a plan whereby he might obtain office or money or honor for himself, but the good of others, as individuals or in society, was the motive that inspired his activity. Benevolence or good *feeling* did not exhaust his energies. It was beneficence or *doing* good that impelled him to exertion and sweetened self-denial.

The number of persons whom he aided was large, and they represented almost every form of suffering and privation. The aged — men and women; indigent students; widows, poor people, the sick, the insane, Indians, negroes, sailors, prisoners, the friendless, — all found in him a sympathizing friend. Aid went with his comforting words from his ever-open, but poorly furnished, purse. It was by the same spirit that he was enabled to aid his brother ministers and the churches. In the spring he spent a day with the church in Malden, where they had no minister; and when they had secured one, he preached the ordination sermon. At Reading when a fast was kept by the church, he was the preacher. In September he went to Bridgewater to preach for an aged and afflicted minister, Mr. Keith, on the Lord's day. These journeys involved time and expense, but he never hesitated on that account.

Early in the year he had a large accession to his library, and besides the volumes there were several hundred single sermons. Books seemed to gravitate to his shelves, as if there was their proper home.

In March he was afflicted with heartbreaking temptations. They took the form of doubt. He was tempted to regard the Christian religion as a ——, and did not dare to write what. A keen intellect questioning the foundation of all opinions and systems, when in a morbid condition from overwork or anxiety or ill-health, will probably account for much of the distressing skepticism which now tortured him. He resorted to prayer, and found relief by putting himself under the personal influence of God. Doubtless the distress of his mind was aggravated by the fact that he was in want of proper clothing for himself and his family, and of other things necessary to a comfortable livelihood. The weekly contributions may have fallen off, or he may have met with losses. His people did not always know his condition, and he was too sensitive to complain. This made the strain on his mind more severe.

On the sixteenth of May another son was born to Mr. Mather, to whom the name of Nathaniel was given six days later at his baptism. This corrects an error in published lists of his children, which place this birth at May 16, 1707. The last is a manifest error, as Samuel was born October 30, 1706, only six and a half months before. This child, Nathaniel, lived only to November 24 of the year of his birth.

In the autumn Mr. Mather drew out at length questions for the morning of every day of the week. The questions were minute in regard to the private and public duties of each day, thus furnishing a directory for the conduct of his life on a regular and continuous plan. Nothing was left out which was necessary to a complete dedication of soul and body to the service of God, and no minute appears to be left for recreation, or even rest, but what was given to sleep. His diversion was mainly change of work ; yet we learn from Sewall's diary and other sources that he was often in company, and that he received many calls, when his conversation was both instructive and entertaining.

One of the publications of this year was comprised in twelve pages, but it contained much matter. It was called " A Golden Curb for the mouth which with a headstrong folly, rushes into the sins of profane swearing and cursing." It was part of a volume later entitled " Batteries upon the kingdom of the devil." The following is taken from the little pamphlet, showing the profaneness of certain phrases which people used who were afraid to swear outright.

You disguise, you curtail, you abbreviate your swearing, as, *Dod*, and many other such strokes in the jargon of oathmongers. . . . This is a poor evasion. What is it that these fictitious words originally signify? In these mongrel oaths, your *Gedso*, is as much as to say, By God's soul. Your *Ods me*, is as much as to say, As God sees me. *'Slife*, is as much as to say, By God's Life. *Zounds*, is as much as to say By God's wounds. Yea, when you say, *Marry*, 't is By Saint Mary. And thus for the rest.

" A Christian Conversation with the great mystery of Christianity ; the mystery of the Trinity in the one infinite and eternal God, practically improved and applied, and plainly brought into the life of Christianity," made a small volume of fifty-five pages. The motto expresses the author's idea of the practical use of the doctrine of

"Three Divine Persons in One Being. *Ipsa visio Personarum Divinarum perducit nos ad Beatitudinem.*" Text, I John 5 : 7; cited by Cyprian in the middle of the third century; also by Tertullian and Jerome.[1] He held not to three substances, but three subsistences. " The divine essence, which is but one, does yet subsist in three relative properties. These are three faces or aspects of the Godhead, which is the old Jewish term for this unfathomable doctrine." He then shows, with the glow of a real Christian, the practical influence and value of the doctrine of the Trinity. It is not a mere speculation. It is not a mode of being which a creature can understand. It is a revealed fact, and a fact which has a rich meaning to a believer. It brings God near to the soul as a Father; it reveals God in Christ to us as a Saviour, as Emmanuel; as God with us, emphatically; and it shows us God the Spirit, as the very life of our souls, creating us anew, and carrying forward the new life unto perfection.

"The Cure of Sorrow," "The Desires of a Repenting Believer," and an "Essay on the Streets of the Holy City" belong to this period, but I have not seen them. The first was in Brinley's Library (pp. 46). The other two are noted in Samuel's list. They are referred to here as showing in how many ways and by what felicitous topics Mr. Mather tried to comfort, improve, and delight the Christians of his day.

One of our author's very useful books was his " Family Religion urged ; or, Serious Considerations offered to the reason and conscience of every prayerless householder, with plain directions how the Gift of Prayer may be sought by persons of the meanest capacity." To this was added a selection of "choice hymns," upon extraordinary occasions, "collected from the works of eminent"

---

[1] This text is omitted in the Revision.

English ministers. It had three editions, in which the title was somewhat varied. He speaks of the " shameless neglect; yea, the woful decay of household piety, and the fearful aspect which this impiety has upon us."

First, we have thirty *considerations* in favor of family prayer. Every one of them clamors for quotation. It would seem that no Christian at the head of a family could resist the appeals to maintain household worship. He opens in this way : —

Since all men are to acknowledge God in all their ways, does not every society owe religious acknowledgments unto God? Or, is it not a profanity for a people in a formal society, never, as such, to express their dependence on the blessed God for his blessings? But is not a family the very first society that by the direction and providence of God, is produced among the children of men? And for such a society *never* to *unite* in acts of piety, is it not a most unnatural profanity and impiety?

The following are the seventh, eighth, and ninth considerations : —

7. If grace be in the heart, can it be long before prayer is in the home? 8. Have we no family sins to be pardoned? No family wants to be supplied? No good things in our families to be thankful for? 9. Did ever any man in his dying hours repent of his praying with his family?

This is followed by "plain and short directions" how the gift of prayer may be sought by persons of the most ordinary capacity. A study of the directions would help any praying man or woman to pray in the presence of others. They are to think of what they have to be thankful for; of what they want; of what wrong they have done; of what duty has been omitted; of the greatness, holiness, and mercy of God. Use the language of the Bible in prayer. I have never seen a book of the kind equal to this in the cogency of its reasons and in its helpfulness to one having the spirit of prayer, but shrinking from its performance.

The decease of the Rev. John Higginson, the "aged pastor of the church in Salem in the 93d year of his age, who went from the earthly Salem to the heavenly," December, 1708, was the occasion of a sermon, which was published early in this year. Mr. Higginson was the son of the first ministe. of the church, and was worthy of the name. The discourse has the title, "Nunc Dimittis, briefly descanted on ; the happy dismission of the holy believer from the work of earth to the joy of heaven." Mr. Higginson is styled the "venerable and memorable servant of Christ." Lord Brougham said that it added to the bitterness of death to think of having Lord Campbell write one's biography ; but it was on the other hand a privilege to be embalmed in the appreciative and scriptural sentences of Cotton Mather.

Sailors as well as landsmen were the objects of Mr. Mather's care. His "Sailors' Companion and Counsellor," a little work of sixty-two pages, was adapted to meet the religious needs of the "Tribe of Zebulon," and to awaken the "mariner to think and do those things that may make his voyage prosperous."

Next we have an essay entitled "Work within Doors," to assist serious minds in self-examination, "conversing with themselves, and communing with their own hearts." Having his eye on the youth as well as the children of his charge, he set before them "Youth in its brightest glory, directing them that are young in age, to become strong in grace, by the word of God abiding in them." This was printed by the desire of a religious society of young men who heard it.

The preaching and publishing of Mr. Mather in 1710 went on with the usual variety and prolific vigor. One

small work of about 200 medium-sized pages has had
many editions, and is eminent in its way. A brief note
on its republications may be interesting. The book was
thus entitled : —

> Bonifacius : An Essay upon the Good that is devised and designed
> by those who desire to answer the great end of life, and to do good
> while they live ; a book offered first, in general, unto all Christians, in
> a personal capacity, or in a relative; then more particularly, unto
> magistrates, unto ministers, unto physicians, unto lawyers, unto school-
> masters, unto wealthy gentlemen, unto several sorts of officers, unto
> churches, and unto all societies of a religious character and intention.
> With humble proposals of unexceptionable methods to do good in the
> world.

The running title, and that by which the book is now
known, was " Essays to do Good." This contained 199
pages ; an appendix relating what had been done for propagating religion among the Indians, enlarged to 206 pages.
The edition of 1710, Boston, was succeeded by how many
in the eighteenth century I have no means of knowing.
It was published in 1805, in 108 pages, by the American
Tract Society. Under the title, " Essays to do Good,"
and addressed to all Christians, private and public, " improved by George Burder," an edition came out in Boston
in 1708, from the latest London edition of 1797, in 148
pages. The same, with additions from Edwards, Sir
Matthew Hale, and others, from the latest Boston and
London editions, was published in Johnstown in 1815.
Another edition, with an introductory essay by Andrew
Thomson, D.D., minister of St. George's, Edinburgh, appeared in 1825, in Glasgow, Edinburgh, Dublin, and London, in 214 pages. The same appeared at Dover in 1826;
also at London in 1842. The Massachusetts Sunday-
school Society issued it in 1845, in 304 pages, with an
appendix, in all 315 pages. This edition is printed from

the original with no additions from editors. That of Burder, which is said to be "improved," is really injured and stripped of much of its strength and beauty by almost numberless changes of words and expressions. The reader who may take it up should never attribute it to Cotton Mather. The testimony of Dr. Franklin to the worth of this work is the more weighty with some because he did not sympathize with the author in his views of religion. He wrote as follows, in his old age, to Dr. Samuel Mather: —

When I was a boy, I met with a book entitled "Essays to do Good," which I think was written by your father. It had been so little regarded by its former possessor that several leaves of it were torn out, but the remainder gave me such a turn of thinking, as to have an influence on my conduct through life; for I have always set a greater value on the character of a doer of good, than any other kind of reputation: and if I have been, as you seem to think, a useful citizen, the public owes all the advantage of it to that book.

I had the intention of giving an abstract of this remarkable book, but it is so crowded with good matter that an epitome would require too much space. As briefly as possible I will say that the dedication to Sir William Ashurst and the preface, like all the rest of the work, bear the unmistakable mark of Mather's hand. The whole is divided into twenty-two sections, with a conclusion. The first section opens with these words: "Such glorious things are spoken, in the oracles of our God, concerning them who devise good, that a book of good devices may very reasonably demand attention and acceptance from them that have any impressions of the most reasonable religion upon them."

In the third section we read how the saints of old sweetly sang, "I was glad when they said unto me, Let us go into the house of the Lord." "Thus ought we to be glad when any opportunity to do good is offered unto us. We should need no arguments to make us entertain the offer; but we should naturally fly into the matter, as most agreeable to the divine nature whereof we are made partakers. It should oblige us wonderfully. An ingot of gold presented unto us, not more obliging."

After many weighty remarks in a most vivacious style, we come to this point in Section X: "First, let every man devise what good may be done for the help of what is yet amiss *in his own heart and life.*" Next, what can a man do "to render his relatives the better for him?" Here come in duties of husbands, wives, parents, children, brothers, sisters, masters, servants; of all in the family relation; with directions for each and all. Then come suggestions as to the best methods of helping the poor by kindness and sympathy, by employment and alms, by religious influences and prayers.

In the thirteenth section the question is asked: "How can we leave the offices of good neighborhood, without interposing a proposal to animate and regulate *private meetings* of religious people for the exercises of religion? . . . The man that shall produce and promote such societies, will do an unknown deal of good in the neighborhood. And so will he that shall help forward another sort of societies; namely, *those of young men associated.*"

Next in order came sections setting forth at length the duties of *ministers* to devise and do good; of *schoolmasters*, to teach and govern so as to give the best possible training; of churches to become more holy, more exemplary, more prayerful, more benevolent, more kind to the poor, more liberal in sending the gospel to the destitute; of *magistrates.* Under this last head we have an account from Basil of an ancient governor, "that he was a most exact observer of justice; but very courteous and obliging, and easy of access to the oppressed ; he was equally at leisure for the rich and for the poor ; but all wicked people were afraid of him ; he abhorred exceedingly the taking of a bribe ; and his design, in short, was to raise Christianity unto its pristine dignity." Physicians, lawyers, officers of every grade in civil and military employment, shipmasters — all have their special duties and opportunities, which are specified. Next, almost every form and mode of removing evils, and doing good by associated action, are anticipated in these methods of Mather. It would seem as if he had been inspired to teach mankind how to bless one another by entering into the spirit of Christ and imitating his example. The work closes with these words : —

I will conclude with a testimony that I shall abide by. Were a man able to write in seven languages; could he converse daily with the sweets of all the liberal sciences, that more polite men ordinarily pretend unto; did he entertain himself with all ancient and modern histories ; and could he feast continually on the curiosities which all sorts of learning may bring unto him; none of all this would afford the ravishing satisfaction, much less would any grosser delights of the senses do it, which he might find in relieving the distresses of a poor, mean, miserable neighbor ; and which he might much more find in doing any extensive service for the kingdom of our great Saviour in the world; or anything to redress the miseries under which mankind is generally languishing.

Though this book is nearly two hundred years old, it is not obsolete nor dull nor useless, but it is full of common sense, rich in invention, surcharged with divine wisdom and benevolence; and it is, moreover, written in a free, lively, and entertaining style, enlivened by wit and redolent of learning. It should rank with the best writings that gave luster to the age of Queen Anne.

The relation of the young to the church as the *spes gregis,* or hope of the flock, was ever resting on Cotton Mather's heart. It was evinced anew by his "Chris-

tianity Demonstrated, in a sermon to my young men,"
spoken in October, 1709, but published in the present
year. It was an "essay to consider the sanctifying work
of grace on the minds of the faithful, as a noble demonstration of the truth of our holy religion." It was an
appeal to all classes, but especially unto young persons to
seek after God. 1 John 5 : 10. He says: "I am undertaking to produce witnesses unto the truth of Christianity. I shall be able to say, the witnesses are at hand.
Hundreds of witnesses are now appearing, 't is to be
hoped, in our assembly." Quite a number were added
to an already large church this year. "A true Christian
has from the work of the Holy Spirit on him, a witness
within himself of the truth of Christianity." He guards
this statement in a way to give it force.

A little work of thirty-six pages, which I have not
found, on a subject which perhaps no other pastor ever
approached, had the sacred and tender title, "Elizabeth
in her holy retirement." It was written to "prepare a
pious woman for her lying-in, or, maxims and methods of
piety to direct and support an handmaid of the Lord who
expects a time of trouble."

At this date Mr. Mather received the title of Doctor
of Divinity, which in those days was a great and rare
honor and one highly prized. On the twenty-fifth of
December he wrote a letter "To the truly honorable and
venerable rector, and others of the University of Glasgow, acknowledging the degree of D.D." That he was
gratified by this recognition of his merits is evident from
his reply and from the preface to his Life of his father,
"The Parentator." None at home could deny his merits,
but some were mean enough to withhold the honor which
he had fairly earned from the renowned University of
Glasgow. It was therefore doubly pleasing. The degree

was accompanied by letters which informed him of the high esteem of scholars and divines in the old country. The honor was attended with a "signet ring," which some of his friends advised him to wear, for the singular reason that it would be in compliance with the fifth commandment, "Honor thy father and mother." The ornament would thus not be an exhibition of vanity, but of filial piety rather. His son remarks: "The Doctor therefore would wear this ring, and made this action, so seemingly inconsiderable, a great engine of religion." It may seem trifling to make ado about wearing a signet ring when college honors are so plentiful and so little esteemed by the public; but even now the reception of such degrees excites so much envy that a considerate man would not carry about his badge unless he had reason, sound or plausible, to justify the act to himself. The son proceeds: "The emblem on the Doctor's signet is a tree, with *Psalm* 1: 3, written under it, and about it, *Glascua rigavit.* The cast of his eye upon this, constantly provoked him to pray, 'O God, make me a very fruitful tree, and help me to bring forth seasonable fruit continually.'"

Another beautiful title of a volume of eighty-five pages was "The Religion of the Morning." It was made up of two utterances at different times. and had relation to religion in early days — the "morning of life." The descriptive title was: "Man eating the food of angels; the gospel of the Manna to be gathered in the morning." Exodus 16: 21: "They gathered the manna every morning." It was enforced "with diverse, and famous, and wondrous examples of early piety; especially, the surprising history . . . of a late son to the physician of the king of Prussia." In reading this little work one can but regret that change of fashion or style in writing prevents its being reprinted by thousands. Manna was gathered in the morning: so with the morning of life. The heavenly manna is for the young. "When young gentlewomen are very pious, and unto all sorts of endowments add this, that they mind religion, and set a bright example of religion, this is their truest beauty, but it puts a beauty on religion too."

The death of a daughter of Judge Samuel Sewall, who was a personal friend of Dr. Mather, though a member of the South Church, was the occasion of a lecture on "Divine Consolations." Job 15 : 11 : "Are the consolations of God small with thee?" The essay was dedicated to the judge. It shows that the consolations of God are abundant and rich. 1. Consolations in the *promises* of God ; 2. in the *pleasures* of piety ; 3. in the *assurance* of hope. The Spirit of God is the Comforter of them that belong to him. 4. Most blessed consolations in the *heavenly* blessedness. These consolations are great 1. in number ; 2. in their nature ; and 3. in their duration.

The "Theopolis Americana" (American City of God), "An essay on the golden street of the holy city," was a sermon to the General Court and dedicated to Judge Sewall. It was a "testimony against the corruptions of the Market place ; with some good hopes of better things to be yet seen in the American world." It brightly exhibits the tendency of the author's mind to rise above the material to the spiritual. "Pure gold in the market place." Revelation 21 : 21 : "The street of the city was pure gold." Not lined with mints and treasuries of bullion, but things infinitely richer. "Glorious things are spoken of thee, O thou city of our God!" "The street be in thee, O New England. The interpretation of it be unto you, O American colonies." He would have the market place of every city and town in America governed by the strictest rules of honesty and godliness.

Dr. Mather was what he styled a "sober chiliast," a believer in the *millennium*, but free from wild imaginations. He looked for the coming of Christ to enlighten the world and bring great multitudes into the church. He supposed that the set time had almost come.

We have a world of reasons to believe that the second woe is passing away, and that we are entering into the seventh day of the Romish Jericho, and that black (but oh! let it be brief!) time, when the vials of the wrath of God, and the most woful plagues that ever were heard of, are to be poured out upon the Anti-Christian world. When that fearful dispensation is over, *then*, *then* that state of the church on earth which will answer the description that is here given of a new Jerusalem [will appear]. There will be a time when Jerusalem shall be literally rebuilt; and people all over the world shall be under the influence of that holy city.

The late Earl of Shaftesbury was animated by this same expectation, and his words often remind one of Cotton Mather, who goes on to describe the ideal city. One feature of it is as follows : —

The " golden street " indicates that all the business in it will be honest, sound, unalloyed by wrong, — in a word, pure gold. All proceedings, transactions, bargains, will be golden ones, or godly ones, in the market.

CHAPTER XVIII.

MANIFOLD LABORS AS PASTOR, CITIZEN, PHILANTHROPIST, AND AUTHOR: 1711–1715.

FROM the records of the church in 1711, we cite a singular cause of discipline, one which I have not met with elsewhere, which may be noted: "John Brewster, having given scandal, by assisting a soldier in deserting from the camp, his repentance and confession was this day — 12 d. 6 m. — publicly offered to the church, and accepted."

The full diary of this year gives us what little aid can be derived from published extracts, and a few names and dates.

We find Dr. Mather carrying forward all sorts of charitable work whereby different classes of people might be benefited, while giving special attention to his children. To show the variety of interests that engaged him, take the following summary. He was now (February 12) forty-eight years old, and in his full vigor.

In March he refers to the education of his son Increase as a matter of prime importance. The lad was now twelve years old, bright, healthy, mercurial, and full of joyous life, but needing guidance. He was the only living son of his mother, and very dear to his father's heart. Of course he must have the best education the province could give him and then be a minister, if God so pleased. Yet for some cause, perhaps something in the boy's temperament, the diary betrays no plan of the father to prepare the son for the ministry. However that might be, it was needful that his education for usefulness should be attended to in time. The young girls — "little girls" he calls them — must be taught housework. This included Lizzie, who was seven, and probably Hannah, who was fourteen. Katy was a young lady of twenty-two, and Nabby had seen seventeen years, and both were doubtless skilled in housekeeping, according to the training in good households in the olden time. At the end of April the father baptized the infant Jerusha, named after Aunt Jerusha Oliver. About here comes in a little scene between two of the young children — Lizzie, seven, and Sammy, five. The boy was cross to the sister, as boys will be. His punishment was to see his sister eat some cake while he had none. He felt sorely and cried, when the little girl, sister-like, with tearful eyes, gave him a part of the cake. Such a scene has lasting influence.

This is a glimpse of home life; but Mather cared for others outside of his family. He invited the children of the parish to his house to be catechized, and they came. He was so gracious in his ways, and so adapted his lessons to the young, that they loved to come. This man had not only clerical authority, but personal attraction.

It was, from the first, considered the duty of the clergy to visit the schools, and about eighty years after this date the duty was put into the Constitution by the pen of John Adams. This duty was esteemed a privilege by Cotton Mather; therefore he took time from his pressing engagements to inspect the schools of the town. He also attended to the support of the grammar school, which included in its course of study preparation for Harvard college. Nor was this all; for in September he was engaged in starting a charity school. I have somewhere read the strange assertion that where the Mathers lived they exerted no influence to elevate society and promote progress. The record of every day of their adult lives refutes the rash statement. At the same time that he was looking after the welfare of the homeborn, he actively favored the formation of a society among the Scotch settlers, whereby their moral and spiritual interests might be promoted.

Cotton Mather anticipated the Seamen's Friend Societies more than a hundred years by taking a personal interest in the sea rovers, and their wives and children, many of whom were in his congregation. Besides, he wrote books for them, and placed them in vessels when they sailed, for the entertainment and instruction of the crews. He also sent some of his practical works to Scotland for free circulation.

In March, May, and other dates, he kept vigils. These began when his family retired, and were kept till near morning, when he was alone with God; and maybe with angels.

In March his mother was seventy years old, and he noticed the event with special marks of honor to one who was worthy to be the daughter of John Cotton. His annual journey to Salem was taken in September, where he preached on the Sabbath, and probably on Lecture day, as was his wont.

Among his numerous correspondents this year was Dr. Francke, of Saxony, famous in his day for learning and for evangelistic work; and also Daniel De Foe, celebrated in all countries where boys can read, and booked for a passage to endless fame.

And all the while Dr. Mather was doing good by advice, by sympathy, and by gifts, beyond his means, to worthy, or, mayhap, unworthy, objects of charity. He believed in doing good to sinners, and he denied himself that he might have the means.

The works of nature were, in his theology, the works

of God, and advancement in knowledge of these works drew him into more intimate communion with his Creator and Preserver. To this mode of learning and teaching the attributes of God he devoted his thought and his pen.

Several war vessels came from England in the spring of this year, and Dr. Mather took pains to be acquainted with the officers and endeavored to "engage them in works of piety." They belonged to a great fleet sent over for the conquest of Canada. In the preceding year Colonel Nicholson, with six English vessels, thirty New England vessels, and four New England regiments, had taken Port Royal. The place was named Annapolis, in honor of Queen Anne. The new expedition was composed of fifteen ships of war and forty transports, under the command of Sir Hovenden Walker, attended by a battalion of marines and by seven veteran regiments under General Hill, who had seen war on a great scale under Marlborough. Its design was to capture Quebec and add Canada to the British dominions. This fleet lay in Boston harbor from June 25 to the thirtieth of July, taking in colonial forces and supplies. The expedition proved a disastrous, if not a disgraceful, failure, owing in part to the incapacity of the commanding officers. The only advantage it brought to Boston and the province was the money paid for stores; but this was many times overbalanced by the loss of life and the wasting of substance. But there was a set of politicians just then at the head of the government in England, of whom the gifted but unprincipled Lord Bolingbroke was chief, who cared little what became of Canada provided they could retain power and pay. He had stopped the splendid career of Marlborough on the continent, and hoped to obtain popularity by a brilliant campaign in Canada. The failure, however, was a disgrace to himself and his party and a bitter result for the province and all New England. There was a passion for the conquest of Canada. No men felt the result more keenly than the Mathers, because they had in mind all the captivities and murders which had come from the incursions of French and Indians, and none more clearly foresaw what sufferings would still come from the same source.

Another calamitous event made this a sorrowful year to the people of Boston. This was the great fire in October, when a considerable part of the business portion of the town was consumed. This is not the place for particulars, but it concerns us to notice the connection of Dr. Mather with it. On the fourth of October he preached a sermon on the fire that had raged the two preceding days. His text was Numbers 11 : 2 : "He called the name of the place Taberah : because the fire of the Lord burnt among them." The title was : "Advice from Taberah, preached after the terrible fire, which, attended with some very lamentable and memorable circumstances, laid a considerable part of Boston in ashes." According to his wont the preacher ascribed the calamity to the holy providence of God in rebuking a sinful people ; and he directed a "pious improvement of so calamitous a desolation." The running title was : "The Voice of God crying to the city."

A narrative that used to thrill the hearers round the winter fireside was the occasion of an "Essay of profitable reflections." John Dare and a company, shipwrecked on a desolate rock on the northeastern coast, had "surprising distresses and deliverances." These called for "awful and useful consideration." Other remarkable occurrences were added, making a little book of about fifty pages. The title was "Compassions Called For";

and it was adapted to affect the heart and awaken an interest in those who "go down to the sea in ships."

The "Memorials of Early Piety" is a choice little work, relating the "holy life and joyful death" of his sister, Mrs. Jerusha, wife of Peter Oliver. It gives some account of her "Christian experiences, and extracts from her reserved papers." He thus speaks of her : —

> She had a great felicity in a more than ordinary strength and sharpness in her eyesight, being able to read by such a dim light as others could not, for which she was thankful to God, and made a good use of it. She became from her childhood a notable mistress of her pen, wrote a fair hand, and rarely misspelt a word in all that passed her hands. She was to her father his amanuensis, and could read his ordinary hand and characters; and transcribed many of his printed books for the press.

One who has tried to read the manuscript of Increase Mather must wish that she had rewritten them all. She kept a diary, and seldom let a day pass "without entering some or other; that was an aspiration of serious piety." Her husband was a goldsmith, a "virtuous young man, one of good reputation for a skillful artist in his calling, as well as for his piety, with whom she was likely to have lived happily, he being very tender of her." She was a true woman, bright, sweet, kind to the poor, devout, and happy.

The following exhibits a phase of ancient New England life, showing how Christian families looked to their ministers in times of bereavement. The Hon. John Foster and his wife having died, his religious family kept a day of prayer, when a sermon was preached to them by Dr. Mather. It was styled "Orphanotrophium, or, orphans well-provided for." It set forth in lively colors the care taken of the children by divine Providence when their parents are removed, with "advice to both parents

and children, that the care of heaven may be more con-
spicuously and comfortably obtained by them."

The adaptation by Dr. Mather of all his discourses to
the condition of the afflicted was evident in the above, as
well as in the following "Persuasions from the terror of
the Lord," spoken "15 d. 2 m.," on Psalm 50: 3: "Our
God shall come." It is a masterly discourse, but I can
give only the motto on the title-page, and a few words
addressed to the parents. The occasion was the "sudden
death of a lad, crushed to death by a cart falling on him."

Sic Deus vias nostras considerat, et gressus dinumerat, ut ne mini-
mae quidem cogitationes, ac verba minutissima, ejus judicio indiscussa
remanerant.

> Quantus tremor est futurus,
> Quando judex est venturus,
> Cuncta stricte discussurus?

"God so considers our ways, and numbers our steps,
that not the smallest thoughts, or least words, may escape
his scrutiny."

> What a trembling there will be,
> When the awful Judge we see,
> Judging all things strictly![1]

Address to my dear friends, that were the parents of the child,
whose death gave life to the following sermon. When the glorious
Lord of our lives took away your lovely son in such a sudden and
awful manner, you religiously said, the *Lord has taken away*. And
you had a thousand considerations to quiet you under such a dispensation. Among the rest, one was the dutiful and delightful behavior of
this child unto his pious, gracious and holy grandmother, who died but
a little while before him, and on her death-bed expressed her satisfaction in him.

A sermon pertinent to any period seems to belong to
this year. It was an "Earnest Exhortation to the children

[1] Dr. Mather is not responsible for this free translation.

of New England to exalt the God of their fathers." The text was taken from the Song of Moses (Ex. 15 : 2) : "My father's God, I will exalt him." The topic is in these words : "The children and posterity of godly parents are under special obligations to exalt their fathers' God." He first exhibits the ways of exalting God, and then presents the obligations to do it with clearness and with cogent application. The following fact is cited as an incitement to imitate the fathers of New England in exalting God, the great Father. A preacher to the parliament, in company with the assembly of divines in Westminster, showing how the fathers of New England honored God, said that he "had lived in a country seven years, in which time he never saw a beggar, nor a man overcome with strong drink, nor did ever hear a profane oath. What happy country was it, think you? It was New England."

Nearly all that can be learned of the life of Cotton Mather for the year 1712 must be derived from his published writings. Those were numerous, and on topics of immediate and practical importance. It may be noted that the *Biblia Americana*, in six huge manuscript folios, was completed, except as additions were made from time to time, in the course of reading, so that the author could turn his mind to other studies. But as his father was now seventy-five years old, and beginning to feel the weakness of age, the larger part of pastoral duties fell to the junior.

A case of discipline had a peaceful solution. William Colman was restored to fellowship, and allowed to seek membership in another church. It is supposed that this was the name of a man who had been very hostile to the pastor.

It is said that the practice of reading the Scriptures in public worship began about this time, in the Congregational churches. In the service of the English Church it was arranged that portions of the Bible should be read every Sabbath. This was specially needful when Bibles were few, and large numbers were unable to read. But after the publication of King James' edition, Bibles were more common, and the greater part of a Puritan congregation could read their Bibles at home. But the reading of Holy Scripture greatly enriches the service in the house of God. One of the peculiarities in the worship in Brattle Street Church was Scripture reading. Probably it recommended itself to other churches, and thus came gradually into use. The exact date of its introduction into the Second Church has not been found.

A matter of great interest to the whole congregation began to be agitated about this time. It was the formation of a new religious society and church at the north end. The matter was in abeyance all the next year, but the church was not organized till early in 1714. It may be noted here, however, that Cotton Mather manifested a friendly spirit throughout, as the pages of the diary for 1713 fully show. But Dr. Increase Mather was troubled by the movement, perhaps because he could not see the need of another church in the neighborhood; yet he did nothing unbecoming his years and position. The junior pastor has been recklessly censured as if he was in opposition to the enterprise, when in fact he was friendly to it and cordially assisted in the formation of the church.

His connection with public events this year calls for no special mention. We may believe that his pastoral duties were zealously performed; that his work in the study was incessant; that his correspondence was large; that he aided all needy applicants for help; that he was "devising" wise plans for the benefit of others; that he kept his vigils and fasts, as aforetime; that he had his trials from evil spirits and unfriendly men ; that he had blessed compensations in prayer, and that his family shared in the affections of his warm heart in the usual abundant measure.

Fourteen writings, at least, saw the light in the year 1712, besides letters and prefaces. They would make up a volume of more than 600 pages in ordinary octavo, pica. Some of these will be briefly referred to, showing as they do the variety with which Dr. Mather entertained his large and intelligent congregation.

One was entitled " Awakening Thoughts on the Sleep of death," in which a tribute was paid to the memory of some that slept in Jesus, especial reference being made to Mrs. Mary Higginson. He showed the meaning of that lively metaphor, "the Sleep of death," the nature of sleep, and the method by which we may enter into a happy rest, when we fall asleep.

Not only were sailors proper the objects of Mather's special interest, but the fishermen who abounded in the north end had in him a friend. We have " The Fisherman's Calling," with a preface addressed to the gentlemen who employ the fishermen. It is a " Brief Essay to serve the great interests of religion among our fishermen, and set before them the calls of their Saviour, whereof they should be sensible in the employments of their fishery." He says of it : " I have here done something like what Peter did ; I have girt a fisher's coat about me. Your fish don't always come so soon as you would have them ; you must bait and wait : your patience must be exercised. In like manner, you must be willing to pray and wait for the desired mercies of God."

We come now to what has been called a Christmas sermon ; one of the earliest — perhaps the first preached from a Puritan pulpit, in New England. It contained this caution, which was sadly needed by keepers of Christmas in those times: "We lay the charges of God upon you, that if any people take *this time* for anything of a riot-ous tendency, you do not associate with them in their ungodliness. The grace of God in sending us a great Saviour, calls for more pious acknowledgments." It was preached on the twenty-fifth of December, and bore the title: "Grace Defended; a censure on the ungodli-ness by which the glorious grace of God is too commonly abused; containing some seasonable admonitions of piety, and concluded with a brief dissertation on that case, whether the thief on the cross be an example of one repenting at the last hour, and on such repentance, received unto mercy."

A mortal sickness raged in Connecticut, and the many deaths of "our brethren there" occasioned "Seasonable Thoughts upon Mortality." Mather was always inter-ested in the affairs and fortunes of this colony. Perhaps he remembered with satisfaction the call he had received, when a very young man, to become the pastor of the important church in New Haven. His intimate friend-ship with some members of the Winthrop family residing in New London fostered this interest in the college, churches, and people of Connecticut.

Perhaps this had something to do with writing his "Repeated Warnings, an essay to warn young people against rebellions that must be repented of; with a pathetical relation of what occurred in the remarkable experiences of a young man who made a hopeful end lately at Lyme, in Conn." To this was added a "Copy of a letter to the author" from the father of the young man, M. G. (Matthew Griswold).

His "Grata Brevitas, a Winter Sermon," was an "Essay to demonstrate that a few words may have much comprised in them, with the most weighty matters of religion"; and his "Pastoral Desires" expressed the "excellent things which a *true pastor* will desire to see approved, and practiced, and abounding among his people." This was designed to be left in families as he made pastoral calls, and was adapted with the author's usual felicity to its purpose. Both of these writings — one of 20, and the other of 116, pages, evinced the wide scope of Cotton Mather's ministry. Nothing escaped him which could be utilized for the good of individuals or the public. We cease to wonder how he could hold the minds and hearts of the congregation as we become familiar with the ingenuity and fertility of his mind and the glowing fervor of his spiritual nature.

It is often said that the resurrection of Christ is the point of attack by unbelievers, in recent years, as they have been driven by the progress of study from every other ground. If they can disprove that, the whole edifice of Christianity will fall. But Mather realized this in his day, as keenly as any in ours. His "Reason Satisfied, and faith established; the resurrection of a glorious Jesus demonstrated by many infallible proofs; and the holy religion of a risen Jesus victorious over all cavils of its blaspheming adversaries," is a compact presentation of the whole subject in forty-seven condensed pages.

If Dr. Mather were on earth now, he would not be incited to publish so often and on such a variety of subjects; but in his time there was a dearth of books adapted to the religious wants of the people. Those that were in vogue were in volumes of considerable size. Tracts were few, in comparison with the deluge of them which now overspreads the land. Therefore he poured forth a stream of sermons, tracts, and little books, for the sake of doing good, regardless of the effect on his reputation as a clergy-

man or author.   In this spirit his " Soul well-anchored ;
a little manual for self-examination," was given to the
public, "to assist a Christian in examining his hopes
of future blessedness."   Prefixed was a short hymn to
" assist the pauses of self-examination."

There is a poetic beauty in many of his titles, as, for
example, " Thoughts for the day of rain "; two essays :
1. " The Gospel of the rainbow, in the meditations of
piety on the appearance of the bright clouds with the Bow
of God upon them ; and 2. The Saviour with his Rainbow,
and the covenant which God will remember his people
in the cloudy times that are passing over them."

In like manner, depicting the " hard way of transgress-
ors," he does it in a " True Survey and report of the
Road," wherein he is able to show all the hardships of
the road that leads to death.

It is admirable with what a variety of address he studied
to interest the young.   Here are three brochures : two
at the close of this year, and one at the opening of the
next.   The title of one is " The Ways and Joys of
Early Piety," with a testimony against some "errors
which many of our children run into."   Another is "The
young man spoken to," which inculcates the "maxims of
early religion."   This was preached on a special occasion,
the death of good Peter Oliver, whose wife Jerusha,
Mather's lovely sister, died a year or two before.   The
third was "The A. B. C. of religion ; lessons relating to
the fear of God, fitted unto the youngest and lowest
capacities."   Appended are " Instructions for children in
verse," and the " Body of Divinity Versified "; the whole
filling about 120 pages.

1713.   A diary for this year, beginning on the author's
birthday, February 12, remains.   A few passages have
been printed in Peabody's Life of Cotton Mather, and

perhaps in other books. Free use has been made of these.

From this year on to the close of Mather's ministry, the average of admissions to the church about twenty-five per year.

The project of forming a new church — the New North — was carried forward, and a meetinghouse was built, though the church was not organized. It was hard for the senior pastor to be reconciled to the dividing of his congregation, and, quite naturally, he felt a reluctance to part with many to whom he had ministered many years, as they grew from childhood to manhood and old age. Possibly he felt mortified by the apprehension that they withdrew because tired of his ministrations; but there is no proof of any such loss of interest in his labors. There was actual need of a new society and house of worship, as the event proved, for the accommodation of an increasing population. Ministers sometimes fail to see such a need, and thereby hinder the growth of churches. The younger pastor seems to have had a better understanding of the situation.

The Mather meetinghouse was either enlarged or preparations were made to enlarge it at this time, and "galleries of the second range" were added. Fourteen were dismissed to help build the new meetinghouse. Probably a building society was formed before a church was organized.

Some items relating to family matters may be grouped together, though they occurred at different dates. In February there were prospects of the espousal of Katy, and also of a sister. This must have been a second marriage, as all his sisters had been married previous to this time, except one, who died in infancy. It was doubtless the marriage of Maria, whose first husband was Barte

Green. She was united to her second husband, Richard Fifield, November 6, 1713. The acquisition of a new brother-in-law and relatives put Dr. Mather, as usual with him, upon "devisings" to do them good. His beloved Katy was now about twenty-four; and, though attractive and accomplished, she died in maidenhood, of consumption, a few years later.

This was a year of great family affliction. Mrs. Mather was taken sick. The measles were prevalent and she became a victim. It was noticed that the perils of childbirth were aggravated by that disease at the time. Twins, Eleazar and Martha, were born, but died in November. On the eighth day of that month appears the following [1] in the diary: —

When I saw my consort easy, and the measles appearing with favorable symptoms upon her, I flattered myself that my fear was all over. But this day we are astonished at the surprising symptoms of death upon her, after an extreme want of sleep for divers whole days and nights together. To part with so desirable, so agreeable a companion! a dam from such a nest of young ones too! Oh, the sad cup which my Father hath appointed me! God made her willing to die. God extinguished in her the fear of death. God enabled her to commit herself to the hands of a great and good Saviour; yea, and to cast her orphans there too. I prayed with her many times, and left nothing undone that I could find myself able to do for her consolation.

On Monday, 9 d 9 m. between three and four in the Afternoon, my dear, dear, dear friend expired. Whereupon, with another prayer in that Melancholy Chamber, I endeavored the Resignation to which I am called. I cried to heaven for the grace which might be suitable to this calamitous occasion, and carried my orphans to the Lord. Oh, the prayers, for my poor children! Oh! the counsels to them now Called for!

10 d 9 m. In the midst of my Sorrowes . . . the Lord helped me to prepare no less than Two Sermons for a public Thanksgiving, which is to be celebrated the day after tomorrow.

11. 9 This day, I interred the Earthly part of my dear Consort. She had an Honourable Funeral.

[1] Peabody, page 302.

Her son Samuel, who was seven years old at the time of his mother's death, in connection with the testimony, as to her character, given on page 301, writes as follows: —

Her husband rejoiced in her as having great spoil, and in finding her, found great favor of the Lord. They lived together in perfect content and harmony over ten years. She died with willingness; the fear of death was extinguished in her. She committed herself unto the hands of her Saviour, and in the same gracious hands, she left her children. She was much beloved and greatly lamented.

If the death of Mrs. Mather occurred on the eighth of November, as some genealogical tables fix it, little Martha died on the nineteenth, because it was eleven days later. He writes of the daughter's death: "Little Martha died at eleven o'clock in the morning." But this was not all. Besides his wife and the twins, he adds: "I am again called to the sacrifice of my dear, dear Jerusha. Just before she died, she asked me to pray with her, which I did, with a distressed, but resigning soul; and I gave her up unto the Lord. The minute that she died, she said she would go to Jesus Christ. She had lain speechless for many hours. But in her last moments, her speech returned a little unto her. Lord! I am oppressed! Undertake for me!" This little hopeful child was only two and a half years old.

This closes another period in the domestic life of Cotton Mather. Of the nine children by his first wife, four only remained to him; namely, Katharine, twenty-four; Abigail, nineteen; Hannah, sixteen; and Increase, eleven. Of the six children of the second wife, two were left: Elizabeth, the eldest, now nine, and Samuel, the next in birth, who was seven. Two "lovely consorts" and nine much-loved children were laid in the spacious tomb given to him by his friends in 1702. Their garnered dust reposed *there*, but this afflicted husband and father was accustomed, in mind, to follow the spirits of his lost ones to God, who gave them. And in respect to all these he had a cheerful and consoling hope.

In all the afflictions above recorded, the labors of Dr. Mather were incessant. Grief for himself never relaxed his service for the good of others. Preaching at home, or at Salem, Ipswich, or wherever wanted, he found time to prepare many short treatises and sermons for the press. Of some of these a brief notice will now be taken.

His "Adversus Libertinos," with the running title, " The Gospel entertained, with the Law established," was one of these. The occasion of this work of forty-nine pages is given in his own words : —

The churches in some southern colonies of our North America, have begun to suffer an assault from some spreaders of Antinomian errors, and sowers of tares and of strifes among them. A valuable servant of God, who hath been, after an exemplary manner, laboring for his name's sake, without fainting, in those colonies, wrote his desire that something might be here composed and published against Antinomianism, with an attestation to it, from the ministers of Boston, and be sent thither for the establishment of the faithful in their most holy faith.

The "Advice from the Watchtower" was an exposé of certain evil customs that had been coming in, with "methods for suppressing them." A "black list" of some of these evil customs was added. This work will appear again.

On the twenty-second of November, the month in which the waves of affliction had gone over his soul, Dr. Mather preached "The Best Way of Living," and gave it to a publisher who had also been "struck with a sudden death upon a vital part" of his family. The "best way of living was to die daily." "One who lives in the midst of deaths, may find cause to say so." "One who feels within him that which bids him reckon his own among the many deaths without him, can't but say so." "One who has in less than two weeks, had five deaths in his family, would be very senseless if he should not say so." He goes on to inquire, from his own sorrowful experience, "What is the dying daily which a Christian is to live in the practice of?"

The same event — death in his family at this time — prompted a sermon from the text Luke 9: 23, and the subject of it was thus stated: "He that would approve himself a Christian, or hope to be found an approved Christian, must be willing to entertain whatever afflictive cross his glorious Lord shall please to order for him." He asks, "What is a Christian? A Christian is one who believes all that our glorious Lord Jesus Christ has revealed. A Christian is one who also obeys all that our Lord Jesus Christ has commanded." "How must a Christian suffer the cross which the Lord Jesus shall order for him?"

We have often observed that Mather's sermons had always an occasion, an object, or a purpose. The two following are in this line. "The Curbed Sinner" was preached on the occasion of a sentence of death, passed on a young man for the murder of his companion. It shows the restraints laid upon men, in the providence of God, to "keep them from sinning against him." And the "Flying Roll brought forth to enter into the house and hand of the thief" (Zech. 5: 1) shows how theft is detected and exposed and how repentance is demanded from the malefactor.

The death of a schoolmaster in Boston, Mr. Recompense Wadsworth, and the sickness that was prevalent in the latter part of the year, suggested the "Lively Description of Death" and his "Christian armed with strength from above."

"A Man of his Word" was preached before the governor and the general assembly in June, at the Boston lecture. It was doubtless intended for the occasion, as it insists upon the oath of the men in public life to be true to the interests of the state. Perhaps some would imagine that there were covert allusions to the governor, as one who was sometimes derelict in duty. The text, from Psalm 15 : 4, is as follows : "He that sweareth to his own hurt, and changeth not." If the preacher had any public man in mind, he made no application. He says that "a good man will be as good as his word. If a good man has given his word, he changeth not ; he won't fall from it ; he won't be false to it. He keeps his faith in his promises, both unto God, and unto his neighbor." He goes on to show how all-embracing is the scope of this obligation to fidelity — to one's word, vow, promise, or oath ; and how the good man, in public as well as in private life, will be true and unchangeable.

A discourse delivered on the thirtieth of September, entitled "*Nepenthes Evangelicum,*" or, evangelical assuaging of grief, was delivered on a most interesting occasion. The Rev. John Wilson was the first minister of the First Church of Boston, and Mrs. Mary Rock, at whose funeral the sermon was spoken, was his daughter. As she was in the eighty-first year of her age, she must have been born in 1632, only a year or two after the settlement of Boston. She is spoken of as a "religious matron," and it is said of her that she was "one of the firstborn, if not the very first of her sex that was born in this famous metropolis of the English America, and who deserves to be honorably mentioned as long as *Boston* shall endure, which I hope will be as unto the second coming of our Saviour." It is hardly supposable, however, that she was the first girl baby of the Puritan immigration that was born in Boston. But what a mass of New England history she must have carried in her mind, taking all she had heard from her parents and all she had herself seen and experienced!

At this time Dr. Mather issued "A New Offer to the Lovers of Religion and Learning, being a Prospectus for the publication of his BIBLIA AMERICANA," in relation to which the Rev. Thomas Prince, who knew whereof he affirmed, wrote thus : —

I cannot forbear expressing my most earnest wishes that that admirable labor of his, *The American Bible*, might soon appear, . . . an extraordinary work that his heart has been set upon from his early days, and has taken him up almost fifty years to compose.

This work will be referred to at greater length in later pages, but it may be said here that its immense size probably prevented its publication. From a rough estimate it would have been four times as large as the *Magnalia*, or eight large octavo volumes, in similar type. But few ministers could afford to subscribe for a single work at such cost as would be remunerative to author or publisher.

An essay with the title " Tabitha Redivivus " to describe and commend the *good works* of a virtuous woman, with some justice done to the memory of that religious and honorable gentlewoman, Mrs. Elizabeth Hutchinson, was one of the publications of this year. Some of the passages are worthy of insertion, because of the noble tribute to the first mothers of New England. " This woman was full of good works." Paul's three glorious words are " soberly, righteously, and godly." The author remarks : —

Both Testaments of the Bible have celebrated the virtuous women of the early ages. Eve, the mother of all that live unto God. The

women that wrestled with faith, and gave glory to God our Saviour —
women that were leaders to others in the praise of God, and that were
mighty blessings to all the people of God: women that were filled
with the Spirit of God, and exemplary for the things that are holy, and
just, and good. . . . As it was in old time, also has it been in our
time. Very many of those matrons who cheerfully bore their part in
the terrible transportation over the huge Atlantic Ocean, into this
horrid and howling wilderness, were such patrons of patience and of
courage in going through that glorious undertaking to take possession
of these uttermost parts of the earth for our Saviour, that wherever
the gospel is preached in foreign countries, what they have done ought
to be told for a memorial of them. And the remainder of their pilgrimage which they passed in this wilderness, they spent in a conspicuous fear of God; and the actions of a prayerful, watchful, humble
walk with him, wherein they obtained a testimony that they pleased
him, and this wilderness became, on the noblest accounts in the world,
a fruitful field. They are gone, and their daughters have rose up and
called them blessed. The two succeeding generations have been also
brightened with numbers of their genuine daughters who have walked
in the steps of that faith, and that zeal for good works, which they have
seen in those that went before them. It is most certain, the virtuous
women in this land have been some of its brightest glories; and so
will they be esteemed in the day when the Lord of hosts will make up
his jewels.

The sermon closes with a just character of a most
excellent woman.

An item of information about the college is found in
the funeral sermon of Rev. Recompense Wadsworth.
When he had been about two years in college (1706)
he made a covenant with God. Some of the students
"formed a society which, laying to heart the too general
decay of serious piety in the professors of it, resolved
upon essays to speak often unto one another, and in
the sweetest methods of brotherly love, watch over one
another; or carry on some suitable exercises of religion
together, wherein they might prove blessings not only
unto one another, but unto many more whom they might
be concerned for."

The materials for 1714 are meager, except what is found in the issues of the press. The diary is entirely wanting. The records of the church are happily free from any stain of conduct needing discipline. On the other side is the bright record of thirty-five admissions. Among those received were the two eldest daughters of Dr. Mather, namely, Katharine and Abigail. The pastor loved all the children of the flock as his own, but there must have been a peculiar joy in welcoming his own daughters into the fold. These daughters were a source of great comfort to their father. He speaks of them, as of his other children, in terms of the tenderest affection. If he had any favorite, which is not discernible, it might have been the eldest, who, besides being affectionate and dutiful, was a brilliant and highly educated girl. Especially were the daughters near to him at this time, for it was a year of widowhood. From November, 1713, to July, 1715, the family were without a mother. It was a time when Increase, now a growing youth, was in special need of the molding power of a wise and pious mother. His own mother died in his infancy, and now he was bereft again when the perils that beset life are most dangerous. His temperament was such that all the influences of home were needed to keep him out of the currents and whirlpools which bear so many away to moral ruin.

There is extant a singular letter written by Cotton Mather that probably belongs to this period. It has been styled a "love letter," and is such emphatically. No name or date is attached to it, but it is addressed to a nameless lady, who is extolled in words of admiration and profound respect. It is supposable that the object of his devoirs was the lady who became his third wife, but of this there is no certainty. The letter is referred to here as one that should be read by any one desirous of seeing all sides of a many-sided man. It is in the library of the Antiquarian Society.

The student of our early history is often struck with the fact that the connection between the mother country and the colonies was very close and involved. Though by the aid of steam and the telegraph we are brought into near proximity to England, our interests do not begin to be so important or interesting as they were at any time before the Revolution. It was almost a vital question with our fathers as to whom allegiance was to be paid. They lived in dread of, and in hostility to, the whole Stuart succession. Under William and Mary they felt secure, looking upon the king as not only the deliverer of England, but as the savior of the American colonies from French domination and the extension of the Roman Catholic Church over the continent. Under Queen Anne there was an uneasy and apprehensive feeling, as she came by degrees under the sway of the Tory party, some of whom were ready to bring in her popish brother, the Pretender, and nearly all of whom were tainted with the politics of the reigns of Charles and James. Though rendering due respect to the queen, there was doubtless a feeling of satisfaction when the news came that the Elector George of Hanover was securely established as the king of Great Britain and Ireland. The government of England was now in the hands of the Whigs; the king was indebted to them for his throne. He had become a great prince, and he made England the bulwark of Protestantism. Our fathers rejoiced in the accession of the house of Brunswick, and from the time of its advent in England we find names of places marking the recognition of its claims upon honor and gratitude. The names of Hanover, Brunswick,

Lunenburg, Nassau, and others were naturalized on our soil. The satires of a great English novelist and critic and the insular pride of Englishmen have led them to belittle the Georges; but the first two were men of respectable abilities and dauntless courage, and they were true to the principles of constitutional liberty and the Protestant establishment.

The sentiment of the time in this province was uttered in the discourse of Mather, entitled "The Glorious Throne," preached September 23. It was a "short view of our great Lord-Redeemer, on his throne; ordering by his providence, all the changes in the world; and most particularly what has occurred in the death of our late memorable sovereign, and the legal succession of the British crown to the illustrious house of Hanover, in a sermon on that great occasion." The plot to bring in the heir of the Stuarts at the death of Queen Anne is glossed over by some English historians, but our preacher seems to have had authentic intelligence that the plans were all formed by the connivance, if not the approbation, of the queen, to proclaim her popish brother. The people of New England rejoiced in the signal defeat of a project that would have changed the history of England and the destiny of these American states.

The history of the twelve years' war, from 1702 to 1714, or during the whole reign of Queen Anne, gives an account of the trials and deaths of our people from the attacks of French and Indians, under the title of "Duodecennium Luctuosum," or twelve grievous years. It was delivered in the presence of the governor and the general assembly, on the thirtieth of September, and was intended to "declare the voice of the glorious God in the various occurrences of that war, which have been thought matters of more special observation." This is, in fact, a continuation of the "Decennium Luctuosum," or ten years' war of King William (1688–1698) in volume ii of the *Magnalia.*

Quite a number of discourses were preached this year as funeral sermons, or in connection with a time of sickness. The decease of his mother suggested the discourse on "Maternal Consolations"; and that of his wife, the one on "The Religion of the Cross." The "honorable and religious gentlewoman, Mrs. Sarah Thing," was the occasion of "A Life of Piety Resolved Upon, and the resolutions wherewith such a walk is to be come into." The winter of the year had been very sickly, and though many passed through the sickness without dying, there had been some deaths of "young persons who had been patterns of piety." A sermon styled "The Perfect Recovery" spoke of the "voice of the glorious God unto persons whom his mercy had recovered from sickness."

One of his little works, in twenty-two pages, had several editions, — seven at least, — the last of which came out in 1750. One was in "English and Indian." It was a "Monitor for Communicants." Though anonymous, it was approved by six ministers, whose names are given, "by the unanimous voice and consent of the whole Association." It was an "essay to excite and assist religious approaches to the table of the Lord." He says of the effort : "It is much to be desired, and how sweet unto our souls would be the desire accomplished, that the table of the Lord may be more generally, and after the most worthy manner, approached unto. The table of the Lord, with his new-born children, like olive plants around it, verily, 't is an excellent sight." This was probably spoken when a large number were received into the church, including two of his own daughters. He closes by urging habitual and thorough preparation for the sacred ordinance.

Other writings were given to the press this year with significant and beautiful titles, as the "Verba Vivivica," or "words of life produced by the deaths of some young persons"; "Vita Brevis, an essay upon Withering Flowers"; and the "Saviour with his Rainbow." I will close the record with a brief reference to "The Sacrifices," which was an "Essay upon the sacrifices wherewith a Christian, laying claim to a holy priesthood, endeavors to glorify God." From 1 Peter 2: 5 the author draws the doctrine that "Every Christian must be a sacrificer; his work is to glorify God, the great God, with spiritual, and continued, and commanded sacrifices."

"What are the sacrifices in the oblation whereof a Christian is to approve himself a priest unto God, a spiritual sacrificer?" He first shows how we depend on Christ the Sacrificer, then specifies all the ways in which Christians are to make sacrifices. Next, the blessed results of sacrificing. "O! come and taste, and see how gracious the Lord will be unto the sacrificer, and be it known unto you, nothing so comfortable, nothing so profitable, as the heavenly skill of sacrificing. Of all our enjoyments themselves, none of them all are so valuable as the skill of sacrificing them all."

No line of diary sheds light on Cotton Mather's life during the year 1715, except about a month, in which an item or two may be found of interest.

In January he decided that Samuel and the daughters must live in the daily use of their pens. This was a point in education. The practice of expressing themselves on paper was found conducive to thought, and precision in conveying it. Increase was put to the study of mathematics, and was sent to fencing and music schools.

At a meeting of the church on the sixteenth of January, "after the withdraw of the pastors," the following vote, drawn up by Colonel Adam Winthrop, was presented; and the church "voted, *nemine contradicente*, that the house of Mr. Thomas Hutchinson, in Ship street, now vacant, be hired for the accommodation of the Reverend Dr. Cotton Mather, at the charge of the church, until some further provision be made for him."

The family had been without a wife and mother nearly two years, when, on the fifth of July, Dr. Mather and Mrs. Lydia George were united in marriage. She was the daughter of Rev. Samuel Lee — a man famous for his learning, who came from England, but after a few years of service returned to the old country — and the widow of Mr. John George, a Boston merchant. The evidences of her accomplishments and of her husband's admiration and affection are abundant ; but her nervous temperament was soon a source of anxiety.

Several discourses this year as well as in the preceding were commemorative or warning or comforting, in cases of bereavement. The death of Rev. Thomas Bridge, late pastor of the First Church, was noticed by "Benedictus ; Good Men described, and the glories of their goodness declared, with some characteristics of one who belonged unto the tribe."

No man honored the laborers among the Indians more than Dr. Mather. Though he never preached to them, yet he evinced his regard for their welfare by writing and circulating books among them. He also took pleasure in extolling the goodness of those who carried the gospel to them in person. In his "Just Commemorations," besides giving an account in brief of the evangelical work among the Christian Indians, he wrote in warm eulogy of Rev. John Cotton, Rev. Grindal Rawson, and others, who preached to English and Indians alike, and wore out their lives in self-denying labors.

The "Blessings and Comforts reserved for pious children after the death of their pious parents; and a commemoration of two such parents," was preached to the "children of an honored and religious family," on a time of prayer in a neighborhood meeting. "Parentalia" was the title, with the running title, "Blessings and Comforts of pious children." The very titles seem to be fraught with sweetest consolations, and a perusal of the discourse shows the wealth of scriptural comfort that a fruitful and godly mind can press into small compass.

Two sermons were delivered on a "Sorrowful spectacle": one by Dr. Mather, the other by Dr. Colman. A miserable woman, sentenced to death for the murder of a spurious offspring, was the occasion. The first was on "The evil of a heart hardened against all means of good." Dr. Colman's subject was "The fearful case of such as in a suffering time, and much more, such as in a dying hour, are found without the fear of God." Some "remarkable things relating to the criminal, proper for all to be informed of," were added.

Another sermon treated of generations of men passing away. It contained "Remarks upon the changes of a dying world, made by one generation passing off, and another generation coming on." It was spoken in the "audience of the general assembly." The third generation from the settlement had now nearly closed, and the preacher could remember many of those who founded Salem and Boston.

Mather's correspondence kept him familiar with the work of Christians in foreign lands. One of his most esteemed friends was Dr. Hermann Francke, of the University of Halle, in Saxony. From him he received information which he published under the heading of "Nuncia Bona e Terra Longinqua, — a brief account

of some good and great things a-doing for the kingdom of
God in the midst of Europe." He writes of Dr. Francke
that "he is the wonder of Europe for the vast projects
he has laid for religion and learning, and his success
in executing them." A postscript was added from Dr.
Kennet, on charity schools. Besides his professorship,
the life of Francke seems to have been devoted to
building up schools, philanthropic institutions, and the
spread of heartfelt religion. He was a man after Mather's
own heart.

A reference to "Shaking Dispensations" will close the
record of authorship for this year, in all about 400
printed pages. Louis XIV of France had been king
more than fifty years, and probably there had not been
a year in the whole period when he was not plotting
to rule England, either by force or bribery. He held the
two Stuart kings in thrall by largesses ; he bribed members of parliament to weaken their own branch of the
government in favor of the monarchy; and under William
and Anne, he kept cabinet ministers, generals, and members of the privy council in pay. England and Holland
were in the way of his schemes of conquest and his
plans for the suppression of Protestantism. William of
Orange seems to have been raised up to thwart his designs. The scheme of Louis embraced the conquest of
North America and the spread of Catholicism all over
its surface. The New England colonies were marked
for destruction. The people of New England felt it in
their bones. The clergy looked upon his reign as that
.of Antichrist. The heart of Mather was oppressed with
the fear of French aggression and success. When Louis
died, on the first of September, 1715, there was a sense
of relief throughout the British dominions, and nowhere
more sensibly than in New England. Mather's feelings

were partly expressed in a sermon on the thirteenth of
October.   It was an "Essay upon the mighty shakes
which the hand of heaven hath given, and is giving to
the world, with some useful remarks on the death of the
French king, who left off to make the world a wilderness,
and to destroy the cities thereof, on the 21st of August"
(O. S.).   Dr. Mather took a correct measure of the sovereign who lived, first, for his own personal glory, and
next, for the extension of French dominions ; but who
not only made a wilderness of other countries in his lifetime, but left to his own nation a legacy of poverty,
corruption, and bloody revolution — a heritage of curses
and evils not yet expended.

CHAPTER XIX.

THE THIRD MRS. MATHER AND THE DEATH OF
KATHARINE: 1716.

FOR the narrative of the year 1716 there are abundant materials in the diary; of these I have condensed some and omitted more. The volume is in the library of the Congregational Association, and the greater part of it was printed in The Panoplist (vol. xvi), though some important parts were omitted, and in some cases the language was altered, though not so as to materially change the meaning. In this volume there is much of recorded experience similar to what has been given already, which proves that the writer's interior life flowed on in its usual channel and with its usual fullness of spiritual enjoyment. Extracts will be made to connect the thread of the life with what is before and what will come after.

Among the twenty admitted to the church this year one was Daniel Willard, the husband of Dr. Mather's daughter Abigail. It was of this young man, a descendant of Major Simon Willard, that his father-in-law wrote, June 6, as follows: " I brought him into a business which is likely to prove superior to what any young man in the country pretends unto. But I must now endeavor that I may be to his advantage in regard of his better part. This must be by the continued admonitions and inculcations of piety."

On the twelfth of February, his birthday, the diary opens thus: "What! and is the fifty-third year of my life this day finished? A life so forfeited, a life so threatened, such a dying life; yea, such a barren one! My God, I praise thee. The display of thy sovereign grace is my admiration, my astonishment. My Saviour, I bless thee; I love thee ; I resolve to serve thee. . . . I am reviving my cares to visit the flock, and I would as soon as I can, get furnished with *Echoes of Devotion*, that I may lodge the book in all the families where I come." The Echoes was a little practical work in thirty-six pages, soon published.

The next day he wrote: "Unto each of my children, present my *Utilia*, with my charges unto them, to make the book very much their companion and counsellor. There are some relatives at a further distance from me, to whom the like present of my *Utilia* may be an agreeable expression of my concern for them." This book treats in eight essays of "Real and Vital Religion, served in the various and glorious intentions of it." The topics are as follows, and the attentive reader will see how very suggestive is each of these titles : "Joshua, or the joyful sound of a Saviour leading into rest. 2. En-Gedi, or the delights of piety. 3. Urijah, or the light of God in the soul of man. 4. Chilion, or thorough Christianity. 5. Bochim, or the weepers of Zion. 6. Shemajah, or the successful petitioner. 7. Azubah, or a believer in a wilderness. 8. Upon Alamoth, a discourse of unknown things."

About this time he had a notion that if he could redeem the time and dress up some sublime thoughts in meter, he might in time have a collection which might prove profitable and agreeable to the Church of God.

February 18. "Relieve a poor man, clothed with rags, at the south end of the town. At the same time, exhort him." He knew the secret of putting relief before exhortation.

Desiring to rise to a higher plane of living, he writes : —

I would now endeavor a greater frequency in forming those thoughts upon every turn, which being applied unto my *actions,* and my *enjoyments,* will bring such a respect unto God, upon them, that I shall indeed live unto him. Upon my *actions.* In this action, I propose an obedience to the glorious God, animated with an apprehension that he knows what I now do under the eye of his glory; and that on the account of my beloved Jesus, it will find acceptance with him. Upon my *enjoyments.* What gives a relish to this enjoyment is, that the glorious God shows me something of his glory in it, and that by this good thing I am assisted and comforted in serving him.

He makes record of one of his modes of "pleasing his wife." He had used the same method with his former wives. It is reasonable to infer that the practice was agreeable to them. "It may not only be a service unto myself, but also greatly serve the interests of piety in my consort, if I should use every morning before I rise, to read a chapter in my dear *Arndt,* and communicate unto her the priceless thoughts occurring in it." The writings of Egardus were held in similar esteem and used for the same purpose.

In following days, he not only circulated his "Tokens for good" among his flock, but sent his *Utilia* and other things to an aged relative in another town and took measures to supply good reading to the eastern settlements, especially Arrowsick and Brunswick while they were without a minister. He included the evangelization of the Indians in those parts in his gifts and plans. He was also devising how to secure a "good justice for a distant plantation," an appeal having been made to him therefor. And even a "poor drone" must have something done for him as well as be provided with employment. Hardest of all a "crack-brained youth must be looked after."

Soon after his errands to heaven were: — "1. To obtain the pardon of my miscarriages; 2. greater measures of piety and sincerity; 3. the divine conduct and blessing to my ministry in every part of it; 4. a smile on the offers of my pen unto the public ; 5. the good estate of my family; 6. the welfare of my son abroad ; 7. the release of my daughter-in-law from her unhappy circumstances ; 8. the comfortable disposal of my daughters in the married life ; 9. the favor of heaven to my flock, the land, and to the British nations, and my dear brethren that are at work for God in Lower Saxony, and other matters." His son abroad was Increase, now on a visit to his uncle Samuel, settled as a minister at Witney, in Oxfordshire. In all these subjects for prayer the burden was for others, but he was rewarded in the exercise. "When I perceived by the breathings of my soul, that I began to live unto God, O the triumphant joy that I was filled withal, to think that now I am assured of everlasting life. The Life of God is what never can be killed."

There is a hint in the following citation for those Christians or others who are in the habit of wondering what particular sin has brought upon them loss or suffering. If Dr. Mather suffered any adversity, he designed to "discover what corruption in him it was intended for the killing of," and so would give "welcome entertainment thereof unto the cross."

Prayers in public for families in affliction were common down to the middle of the present century but now are scarcely ever heard, except in general. The reader will see by the following that the "bills for prayer" and the prayer itself had a meaning in former times. Dr. Mather "would continue the public prayer for special occasions, which were mentioned in the bills put up in the congregation, to be more adapted, more expressive, and more useful than heretofore. Would spend more time in making an exquisite provision for that purpose."

He took measures to get the work styled "*Medicina*

Mentis" into the hands of ministers and college students; and he resolved to "exhibit a little sum of money to be given to such lads at school as would get by heart the 'Maxims of the everlasting gospel.'"

After visiting the prison he writes: "A miserable man in the prison cried out to me for my compassions. I must clothe him, and help him what I can."

From the following we may learn much of Mather's religious life: —

> That sort of prayer, or that elevation of mind in prayer which is in the *Venus Christianismus* called *supernatural prayer*, is what I would exceedingly aspire unto, and grow more experienced in. I would soar towards it in great essays at the *sacrificing stroke*, which with a self-annihilation will bring one towards a union with God, and an acquiescence in him, and in his will. And when I feel in this way, God becoming all-in-all to me, I would be entirely swallowed up in him.

A sentence dated March 6 should be inserted to the credit of Mrs. Mather. "Very much inculcate on the children the lessons of thankfulness to the glorious God, for his having provided so wonderfully for them, when he had made them orphans, and now bestowing an excellent mother upon them."

Many of his flock were connected with the sea and often were the subjects of his prayers; but he felt that their friends at home should be prayed for as much, since their anxieties and privations were great in the absence of their husbands, sons, and fathers.

March 7 was spent in the "exercises of a secret thanksgiving unto the glorious God." He began by "reviewing his life and confessing his sins." After this he entertained his family with meditations on the One Hundred and Thirty-eighth Psalm, and with them celebrated the favors of heaven to the family (especially in the excellent mother that he had bestowed upon it). Then come these words, doubtless inserted some time after: ["Ah! quam deceptus."] The reason for this will appear in due time. He proceeds: "I distinctly adored the divine perfections, and breathed after such dispositions and behavior in myself as they call for. I beheld each of these persons in the Godhead, shining with all those perfections, and very particularly the God-man, who is my Saviour. And I triumphed in the enjoyments of such a Saviour." Next he gave thanks for many blessings, but we note only one or two particularly as they bear on his situation as a minister. A large number had left his congregation a year or two before, and there were fears lest his audience would be much reduced: but his thanks indicate the contrary. "The strange prolongation of my life, my health restored, and strength renewed, — my employment in the ministry of the gospel, and in so large an auditory, and with an utterance bestowed in such an abundant measure upon me; my marvellous opportunities to be serviceable unto the kingdom of God by way of the press." He had continual cause for gratitude and evidence will accumulate that his course went on shining more and more unto the closing day.

Other exercises followed, when we came to the following entry: "After this, I carried my lovely consort with me into my library, and there we together offered up our praises unto God for his blessings; especially spiritual blessings; and for his bestowing us upon each other with surprising dispensations of his Providence." Then he gratefully recognized the ministry of good angels, and concluded with resolves to be more prayerful and studious.

Dr. Mather's heart was set, at this time, upon "exciting a religious influence upon the students at home," and upon addressing his friends in the Frederician University. A poor student is to have his case presented to a society of gentlemen that he may be assisted in his education; and a "miserable man under distraction" must have kindness done for himself; and another family must be supplied.

Referring to a number of persons who were qualified for church membership but who had delayed to come forward and must be called upon, he exclaims: "But oh! how seriously am I to consider the great flock as consisting of a people for whom I am to do the best that they may live unto God." He speaks of "animating the visits of his dear consort unto the poor in the neighborhood"; of supplying other "engines of piety" to his kinsman at Windsor (Rev. Dr. Samuel Mather); of introducing "more religious influence into the schools of the town"; of renewing the "expired charity school," and of relieving "several poor afflicted ones."

In March a society of "young men in the more southern part of the town" solicited a sermon from him. Probably this society was outside of his congregation, as the "more southern part of the town" was then the section supplied by the First, South, and Brattle Street churches. The sermon was published at their request with the title: "The Resort of Piety; our Saviour exhibited as a Tree of Life, which all may and must resort unto."

From the following words, dated March 22, we find one of the perplexities of Dr. Mather in his efforts to do good: "I would set forward good motions among the ministers; but there is one humorsome, furious, boisterous man among us, who confounds all my intentions that way. I am utterly dispirited for doing anything among the ministers in our vicinity." And yet he persevered and the ministers generally coöperated. The "boisterous man" was, it is supposed, the pastor of the South Church, who took sides with Governor Dudley and resented Mather's letter to him. He said that "if he were as the Govr he would humble him [Mather] though it cost him his head."

At this time he had several aged men in want to be looked after ; made his table more emphatically a place of worship ; aided his father in writing a book for old men ; provided for an aged handmaid of the town in poverty. His beneficence was all-pervasive, and could not be hindered by the "humorsome, furious, and boisterous" brother minister.

There is food for thought in the following reflection : April 1. "Among my essays to glorify my Saviour, this may be one. I will consider the gods of the ancient pagans ; the several glories which the poor idolaters did ascribe to them, and the several favors they did expect from them. Then my soul shall make my boast in my Saviour. In him will I see all these ; all in him."

At this time, early in April, Dr. Mather was planning to make the meetinghouse more commodious, showing us that his hearers were increasing : and he was inciting his children to do more than before, to visit and comfort their aged grandfather. His relatives in many and distant places were often remembered in acts of kindness. The Bermudas cried to him to "provide a good minister for them." He incited the "Commissioners of Indian Affairs" to do more for the benefit of those poor creatures ; and on the 7th he wrote : "I will take a poor, fatherless child to lodge and feed in my family, and watch opportunities to do him further kindnesses."

In the following we see how a bitter enemy became a friend, though Mather shrewdly suggests that he had an object in his change of treatment : —

A strange thing befalls me. A monster of a man, and one of the wickedest of men, and who went away to London many months ago, full of malice against me, and against the country ; and one from whom I expected the publication of bitter libels against me, and one whom I have often carried unto the Lord, with desires of divine restraint upon him, addresses me with letters full of respect, bewailing his former disaffection, protesting that he has not spoken one disrespectful word of me since his going away, and intreating my favorable opinion of him, and assuring me that I suffer no incivility from him; at the same time, he sends me over an instrument that he has published for the service of the country. Doubtless God has brought him to feel some occasion for his being on good terms with me. There is in this thing, *the finger of God.*

On the 10th, Samuel's fever was a "call to endeavor much good to him, and all the family," and on the 14th a "miserable woman," that is, a woman in misery, "wants to be relieved on many accounts; and whose passage to London is paid for; I must bear expenses for her."

In another sentence we learn the object of his teaching. He would "endeavor more exquisitely than ever, in catechising, to teach the skill of *living to God.*" Filling the children with knowledge was not enough. They *must live to God.*

We next have, on the 17th, a glimpse of the temperament of his wife as well as his method of aiding her in her flights of devotion "My religious and excellent consort wants, with some exercises which oblige me, (and Oh! how happy am I in the conversation of so fine a soul, and one so capable of rising and soaring to the higher flights of piety,) to treat her very much on the point of having a soul wherein God shall be enthroned, and all the creatures that have usurped his throne, ejected and famished; and having a will utterly annihilated before the will of God."

A society of pious, praying youths at college caused him to study ways to promote their usefulness.

News came, April 21, of the sickness of Increase at his uncle's in England. The severity of his rheumatism was such as to deprive him of the use of his limbs for the time. The father writes: "Oh! the anguish with which

I am to cry unto God, that he would yet be gracious to this poor child, and make him a new creature, and a useful man, and return him unto me." At the same time he was making "new applications unto a kinsman," that he might in "good earnest come into the life of God." Perhaps this "kinsman" was his brilliant nephew, Thomas Walter.

His far-reaching benevolence inspired his correspondence with the Danish missionaries at Malabar and caused him to send "certain books of great improvement and influence to the famous Frederician University" at Halle. He hoped these would have a "tendency to correct the present wretched methods of education there." Dr. Mather was not satisfied with the religious condition of Harvard College and from the above it appears that he thought the "methods of education" at Halle were susceptible of improvement. The authors whose works he would send to the "poor college" were Arnd and Francke and Langres and Boston.

An aged handmaid of the Lord, in Boston, a poor woman at Malden, and an aged relative at Fairfield, Conn., were all to be kindly regarded.

May 8. This date brings into view a new and more exquisite cause of suffering to a tender father's heart. "My dear daughter *Katharine* is ill, and in much hazard of going into a consumption. I must have her condition seasonably looked after. Much prayer must be employed for her. Her mind must be comforted."

Another child was the cause of a different and more severe kind of anxiety, though at just this point in his life inspiring some hope. This was Increase, of whom the father writes, May 22: —

This day my son, [now seventeen] returned to me, much polished, much improved, better than ever disposed, with articles of less expense to me than I expected, and, which is more wonderful, with an excellent business prepared for him immediately to fall into. I am astonished at the favors of the prayer hearing Lord. Oh! my Father! my Father! how good a thing it is to trust in thy Fatherly care! But Oh! what shall I now do to fix the returned child for the service of God?

There was, this month, a poor negro in the prison under sentence of death for burglary. He was executed on the first of June. The wishes of the condemned were generally, if not always, favored in the choice of a minister, and Dr. Mather was often requested to be present and help the prisoner *in* his dying hour, as he often, while in prison, tried to prepare him *for* the hour of death. On this occasion he preached and instructed the guilty man how to do good as well as find good in his death.

Dr. Mather prepared a motion to be offered in the general assembly providing that "no family in the country be without a Bible and a Catechism; that all children of a set age be found able to read, and that there be inspectors for this purpose."

The ways of a boy are not an infallible indication of what he will be when a man. Increase died soon after he made a change for the better, but Samuel lived to a good old age. He was so devoted to play that his father (June 26) wrote: "I must think of some exquisite and obliging ways to abate *Sammy's* inordinate love of play. His play wounds his faculties. I must engage him in some nobler entertainments." This boy became a hard student, an inveterate "dig," and continued so to old age, a man of extensive learning. A few days later he wrote: "My son *Samuel* I entertain with further and riper thoughts for an exquisite improvement in his education."

The calls upon Dr. Mather's time, attention, and sympathy by all sorts of persons, among his relatives and strangers and poor people and prisoners, was enough to

exhaust the patience and endurance of an ordinary man;
but this man did not cease his kindly ministries, and even
the loss of hearers did not sour his temper. He says:
"The humors of many in the flock, who easily withdraw
from the assembly, afford me such an exercise for a patient
sacrificer as may have happy consequences." Doubtless
the fact that newcomers filled the vacant seats had a tendency to promote his cheerfulness. In the middle of July
he notes that, with the exception of the sickness of his
two daughters, he enjoyed, "upon all accounts, a most
wonderful prosperity. Blessings without number, with
my own health and strength strangely recruited."

Some young men, "associated for the purposes of religion," requested for publication a new discourse to them,
entitled "Early Piety Demanded; a very plain and brief
essay to demand piety from all people; more especially
from young people." These "societies for the intentions
of piety," in the city of Boston, were a great encouragement to him, and the fidelity with which the young clung
to him must have been a comfort when unreligious men
threw impediments in his way.

For the sixth of August we read: "I would send for
the negroes of the flock, which form a religious society,
and entertain them at my house, with suitable admonitions
of piety."

This is followed by a manifest concern for his own
children. "The methods of seeking *first* the *kingdom of
God* in the management and government of my family,
ought more distinctly to be thought upon, and further
improvements must be made in them." Hannah and
Increase had not yet come into the church. Neither had
the two younger children.

Similar was his desire for the spiritual welfare of the
other children of the town. "I will go on with my pro-

posals for religious education in the schools, and if I can, bring in the other ministers to favor them." This object had long been upon his mind.

Of the same date is the next extract: "It shall be considered whether the *religious societies* of young men may not have their quarter-nights all together; or, if they may not, on those nights hold their meetings in one or other of our public meeting-houses; and whether a sermon preached on that occasion by one of the ministers, may not be a great service among the youth of the town."

The eleventh of August was a day of private supplications, and some of his thoughts on that day are here given because at different periods eminent Christians have had similar hopes and expectations. Sometimes they have looked for the speedy coming of Christ in person to reign on earth; and sometimes the expectation has been fixed on a great and continuous outpouring of the Spirit. The latter was what the Christians in large numbers were looking for eighty or ninety years ago, when the Foreign Missionary Society was inaugurated by Carey and Marshman in England, and by our Congregational missionaries a few years later. For such a development Dr. Mather prayed; but he also looked for the second coming of Christ at the opening of the millennium.

He writes, August 11: —

I went unto the Lord with my humble memorial concerning the state of his kingdom, the approaches whereof are by his faithful servants greatly looked and longed for. I represented that there were servants of his industriously at work for his kingdom in the world. Among these I particularly mentioned those of the Frederician University and those of the Malabrian Mission. But we can do very little. Our circumstances are insupportable; our difficulties are infinite. If he would please to fulfill the ancient prophecies of *pouring out the Spirit on all flesh*, and revive his extraordinary and supernatural operations with which he planted his religion in the primitive times of Christianity, and

order a descent of the holy angels to enter and possess his ministers,.
and cause them to speak with the tongues of men, under the energy
of angels, fly through the world with the *everlasting gospel*, to preach
unto the nations, wonderful things would be done immediately. His
kingdom would make those advances in a day, which under our present
and fruitless labors, are scarce made in an age. I pleaded that his
word had given us reason to hope for a return of those powers, and for
the making bare the arm of the Lord, before the nations. And he has
promised the Holy Spirit unto them that ask him. I pleaded that his
diligent servants, having preferred the *sanctifying influences of his Holy
Spirit* above any *miraculous powers*, and been humbly willing to
undergo any fatigue for the service of his kingdom, seemed somewhat
prepared for these favors of heaven. And having made this representation, that order may be given by the glorious Lord for a descent of
his mighty angels, to give wonderful shakes unto the world, and so
seize upon the ministers of his kingdom as to do things which will
give an irresistible efficacy unto their ministry, I concluded with a
strong impression on my mind, — *they are coming*; they are coming;
they will quickly be upon us ; and the world shall be shaken wonderfully.

It would seem that some Christians in every age had to
learn that the Lord has "kept the times and seasons" in
his own hand.   And yet it was but a few years when the
Holy Spirit came with such mighty efficacy — even before
Mather's death; and later in the days of Edwards, White-
field, and the Wesleys.

In going to a picnic Cotton Mather got a ducking.   As
he looked at it, "a singular thing" befell him on the 14th.
He was asked to ride into the country a few miles to
take the air, and to "join in the diversions of a famous
fish pond."   It so happened that his foot slipped and he
fell overboard. This is an event common enough to
cause no remark, but it set Mather to thinking about the
meaning of the providence and to inquiring, "Am I
quickly to go under the earth, as I have been under the
water?"

A hint may be derived by the hard-pressed minister
from the following.   Dr. Mather had about this time got

into the way of giving his first thoughts, after a prayer, upon rising in the morning, to passages of Scripture, with a view to sermons ; and he remarks : —

I am apprehensive that the chief work I have to do is to preach the gospel of my Saviour, and it calls for my first thoughts ; the clearest and brightest of my intellectual powers. And by thus ordering my studies, I may not only have my sermons very seasonably prepared and finished, but I may also get ready beforehand, a collection of treasures for all occasions. My flock may find the benefit of my coming into such a method of my studies.

Here we have one secret of the unflagging interest of his preaching to the same flock during forty-five years.

A service held on the 23d shows the intimate connection between the province and the mother country in those old times. It was a day of general thanksgiving "for the victories over the rebels." The Pretender landed in Scotland in 1715, but after brilliant successes his forces were utterly broken and scattered by the Duke of Cumberland in the spring of this year. But as the prince was not captured, and detached parties of his friends were lurking about, the celebration of the suppression of the rebellion had been delayed a few months. Whatever division of opinion might have existed in England and Scotland, the people of New England were practically unanimous for the house of Brunswick as against the Stuarts.

A record like the following helps us to see the impression made by Mr. Mather's life and writings on the mind of an aged minister : " A holy and aged servant of God, the minister of *Bridgewater*, Mr. Keith, who has not been in this city since above seven and twenty years ago, is come to sojourn with me till the latter end of next week. And his principal intention is, to enjoy the consolations of my family. I must now allow much of my time to this excellent friend, while he stays with us. But I would redeem the time to render him as useful as may be in the city before he goes; and study to be as useful to him as ever I can." He arranged to have his "aged friend" preach to one of the religious societies of young people on Sunday evening.

The custom of beginning the Sabbath on Saturday evenings led to social enjoyments rather than religious observances on Sunday evening. One of Dr. Mather's methods of reclaiming the Sabbath evening was to have the meetings of the young people's religious societies at that time as often as possible. To help this movement he gave to the public a little treatise entitled "A good evening accommodated with a good employment; or some directions how the Lord's day and evening may be spent religiously and advantageously, with some persuasives to spend it so."

On the eleventh of September we read: "*Nabby* is near her marriage. There are several steps of prudence and of piety of which I am to be solicitous on this occasion." On the 18th he adds: "I am giving her away to a hopeful young gentleman, who is to-morrow to become her husband. But I am in several ways, to give her up also to God, and do the best I can to render her a blessing to her husband, and in the city." A day later: "My *Nabby* was married (by my father) to Daniel Willard. God be gracious to them."

The cases of friends, relatives, neighbors, or strangers who were needing sympathy, advice, or aid, were continually appealing to Dr. Mather, while his daughters Katy and Nabby were moving forward to such different events. Here is a case sure to call for his deepest interest: "The daughters of a worthy minister, sometimes of *Middleborough*, in Holland, are now arrived here, in the quality of servants. They are objects of much compassion and charity, and I shall treat them accordingly."

The situation of Christian Indians at Yarmouth called for his consideration ; and the encouragement of children in the charity school to learn rapidly to read the Bible prompted the gift of Bibles to good and studious scholars. And still the press was utilized to reduplicate his influence for good. He writes, on the 27th : " I would look out for some assistance to encourage the publication of the work which I am now sending to London, on *The Work of the Day*, whereof I have great expectations." Half a dozen other works, at least, added to the bulk of his publications this year, and in like measure to the author's usefulness.

One of the great trials of Dr. Mather's life, and the spirit with which he bore it, is indicated in the following lines : " I glorified the Lord this day [October 6] with the sweetest acquiescence and resignation, in the case of the *Biblia Americana* whereof I received advice this day that the publication thereof is to be despaired of." As already stated, that work was too great for any bookseller at home or abroad to publish at his own risk, and probably but a small number of ministers or laymen would have been able to buy the volumes by subscription ; yet it would have been of more value to many ministers than their whole library, the Bible excepted.

The new governor, Samuel Shute, arrived in October. On the 5th, Dr. Mather writes : "As I would improve my acquaintance which I am like to have with him, for all the good purposes imaginable ; so, because there arrives with him a new Commission for our Indian affairs, which constitutes him one of the Commissioners, I would prosecute some further good purposes in this relation."

The next reference to Governor Shute is on the 11th : "Being to preach, this day, in the audience of our new governor, and with much expectation from the auditory, I contrive a recapitulation of *Tokens for Good*, as the whole Protestant Interest and our own country has to comfort us. And with as much insinuation as may be, I gave our governor to understand what sort of conduct in him we hoped for. God was graciously with me in the action, and it found much acceptance both with the governor and the people." Mr. Mather states that his access to the governor inspired him with the hope of serving the interests of the people, defeating the "countermining intentions" of certain gentlemen, and concerting measures for the benefit of the Christian Indians.

There were Jewish families in Boston, and at this time (the autumn of 1716) there had been "strange impressions of grace" on their children. The facts in relation to this phenomenon are scanty. Mr. Mather resolved to "improve it for an increase of piety in his flock, and among the young people."

Bearing his seafaring friends on his heart, he published the "Thankful Christian," with some suitable meditations that might have a tendency to make them sensible of their obligations to turn unto God. It was specially offered to the "numerous tribe of whale catchers," calling them to express "their gratitude unto God their Saviour."

The kindliness of Dr. Mather reached out in all directions, but the case to be mentioned was one of many misfortunes which came from his third marriage: "My daughter-in-law and her children [who had no legal claim on his bounty], shall be entertained at my house until she marries, and I will endeavor to serve her in all her interests, and also to befriend the pious education of her children."

Here is a record redolent of the times : " There has lately been in the town, an apparition of a dead person.

It is a thing so well-attested, that there can be no room to doubt of it." More than half a century later, Dr. Samuel Johnson believed in the "Cock-lane ghost" in London. The following suggestion of Dr. Mather was so sensible that one would be glad to learn that it was acted upon : " It may be a service to piety for me to obtain a full relation of the matter, and have the persons concerned therein to make oath unto it before a magistrate."

How many ministers can bear witness to the experience recorded November 26 ? " I have often seen it, that my exercises, temptations, calamities are made singularly serviceable to the edification of the flock. They lead me to discourse on subjects, and communicate meditations and experiences which God makes useful to his people. I must exceedingly and exquisitely contrive how the terrible trials come upon me in the condition of my lovely *Katy*, may be made profitable."

Many things occupied the anxious father during the first half of December, though nothing kept him from doing all that was possible by way of preparing his daughter for her upward flight. One object of great interest was Eliza's education. He sent books in considerable numbers to relatives in Ireland. He assisted his brother-in-law, Walter (out of health), minister of Roxbury, and encouraged his nephew, Thomas Walter. He was busy in preparing the *Ratio Disciplinæ*, in the hope that it "would serve the kingdom of God," as it did for three or four generations, and is still useful. And finally, on the 15th, he writes : " I will persuade some of our physicians to bring the *cold bath* into fashion, whereby many fever-sick, miserable people may obtain release under some maladies which now remain incurable."

The name of Katy appears often in the diary of the

months passed and now it is time to gather up the references which tell us of her last days on earth : —

Sept. 4. Ah! my dying daughter! my dear, dying daughter! what
shall I do for thee, that thou mayest, in thy death, glorify God?

8. One very singular, and very depressing matter of supplication,
was the condition of my dear *Katy*, who is in dying circumstances.
Oh! what a sacrifice am I now called unto! At the same time, I have
cause to rejoice exceedingly in the favor of God, that the child enjoys
an admirable serenity, and gloriously triumphs over the fear of death.

23. The Angel of death stands with a drawn sword over my family
in the dying state of my dear, good, wise and lovely *Katy*.

25. My lovely daughter *Katharine* draws now near unto her end.
I must use all possible methods to render the period of her life, not
only comfortable to her, but also profitable to the people of God.

26. My dear *Katy* is utterly given over. Physicians can do no more
for her. A consumption doth waste her, wherein the assaults of a fever,
in the shape of a quotidian ague, exasperates the malady. But her soul
is not full of troubles. I cannot but wondrously rejoice in the favors
granted unto the soul of the child, which is from above so irradiated,
that she triumphs over the fear of death. Death is become easy, yea,
pleasant to her. She rather chooseth it, and has a contempt for this
world, and a most surprising vision of the heavenly world.

There is something singular in the next sentence as the
father puts it : "It is very strange to me : — the child feels
herself a-dying, but has a strong and bright persuasion of
her own recovery. I have none."

The diary continues as follows, beginning with the third
of November : —

The dying state of my poor *Katy* was a special article of my supplications.

13. My dear *Katy* being brought now so low that she cannot attend
the family sacrifices with us, I must pray daily with her in her chamber.

27. Such is the condition of my family, in regard of my dear *Katy's*
dying circumstances, that I am called of God unto more than ordinary
methods for the quickening of piety in my family. O that I may be
directed of God, what I am to do upon this infliction.

December 1. The dying state of my dear *Katy* made a grand article in the supplications of the day. It was this day, seventeen years ago, that her mother expired.

7. Thanksgiving Day. Move my dying child that she speak such things, especially unto her two brothers, as may leave a precious and lasting impression upon them.

11. My lovely *Katy* desires mightily that her death may glorify God.

Lord's Day Morning, 16th day. A little after 3ʰ A.M., my lovely daughter *Katharine* expired gloriously. The things which her dear Saviour has done for her, afford a wonderful story. But because I relate it in other papers, I shall here insert nothing of it. Much of my time, of late, has been spent in sitting by her, with essays to strengthen her in her agonies, wherein God graciously assisted me.

The further particulars concerning this lovely young Christian are given in "Victorina; a sermon preached December 23, on the decease, and at the desire of Mrs. [Miss] Katharine Mather, by her father." To this was added a "further account of that young gentlewoman, by another hand." This was her young cousin, Thomas Walter. A poem and other matter fill out the precious volume.

Katharine, the second child of Cotton and Abigail Mather, was born September 1, 1689, some time after the death of her sister Abigail. Her father wrote as follows concerning her death : —

You may not expect of me so much as one word for the applauding of my departed child; not so much as the least intimation, as if she excelled any of the many daughters among us who have done virtuously. So far from doing like Cicero, whom Lactantius justly reproached for his ridiculous intention of an apotheosis for his daughter upon her leaving of him.

All that I shall do is to recommend unto you that piety which it was her dying desire to have urged upon you; and that, not by relating how far that piety might shine in her exemplifying of it, but by a short relation of the end which it brought her to; an end which God would have a mark set upon.

In the introduction to the sermon preached after her decease he writes : —

When great sorrows are, by a righteous and holy God, brought upon them that serve him, it is a great alleviation of their sorrowful burdens, and consolation under them, if he make them serviceable to the interests of his kingdom in the world; subservient unto the best of interests. This happy circumstance marvellously takes away the bitterness, and throws a dulcifying branch of the tree of life into the waters of Marah.

A lamb inexpressibly dear to him, who had nourished it, (and it grew up together with him, and with his children,) had his passion for it so described, it was unto him as a daughter. The death of such an one, and especially if there has been in such an one, a constellation of everything that could endear a daughter, cannot but be a killing thing unto a parent.

But if by such a death as this, piety shall be more enlivened among the survivors, and recommended with a more lively efficacy, to them whom it should speak to, we have the blessing promised, "Light shall arise in darkness."

He then says that it was his daughter's dying wish that God might be glorified by her death. She was singularly modest, but greatly desired that what God had done for her should be made useful to the young. He adds: "Nor can there be left many tears to fall into our lacrymatories, when we are not only well satisfied that our children are gone into their chambers with peace, but also perceive them to outlive their funeral in the perpetual usefulness of their preserved speeches and patterns unto the living."

His text was Proverbs 3 : 17 : "Her ways are ways of pleasantness, and all her paths are peace"; and he shows the delights of piety from the life and joyful death of a young person, "who sometimes on her deathbed, with a lively zeal, uttered that wish of her soul, 'Oh! that my death might glorify God.'"

The sermon is admirable, and would be useful if re-printed.

The "Account oi Mrs. [Miss] Katharine Mather, by another hand," is ascribed to Rev. Thomas Walter, her young cousin, who died after a short ministry. He assures the reader that he avoids painting her in false colors, but keeps far within bounds. Premising that she was a good Latin scholar, I will quote the following about her education and accomplishments: —

> Of her first years, all the notice I shall take will be this. As a prom-ising soul, and a good and ingenious disposition are polished and perfected by a good education, so this young gentlewoman was happy in an education that was polite and agreeable to the circumstances of a gentlewoman. Her proficiency in the qualifications which render such an one accomplished in the more genteel part of the world, was not inconsiderable. Such were her accuracy at her needle; her dexterity at her pen; her knowledge of what concerns the table; her skill in music, both vocal and instrumental; to which she added this, that she became in her childhood, a mistress of the Hebrew tongue. She had also attained to a considerable knowledge of the Sacred Geography.
>
> What added a lustre to all the rest, was that she never, in the least, affected ostentation. Her humility was an agreeable and lovely shade to set off her valuable accomplishments. Clothed with humility, though not affecting singularity, while maintaining sobriety in her clothing.

The biographer states that she affected — that is, de-sired — obscurity and retirement to a fault, yet she was not "morose, but of a very gentlewomanly temper and carriage. A particular air of civility and discretion was observed to run through her whole carriage and conduct."

She was one of "very few words; but when she spake, it was to the purpose; what she uttered, was usually very expressive and significant." He then speaks of her piety, partly in her own written experience; also, of her char-ity, though she avoided observation. But one instance is memorable. A miserable woman was in prison, under sentence of death for murder. She could not read, and "was wretchedly for it, for spending her time after her condemnation. This young gentlewoman went, and spent several afternoons with this condemned woman, and reading to her the Sacred Scriptures, and such books as were suitable for her. Adding with a becoming modesty, such instructions as she thought proper for one in her condition." On one occasion, being shut up in close prison, the circumstances were such as caused her to fall into a swoon; but this did not discourage her. A number of religious young women were induced to follow her example.

She loved good reading. Two books of John Arnd, entitled "Of True Christianity," were among her favorites. Arnd was born in 1555, and lived till May, 1621. The work which Katharine Mather enjoyed was in two parts: "1. The whole economy of God towards man; and 2. The whole duty of man towards God." It was written in German and Latin. It was translated into English, and in 1712 published in London; republished in Boston, 1809. Some of the editions are illustrated with fine engravings. It was of this work that the excellent Boehm said: "It was blessed for the bringing of hundreds of thousands of souls home unto God and Piety, a hundred years ago," that is, in the latter part of the author's life. It is indeed a most admirable work, and would be greatly useful now, if it were not that the numberless issues of the modern press crowd it and other excellent books out of use and out of sight.

Mr. Walter quaintly writes: "It is said that the Egyptians were wont to put within the cavities of the breasts of the embalmed bodies of their dead friends, the things which they most loved in their lifetime; as books, medals, Jewels, and other things. Were this gentlewoman to be so dealt withal, her breast would now have lodged in it the two books of the famous German divine, John Arnd."

After giving points of her character and piety, he states some of the facts concerning the close of her life. On the fifteenth of December, it was evident that the end was near. She said, "I have nothing to do but to resign and rejoice"; again, "My love to my Saviour, 't is strong as death, and I am ready to go through any death unto him." As the hour drew near, "O my lovely Jesus, I love thee beyond all expression!"

She said unto her excellent and obliging mother, whom she would not suffer to be called a mother-in-law, but a mother-in-love unto her, "I love my friends very well, but my lovely Jesus is more worthy of my love than all of them! Madam, I love you dearly; but I love my Jesus more than you."

It was thought she might continue a day or two more, but she said she had received this intimation from above: "This night thou shalt be with me in Paradise." A little after midnight, to her sister, demanding of her whether, while she was in this bodily distress, all was quiet and easy within, she replied, "My soul is in perfect ease!" Upon which she sweetly expired, and resigned her soul into the hands of a glorious Redeemer.

Sic Rosa, sic Violae prima moriuntur in herba,
Candida nec tota Lilia mense nitunt.

I have given so much space to this little memoir of Katharine Mather for two reasons. First, because the best eulogy of her father was such a child. The keen light of intellect, the love of learning, the elegance and refinement of character, the sweetness of disposition, the readiness to do her duty to every class, the seraphic piety, all were in some measure the effects of his teaching and the results of his daily personal influence. "The glory of children are their fathers."

The other reason is that it is a delight to me to look back nearly two centuries into the life of ancient Boston (which many take pleasure in representing as gloomy and superstitious) and to find there such an exhibition of female loveliness. We instantly recognize in this "young gentlewoman" one who could take her place in the highest and most cultivated circles of the present day and be a leader there, while finding her chief delight in the offices of piety at home, or among the outcast objects of benevolence. As she derived honor from her father, so she reflected it back upon him. "Children's children are the crown of old men."

The last few pages of the *Victorina* were filled by a poem signed by J. P., whose name is unknown. A few of his lines are copied, because they reveal some traits of Miss Mather not given elsewhere. Remember in reading that the fair subject was comely in person : —

> The charms I sing not of a comely face,
> Nor the fair beauties which a body grace.
> Soar high, my Pen! the work for thee designed,
> Leads to the brighter glories of the mind;
> A mind that with its early vigor shone,
> Bright as the clear beams of the early sun;
> Beams which contracted by provokëd wit,
> No burning glass would strike and pierce like it;
> And yet uniting with the gentler air
> Of goodness, did the scalds of Satyr [satire] spare.
> With a quick flight, and with uncommon ease,
> It ran the round of female sciences.
> But not pleased so, her greater genius bent
> On higher points; in them her hours she spent.
> With liberal arts and various skill adorned,
> Her soul a trifling conversation scorned.
> To skill in languages disposed to rise,
> She first seized on the tongue of Paradise.

CHAPTER XX.

IN this chapter will be condensed the events in the life of Cotton Mather and his family for the years 1717–1719. The record of admissions to the church indicates the pulse of spiritual life. Two persons were dismissed that they might bear "their part in laying the foundations of a new church in the south part of the town." This was styled the New South, and its edifice was on Summer Street down to a recent date. The vote dismissing the two members was passed on the sixth of January. A reference to the movement for a new church is in the diary of September 13 of the preceding year, in the words following: "There is extreme hazard of a mighty flame arising in the town, from the proceedings of the new church in the south part of it, unto the choice of a minister unacceptable unto the rest. I would seasonably interpose, as far as may be, to prevent the devices of Satan." The organization of this church, according to Clark, was not completed till 1719. Perhaps a colony was formed, but a pastor was not agreed upon before that year.

On the sixth of October, 1716, "at a meeting of the brethren of the [North] Church: In consideration of the great age — 77 — to which our venerable pastor is arrived, by the good hand of God upon him, and by his many services to the public, whereof we have a grateful remembrance, and from our desire to have his life prolonged, and rendered comfortable, and that we may enjoy his public labors in such a way as may be most easy to him, etc., proceed to provide a further supply." Action was postponed.

There is a diary for this year in the library of the American Antiquarian Society, to which the reader is referred. It is replete with the experiences of the writer, besides giving the main facts of his family and parochial life. We shall make use of a few facts and dates.

On the twelfth of February (O. S.), it is recorded that the elder pastor of the (old) South Church, Rev. Ebenezer Pemberton, was dead. Dr. Mather was called upon by the junior pastor, "a dear son," Rev. Joseph Sewall, to preach the funeral sermon. It was the part of this colleague to preach on the occasion, but he was urgent in his request, and Mather complied. What made it difficult was that the deceased minister had been a great trial to him, as we learn from another record, and had been in the habit of opposing and hindering his plans of usefulness.

In this year Cotton Mather proposed to his brother Samuel, then settled in Witney, Oxfordshire, to retreat to New England "if storms should arise in the old country." The defeat of the Pretender had not killed the hopes of his friends and of the enemies of England, and not till 1719, when the plan of a Spanish invasion proved abortive, did the fears of new rebellion subside. The reinstatement of the Stuart family would have been the ruin of the dissenting churches.

Dr. Mather sent to Geneva some copies of his work, printed the previous year. It had a Latin and an English version. "The Stone cut out of the Mountain; The kingdom of God in those maxims of it which cannot be shaken." "Lapis Monte excisus, atque Regnum Dei, ejusdemque Principia in eternum stabilienda." He had the hope that the present of the book might be a "seasonable action."

The "great snowstorm" of February 23, 1717, is alluded to several times in our author's writings. Perhaps his account of it is the best in print. It was mentioned in many records of the time, as in letters, almanacs, diaries, and publications. It was the *great storm* of a century, and has never been equaled in our annals.

The diary bears witness to the writer's watchful care over the education of his younger children; his distressing anxiety about Increase; his tenderness towards his wife, and his respect for her mental and moral qualities, as evinced by the books he shared with her; his care for poor widows and indigent students; his interest in the welfare of his domestics; his "devising" for the evangelization of the eastern Indians; his fostering of the evening and charity schools; and his spirit of union with all the ministers of the town in all their united measures for the spiritual good of the whole people.

The respect and reverence which he showed to his venerable father, and which he taught his children to render, was beautiful. He had his father often at his table and wanted him oftener. It was "one of the most grateful spectacles in the world."

A man was executed for murder in Boston on the thirteenth of July. He had been visited by Mr. Mather, who, at his request, preached a sermon just before the execution, on a text selected by himself (Matt. 10: 28). This was published under the title: "The Valley of Hinnom; the Terrors of Hell Demonstrated; and the methods of escaping the terrible miseries of the punishments on the wicked there declared." It was delivered in the hearing, and at the request of the man (Jeremiah Fenwick), under sentence of death. One doctrine of the sermon was that the terrors of conscience will be the chief ingredient in the fires of hell.

His *Malachi*, written and published to "promote union and communion between all that would meet and serve those advances which the kingdom of God is now making in the world," was in ninety-three pages. It had a second edition in 1767, in Philadelphia. It presented the "maxims of piety in the everlasting gospel, which are to be the glorious rules of behavior, the only terms of communion, and the happy stops of controversy" among all who would promote Christian union.

It may be noted here that Dr. Mather wrote down about as many "devisings for good," each month, as there were days in the month; and generally, if not always, these devisings or plans were carried into action. His benevolence was not mere sentiment, nor was it wasted in the dreams of a refined but useless sensibility.

His first grandchild, the firstborn of Mrs. Willard, was baptized in August. On this occasion he preached a brief sermon on the "conspicuous blessings with which the people of God, and their offspring, are known to be blessed of the Lord." It was published with the title, "The Tribe of Asher," in fifty-four pages, without the author's name.

On the sixteenth of October he refers to a "base libel, full of slander, by a furious, venomous, rancorous man," and records the purpose to do what good he could for him.

The decease of Mrs. Hannah Sewall, the "religious and honorable consort" of Samuel Sewall, Esq., was the occasion of a sermon which was given to the public, with the title, "The Valley of Baca; or the divine sovereignty displayed and adored, more particularly in bereaving dispensations." The wonderful beauty of the Scripture is set forth, and then the wealth of comfort to the mourner, in the whole psalm (Psalm lxxxiv), is displayed.

In the latter part of October Samuel was sick. His condition improved, but on the 5th of the next month he had a relapse, causing alarm. He recovered, however, and the next we hear of him he had joined himself to the company of "sober and pious lads." He was now twelve years old. It was a time of severe sickness in the town; and the diary states that within about two months at the close of the year more than twenty members of the church had died.

One of the most honored friends of the Mathers was the Hon. Wait Winthrop. He was major-general and a member of the council, and his position in the town was among the most prominent. His decease on the ninth of November called for a funeral discourse in accordance with general custom; the subject was: "Hades looked into; the power of our great Saviour over the invisible world, and the gates of death which lead into that world."

A few days later, the execution of six pirates led to the sermon entitled "Instructions to the living from the condition of the dead; a brief relation of remarkables in the shipwreck of above one hundred pirates who were cast away in the ship Whido on the coast of New England." Some were let off by the authorities because they had been captured and forced into piracy, but six were condemned and executed. It was a great event in Boston, and crowds from the country increased the throng which viewed the closing scene. Pirates infested commerce on our coast as well as other portions of the sea in those times, and it is stated by Dr. Mather that the pirates sometimes made the captive sailors whom they forced into service show their consent by cursing Cotton Mather. To be cursed by pirates was an honor to the sin-hating minister. But these same pirates, when in prison and facing death and the judgment, made choice of this minister for their religious guide. He visited them in prison, set before them their wickedness with uncompromising fidelity to the truth and to their souls, showed them an all-mighty Saviour to the penitent, and went with them to the scaffold as a friend.

Among other publications of this year may be named: "The Case of a Troubled Mind," which had a second issue in 1741; "A Brief Account of the State of the Province, civil and ecclesiastical, by a Lover of his country"; "Anastasius, or the Resurrection of Lazarus improved"; "Iconoclastes, directed against the subtle Idolatry which alloys the goodness of many Christians"; "Febrifugium, an Essay for the cure of ungodly anger"; "Piety and equity united, in two Essays: 1. The Desires of piety; 2. The Measures of equity"; "Raphael, or the Blessings of a healed soul considered"; and "The Voice of the Dove, with Memoirs of Mr. Robert Kitchen." The case of a student who died in college is mentioned by Dr. Mather, and it is supposed that his name is given above.

The interest of Dr. Mather in the new South Church will be remembered. It was shown further by the fact that he was chosen to preach the sermon at the dedication of the meetinghouse in the early part of the year. The title is characteristic of the preacher: "Zelotes. A Zeal for the house of God, blown up in a sermon unto an assembly of Christians." It was on a day of prayer (January 8), "kept by them at their first entrance."

The sentiment of the sermon, and some facts about the Boston churches, will be read with interest even now. Zeal for the house of God will do all that is possible for the good of the Church of God. He then refers to the number of churches in the town. Six or seven were Congregational. The French church was essentially the same. Besides there were the Baptist and Episcopal churches — one of each. The last two, he states, do not express communion to such a degree as the others, yet "all the ten carry on so lovingly, so peaceably, and so decently, and all the offices of good neighborhood are in so distinguishing a manner cultivated among them, as to give unto the bigots for uniformity, a sensible rebuke of their bigotry, and a notable instance how consistent a variety of rites in religion may be with the tranquillity of human society."

The condition and prospects of Increase, the son of such high hopes and such cruel anxieties, seemed full of promise, last year, when he returned from England; but soon the levity of his character broke out anew and caused his father, with all the family, grief and shame. The young man was accused of a disgraceful sin and crime. Though candid men, after inquiry, did not believe him guilty, yet he confessed to his father guiltiness of some kind, which overwhelmed him with anguish. This was the "skeleton in the family." Losses, bereavements, enmities, slanders, and hard toil could be borne, but this pierced the parental heart.

Except a few entries in the first weeks of the year 1718, there are no more diaries until 1721, from which to draw material for our biography. Nor do the records of the church furnish much besides the annual additions during the same period. We know that pastoral work and earnest prayer must have filled the year, because the additions to the church in 1718 were twenty-six. All these, after conversion, had to be prepared for a public confession, by faithful examination and instruction with reference to that important event in their lives.

The interest which he felt in the college at New

Haven has been held up as a matter for reproach. It has been ascribed to envy and resentment, because others had been more honored by the college at Cambridge. It is not to the honor of any writer to impute such a spirit to Cotton Mather. Doubtless he knew when he was insulted and undervalued by inferior men, but he was of a much loftier type of character than to be governed by wounded pride. He had reasons for being concerned for the prosperity of the New Haven institution, aside from the consideration with which he had always been treated by friends in Connecticut. He knew that the good people of the "land of steady habits" had not only sent their sons to Cambridge for education, but had contributed of their poverty to its endowment. But chiefly he knew that many who could not afford to come so far from home as Harvard College would be accommodated by an institution near at hand. And as he appreciated the value of learned men for the ministry and for public affairs, so he desired that a large number should be raised up in the sister colony. His mind was of a broader make than that of some of the leading men of those days in the Bay, who sought to make all the other colonies into satellites of the older colony. This led him at this date and at other times to inquire what he could do for the college at New Haven. And while taking the distant college into the scope of his vision, he was busy in "erecting a charity school" for the negroes of Boston.

A few excerpts follow from the scrap of diary between the twelfth of February and the eighth of March inclusive, which will lighten up about a month of this spring. He began the fifty-sixth year of his life really believing it would be the last. The day was set apart for devotions, with fasting before the Lord. The record of the day is

long, and reports bitter contrition and confessions in review of his sins; but there is little new in the experiences.
One item must be noted. He represents himself so dead
to this world and so willing to disappear from it and so
wholly swallowed up in God, that among other effects
of this mood he was inclined to destroy these memorials
of his life and write no more. He would never again have
his picture drawn, and repented that he had ever sat for
some draughts of it. Let God alone keep any remembrance of him. But the thought that these records might
be of use to his son, in teaching him how to do good,
induced him to continue writing.

The "cursed, senseless party spirit" that abounded led
him, on the 13th, to procure an interview with a number of the members of the assembly. He invited them to
his house. His influence with the delegates from the
country towns was always great.

The widows of his church were numerous. One fifth of
the communicants were bereft of their husbands — sunk,
many of them, in the ocean. He preached for these sorrowful women a sermon "full of counsels and comforts."
The title was: "*Marah* spoken to: An essay to do good
unto the Widows."

On the 18th he records his gratitude for the restoration of his "invaluable consort." This opens the way
to make a statement, once for all, of the sad and wearing affliction that came upon him and his family through
the derangement of his third wife. There are intimations in Dr. Mather's writings that she was a lady of
uncommon virtues and accomplishments; and in the life
of his father, by Samuel, she is spoken of in terms of
respect and affection. As she outlived her husband five
or six years, or until Samuel was old enough to know her
character, his testimony may be trusted. This is the lady

whom Katharine would not have called "mother-in-law," but "mother-in-love." Some of the last years of her husband's life were not made miserable, but comfortable rather, and happy, by her wifely conduct and ministrations. This fact being understood, the statement may now be made, that during a few years the conduct of Mrs. Mather was such as can be explained only on the supposition that she was deranged. This was not perceived at first, but by degrees her husband appears to have settled down into that conviction. The treatment of himself and his daughter Hannah was so cruel and intolerable that he cried out in anguish. Nervous disorders were not understood then as they are in our times, when persons in such a case would be taken at once to a private hospital with hopes of speedy alleviation. Her troubles lasted several years, with alternations. Some of the records are in Latin and some in English, but in Greek letters. No word will be quoted. At one time the poor distracted woman would be in an awful rage, and then would overflow with such profuse expressions of fondness as to be unendurable. Then the spasm would pass off, and all would be serene. Life in the family would flow on in a peaceable and gentle current. But, as already said, the "stormy latitude" was passed in a few years, and the remainder of their married life was happy. It remains to be said that the awful trial only revealed the depth of affection, and also of Christian principle, in his heart, which enabled him to treat his unfortunate wife with the utmost patience and tenderness.

His brother-in-law, Rev. Nehemiah Walter, of Roxbury, suffered much from sickness and, as a result, from depression of spirits. He was in this case at the present time; therefore, he being laid aside from preaching for a year, Dr. Mather invited him to "come and sojourn in his house, and so have the care of some physicians" in Boston.

The following words show us that Dr. Mather's severe judgments of himself should be taken with some grains of allowance : " Sloth, wicked sloth, cursed sloth "; and this when he was doing the work of several ordinary men !

On the twenty-fifth of February he had a service of thanksgiving for the "healing of his consort." It was temporary.

The next day he notes the fact that his "church had some motions towards inviting his kinsman, Thomas Walter, to come to the assistance and succession of the ministry" with them. Five days later there is another reference to this motion : —

Danger of the church going into confusions, not to be thought of without horror. All the brethren of the church except four or five gentlemen, who must always be the rulers of all, are fond of inviting Mr. Walter into the assistance and succession of the ministry. Last October an excellent man was given up to please these men. There is now a more general desire, and a very vehement one, for this person, who is one of rich and rare accomplishments, and such another cannot presently be hoped for. But these gentlemen clog all the motions. Roxbury is like to seize upon him. Oh ! the wisdom ; oh the patience ; oh the prayer, I am called unto.

Young Walter was settled in Roxbury as his father's colleague. He was considered by Dr. Chauncy, as we have seen, one of the ablest and most promising young men that ever came under his notice.

Among the items belonging to the year preceding this date, March 8, these are some : he sent money to the school at Malabar ; put some copies of his *Raphael* into the hands of physicians, to be given to their patients on recovery, at their discretion ; befriended a poor woman who was greatly oppressed for speaking the truth ; made journeys to preach, attend councils, and settle difficulties ;

was deeply interested in the education of Samuel and Eliza; solicitous about Increase, and grieving for Hannah because of her trials from her distracted stepmother. The state of the college was a grievance, because it did not come up to his idea of what it might and ought to be, as a Christian seminary. The Indians and the negroes enlisted his good will and assistance, and he sent letters and money to the Frederician University in Saxony. At the same time he wrote to gentlemen in Connecticut urging the gospelizing of their Indians. The number of Indians in that colony was small, and mostly confined to the Mohegan tribe.

This fraction of a diary shall furnish us this passage relating to the ministry of angels : "March 7. Given up to meditation on the Angels :—their number, greatness, holiness, glories, services; and the infinite glory of God in being worshipped by such beings. And the greatness of God before whom angels are mere shadows and nothings." This in private. In family devotions he "expressed unto God what, as a family, we were unto the angels. Cried unto God the Lord that the ministry of the holy angels might more than ever be allowed to him. Prayed God to influence the angels to befriend his health, to supply his wants, to direct his studies and all his motions; to help him resist temptations, to raise up powerful friends to his designs, and especially to incline suitable persons to publish several great works, prepared for the church of God." He then prayed that the family "might fare the better for angelic ministrations," in several particulars.

Dr. Mather evidently believed that angels were employed by their Maker in doing his will as much as, and more than, human agents. And who knows enough about force or power in all its agencies and applications to say how the infinite, personal, and intelligent Force which works for righteousness carries out His kind designs?

A Baptist church had been established in Boston in the year 1665, by four or five seceding members from the church in Charlestown, and a few who had been connected with Baptist churches in England. They had a troubled and troubling life, but in 1680 secured a place of worship. The want of Christian courtesy which had hindered their obtaining a building lot had not the sympathy of the Mathers, and now, on the twenty-first of May, 1718, they both joined in the services at the ordination of a minister — Rev. Mr. Elisha Callender — over this church. The sermon preached by Cotton Mather on the occasion bore the title: "Brethren dwelling together in unity: The True Basis for a union among the people of God, a sermon preached at the ordination" of Rev. Elisha Callender. His text was Romans 15 : 7 : "Wherefore receive ye one another, as Christ also received us to the glory of God"; and his topic was: "They whom our great Saviour will one day receive to the glory of God in the heavenly places, ought upon the terms which qualify them for that glorious inheritance, now to receive one another with the regard due to the heirs of that eternal blessedness." The discourse was a very clear, scriptural, and loving statement of the ground of union between true believers.

"A Man of Reason" was one of this year's publications, but the matter was prepared several years before. It was a brief essay — thirty-two pages — to "demonstrate that all men should hearken to reason ; and what a world of evil would be prevented in the world, if men would once become reasonable." A sample will snow the quality of the work : —

There is in every man an admirable spirit. In that spirit there is a faculty called *Reason !* 'T is that faculty which is called, *Prov.* 20 : 27, the spirit of a man which is the candle of the Lord. By the light of this precious and wondrous candle, it is that we discern the connection

and relation of things one to another.   There are certain ideas im-
printed on the spirit of man, by the God who forms the spirit of man
within him.   These awakened and brought into exercise by observation, are the Principles of Reason.

And the following lines give an interesting account of
the fortunes of the manuscript : —

About nine years ago I formed a brief Treatise, which I entituled,.
A Man of Reason.   One who pretended much friendship to me, carried
it for England, with a declared purpose to publish it there.   The
French took him, and he lost all that he had with him.   Only one
day at his lodgings in France, his landlord brought this manuscript
unto him, telling him, " I can get no good by it; it may do you some
good."   He carried it over to Bristol with him, and there left it carelessly in a hand unknown to me.   After some years, it was by the
mediation of my friend, Mr. Noble, returned unto me.   Here it remained some years, until a religious society of young men asked me
lately to give them a sermon; and this was the sermon (which with
some other strange circumstances, that at the instant brought it into
my hand, though I had lodged it with one that was now gone a
voyage from us), I gave unto them.   The young men at last commit
it unto the press; and it looks as if it were designed for some good in
the world.

" Providences asserted and adored " was a sermon occasioned by the death of several persons who were drowned.
It appeared without name.   Another sermon of this year
went through four editions, under the title, " Early Piety,
exemplified in Elizabeth Butcher of Boston, who died
when eight years and eleven months old."   It is evident
from many cases of this kind that early piety was far
more common in the early generations of our history
than has been supposed.

Rev. Thomas Barnard, or Bernard, as Mather writes
his name, was a native of Hartford, Conn., a graduate of
Harvard College, and minister of Andover about thirty-six
years, dying in 1718.   His funeral sermon was preached

by Dr. Mather, whose topic was, "Vanishing Things: An Essay on the dying man, known in his place no more." He speaks of the pastor as "shining yet humble." The eulogy is perfect. He was a scholar in the best estate of man as a minister of the gospel, and in it he was *shining*, and at the same time *humble*.

Another work belongs to this year, which demands more space than can be given to others, which may be equally valuable. This is unique, and is known as "Psalterium Americanum." It is the Book of Psalms in a translation "exactly conformed unto the original, but all in blank verse, fitted unto the tunes commonly used in our churches ; which pure offering is accompanied with Illustrations, digging for hidden treasures in it ; and Rules to employ it upon the glorious and various intentions of it." Some other portions of the Bible were added, to "enrich the cautional."

Dr. Sibley quotes the following from a writer whose name is not given : —

In this singular publication, which is a close translation of the Hebrew, Dr. Mather has not only disregarded the modern practice of breaking the lines, whether rhymed or not, but he has run out (to use a printer's phrase,) the whole matter; so that, while each psalm looks exactly like prose, and may be read as such, it is, in fact, modulated so that it may be sung as lyric verse. The learned doctor says that in the " twice seven versions " which he has seen, the authors put in a large heap of poor things that are entirely their own, merely for preserving the " *clink of the rhyme*, which, after all, is of small consequence unto a generous Poem, and none at all unto the melody of singing."

In an introduction of thirty-five pages there is some fine writing upon the beauty and sublimity of the Psalms, and their fitness for the "service of song in the house of the Lord" ; and an explanation of his design and method in preparing this version. He writes : —

The version is fitted unto all the common tunes, the notes whereof are eight and six. Some are accommodated for a well known longer note by putting in two syllables of the black letter [italic is used here] which are without any damage to the truth of the translation, found enclosed between two such crotchets as these [ ] — and which, being left out, the metre with the sense yet remaining entire, is again restored unto the usual eight and six. And some of them are so contrived, that by leaving out what is in the black [*italic*] letter between the two crotchets, [ ] which may be done without any manner of damage, they are accommodated unto a well known shorter metre.

Here follows a part of Psalm ii, in 8s and 6s : —

1. The nations, why do they concur | with such tumultuous rage ! | and why the people meditate | a thing that is but vain?
2. Kings of the earth do set themselves, | and rulers do consult | against the eternal, and against | [Christ] his Anointed one.

The word *Christ* is inserted in the last line to fill out the measure, but it does not change the sense; rather, it makes the meaning more specific.

Take now the first three verses of the One Hundred and Forty-fifth Psalm. The italic is inserted in this example to fill out the measure : —

1. O Thou that art my God, the King, | I 'll thee extol [*and set*] on high, | and I will speak well of thy name | to [*endless*] ages still to come.
2. All day, and every day, I will | keep [*ever*] speaking well of thee; | and I will celebrate thy name | to [*endless*] ages still to come.
3. Most great is the eternal God, | and greatly to be praised [*is He,*] | and of his greatness there cannot | be [*ever*] any searching out.

The following version of the first three verses of Psalm ciii may be sung in long or common meter, according as the *italic* words are used or omitted : —

1. O my awaked soul, do thou | bless [*always*] the eternal God; | and all my inward powers the name | of his pure [*spotless*] holiness.
2. O my awakened soul, do thou | bless [*always*] the eternal God ; | and O forget not any one | of all his [*precious*] benefits.

3. 'T is he who gives a pardon to | all my [*most vile*] iniquities | 'tis
he who gives an healing to | all thy [*most sad*] infirmities.

To those worshipers who longed to avoid the Scotch
method of singing without any regard to meter; or the
use of The Bay Psalm Book, whose rhymes were often
horrid, this arrangement must have afforded grateful
relief. The sense of the original is preserved; the verses
are left as in the Common Version; the attempt to rhyme
is given up, but the meter is generally smooth and pleasant. The perpendicular line marks the end of the staff.
Soon the version of the Psalms by Dr. Watts, and his
own Book of Hymns, superseded the psalms and hymns
before in use among the churches.

No diary exists to guide our steps in the year 1719, but
we have no reason to doubt that Dr. Mather's interior experiences this year were similar to those which he had in
preceding and succeeding years. There were no changes
in his family, unless, perhaps, the death of one of the little
girls of his daughter, Mrs. Willard. Samuel was a lively
boy, and was studying geography, astronomy, and mathematics, as well as Latin and French, as much as his love
of play would allow. Eliza also showed a desire to study
French with him. Nothing definite is known of the deportment or employment of Increase (now about twenty)
unless he was in the secretary's office, where he was at
one time engaged.

As Dr. Increase Mather was now eighty years of age, it
is not probable that he could render much assistance in
the way of preaching, though his presence and his prayers
were a benediction.

In Drake's Boston it is noted that the *aurora borealis*
was first seen in these parts on the seventeenth of December. No man in the province would have beheld it with

more eager interest than Cotton Mather. An anonymous publication with the title, "A Voice from Heaven; An Account of an uncommon appearance in the heavens, with remarks upon it," is ascribed to him by Dr. Prince. It is marked P. in his catalogue, but is not found among the books of Prince in the public library.

The year was begun by preaching, on New Year's day, a sermon on "A New Year well-begun; an Essay offered to provide a good work for such a day, and advice how a good year may certainly follow the day." It was dedicated to John Winthrop, Esq., of New London, where it was printed. An extract from Sir Richard Blackmore's poem, entitled "The New Year's Day," was added. The text was Psalm xc: "So teach us to number our days, that we may apply our hearts unto wisdom." A passage will show the drift of the discourse: "Very frail, very short, very soon spent, is the life of man. And the rolling of his life along is like the telling of a story; the years of his life pass away like a story." This is the conclusion : —

Wherefore, get into such a state and frame of mind, as to be ready for the coming of the Lord unto you, in all the dispensations of his providence. As the years of change are all in the right hand of the Most High, so are all the changes of the year. Become reconciled unto God, and then, whatever happens, you may say, " God has meant it unto good." Realize the providence of a dear Saviour, at work in all that befalls you, to convey thereby unto you the blessings of a healed soul. Become dead with your crucified Redeemer; dead not only unto the comforts, but also unto the troubles of this world; and then the most killing things will never hurt you. You will only say, " My dear Saviour loves me when he kills me." A heart established with the love of God, will make a good year for you, and make light arise in all your darkness, whatever events the year may be darkened withal.

On the twelfth of March he preached in the audience of the governor and General Court: "Concio ad Populum;

or, A Distressed People entertained with Proposals for the relief of their distresses." The running title was "The Valley of Vision in the Valley of Achor." This valley is the door of hope. The text (Prov. 29: 18) is both warning and comforting: "Where there is no vision, the people perish: but he that keepeth the law, happy is he." He first pointed out the distresses and evils which afflicted the people, and then suggested means of relief: 1. A society for the relief of public distresses; 2. frugality; 3. industry.

Several ministers joined in a "Testimony against evil customs." It was attributed to Mather and was signed by him, Benjamin Colman, and Benjamin Wadsworth, with the concurrence of others. Some of the evil customs that had come in, or old customs which were being turned into an abuse, were specified, as follows: — 1. Lewd and rude practices; 2. Ordination frolics in the evening, after the service; 3. Weddings — immodest irregularities; 4. Lectures, followed by resort to taverns; 5. Trainings; 6. Commencement feasting and follies; 7. Huskings.

The ordination levities, in the shape of parties and dances, prevailed in some places till after the present century came in; and the ancient trainings, whether of single companies or of regiments, were always attended by hard drinking, and often with drunkenness. When officers were elected, they were expected to "treat all round," and thus habits were formed which brought many bright young men to an early and dishonored grave. This paper showed how evil habits had grown and become obdurate, and urged their abandonment at once.

The "Tryed Professor" and "Vigilius" have the same end in view substantially. The latter is fitted to awaken men from natural sleep in the hours of devotion; and the moral sleep, wherein the "souls of men frequently omit the duties, and forfeit the comforts of religion in earnest"; and the former is a "brief essay to detect and prevent hypocrisy, and make sure of sincerity in the profession of religion."

False swearing and perjury were treated of by our preacher, before the General Court, probably with the intention or desire of effecting some legislation that might tend to diminish the evil. "The Religion of an Oath" was the topic, and directions were given "how the duty of swearing may be safely managed, when it is justly demanded; and strong persuasives to avoid the perils of perjury." The laws of Denmark in relation to oaths were explained for information. The sermon is an indication as to the morals of the time, and of the scope of the Puritan ministry in the usage of a fearless yet god-fearing man.

The next discourse witnesses to the variety which characterized the preaching of old times. The subject was "A Glorious Espousal." It exhibits the essence of the espousals of Christ to his church, and "thereupon recommends a good carriage in the married life. What could more seasonably be presented when marriage is upon celebration?"

Here is another of Mather's peculiar title-pages, which is full of meaning: "Desiderius, or, A Desirable Man Describ'd; in the character of one worthy to be a man greatly beloved; and an example of one who lived very much desired, and has died as much lamented; given in some commemoration of the very valuable and memorable Mr. James Keith, late minister of the gospel in Bridgewater." This minister, whose age was seventy-six, has been mentioned in previous pages, in terms which evince the respect, reverence, and affection of his friend Mather.

One or two letters on public and political matters have

not been found, but a long sermon still remains and still is
instinct with life. The title is "Mirabilia Dei: an essay
on the very seasonable and remarkable interpositions of
the Divine Providence, to rescue and relieve distressed
people, brought unto the very point of perishing; especially relating to that twice-memorable fifth of November;
offered in the audience of His Excellency the Governor,
and the General Assembly of the Massachusetts Province,
N. E., on the fifth of November, 1719." This was the
anniversary of the Gunpowder Plot. It was a subject
suited to the occasion. The English nation had been
in peril from a great scheme of invasion and rebellion
this very year, and the colonies were in a distressed condition. The historical strain of the sermon was suited
to the preacher's genius and knowledge, and the members
from the country — the far larger part of the assembly —
would listen with rapt attention to his historical lore.

The text was Genesis 22 : 14, which shows the watchful regard of God for his people. As the nation had been
in dangerous circumstances, it was pertinent to show how
God had interposed for his people in all ages. The
inference was, to take courage. He referred : — 1. to the
case of Abraham and Isaac by the altar of wood ; 2. of
the people of God in Egypt, and at the Red Sea. Then
he illustrated from individual history : — 1. The One Hundred and First Psalm of David, who wrote : "I will sing
of mercy and judgments"; 2. he instanced other Old Testament characters, as Jacob, Sarah, Daniel; 3. he referred
to great events in English history, as the Armada, the
Gunpowder Plot, the coming of William III, and the plot
to bring in the Pretender, on the death of Queen Anne,
from which peril the nation had recently escaped. He
says: "Everybody now knows that there was a design
with a strong hand carried on, to put by the succession to

the crown." Next he referred to New England history, closing with King Philip's War, which some of his hearers remembered, and with the story of whose horrors all were too familiar. In view of all these great interpositions of God for his people through centuries, he closes with the exclamation, "O Thou hope of New England, and Thou Saviour thereof in the times of trouble, with encouraged hopes will we keep looking up to Thee."

CHAPTER XXI.

A CHRISTIAN IN THE FURNACE: 1720–1721.

THE year 1720 was full of trouble and anxiety to Dr. Mather. The ingratitude of relatives by marriage, and the entanglements of an estate which he had been requested to administer upon reduced his strength and nearly overcame his fortitude. It appears that nothing but faith in God kept him from mental distraction. The diary — perhaps happily for us — is wanting. It must have been, for several months, a record of ill health, domestic infelicity, mourning over a wayward son, comparative unfruitfulness in his pastoral work, and suffering from pecuniary embarrassment, brought upon him by the misconduct of others.

The four years, 1719–1722 inclusive, give an average of less than eleven admissions per annum, which is much less than the average of his whole ministry. It was, in comparison, a dark period in Dr. Mather's pastorate as well as in his life. The business entanglement and the vexations growing out of it were an addition to all the griefs which a distracted wife and an unworthy child — both dearly loved — brought upon his sensitive heart.

Two essays marked the close of the preceding year and the opening of this, with these titles, respectively: "Youth Advised; an Essay on the sins of Youth"; and "A Brother's Duty; an Essay on every man his brother's keeper." These are in the list of his son Samuel, but not found in any public library at present.

Two or three funeral sermons may be arranged together, especially as they all were delivered near the same time, and that the beginning of the year. "A Year and a Life well-concluded" was delivered on the last day of 1719, and printed soon after. It was a "Brief Essay on the good things wherein the last works of a Christian may be, and should be, his best works."

The Rev. Mr. Joseph Gerrish, of Wenham, "was received where the weary are at rest," on the sixth of January, in the seventieth year of his age. The discourse on his decease was entitled "Detur Digniori: The righteous man described and asserted as the excellent man; and the excellences of such an one demonstrated."

"Undoubted Certainties: or, Piety enlivened from the view of what the living do certainly know of death approaching," was a sermon on the death of Mrs. Abigail Sewall, preached on the fifth of June, the text being from Ecclesiastes 9: 5: "For the living know that they shall die," etc. First point: "We know that we *must* die. 2. *How* should we know it? or, with what effect? So as to put it to good use. History mentions an excellent person, who dying very suddenly, was found sitting in his chair. Some would have made a rash interpretation of it. But God ordered it that he was found with a book lying before him, and his finger pointing to these words: 'Whatever death a righteous man may be presented withal, yet he shall be in rest.'"

"The Quickened Soul," referring to the "withered hand revived and restored," was "aimed more particularly at the direction of them whose conversion to piety may be in danger, through wretched and foolish pamphlets, which the enemies of grace and of souls, industriously scatter about the country." Dr. Sibley suggests that perhaps it refers to John Checkley's "Choice Dialogues between a godly minister and an honest countryman, concerning election and predestination."

An anonymous publication of this season, with the title "The Salvation of the Soul considered," is supposed to be the work of Dr. Mather. The title of another is given as his, though without name, because the style of the title reveals his hand, and the hand of no other man. It is "Coheleth : A Soul upon recollection, coming into incontestable sentiments of religion ; such as all the sons of wisdom will and must forever justify; written by a fellow of the royal society, offering the advice of a father, going out of the world, unto a son coming into it." His son Samuel was about entering the college and so the world, and that may be the personal reference. "Coheleth" is the "preacher," as the word is used in Ecclesiastes 1 : 1 ; one who upon "recollection" or review of his experience, comes into "incontestable sentiments of religion."

We come now to the special afflictions of the year, and of the years just before and after ; but our attention will be mostly fixed upon an anonymous letter which has been ascribed to Dr. Mather. In the diary of 1716, November 30, are these words : "We are now getting towards the clearing and settling of the estate. I would propound unto my wife what special service for God and his kingdom she will do, in case the administration be well finished, and she find any effects remaining that may render capable of doing anything." This probably refers to an inheritance of his wife, from her father or her former husband. It is not of any use to trace out the history of this "administration," or even to refer to it at all, except so far as it is connected in some way with an attack upon the character of Dr. Mather. In one of his entries he states that he had unwittingly become bound to pay the debts of his wife's late husband, and in a letter about to be quoted, the writer (supposed by some to be

Cotton Mather) speaks of the "perplexities of the administration" of an estate. All we need to understand is that in his troubles a letter was written by some one which has been made the occasion of severe insinuations, cruel charges, and unmanly sneers against him. It is a (supposed) letter to the Honorable Judge Sewall, April, 1720. It is printed in Massachusetts Historical Society Coll. 32, 122. This is introduced and followed by remarks from the then president of the society, Mr. Savage, highly derogatory to Dr. Mather. These will be considered after reciting the letter, word for word. The original is now in existence, and the following is a copy corresponding with that in the collections. One or two corrections are suggested in brackets.

[Supposed] Letter from Rev. Cotton Mather, D. D.
Honorable Sir.

As soon as your hon'r has considered ye contents hereof, I request you, (for several reasons,) to burn it. I being lately in ye company of Dr. Mather, was made sensible of some things, w'ch I tho't I might do well to lay before your hon'r, and the rather because he is a person that you have some value for. I am not without feare that ye heavy and many troubles that oppress him, may have such an effect upon him, that we shall quickly lose him, except redressed speedily; and indeed, had it not been for some singular attainments w'ch I suppose he is master of, he never could have borne up so well as he has. Your Honor, I believe, is not [un]acquainted with his troubles, but I find that w'ch most overwhelms, is ye wretched Administration, as he calls it, in w'ch he has been ensnared, by his love to some whom he finds full of ingratitude. Your hon'r can deliver him, if you please, and if Incapacity to Administer be a just cause for a judge to lay aside an Administrator, you have it alredy before you; or if you think you have not, you will, (it may be,) have it either in the Death, or in something worse than that soon coming on that distressed, tho' worthy Gentleman. I am informed by those who have it from Boydell, that ye accounts of ye Administration given in, are beyond expectation fair and clear, and to your hor'rs satisfaction.

Every one that I speak with are of opinion, that ye managers deserve to have more allowed them all that Mr. Whittamore has applyed for his own support in the business, for the Incredible fatigue w'ch they have undergone. But if so much be not allowed them, ye Doctor must pay it of his pocket, w'ch I perceive he is ready to do, rather than the orphans should be defrauded of a penny. But until your hon'r shall release him, his condition, as he says, and I partly know it, is intolerable. Every one that knocks at his door, surprises him, that his heart dies within him, as he says, fearing there is an Arrest to be served on him, or somebody to dun him for a Debt, due from an Estate, which he never can be the farther [farthing] the better for. Old Mrs. Fyfield keeps worrying about ye ruins that her estate must suffer, because of her husband's suretyship.

Your honor gave the Old Doctor (Increase) some hope that you would deliver his son out of his extreme distresses. He says you told him it was in your power, and then he adds, I hope the good judge will think tis his duty.

The brave and good Old Doctor, who is languishing for Heaven, does also vehemently long for your hon'r to deliver his son. But this morning I find the distressed Gentleman, viz. ye young doctor almost sunk into a total dispair of any deliverance; he says the affair labors as if it were incharnted; they have been two years in doing what might have been done in less than two months. The Doctor speaks of your hon'rs judgment and goodness, with ye greatest respect, but he seems to be apprehensive of a strong plott laid to ruin him, by them for whom he always had the bowels of a tender father. He is commonly Informed that your Nephew stirs up people to arrest him, and has given the Doctor reason to think that he has consulted with an able lawyer to molest him for maleadministration. He is told that Mr. Faneuil's arrest was contrived on purpose to prevent your hon'r from delivering of him, w'ch arrest, tho now dropt, (by the good persuasion of my great and good friend,) will be speedily renewed for that purpose. His tirrible wife (whose character Mr. Jon. Sewall has given, as ye Doctor understands, to others, and can give to your hon'r, if he pleases,) will have a great estate, whether there be one or no. The women talk like mad people about it. The story of a sham Inventory Mr. Boydell can tell your hon'r.

The estate has already fared much the worse, as I am informed, because your Nephew refused to act as an attorney in the administracion, and will do so more and more. It seems his wife wont let him act, and the Doctor thinks its from an ill-intention to plague the doctor.

Considering some strange things that your Nephew knows relating to his predecessor, the doctor has often wondered at his barbarous carriage towards him, (whereof I believe the Doctor can give your hon'r a strong Instance,) and that he is not afraid of dreadful consequences. The Doctor thinks your Nephew studies all ye Litigious arts he can to defeat your hon'rs just and good purposes to deliver ye poor afflicted servant of God, and the Doctor expects he'll be successful in them, w'ch causes the doctor to be so dejected that it would move your hon'rs compassion to a great Degree, were you to see him. The Doctor, I perceive, esteems your hon'rs conversation above any in the Land, and would have waited on you often, but his dejection att this wretched administrac'on so dispirits him, that he is fit for to speak with none, to talk of nothing. His burthen certainly is almost insupportable, for he would fain have preached a Lecture sermon, to stir up devout persons to pray for ye conversion of ye Jews, on ye next week, but he says this wretched administrac'on undoes him : he cannot fix his tho'ts and must let it alone.

Good S'r. Make haste with your helping hand to this distressed, afflicted minister of Christ, and save him from the plotts of those who, you may see, would ruin him. I beseech you, S'r, let [not] your nephew, or by him, his wife, be to hard for you.

I am your hon'rs most humble
and obedient serv't &c.

[Rec'd Ap. 13, 1720   To
past 9 at night.]   The Hon. Judge
                                     Sewall.
                                     These.

On the outside of the letter, folded in the usual way of folding letters, Judge Sewall wrote: "Rec'd Apr. 13th 1720, in behalf of Dr. Cotton Mather."

One complaint against Dr. Mather is that he wrote an anonymous letter. But ∙an anonymous letter may be a very innocent thing. It depends on its spirit and design, whether it is harmless or blamable. A letter without name may be written to give needful information, to warn of dangers to further a good design, when the writer has reasons for concealing his name. Viewed in this light, the letter is without sin.

But it is said that in this case there was an ingredient
of falsehood in concealing the writer, while making the
impression that the letter was written by some one else.
This would be a grave offense to morality, if the conceal-
ment was real, and not merely a modest veil which the
receiver would see through at once and recognize the
real writer.   If Judge Sewall ever supposed that Cotton
Mather was the author, what would have been his conjecture as to the design of anonymity?   Would he not have
said, "Dr. Mather is in deep distress; he wants help; but
in his sensitiveness he tries to conceal the secrets of his
heart by covering up his name and agency in this letter"?
Something like that, doubtless.

But there is no proof that Judge Sewall ever thought
or imagined that Dr. Mather wrote the letter or inspired
it.   He merely wrote on the outside of the letter, with
the date, these words: "Rec'd in behalf of Dr. Cotton
Mather."   And that, in all probability, was what he thought
of it.   If he had imagined that there was anything wrong,
or even questionable in the letter itself or in its mode,
who can doubt that he would have complied with the request to burn it?   Who can doubt, knowing the unbroken
friendship of the two men for nearly half a century, that
he would have seen Dr. Mather and conversed on the
subject, and returned the letter or destroyed it, if it was
open to censure?   The fact is that there is no proof to
satisfy a candid mind that Cotton Mather wrote or had
anything whatever to do with the "supposed" letter.

In the first place, it is not written in the style of Cotton
Mather, or in any of his styles, for he had two or three.
The style of the *Magnalia* is entirely different from that
of many of his printed sermons and thousands of his
manuscript pages; while many of his letters differ in style
from the preceding "composures."   They are written in

a swift, *currente calamo,* and almost rollicking style, over-
flowing with quips and quirks, and a somewhat ponder-
ous fun, all mingled together. Now this "supposed"
letter has but the slightest resemblance to anything of
Mather's extant.

Nor is it supposable that Dr. Mather would put so many
commendations of himself into such a letter, if ever so
much impelled to write it. They are unnatural, as in the
sentence which speaks of "some singular attainments."

But, thirdly, the tone and spirit of this writing are wholly
repugnant to all we know of the morbid sensitiveness of
the man to any such revelations of himself. Whatever
he may have put into his private diaries, designed for
his sons' perusal, he had such a high sense of honor, such
a keen pride of independence, that he never asked his
people for a farthing of money for his own use. He left
it with them to fix his salary and the mode of raising it,
and though liberal in the extreme in giving, he never,
even when in extremest want, asked for help or let his
people know of his pinching circumstances. His honorable pride almost bordered on simple disdain of friendly
aid. He would not stoop to ask for charity. It is a
shining fact in the history of men, that we have here
a man who never sought anything for himself from mankind. He never uttered, so far as we know, a desire for
any office, promotion, or honor. He never intrigued or
figured for parish, professorship, or presidency of the college. He never opposed the promotion of another man
from personal reasons. There is not in his published or
his manuscript writings, or even in the gossip of his opponents, a line of proof that he was self-seeking. If treated
unkindly, he retired into himself, and his great heart fed
upon its griefs, until he found communion with God. He
sought ways to do special acts of kindness to his enemies

as well as to pray for them. And y⸤⸥ we are told that
he, in this "supposed" letter, poured out his sorrows and
made known his embarrassments — lifted the cover from
his secret soul — for the purpose of obtaining pity! The
supposition is absurd ; the assumption by Mr. Savage and
others that he did this betrays a total ignorance of the
man or a strange prejudice against him.

There is a supposition which readily explains the whole
matter. The letter was not written by Cotton Mather, but,
as it purports, by a friend who was intimately acquainted
with the affair in question. The writer was a friend,
was often in the company of the "old doctor" and the
"young doctor," and had heard this business talked over
until he knew it well. He was so distressed by it himself as to be impelled to seek the intervention of Judge
Sewall in removing the difficulty. Now, the question is,
Was there such a person? And the answer is, There
was just such a man, who in his person filled every
demand of the occasion. That man was probably young
Thomas Walter. He was the son of Rev. Nehemiah
Walter, of Roxbury, by his wife, Sarah Mather, daughter
of Increase and sister of Cotton Mather. Young Walter
was something over twenty years of age. He was a
graduate of Harvard, and one of the three spoken of
by Dr. Chauncy as a very brilliant young man. Walter
was a student of Cotton Mather, for whom Mather was
solicitous and of whom he was proud. Walter studied
divinity with his uncle, and learned much from his conversation on all subjects which interest and charm inquiring
minds. He was at home in his uncle's house almost as
much as at his father's in Roxbury. All but a few —
"four or five men" — wanted him as successor of Dr.
Increase and colleague of Dr. Cotton Mather. He was
settled as colleague of his father in 1718; but his inti-

macy with the family of his uncle was not affected by
this event. He prepared the memoir of his fair cousin
Katharine, and a year after the date of this letter he
came to the house of his uncle Cotton to have the small-
pox by way of inoculation; and it was while lying sick in
his uncle's study that the hand grenade was tossed into
the chamber window. These facts are recalled to show
how intimate he was in the family, and how qualified he
was to do precisely what was done in the writing of this
letter. This theory fulfills all the demands of the case
and leaves the reputation of a noble and godly Christian
man and minister free from the shadow of a suspicion of
wrong doing. There is not a smell of fire on his garments.

Passing into the year 1721, this year, if we may use
one of Dr. Mather's phrases, might be styled an *annus
luctuosus* — a year of grief — in his life. Much as he
had to endure heretofore, of bodily weakness, of sickness
and death in his family, of grief for the misfortune of his
wife and the misconduct of his son, and of enmity and
slander from the world, perhaps this year gathered into its
days the greatest accumulation of woes. But in "all this
he sinned not, nor charged God foolishly." Though he
had much to endure, yet there is no evidence to sustain
the assertion that has found its way into some accounts of
his life, that he was abating his Herculean labors in the
service of God and man or that his influence for good was
waning. One of the events of this year will give him a
place on the bright roll of the greatest benefactors of the
human race, as it made the year one of the most memorable in a busy, but useful and happy, life.

The number of admissions to the church was small, but
evidently there was great preparation for a large accession
in the following year.

On the eighteenth of January there was a meeting of the Indian commissioners at the house of Judge Sewall, as we learn from the latter's diary. It was to pray for God's blessing on the work among the natives. Dr. Mather and his wife were present, which fact assures us that she was having a lucid interval. There was a large party at dinner, some of the gentlemen being accompanied by their wives. "Dr. Mather prayed and preached excellently." Dinner parties were frequent in those days, and ministers were in general request. Judge Sewall used to make a note of the services of different ministers. He was their friend, and it is noticeable how often he writes of the "excellence" of Dr. Mather's sermons and prayers.

The doctor opens the diary of his fifty-ninth birthday, which was the Lord's day, with these words: "This year, which, oh! the wonders of the Divine grace and goodness, and patience, that has brought me to!—began with a day which obliges me to enter into the *Rest of God*. And very probably it may be the year of my entrance into *everlasting* rest."

He thanked God for all the blessings of his life and upon his services. He confessed his unworthiness and lamented his unfruitfulness. He made his *flight* unto the great sacrifice of his Saviour for pardon, and prayed for the smile of God upon him in the year to come, and for a soul prepared for all that might come upon him. And specially he prayed that he "might know more of Christ, and how to exhibit him to others."

In dressing he considered the various blessings of his various garments to him, and from thence formed agreeable thoughts of the benefits to be found in the enjoyment of his admirable Saviour, and in doing so he put on Christ.

He had been ill, and this being the first day of his

going abroad, he preached a sermon on the words in
1 Chronicles 29: 15 : "For we are strangers before thee,
and sojourners, as were all our fathers : our days on the
earth are as a shadow, and there is none abiding."

One of his "devisings" was to improve the Thursday
lecture by inciting the ministers to preach on connected
subjects, and such as the *cause of piety most called for.*
This suggestion was adopted, and a volume of sermons
was one of the results. The title was "Early Piety."

The starting of "religious societies in every plantation
for the reviving and preserving of piety " was on his mind
at this time. Families were pushing out into the wilds of
Maine and New Hampshire and the hill towns of Massachusetts, and they needed help in securing the preaching
of the gospel.

His negro servant desired baptism, and he took measures to prepare him for the solemnity. A former servant,
Onesimus, disappointed his hopes and became dissipated.
This was an exception to the general rule, that his servants became Christians while under his roof.

About this time Dr. Mather was anxious to have
"something done to get the gospel into the Narragansett
country." Nearly all that part of Rhode Island directly
west of Narragansett Bay to the Connecticut line was
" destitute of gospel privileges." After the "great swamp
fight," when Massachusetts and Connecticut troops made
a conquest of the region, the wilderness was entered by
people who had very little value for the institutions of
religion ; and those who had were so detached that it was
difficult to gather congregations and build houses of worship. Hence the need of sympathy and aid from the
more civilized and Christianized colonies.

There is a thought in the diary of the 27th, which
is a gem in some page of Bulwer, about the "life of

our thoughts, and the life of our actions ": different, but going on at the same time, every day Mather wished to give a practical turn to the thoughts. He states that many of his hearers had employments which kept their hands busy while their minds had much leisure. He would suggest methods to these people by which their minds might be busy with good things.

Two treatises occupied his pen in these weeks. One was entitled "*India Christiana*," growing out of correspondence with missionaries in the East Indies; and consultation about evangelizing the American Indians. It was the substance of his discourse at the house of Judge Sewall, above noted, on the eighteenth of January. Home and foreign missions were familiar to his mind. Additions were made to the discourse by the letters to and from Ziegenbalgh, Grundler, and others, making a volume of ninety-four pages.

The other treatise was "*Honesta Parsimonia*," an "essay on Time spent as it should be," urging to spend the time so that a "good account may at last be given of it." He desired to "disperse this pamphlet among the scholars at the college." The *India Christiana* was sent into "several parts of Europe, with designs to serve the kingdom of God."

In the essay on time is the following remark: "Whosoever compels another to lose his time, does him, an injury. He who allows himself to lose his own time, does himself an injury. The loss of time! 't is a damage; 't is a wrong to be complained of; 't is a thing which the law of God will animadvert upon."

In March Dr. Mather was moved to indignation by the "cursed pamphlets and libels" with which wicked men were endeavoring to poison the country; and on this he wrote: "An excellent young minister, as bright a thing as ever the town produced, is particularly insulted and abused by scurrilous and scandalous libels." Mather would encourage him; and he desired also that the government would put a stop to those publications. We have still the curse of "scurrilous and scandalous libels," by a portion of the press, but have found that it is not wise to suppress them, except so far as the law of libel may operate.

In regard to his two sons, we find this on the seventh of March: "*Sammy* must be urged to diligence," and after stating that he had paid a bill for a "further accomplishment for Creasy to render him a more finished gentleman," he adds: "Oh! when, when shall I say *Christian* must be paid for?"

How many ministers have ever conceived such a service as the following note specifies? "May I not visit the watch-house, persuade the watchmen to spend the time in devout exercises, and in reading good books when not abroad upon their duty?"

Dr. Mather was busy in these days in trying to get a well-qualified young gentleman into the college as tutor; in "visiting several aged people to help them to prepare for death"; in mending the "singing of the congregation"; and in sending his youngest son to college; writing at the same time letters to some "superior students, asking them to aid the boy in being a good student."

The following, under date March 16, refers to the distracted state of public opinion, and the prevalence of party spirit. It is instructive to know this, even without knowing the cause of contention.

There is a very wicked party in this country, who fill the land with strife and sin, and who are drawing the people into continual snares, and into such actions and follies as are a blemish upon us, and threaten to bring horrible oppression and slavery upon us. Unless the Lord should remove in a wonderful way, two or three men, who are the very soul and staff of the wicked party, the country must be ruined, and the churches reduced to wretched circumstances.

Dr. Mather carried all these troubles to God. Then he continues : —

Within these few hours God has, in a marvellous manner, and at a very critical moment, smitten with an apoplexy, one who has been, and would still have been, the great hinderer of good, and misleader and enchanter of the people, that there was in the whole house of representatives. Methinks I see a wonderful token for good in this matter.

Judge Sewall mentions Dr. Mather under several dates about this time : —

9th. Very thin Lecture because of a great storm. Dr. C. Mather preaches from *Matt.* 12 : 20, bruised cane, etc. excellently.

16th. At night Dr. Mather preaches in the school-house to the young musicians, from *Rev.* 14 : 3. "No man could learn that song." House full, and the singing extraordinarily excellent, such as has hardly been heard before in Boston.[1]

23d. Dr. C. Mather preaches; give Solomon my son, a perfect heart, in a very great auditory.

The "Accomplished Singer" was a publication of this year, and probably it was the lecture above noted. It contained "instructions how the piety of singing with a true devotion, may be obtained and expressed; the glorious God, after an uncommon manner glorified in it, and his people glorified." It was "intended for the assistance of all that would sing psalms, with grace in their hearts; but more particularly to accompany the laudable endeavors of those who are learning to sing by rule, and seeking to preserve a regular singing in the assemblies of the faithful." This shows that Dr. Mather — as might be expected of one so enlightened and so open to everything

---

[1] Dr. Mather had been " mending the singing."

new which promised good results — was in the front rank of those who held advanced views of the improvement of church music in this country. He remarks further : —

There is no exercise of piety more unexceptionable than that of making a joyful noise of singing in the praises of our God; that of signifying our delight in divine truths by singing of them; that of uttering the sentiments of devotion with the voice, and such a modulation of the voice as will naturally express the satisfaction and elevation of the mind, which a grave song shall be expressive of.

On the last day of March it is noted as follows : " My Christian Philosopher, (in a vessel blown off our coast last winter,) is this week arrived from England, — a hundred of the books are come. I may glorify God especially by getting our colleges filled with them." This was a "Collection of the best discoveries in nature, with religious improvements."

The "Christian Philosopher" has been highly commended by those competent to judge. It is in 312 pages, and is divided into thirty-three essays: Of the Light, Stars, Fixed Stars, Sun, Saturn, and four other Planets (the outer planets had not yet been discovered), Comets, Heat, Lightning, Earth, Animals, Man. The book was quite up to the learning of the times. The author referred to the most able and learned writers of the age. The volume is both interesting and devout. All God's works were made to glorify him. There were several editions, the last of which was in 1815.

April 14. "A wicked house at one end of the town, which proves a snare and a ruin to young people; procure the extirpation of it."

May 13. "A miserable negro under sentence of death for the murder of his wife, must be visited, instructed, counselled." This negro was hanged on the 25th. He had been instructed and baptized, and, as the record says, had "rendered himself a pretty noted fellow." A vast assembly attended the public service, and Dr. Mather took occasion to utter many things which he hoped would make a good impression, especially on wicked and froward husbands. The sermon was printed with the title "*Fremenda*: The dreadful sound with which the wicked are to be thunderstruck," etc. To this was added a "conference between a minister and the prisoner, on the day before his execution."

The various troubles that came upon Dr. Mather about this time were enough to crush him if he had not been upheld by divine assistance. He writes, May 14: "Inexpressible; inexpressible consolations," from finding his will swallowed up in the will of his Saviour. He believed that the "holy angels would take pleasure in him"; and that "God would show wonders to the dead."

On the 21st he wrote in this pleasant strain: — "The time of the year arrives for the glories of nature to appear in my garden. I will take my walks there on purpose to read the glories of my Saviour in them. I will make it an emblem of *Paradise*, wherein the second Adam shall have acknowledgments paid unto him."

He resolved to "preach about the glorious miracles of the Saviour," and to press on his people the duty of "seeking objects of compassion."

In June his mind was occupied with matters of interest far and near, individual and national. His African servant was afraid of the smallpox, and so must be "brought into a thorough Christianity." Then his view extended. "Ungospellized places, especially in Providence [Plantations] must be compassionated." His "American Sentiments," on the controversy about the Godhead of Christ, was published and scattered through the nation, that is, England. The "South Sea Bubble" suggested preaching on the "Snares of a worldly mind," illustrated by the "miseries brought on a foolish nation by that financial delusion."

The eruption of a volcano, making an island in the Mediterranean, set him to writing what might be of use in more ways than one. "A Just Alarm to a secure and sleepy world." And "behold at the time when he was writing, a bookseller came and desired to have something on the subject. A vessel came into the port of Boston and brought a report of this wonderful occurrence." Dr. Mather gathered the facts, and embodied them in a discourse. The facts were sent to England; perhaps to the Royal Society. He added a brief history of the other "ignivomous mountains at [that] day flaming in the world."

On the 14th, the wife of Rev. John Webb, minister of the New North, died, and Dr. Mather was called to preach on the occasion, which he did on the 17th. His theme was "Genuine Christianity; or a sure Christian, both in life and in death, glorifying the most glorious Lord." He hoped it would "introduce a more favorable condition of things in the churches." Only three sermons preached in that house had been printed, and he was the author of them all.

Another affliction that came nearer to his heart was the death of his Abigail, "Nabby" or "Nibby," as he loved to call her, the wife of Daniel Willard. Two sermons were occasioned by the loss of this "lovely daughter." One was "Silentiarius; a brief essay on the holy silence and godly patience, that sad things are to be entertained withal." She died on the twenty-first of September. On the preceding Sunday his theme was "The Refuge of the distressed." He had now but two sons left and two daughters, of all the fifteen children.

On the third of October he noted that he would have his *Table-Talk* facetious as well as instructive; yet he would have it intermixed with something from the Bible.

5. This week he finished his French letter, " *Grande Voix du Ciel à la France, sous la Verge de Dieu.*" He regarded France as suffering under the stroke of God for its manifold sins.

26. A fever seized him towards evening, brought upon him by colds taken in night visits and by the poisons of infected chambers.

Dr. Mather has been accused by writers in a preceding generation of cherishing anger and revenge towards opponents. He was, without doubt, a sensitive man and smarted under unjust aspersions, but he was far from malevolence or revenge. The following passage indicates his watchfulness against any indulgence of resentment : —

> I was jealous of myself lest I should harbor or admit any tendency towards the least wish of evil, unto such as may have distressed me, in the contradiction of sinners which I so much meet withal. And if I find, at any time, the least sudden indication that way, I must immediately suppress it, and oppose it, with a contrary wish of all good unto them.

He notes, on the 10th, that during many years, at his own single expense, he had maintained a *charity school* for the instruction of the negroes in reading and religion. A lieutenant in a man-of-war, a stranger to Dr. Mather, in "order to put an indignity upon him, called his negro slave by the name of Cotton Mather." It was one of many instances in which he had been abused and injured for doing good. He trusted that he should get all his harvest of good in another and a better world.

The above anecdote of the lieutenant is also a specimen of the insolence with which many British officers in the civil, military, and naval service treated the people of the province.　Moreover it was the pleasure of a portion of these officials, generally belonging to the National Church, to show their contempt of "dissenting ministers, so called."　In truth, this high-bred, but ill-bred, insolence on the part of the servants of the crown was a great factor among the causes which finally goaded the colonies to throw off the British yoke.

A fact in family history sometimes lurks in a record of devotion.　Thus, on the twenty-seventh of December, "when praying for his children, he would remember his two grandchildren."　This indicates that two of the four children of his daughter Abigail had died before this date; a fact which I have not found elsewhere.

The next day Dr. Mather records a curious "device of wickedness."　A vile set of men had contrived to write on the backs of the "Bills of Credit" what he calls "poisoned mischief"; that is, "irreligious remarks."　He adds: "Quere, would it not be well to write Scripture references, as *Matt.* 16: 28?"　This is the verse: "Verily I say unto you, There be some standing here, which shall not taste of death, till they see the Son of man coming in his kingdom."

CHAPTER XXII.

MANY items in personal history, and the titles of several works, have been stated in the order of time, closing with the twenty-eighth of December; but a large number of entries in the diary for 1721 have been passed over. There were, however, many events in that year which may be referred to without precisely giving the day or the month. One item in the year's history extends over several months. Selections will be arranged in several paragraphs, for convenience.

1. We have seen that the formation of the New North Church, in 1714, was the occasion of solicitude to both the ministers of the "Second" or "Old North," though the junior pastor was less anxious than his father. The result had been good, and both houses of worship had been well filled. There was entire harmony between pastors and people. But now, the project of founding another church at the north end gave rise to great commotion in that part of the town. On the first of May, Dr. Cotton Mather writes: "I must now, more than ever, look on my flock with a sacrificing eye. 'T is incredible what numbers are swarming off into the New Brick meeting-house." But being called to preach in reference to the movement, he proposed to take his farewell of those leaving, with a "solemn warning that they do not perish, after all they had received in his public ministry."

The cause of forming a new church was a contention in the New North about settling a minister. The Rev.

Peter Thacher, the pastor of the church in Weymouth, was invited to become the pastor of the New North, in 1719, by a vote of thirty-four out of forty-four. This was on the ninth of September. The next week, the congregation met to vote on the question, when six members of the church and thirty-nine others of the congregation protested, and immediately withdrew. Forty-six persons remained, and all voted for Mr. Thacher. This was the origin of a contest which involved all the churches and ministers of the town. The protesters took the ground, now that they were in the minority, that it was wrong to call a minister to leave a people who was esteemed by them. The other churches sympathized with this view, so that the council called to settle Mr. Thacher was very small, as the larger number invited declined to attend. But the church went forward, and had services of installation. This was the signal for a break, and the defeated party began to prepare for a new organization. It was carried forward during the next two years. A very large brick meetinghouse was built, and the New North congregation was divided. The enterprise drew in a large number from the Second congregation, — that of the Mathers, — including church members. The New Brick was embodied, and the Rev. William Waldron was ordained on the twenty-third of May, 1722. It was supposed by many at the time that the population on the "island" was not large enough to fill the three houses of worship, and the ministers of the North Church, as well as the pastor of the New North, very naturally felt the loss of those who withdrew. Hence Dr. Cotton Mather spoke of looking on his flock with a "sacrificing eye." His father, also, as said above, "took too much to heart the withdrawal of a vain, proud, foolish people," and he must try to comfort the good old man.

On the eleventh of May he writes that as his auditory
was to suffer a very great abridgment he must do more
by his writings. But his fears soon subsided. When he
saw so many departing, he could hardly resist the thought
that some coolness, or at least indifference to him, was
one of the causes; but this seems not to have been the
case. There appears to have been room for the new enterprise. Before the month was out, Dr. Mather found himself surrounded by a large congregation. On the 15th he
writes: "I had yesterday a very considerable auditory.
The people drawn off, was hardly to be missed in the
great congregation." He prayed that those who remained
might be more than ever united in love, and have such
visits of grace as to make them say, "'*T is good to be
here.*"

It has been said that this movement was a kind of revolt
of the enterprising middle class at the north end against
the domination of the more wealthy and influential families, and owed its popularity to that fact. Be this as it
may, the affair ended much better than Dr. Mather had
feared. Just before the new society moved into their new
sanctuary, he wrote: "April 30. Another great trial. A
party has formed a new society, built a large meetinghouse, — the finest in the country, — enraged, violent, boisterous men, to fill the house, prevail with a mighty number
of the flock to join them." He felt it deeply, that so
many left him and his father, and he prayed: "O Thou
Comforter, who alone can relieve my soul, be thou not far
from me."

Dr. Cotton Mather was invited to preach the first sermon
in the church, at its dedication. This shows the respectful
sentiments of the new society towards him. The sermon
was printed, with the title, "A Vision in the Temple: The
Lord of hosts adored, and the King of glory proclaimed,

on a day of prayer kept, May 10, at the opening of the New Brick meeting house, . . . by the ministers of the city with the society which built it, and this day swarmed into it." He made a solemn appeal to them, and especially his former hearers, in the name of himself and his father. All showed cordial feeling, and a deep interest in the welfare of the new society. The new church was not organized till the spring of the next year. The Old North sanctuary was soon filled so well that the pastors were encouraged. Doubtless special efforts were made by all three societies to induce people to attend public worship, and thus not a few who had neglected the house of God were drawn into the circle of Christian influence.

2. The "wretched administration" was still unsettled, and the conduct of some of his relatives by marriage still weighed down Dr. Mather, as with the weight of a millstone. July 7 he wrote that his "children-in-law, assisted by cruel and crafty adversaries, had laid a deep design for his ruin." He prayed, saying, "My God will hear me." And two days later he speaks of his *poverty*. What little he had owned had been sold, and the money was gone to pay debts not incurred by himself. He did not own a rod of land in the world. His salary was too small for his support in comfort. He met with many wants and straits, "in diet, much; in habits [clothing], more." Strange things occurred to pull him back and keep him low, "if at any time he had begun to lay by anything for the relief of his neighbors." There were deviations in the state of Mrs. Mather's health, affecting his comfort and causing deep anxiety. But still he felt that he had a glorious Christ. "Domine, ubi Omnia mea, Tu scis."

3. Sickness in his family and among his kinsfolk wore upon his strength and exhausted his spirits. On the nineteenth of September he records : —

My lovely Nibby, who was delivered of a daughter on the Lord's day, is now in dying circumstances. Daily with the dear child, assisting and comforting her.

24. O Lord, I am oppressed; undertake for me; my text, because I am tried by the dying circumstances of my family.

The newborn grandchild was to have been baptized in the afternoon, and the water was brought; but the child died in time of public service.

26. To strengthen a dear child in the agonies of death, is a sad work again called unto.

Between ten and eleven in the evening, "the poor child — Mrs. Willard — died a long, hard death."

4. There are many entries respecting Increase, which cannot be repeated; nor is it needful. He was faulty in many things. Though of an active temperament, he was slothful as to all good. He was often in bad company; at one time in a night riot with parties which exposed him to the perils of the law. At another time, hearing his father traduced by one of his godless companions, he resented it with "violent and passionate resentment," knocking the graceless fellow down, by which act he "exposed himself to much danger," and his father to "much trouble." Let us set down this jealousy for his father's honor to the young man's credit. But the whole record, as it affected the father, was one long wail of anguish. He writes, April 23 : —

O dismal case! O doleful case! I am a man of sorrows, and acquainted with grief. But I am now afraid of my sorrows! It looks as if there were certain sorrows wherein the sentence of heaven has put me into a state of punishment. I am punished less than my sins deserve. My crimes have procured an order from God, that I must languish under these heavy sorrows, and heaven is become inexorable. No cries, no prayers, no tears must prevail for the removal of them.

Under the pressure of his troubles, especially two of them,— the misconduct of his son and the madness of the people on account of his favoring inoculation for small-pox, and above all the fear that heaven was offended,— his whole being seemed to tremble and quiver with agony. "But if I am, indeed, in a state of punishment," he writes, "and my iniquity shall not be purged with sacrifice and offering, in this condition, how am I to behold myself, and glorify God?" He would accept the punishment, and humbly take part with God against himself and his in-iquities, with the acclamation: "Just art Thou, O Lord, and just are all thy judgments." The broken spirit and the contrite heart are evinced in the following prayer, on the 23d, at the baptism of a child, in the afternoon service :—

O our dear Saviour, hast thou not commanded us to bring our chil-dren unto thee? Yes; and in obedience to thy command, we do it. But shall dust and ashes plead with thee? Lord, why dost thou call for our children? Was it that thou mayest put them over unto Satan to take possession of them? Was it that they might be given up to blindness, and hardness, and madness? Was it that they might have the distempers of their souls lie uncured, when one gracious word of thine can cure them? Or was it that they might still have their hearts confirmed in their sins, when one touch of thine Almighty arm can give a new bias to their hearts? No, No; Thou hast called for them, that by thy wondrous power, they may become disposed for the service of our God. O our God, our God, we will yet believe that we shall see thee doing wonders for them.

He adds: "I could not but think on poor Increase, when these expressions were thus educed from me."

5. The prevalence of the smallpox in the family of Dr. Mather and in the town, and the trials incident thereto, will form a passage both dark and bright in this narrative: dark, so far as it relates to the disease and to the cruel madness of a portion of the people; but bright, as it reveals

the quick intelligence and the sweet benevolence and the dauntless courage and the Christlike spirit of Dr. Mather. The narrative will be drawn from his diary and from other contemporaneous authorities.

The first mention of the epidemic, in 1721, is under the date of May 26. "The small-pox, a grievous calamity, has now entered the town. The practice of *Inoculation* has never been used in this country, nor in England. How many lives might be saved by it?" Dr. Mather would procure a "consult of physicians," and lay the matter before them. He made an effort in that direction, but the physicians, with one exception, had no faith in the alleged preventive.

The following passage must not be withheld, as it helps us to understand the many-sided nature of the man. In a sermon, some while before, he had foretold the coming of some calamity to the town. He must now humble himself before God, lest some vanity of mind might arise from the fulfillment of his prediction. It would be well if all supposed prophets cultivated the same humility.

The smallpox called for special action from him, as he had two children liable to the distemper. What should he do? Must he take them out of the town? He must be prepared to resign them to the Lord, if they were to be taken away. Moreover, he would be exposed by the "horrid venom" of the sick chambers which he must expect to be called to visit. The children, Samuel and Eliza, soon "had terrors of the contagion breaking in upon them." He would, therefore, "quicken their flights unto their Saviour."

On the thirteenth of June, his son, aged about eighteen, had come home from Cambridge, where the disease was spreading, and was "loth to return." His state, and that of Eliza, about sixteen, who was in greater fear than he, "must be improved in the interests of piety in them."

There were "miserables neglected and perishing in sickness," and he felt bound to look after them. One of his devisings for doing good was to "write a little book on the small-pox, exhibiting medicines and methods" for the managing of it. He thought it might, perhaps, save the bodies and the souls of some people.

In July his cares increased. It occurred to him that he could suggest passages for the public News-Letter that might be of benefit to the readers, and he felt the obligation of comforting and directing "many people under grievous consternation from the spreading small-pox." There was occasion for all his kindness, because, as his record reads, "widows multiplied."

Dr. Mather found no success with the physicians, except Dr. Zabdiel Boylston, who had the boldness to make a trial of the inoculating process. It was an act of moral courage, as the doctors were united in rejecting the new method, and thereby increased the opposition of the public. "People," says Mather, "took a strange possession on this occasion. They rave, they rail, they blaspheme; they talk not only like idiots, but also like franticks. Not only the physician who began the experiment, but I also am an object of their fury, — their furious obloquies and invectives." But he had his consolations. "My conformity to my Saviour in this thing fills me with joy unspeakable and full of glory."

The state of the people called for redoubled exertions from tnose who regarded the bodies or the souls of men. Some fled to other towns, and to them he sent "books of piety." He visited, as far as possible, the "meetings of young people, on Sunday evenings, and entertained them with prayers and sermons," that were adapted to their condition. "Neighbors in very particular circumstances were to be visited." He prayed for the town "under the judgments of heaven, and ripening for more." He also prayed that "God would requite good for all the evils shown him by a deluded people."

An extract from the diary of July 27 is helpful to an understanding of the state of the town, and the writer's own feelings at this time : —

The monstrous and crying wickedness of the town,— a town at this time strangely possessed with the devil,— and the vile abuse which I do myself particularly suffer from it, for nothing but instructing our base physicians how to save many precious lives ; these things oblige me, in the fear of the divine judgments, to fall down before the Lord, in most earnest supplications for his pity and pardon to a people so obnoxious to his displeasure. . . . I must mightily take heed unto my own spirit, and watch against all ebullitions of wrath, lest, being provoked, I may speak unadvisedly with my lips.

In his multifarious reading, Dr. Mather had met with accounts of the good effects of inoculation among the Africans and Arabians; and the reports of Lady Mary Wortley Montague, of what she had learned in Constantinople, while her husband was British minister there, were confirmatory. Moreover, previous to this, he had learned from African servants — natives — that inoculation was practiced successfully by the Arabians. He therefore thought the process worth trying. Having informed the physicians of what he had learned, he was much chagrined and disappointed when they treated his suggestions with neglect. Possibly he hoped that his having been a medical student in early life might have saved him from being considered an intruder in the field that belonged to them. But if so, he was soon undeceived, and found the whole body of the faculty, Dr. Boylston excepted, arrayed against him. A Dr. Douglass, who lived in Boston some years and then returned to the old country, a man of some ability as a writer, but a prejudiced and unreliable man, attacked him rudely and ridiculed him in the most severe and ribald style. This man held out, in spite of the most convincing facts, for a long while; but when he left the country, he angrily yielded the confession that Mather and Boylston were in the right. It must not be forgotten that the ministers in the town, perhaps without exception, favored the introduction of the new method, and Mr. Colman wrote in favor of it; but as Cotton Mather took the lead in the movement, and strenuously urged it upon the people, the public clamor was raised against him and abuse was showered on his head without measure. His own venerable father, now eighty-two years old, embraced the new views and stoutly encouraged his son.

When the danger increased, and he felt the pressure of duty to have his two children inoculated with the virus, the opposition rose to a threatening height. It is incredible now, what a furore there was in the town, including his own society. They told him he would be the murderer of his own children. On the first of August, we read : "Full of distress about *Sammy*. He begs to have his life saved by receiving the small-pox in the way of inoculating." There were ten experimental cases already in the neighborhood. The father writes : "If he should die by receiving it in the natural way, how can I answer for it? On the other side, bitter opposition and prejudice against my ministry, if the boy should be inoculated. If he should happen to miscarry under it, my condition would be insupportable."

The lines following, August 16, show that the trial time had come : —

At last, my dear *Sammy* is now under the operation of receiving the *small-pox* in the way of transplartation. The success of the experiment among my neighbors, as well as abroad in the world, and the urgent calls of his grandfather for it, have made me think that I could not answer for it unto God, if I neglected it. At this critical time, how much is all piety to be pressed upon the child! More easily, perhaps, because his dearest companion and chamber-fellow in college, died this day of the small-pox taken in the common way.

On the 22d, it is written that his son had received the smallpox, in the way of inoculation, and was under the fever necessary to produce the eruption; but now there was reason to fear he had taken it in the natural way. He had had but one infusion, and one so small as to be hardly worth the name. "If he should miscarry, (besides the loss of so hopeful a son,) I should also suffer a prodigious clamor and hatred from an infuriated mob, whom the devil hath inspired with most hellish rage."

On the 29th, the case "was critical," being endangered by an "ungovernable fever." The next day, the diary notes that Mr. Willard, his son-in-law, was delirious in his fever, and that his daughter Abigail, Willard's wife, was "hazarded with several infirmities"; Hannah had a violent fever upon her, so that her life was in danger; and that his sister's family had the smallpox, including son, daughter, and grandson. By these things Dr. Mather was "called unto abundance of duty."

It is improving to learn how a good man bears himself in such a "sea of troubles." He writes: "Long meditation about the children." How desirable and delectable they were! And how much better was Christ! And the children, if taken from the good things of this world, which he would gladly have seen them rejoice in, will be taken by the Saviour unto himself and unto better things.

Towards evening, the child's fever rose to a height which distressed all. But he, "under an impression of such violence upon him, as if it came from some superior original, fell into an unpacifiable passion to have a vein breathed in him. We gratified him, and he had not one uneasy hour after it. His recovery went on to admiration."

From this time Samuel had a gradual recovery ; but his two sisters grew worse, till the lives of both were despaired of. On the fifth of September it was written : "*Nibby* in dangerous circumstances, and *Nancy* dying." But on the eighth, to the surprise of all, Nancy's fever broke, and she recovered. Mrs. Willard lingered a few days, had a child which soon died, and then she too was gathered into the heavenly garner, as stated on a previous page.

In all this, Dr. Mather was busy in comforting a sister and other relatives in their bereavements, and writing about the "terrible things God was doing to France," and getting out a " Pastoral Letter to friends visited with sickness."

Increase appears again in the diary. The father had been compelled to send him away from the family, as a mark of displeasure, and in the hope that such a step would bring him to reflection. He was a victim to "a vile sloth," and under the " power of Satan," but the father's heart yearned for him. " I will invite him again to live with me, that I might have him under my eye continually." He was now twenty-two years old.

As Dr. Mather's own family became free from sickness, cases multiplied in the town. One day he prayed seventeen times with the sick or afflicted, and on another with twenty-two.

The month of October was the harvest time of death, and Dr. Mather was occupied in comforting the mourners. He had three children with him at this time. Perhaps Increase had not yet returned to the household.

On the 7th it is recorded: " The distemper seems now at its height. The '*bills*' in the Old North church for the sick, last Sunday, were 202 ; and on the 8th, which was Sunday, they numbered 315." Prayers at home and with the sick on one day, at this time, were offered thirty-one times. No wonder he exclaimed, "What shall I do?"

And the record goes on in the same strain. On another day he "offered about thirty prayers." He distributed money to miserable families, with which his "dear Green-wood" supplied him. On the 20th, 180 notes for prayer were presented. At length his own strength seemed to be giving away. A fever seized him towards evening on the 26th, brought on him by "colds taken in night visits, and by the poison of infected chambers." He adds: "Is my hour come? It is welcome."

Early in November young Thomas Walter came to his uncle's house to go through the process of inoculation. By the 6th, the number of "bills" was reduced to fifty. Dr. Mather provided a "variety of employments by which his children could enrich their minds with valuable treasures;" and gave continual charges to the young people recovered from the smallpox, coming in his way, to live unto God.

We come now to a passage in the diary which records the degree of superstitious fear and hate to which some had been wrought up by their ignorance and their prejudice against a great public benefactor. On the 14th the feeling of some towards Dr. Mather was exploded on this wise: —

While my kinsman of Roxbury was at my house, down with the small-pox, towards three o'clock in the morning, some unknown hands threw a fire-grenado into the chamber where my kinsman lay, and which used to be my lodging room. The weight of the iron ball alone, had it fallen on his head, would have been enough to have done part of the business designed. But the grenado was charged, the upper part with dried powder, the lower part with a mixture of *oil* of *turpentine and powder*, and (what else I know not,) in such a manner, that upon its going off, it must have split, and probably, have killed the persons in the room, and certainly have fired the chamber, and laid the house in ashes. But "*this night there stood by me the Angel of God, whose I am, and whom I serve.*" As the grenado passed into the window, the fuse was shaken off, by hitting the iron in the middle of the casement, and fell upon the floor, and the fired wild-fire in the fuse was cast on the floor without firing the grenado. A paper was fixed to the missile, with this writing: " Cotton Mather, you dog; damn you. I 'll inoculate you with this, with a pox to you."

Dr. Mather's remarks upon this exhibition of malice growing out of a feverish and unjust state of the public mind, as they reveal the state of his mind in view of his danger, must have a place. Perhaps he overrated the danger, and possibly his exaltation was heightened by the strain on his nervous system ; but making all proper allowance, there are few passages of autobiography which surpass this in interest and in greatness of soul : —

I have been guilty of such a crime as this. I have communicated a never-failing method of preventing death and other grievous miseries, by a terrible distemper among my neighbors. Every day demonstrated that if I had been hearkened unto many persons' lives, (many hundreds) had been saved. The opposition to it has been carried on with senseless ignorance and raging wickedness. But the growing triumphs of truth over it, threw a possessed people into a fury which will probably cost me my life. I have proofs that there are people who approved and applauded the action of Tuesday morning, and who give out words that, though the first blow miscarried, there will quickly come another, that shall do their business more effectually. Now, I am so far from any melancholy fear on this occasion, that I am filled with unutterable joy at the prospect of my approaching martyrdom. I know not what is the meaning of it. I find my mouth strangely stayed, my heart strangely cold, if I go to ask for a deliverance from it. But when I think on my suffering death for saving the lives of dying people, it even ravishes me with a joy unspeakable, and full of glory. I cannot help longing for the hour when it will be accomplished. I am even afraid almost of doing anything for my preservation. I have a crown before me, and I know by feeling, what I formerly knew only by reading, of the divine consolation with which the minds of martyrs have been sometimes irradiated. I had much rather die by such hands as now threaten my life, than by a fever; and much rather die for my conformity to my blessed Jesus, in essays to save the lives of men from the destroyer, than for some truths, tho' precious ones, to which many martyrs testified formerly in the fires of Smithfield.

He filled out the month in the line of promoting inoculation; he drew up and communicated to the physicians about the country the "method of proceeding" in that operation; and in writing to Europe, sent many things which he hoped would "serve the kingdom of God," and among others, a more "distinct account of the *small-pox* inoculated." His hope was that in time hundreds of thousands of lives would be saved.

The last Friday of the month was spent as a "day of supplications," in which he "received many sweet influences of heaven," assuring him, he writes, "that my sins are pardoned, and that I should be rescued out of wretched encumbrances that lie upon me, and that my domestic wants and straits shall be relieved."

In December he speaks of his "auditory strangely reviving and increasing," so that he was put to further service to unite them, and yet further augment them. The formation of two new churches in his neighborhood within a few years, it would seem, had left him a large audience and a strong hold on his people. There must have been a reaction from the violent opposition that had been raging. That was inevitable, because his vindication was so complete; and yet his triumph enraged a certain class of enemies more than ever.

On the 22d he "communicated to some of the best ministers, papers which might have a tendency to raise them to higher measures of holiness and usefulness." He also prayed for final deliverance from the incumbrances which his "unhappy administration" had brought upon him, and he finally put the papers into the hands of Judge Sewall.

The following bit of speculation thrown out here may be taken as a curiosity: "I consider that whatever comes into my mind, has a substance grow unto it there. The thing receives a notional substance there, which is, indeed, all that a mind of no higher power than mine, can give to it."

Common justice would require that a man who had introduced a great improvement in medical practice, whereby the ravages of a loathsome and deadly disease had been reduced to a minimum, should receive due credit. And if this man pursued his way against opposition and amidst obloquy until the new method was fully established, his praise should not be in grudged and stinted measure. But Dr. Palfrey (book v, chap. ii) leaves the impression that Mather acted only a subordinate part, and that with "characteristic acerbity." He says that "Dr. Zabdiel Boylston, against great opposition, undertook to introduce that safeguard," etc. Again, "Among the writers on this side, besides Dr. Boylston, Dr. Colman was prominent, arguing the case with courtesy and moderation," etc. In contrast were "the Mathers, father and son, especially the latter, with the acerbity characteristic of them." But fortunately for the interests of truth and justice, Mr. Samuel G. Drake, author of an excellent history of Boston, seems to have been better informed, or more willing to treat Cotton Mather with fairness. The following is his account under date of 1721 : —

"Inoculation began to be practiced, and Dr. Zabdiel Boylston was the man who, almost single-handed, stood forth and buffeted the storm which the practice called forth, the violence of which is hardly conceivable in this age. The physicians were generally against him." Then he adds : " It is remarkable that Dr. Mather was on the side of inoculation, and encouraged Dr. Boylston to put it in practice ; and it may be pretty safely inferred, that without the countenance and influence of the former, he never could have succeeded, and even his life would have been in as much jeopardy as his reputation."

Dr. Boylston himself, with true magnanimity, recognized the service of Cotton Mather in these words : —

Dr. Mather in compassion to the lives of the people, transcribed from the Philosophical Transactions of the Royal Society, the accounts sent them by [two celebrated physicians] of inoculating the small-pox in the Levant, and sent them to the practitioners of the town, for their consideration thereupon. Upon reading of which I was very well pleased, and resolved in my mind to try the experiment; well-remembering the destruction the small-pox made nineteen years before, when last in Boston, and how narrowly I then escaped with my life.

The prevalence of the distemper, and the efficiency of the preventive, will be seen by the following figures. It was estimated that there were about 12,000 inhabitants in Boston in 1721. It was thought that nearly 1,500 left, to escape the contagion, leaving 10,568 in the town, 4,549 north of the mill creek, and 6,019 south of it. Out of 5,759 who took the disease in the natural way, 844 died. Out of 286 inoculated, only six died. That is, of the first class not far from one in 6.8 died; of the latter class, only one in 48.

During this and the preceding year, Dr. Mather sent about 1,000 pages to the press. Of these pages, 200 were published in 1720, and 800 in 1721; but there is reason to believe that the number written in each year was nearly equal. For example, the "Christian Philosopher" was printed in England in the latter year, but it must have been sent over before.

CHAPTER XXIII.

THE methods of church discipline and of procedure in former times, in the cases of infants whose pious parents are dead, are instructive ; and it is interesting to learn how the early churches of New England met new demands on their charity and wisdom. The following cases belong to the early part of 1722.

Two persons who had been under censure —one nearly twenty, and the other over twenty years — expressed penitence, and were restored. There must have been much patience used in regard to these persons, and persistent effort to bring them back to duty, instead of the unseemly haste with which offenders are sometimes dealt. The ancient ministers did not proceed to extreme measures before they had tried the " second admonition."

The child of a pious woman who died before the baptism of her child, but who desired that it might be baptized and dedicated to the Lord, came before the church, March 27. The grandmother, a pious member, presented the child, and promised before the Lord to adopt it as her own and take faithful care of its religious training. On another occasion an orphan child was presented by a grandparent, as *in loco parentis*, and was baptized "into the Father, the Son, and the Holy Ghost."

The ingathering of the church this year included the pastor's Benjamin, his Samuel, aged sixteen, and now well along in his college course. This was a great delight to

484

the father, but was accompanied with tender solicitude for the two daughters who had not yet acknowledged their Lord.

The year began with the note that "some of the flock were greatly interested in the question, when shall the will of the Lord be done on earth as it is in heaven?" Perhaps they were Second Adventists. They asked him privately about it, and he arranged to have such persons meet at his house, once a fortnight, to consider the subject.

Increase continued to be a cause of great anxiety to his father, who yet had hope to labor with and pray for him. "Ah! poor Creasy! poor Creasy! yet will I not utterly give him over." One of his "supplications" on the 5th, and probably every day, was that "son Increase might yet have a new heart given him." He also studied how to supply him with matters to be inserted in his "Quotidiana," saying, "I would hope to spread some nets of salvation for him."

On the 13th we are informed that an "abominable people at Marblehead, will not let their minister save his life from the smallpox by inoculation." Whereupon Dr. Mather offers to "receive and cover him" in his own house.

The next day he wrote: "This thought is very impressive upon me. When I am going to prayer, I am going to heaven. Lord, make it more so. With what love, and hope, and joy ought I to repair thither on all occasions."

The following record reveals a morbid state of mind. Dr. Mather was naturally sensitive, and any act of unkindness grieved him. There is every reason for believing that he was held in high esteem by the ministers generally; but in what follows, it appears that he had taken up the unpleasant conviction that his opinions were despised, and his suggestions were rejected, because of personal dislike. On the fifteenth of January he made a statement in a meeting of ministers, in which he referred to the fact that, though all his public life (now more than five and forty years) he had tried to do good in all companies and on all occasions, yet it had come to pass that opposition had so risen against him that he could do no more, except among his own people. He had some opportunities abroad, but he said: "At present, *I have done! I have done! I have done!* treating you with any more of my proposals. If they should be never so good, yet if they be known to be mine, that is enough to bespeak a blast upon them. Do you propose as many good things as you please, I will second them, and assist them, and fall in with them to the best of my capacity." It is added that "an ingenuous young person in the company (Mr. William Cooper) made the first, and a quick response to me, in these words, 'I hope the devil don't hear you, Sir.'" The responses of the other ministers are not given, but their general tenor can be imagined. It is certain that Dr. Mather did not cease from "good devisings," or from making them known to his brethren.

At this time he feared that "some inconveniences might befall the college," and he pondered the question, whether he "could privately give some advice that might be serviceable." A few days later his "help was asked about some things a-doing at the college," and on the eighth of February he states: "I have a wondrous prospect of restoring peace to the country by accomplishing some unexpected reconciliations."

With the following paragraph the diary closes for about two years : —

Feb. 10. An aged gentlewoman, eminent for her bounties to all sorts of persons, — I have been myself a sharer in them — is fallen into the lowest poverty. Extreme wants and straits have overtaken her. And none of the ingrates that have partook in her bounties, will now do anything for her. I send her some supplies, but lie entirely concealed from her. I stir up some others to do for her.

The life of Dr. Mather was varied as usual, this year, in his parish work, in his publications, and in his connection with the public. One is amused to find that one of his publications of the previous year was sent as a present, by an eminent chief justice, to a lady whom he was assiduously courting. In his diary for January 25, Judge Sewall wrote : "I enclosed to Mrs. Mary Gibbs, last Monday's Gazette, two fair 5£ bills of credit, and *India Christiana*, very well bound, gilded on the edge, inscribed to her with my own hand."

The "Angel of Bethesda" was one of numerous essays, large and small, which came from Mather's prolific pen in 1722. The angel is presented as "visiting the invalids of a miserable world." The treatise is anonymous, but the words "by a fellow of the Royal Society," revealed the writer. The running title was " *Nishmath Chajim*, or The Breath of Life." Says the author : —

There is a spirit in man ; a wonderful spirit, which from very good authority, may be called *Nishmath Chajim*, the breath of life, which may be of a middle nature between the rational soul and the corporeal mass, and may be a medium of communication between them.

It is a very curious piece, full of old-time learning. Space can be given for only a short passage : —

The great God who formed all things, and who, after a singular manner, formed the spirit of man within him, has endowed this *Nishmath Chajim* with wondrous faculties, which yet are all of them short of those powers which enable the rational soul to penetrate into

the causes of things, to do curious and exquisite things in the mathe-
matical sciences, and above all, to act upon a principle of love to God,
and with the views of another world. This may be the seat of disease.

The new congregation at the north end was some time
in its inchoate state, and a church was not gathered into
its New Brick meetinghouse, and a minister ordained, until
the twenty-third dav of May, when Dr. Mather preached
the ordination sermon of Rev. William Waldron. His
topic was " Love Triumphant "; and whatever may be said
of the treatment of it, his action in reference to the enterprise was an exhibition of triumphant love. " Since love
is of God, it becomes Christians to be exemplary in the
grace of love; pastors to love .their people; people to
love their pastors; all Christians mutually to love one
another."

The variety and adaptation of Dr. Mather's sermons,
pamphlets, and books is a constant surprise, proving that
all his public efforts were thoughtfully designed for an
end.   Here are the titles of three discourses for the
benefit of young people, within three or four months.
One was " Bethiah ; the Glory which adorns the daughters
of God ; and the Piety wherewith Zion wishes to see her
daughters glorious."   Next, on the fourth of June, came
" Columbanus ; or, The Doves flying to the windows of
their Saviour. A sermon to a society of young people."
And, on the fifth of August, Lord's day evening, he
preached " Pia Desideria ; or The Smoking Flax, raised
into a sacred flame, in a short essay upon those pious
desires, which are the introduction and inchoation of all
vital piety, delivered unto a religious society of young
peopie."   Another discourse may be put in the same class,
as it appealed specially to the young.   It bore the title:
" Sober Sentiments, in an Essay, July 19, upon the vain

presumption of living and thriving in the world, which does too often possess and poison the children of the world." It was caused by the "premature and much-lamented death of Mr. Joshua Lamb, a student in Harvard college," who died of a fall received a few days before. Thomas Walter furnished an appendix.

Two other sermons, related in subject matter, are upon the ministry. One is entitled "The Minister," and was preached before the anniversary convention of ministers from several parts of New England, May 31, and published at their request. It was upon the "Services of an able Ministry." The second was a reprint of "Repeated Admonitions, in a Monitory Letter about the maintenance of an able and faithful ministry, directed unto those people who sin against and sin away the glorious gospel, by not supporting the worthy dispensers of it." It had the "pious concomitancy" of the general assembly. A third edition came out in 1725. Our fathers knew by experience that new settlements which remained destitute of church privileges relapsed into a sort of heathenism, and that wherever a worthy minister was sustained, all the elements of good society soon gathered around him.

Three other discourses came before the public, all cognate in spirit, which may be grouped together in this place. "Divine Afflations" was an effort to "describe and bespeak those gracious influences of the Holy Spirit, which will produce and confirm the eternal happiness of those who find that blessed spirit of life so entering into them, and making them live unto God." Again, "The Soul departing" related to the "state of the dead." It was written to answer the solemn inquiry, "How the children of men are at their death disposed of." The recent "decease of some desirable friends" was the occasion. This was followed by "Caelestinus: A Conversation in Heaven, quickened and assisted with discoveries of things in the heavenly world." Some "relations of the views and joys that have been granted to departing saints" were added. This was "recommended to the people of God by the very Reverend Dr. Increase Mather, waiting in the daily expectation of his departure to that glorious world."

The venerable Increase Mather, though aged and feeble, was still called on to write and pray. Judge Sewall (date September 25) records that at a fast kept at the Old North Church, to "pray for the pouring out of God's Spirit on New England, especially the rising generation, Dr. I. Mather prayed, but so low that I could hardly hear a word; was spent."

Two or three items in the judge's diary near this time give us a glimpse of Cotton Mather. At the fast above noted he preached in both parts of the day, from Matthew 9: 18: "Life to the ruler's daughter." On the 19th, the judge sent to him "an Angel, and two Crowns, for assisting the Council in the close of the Sessions." The council requested the clergymen to open the sessions with prayer, and paid them for the service. An "angel" was a coin worth about ten English shillings.

In December, when Christmas was drawing near, Governor Shute, who was an English churchman, though of a liberal spirit, was desirous of having the court adjourned for the day. The judge was opposed to it, as contrary to the custom of the country. On the 20th he invited Dr. Mather to dine. "After dinner, I consulted with him about the adjournment of the court. We agreed that 't would be expedient to take a vote of the Council and Representatives about it." They well knew that the representatives would not vote to adjourn.

Here is another peep into the life of 1722. The

Register (of probate ?) was about to sail for England, and the question came up, Who should fill his place? There were several candidates, and the judge would have been glad to get a berth for Dr. Mather's son, if possible. The record of October 19, in part, is: "Mr. Rolfe is made Register. I tried, before the Council met, and found if I had used my interest for I—— M——, it would not have passed." This shows that Judge Sewall had enough confidence to trust young Increase in the office, but the majority preferred another.

The first notice of Dr. Mather which we note after the coming in of the year 1723 is found in the diary of Judge Sewall, January 11: "The Lt. Gov. [William Dummer, acting governor,] dines at the Green Dragon upon the Council's invitation. Dr. Mather prayed excellently in the Council, for the Gov'r, Lt. Gov'r, Council, Representatives, upon the change of the government." Governor Shute had slipped off unexpectedly to England, and Dummer acted as governor several years.

This year was one of interest to the North Church, because of the decease of the senior pastor, and the calling of a colleague to his son Cotton. Action was taken with reference to an associate while Dr. Increase was yet alive, but only lingering, as it were, on the threshold of the heavenly world. On the tenth day of the fifth month, the record is: "Seeking a supply for an assistance and succession in the ministry." No conclusion was reached.

Under date of August 23, the diary of Judge Sewall reads: "Dr. Increase Mather dies, just at noon, after long and grievous illness." Six days later he was buried in the tomb of his son, "attended by a vast number of followers and spectators." His age was eighty-four years, two months and two days. The last three weeks of his "grievous illness" are condensed in the following paragraph from the pen of his son.

At last he began to fall into the torments of the wheel broken at the cistern; which yet became not intolerable, and forced no ejulations from him, till about three weeks before he died. Under these, about three days before his expiration, coming out of a dark minute, he said, " it is now revealed from heaven to me, that I shall quickly, quickly, quickly be fetch'd away to heaven, and that I shall dy in the arms of my son." After this, he kept very much calling for me ; till Friday, the twenty third of August, in the morning, perceiving the last agonies now come upon him, I did what I could, after my poor manner, that he might be strengthened by such quickening words as the lively oracles of our God have provided for such occasions. As it grew towards noon, I said unto him, " Syr, the Messenger is now come to tell you : This day thou shalt be in Paradise. Do you believe it, Syr, and rejoice in the views and hopes of it?" He replied, "I do! I do! I do!" — and upon these words, he died in my arms.

The same filial pen tells us of the funeral : —

On the seventh day after this, he was laid in the *Cave of the Treasure*, and God honored him with a greater funeral than had ever been seen for any divine, in these, (and some travelers at it said, in any other) parts of the world. The Hon. William Dummer, Esq., who was then Lt. Governor and commander-in-chief; and his honorable, ancient, cordial friend, Samuel Sewall, Esq., the chief Judge of the province; with the president of the college, and three of the principal ministers, were they that held the pall ; before which one hundred and threescore scholars of the college, whereof he had once been the president, walked in order ; and there were followers of every rank, (among which about fifty ministers) and spectators that could not be numbered ; all with an uncommon sadness in their countenance, and a most serious aspect ; concurring to the fulfillment of the text, on which Rev. Thomas Foxcroft, whom he greatly loved, on that day entertained a great auditory with a very acceptable sermon — Text 2 Chron. 24: 15, 16 : — "He was full of days when he died ; and they buried him — honorably — because he had done good in Israel." Indeed, he might on " many accounts be called, the Jehoidah of New England."

The "first fathers" of New England, in Church and State, hold a distinct place in our history and are held in a veneration all their own; but the number of worthies in all the generations since — whether divines, statesmen, diplomatists, or scholars who rank with Increase Mather are very few. None equaled him in varied abilities and accomplishments before Jonathan Edwards appeared, except his son Cotton, and Benjamin Franklin; and when we consider his long pastorate of over sixty years, his presidency of the college, his public mission in England, and his numerous works which informed and guided his own generation, we cannot deny him a place among the chiefest of our great and useful men.

The death of President Mather was honorably noticed in many pulpits, as he was held in general esteem and veneration. Some of the clergy had been students of his, and through them his influence was perpetuated. His son delivered a characteristic sermon on the occasion. Title, "A Father departing; or the departure of the venerable and memorable Dr. Increase Mather; by One who, as a Son with a Father, served with him in the gospel." Early in the next month he preached another sermon, part of which is given in "Parentator," wherein the son describes his father's ministry. Text, Revelation 3: 3: "Remember therefore how thou hast received and heard." In coming to the concluding part he used these words: —

The Pastor, who this day, sixty two years ago, preached his first sermon to the North church in Boston, has of latter years, ever spoken of you as a loving people. The expressions of your love to him were notable, and were numberless, and were such as greatly comforted him. What you expressed in the last years of his life, and especially after he became an emerited soldier, and singularly at his departure, is what I know not that any church has ever equalled. In a very public manner, I now do, and in a more public manner, I hope I shall render you the thanks which are to be expected on the occasion. But I am now to tell you, that the most significant way of expressing your love will be, to remember how you have received and heard, in the ministry of that burning and shining light wherein ye rejoiced for so long a season.

He then, under seven heads, exhorts the hearers to remember the main points of their late pastor's preaching. It was a sermon of great tenderness and power, and the words are still instinct with life and energy.

In regard to a supply, the church voted, September 1, for delay. On the second of October, the "church voted, and chose, by thirty-four, Mr. Joshua Gee." November 12, "Mr. Gee's favorable answer was read." On the 25th, the church "fixed upon Dec. 18, for ordination." Voted to "invite the six churches of the united brethren in this town, and the church in Roxbury, to the ordaining council." The following partial program was adopted by the church: "Voted, that Mr. Waldron, Mr. Wadsworth and Mr. Sewall be desired, with the Pastor, to join in the imposition of hands; the Pastor to give the charge." The other parts were left with the Council to arrange. It was now about sixty years since Increase Mather became the minister of the North Church, and nearly forty years since his son Cotton, after two or three years' assistance, had been ordained as his colleague.

The publications of Dr. Mather this year were less than usual in number, and all of them were small, not one exceeding thirty pages, and all together making only about 200 pages. Funeral sermons led the way. One was delivered on the fourteenth of April entitled, "Euthanasia: A Sudden death made happy and easy to the dying believer, exemplified in John Frizell, Esq." The running title was, "On dying very suddenly." Mr. Frizell was a merchant, and from Sewall we learn that he had a "very great funeral." For some unexplained reason the city of Glasgow, in 1710, "sent over and made him a burgess, and guild brother." This was doubtless a much-valued mark of respect or gratitude, perhaps of both.

The death of Rev. Joseph Belcher, the reverend and excellent pastor of Dedham, called forth "A Good Character; or, a walk with God characterized"; with a running title, "A Holy Walker."

An essay on "Remarkables in the Ways of Wicked Men" cannot be found. It is in the list made by his son Samuel. It would be interesting to see how the subject was treated by one who had an infinite fund of incident and anecdote regarding all sorts of men, in all ages of recorded biography.

We have often been reminded of Dr. Mather's deep interest in the fortunes of those who went "down to the sea in ships." His house and his church were not far from deep water, and he used to take a turn occasionally to the wharves as one drawn thither by sympathy with mariners. Many families connected with the ocean by commerce, or as officers and sailors, were in his congregation. A "young gentleman taking a voyage to sea" requested a sermon of him on the occasion. He complied, and treated of "The Lord High Admiral of all the Seas adored; a brief essay upon the miracle of our Saviour walking upon the water; with admonitions of piety profitable to all, but very particularly agreeable to them whose business calls them to sailing on the water." We here see how near this preacher was in the habit of bringing Christ to his hearers and of leading them to associate him with all their ways and works.

Sermons which reveal the sins of past times are material for history as well as biography. Such a discourse was that with the title: "The Pure Nazarite: Advice to a young man concerning an impiety and impurity, (not easily to be spoken of) which many young men are, to

their perpetual sorrow, too easily drawn into. A Letter
forced from the press, by the discoveries which are made,
that sad occasions multiply for the communication of
it." This was a subject which required all his delicacy
as well as fidelity to handle with profit.

There was a "great and memorable storm" in the early
part of the year (February 24) in which "many, and heavy,
and unknown losses were suffered." This caused him, in
the time of the storm, while it was raging, to preach on
"The voice of God in a tempest." The whole audience,
from their connection with the sea, must have listened
with thrilling interest.

At this period in our religious history strenuous efforts
were made to extend and strengthen Diocesan Episcopacy
in Boston and New England. There was a memorable
controversy in New Haven at the Yale College commencement in 1722. The president, Mr. Cutler, who had
become an Episcopalian, had, with a few others, planned
for a large defection in the Congregational ministry and
churches; but the plan failed, and Mr. Cutler soon appeared in Boston. Things had changed now from what
they were at the first settlement of Boston, when Laud
and the high church undertook to extinguish nonconform-
ing churches. The day of toleration had come in England. But the men engaged in bringing Episcopacy into
Boston were of the narrow, high, exclusive type, who
denied the validity of all non-episcopal ordination, and
made themselves specially offensive by their lordly claims
to superiority.

Times have changed again, since then: for now men
of all evangelical denominations coöperate in many ways
in promoting the cause of their common Lord, without
abandoning their own peculiar views and methods. Dr.
Mather felt it to be his duty to utter "Some Seasonable

Inquiries concerning Episcopacy, for the consideration and satisfaction of them that are willing to weigh things in even balances ; and for the establishment of the Reformed Churches, lest being led away with the error of the day, they fall from their own steadfastness." As a matter of history, the falling away took another turn toward the close of the century, but the Episcopal movement made but little gain until some years after the Revolution.

Cotton Mather was a great letter writer, but only a few specimens, comparatively, of his correspondence have seen the light. His style of writing, when talking to a friend with pen and ink, was so like himself, but so unlike his elaborate " composures," that an example may well find a place occasionally in this memoir. His descriptive power is also well illustrated in his account of the great storm, February 24, 1723, during which he preached "The Voice of God in the Tempest." The letter was written, it is supposed, to John Woodward, Secretary of the Royal Society, in London.

Sir, — The reading of a storm is not so bad as the feeling of it. I shall therefore think it no trespass on civility to entertain you with a short relation of a storm and tide, wherein these parts of the world saw what no man alive remembers to have seen before, and suffered incomputable damage. It was on Febuary 24, 1722–3, when our little American philosophers observed an uncommon concurrence of all those causes which an high tide was to be expected from. The moon was then at the change, and both sun and moon together on the meridian. The moon was in her perigee, and the sun was near to his, having past it but a little before. Both the sun and moon were near the equinoctial, and so fell in with the annual and the diurnal motion of the terraqueous globe. There was a great fall of snow and rain, the temper of the air was cool and moist, and such as contributed to a mighty descent of vapors ; and cloudy atmosphere might also help something to swell and raise the waters. Finally, the wind was high, and blew hard and long, first from the southward, and it threw the southern seas in a vast quantity to the northern shores ; then veering easterly, it brought the eastern seas also upon them; and then, still veering to the northward, it brought them all with yet more accumulations upon us. They raised the tide unto an height which had never been seen in the memory of man among us. The tide was very high in the night, but on the day following, it being the Lord's day, at noon, it rose two feet higher than had ever been known unto the country; and the city of Boston particularly suffered from it incredible mischiefs and losses. It rose two or three feet above the famous long wharf, and flowed over the other wharfs and streets, to so surprising an height, that we could sail in boats from the southern battery to the rise of the ground in Kings Street, and from there to the rise of the ground towards the North meeting house. It filled all the cellars, and filled the floors of the lower rooms in the houses and ware houses in town. The damage is inexpressible in the country, in the inside of Cape Cod. The tide rose four feet, and without, it rose ten feet or a dozen feet higher than ever was known. At Rhode Island and Piscataqua they fared as we did in Boston. At Hampton the sea broke over the natural banks for many miles, and continued running over for many hours. Almost all over the country, the artificial banks of the sea were broken down. The marshes were overflown and overwhelmed; mighty stacks of hay, some removed, some destroyed; many acres of marsh ruined, being either torn up thro' the rage of the water, or covered with the sand from the road. This is the sum of the story; if there be nothing in it worthy to be remembered than as waters that pass away, (or anything like the memorable November storm, that filled the English world with horror, twenty years ago, and whereof a large book was written,) yet it may lead a person of your sagacity to some considerable speculations, and more particularly, tho' I have mentioned what our small philosophers here may dream of the causes of such occurrences, yet you will also consider how far the subterranous heats and streams below the bottom of the ocean, rising thence and passing through it, and causing the deep to boil as a pot, may further contribute unto them. However, as for a tempest, so for a letter about one, you may think the shorter the better, it shall therefore, now be over. I will add no more, and you shall be sensible of nothing more but a swelling tide of esteem and affection for you, in the breast of, Sir,

Your hearty friend and servant,   C. M.

September 24, 1723.

Here, at the close of the life of President Increase Mather and near the end of the life of his son, Dr. Cotton

Mather, is a convenient and fitting place to refer to the contemporaries of both, from 1680, when the latter began to preach, to his decease in the early part of 1728. The list will include the ministers of Boston, and others in the vicinity as well as some in other parts of the province. Some of these were settled before Cotton Mather, and others survived him.

The First Church, formed in Charlestown, July 30, 1630, and removed to Boston soon after (the majority having changed their residence) consisted of only four original members, namely, Governor John Winthrop, Lieutenant-Governor Thomas Dudley, Mr. Isaac Johnson, and Rev. Thomas Wilson. Two days later, five more united with them. Not long after " sixty-four males and half as many females" became members. The ministers in 1680–1728 were: Rev. James Allen, 1668–1710; Joshua Moodey, 1684–1692; Joshua Bailey, 1693–1697; Benjamin Wadsworth, 1696–1725; Thomas Bridge, 1705–1715; Thomas Foxcroft, 1714–1769.

The Rev. Benjamin Wadsworth was chosen president of Harvard College in 1725, and held the office till 1737. It is said of him that he was "highly and justly respected for his ability and his attainments, the unpretending quietness of his manners, and the resolution and firmness of his character." Rev. James Allen was one of the ministers excluded from the English Church in the early years of Charles II by what was called the "St. Bartholomew's Act." All of the pastors of the First Church were superior men. Most of them were colleagues under the old plan of teacher and pastor.

The ministers of the Second, or Old North, Church were: Increase Mather, 1664–1723; Cotton Mather, 1684–1728; Joshua Gee, 1723–1748.

The ministers of the Old South Church, founded

in 1669, were Thomas Thatcher, 1670-1678; Samuel Willard, 1678-1707; Ebenezer Pemberton, 1700-1717; Joseph Sewall, 1713-1769; Thomas Prince, 1718-1758. All of these men were prominent; most of them distinguished. Samuel Willard, a descendant of Major Simon Willard, good as well as famous in his day, and long after, became vice-president and acting president of the college in 1701, and retained the office till his death in 1707. He was, says Samuel A. Eliot, "a man of distinguished ability, and a divine of extensive learning and uncommon powers of elocution." He was the author of the "Compleat Body of Divinity," in more than 900 pages, folio. An idea of the bigness of the work may be formed from the following figures. There are 914 double-column folio pages in the volume. There are 134 lines to an average page. There are about 8.4 words to a line. This gives 1,028,798 words to the whole book. Short lines and breaks in the pages and headlines are not counted. Any one can find the number of volumes of any specified book that would equal this "Body of Divinity" in contents. The comparative size of the volume may be shown by an example or two. In the *Magnalia* ,there are 661,848 words, more or less, or nearly seven tenths as many as in the book in question. In the manuscript copy of the "Illustrations of the Scripture," or "Biblia Americana," there are as many as 2,888,000 words, or, in round numbers, as many as in two and one-half such works as Willard's. The work (of Willard) is in 250 "Expository Lectures on the Assembly's Shorter Catechism." It was not published until nineteen years after the author's death, which is thought to be "without a parallel in the history of theology." It was the first folio issued from a New England printing office. The folio edition of the *Magnalia* was issued in England.

The work was published by a subscription. It is prefaced by a " Character " from the pen of his colleague, Mr. Pemberton, in which he says, " In him [Willard] bountiful heaven was pleased to cause a concurrence of all those natural and acquired, moral and spiritual excellencies, which are necessary to constitute a great man, a profound divine, a very considerable scholar, and a heavenly Christian."

Joseph Sewall was chosen president of the college after the death of President Leverett, but declined. Thomas Prince was the author of " Annals " which have laid all subsequent writers of our history under obligations.

The pastors of Brattle Street Church were: Benjamin Colman, 1699–1747; William Cooper, 1716–1743. Both were eminent in their day, but Colman is held more in remembrance, owing to his connection with the origin of the church.

The New North had for its ministers, John Webb, 1714–1750; and Peter Thacher, 1723–1729.

The minister of the New South was Samuel Checkley, from 1719 to 1769; and the New Brick Church at the north end enjoyed the labors of William Waldron from 1722 to 1727.

The church in Charlestown had the following pastors in the period under review: Thomas Shepard, Jr., 1680–1685; Charles Morton, 1686–1698; Simon Bradstreet, 1698–1741; Joseph Stevens, 1713–1721; Hull Abbot, 1724–1774. Shepard and Morton were men of high rank in the ministry and as scholars.

Watertown was ministered to by John Bailey, 1686–1697; Thomas Bailey, 1687–1689; Samuel Angier, 1697–1719.

John Higginson, son of the first pastor of that name, was over the church in Salem from 1660 to 1708.

Newton : Jeremiah Hobart, 1674–1712.

Dorchester : John Danforth, 1682–1730.

Roxbury : John Eliot, 1632–1690; Nehemiah Walter, 1688–1750; Thomas Walter, 1718–1725.

Samuel Danforth was at Taunton ; Jeremiah Shepard at Lynn, and James Sherman at Sudbury, while Cotton Mather was in service.

In Lancaster between 1690 and 1748, were John Whiting, descendant of Whiting of Lynn ; Andrew Gardner and John Prentice, the latter from 1708 to 1748.

At Plymouth was John Cotton, son of the John of Boston ; and in New Hampshire, Roland, a grandson. The former from 1669 to 1699, and the latter between 1694 and 1722.

The Mayhews made their names immortal in connection with the conversion, the civilization, and the government of the Indians on Martha's Vineyard, between 1689 and 1756.

CHAPTER XXIV.

THIS is the last year (1724) in which we can draw from the diary, beginning with the twelfth of February, the birthday of the author, and extending to the same day in the next year. The record is quite full, but the excerpts will be much restricted, inasmuch as many entries have lost their interest by the lapse of time.

Turning first to the church records, we notice the presence of the new minister, Mr. Gee, who, on the fourteenth of February, administered baptism. The record reads : "The first baptism administered by Mr. Gee, and indeed, the first that has been administered by any hand but those of Mathers (father and son), in the Old North church, for more than half a hundred years together."

The diary begins, February 12, in this strain : "O wonderful ! O wonderful ! O the wonders and praises with which I am to consider the favors of the gracious God, who hitherto has helped me." As this is the last record of Dr. Mather's experiences in his study to be quoted, it will serve to show the state of his mind, when nearing the end, to make from it a few citations.

This birthday was partly spent in thanksgiving. "Enjoyed a most comfortable, yea, an astonishing presence of God. No pen can express my enjoyments and my elevations." He began by recognizing his nothingness; accepted the offerings of God, and resigned himself to God. He thought of the perfections of God, the Father, Son and Holy Ghost. He gave thanks for blessings; specially that he had lived so long, and had been "preserved from the grievous diseases which carry horror with them." He praised God for "discipline and afflictions." He was thankful for blessings on his ministry, and for spiritual blessings in general.

Then he settled points in which he must be, more than ever, the Lord's ; next, sang psalms, after which are these expressions : "But O the expansions of a soul mounting up to heaven, as with the wings of eagles ! And O the assurances and mercies reserved for me ! My pen is not able to relate them." A few days later, he wrote : "Devotions of the day full of a divine life. Prayed, not so much for blessings, as to be willing to go without them."

The diary has the usual notes of designs and efforts for usefulness, both for individuals and the public ; but the items have no special interest now, except as they indicate the unceasing benevolence of the man. A few examples will serve our purpose. He wrote an "elegant epitaphium" for his father's life. Distant relations enlisted his efforts for their spiritual good. He set his new servant upon "learning the ways of piety." He sent his "Visit to the Widow" and other books to those whom they might benefit. His children were "instigated to be a blessing to one another." An eminent man had committed suicide, and Judge Sewall was anxious to have an improvement made of the event, by some publication showing the sin of self-murder. Therefore he requested the Notes of a sermon preached by Dr. Increase Mather, more than forty years before, upon "Self-murder." Cotton Mather looked it up, and it was given for publication. He made efforts to reclaim a minister from intemperate habits, and was solicitous about students in college, some of whom belonged to his congregation.

His public services in his own church, at the Lecture, and in other places, were as frequent as in his earlier life ;

and his heart yearned for the highest good of his remaining children, with apparently increasing intensity. His prayers were not forgotten, but "availed much."

In noticing, with as much brevity as possible, a few distinct events that marked this year, it may be said that some of them constituted a crisis, or perhaps more strictly a change, in his life. Some things that had been burdens were taken off his neck, and some were followed by hope and joy.

One of his designs was to have a new edition of biographies of eminent and pious dissenters to follow Clark's Collections of forty years before. He would send the proposal to London. His own biographies of New England worthies rank high in that department of literature.

One of the chief works in this line was his "Parentator; or, Remarkables of Dr. Increase Mather." It is a work of unfailing interest, in 244 small pages, and written with a rapid pen, but crowded with matter illustrating a busy and a noble life. I found a very old copy of the first edition about thirty years ago, and went through it the first day. Repeated readings have endeared the book to me. It is strange that some bookseller does not issue a new edition with notes, just enough to elucidate a few points obscured by the lapse of time.

The following "singular experience" in the diary for May 1 is given, as it exhibits a phase of character. It is not necessary to affirm that the experience "was real, or in accordance with the spiritual intercourse of heaven with earth," unless to meet the doubts of those who call all such sequences mere coincidences : —

On the last Lord's day in public prayer, I was led out of myself, as it were, to pray that the pirates who infest the coast, might have some remarkable thing done unto them. This prayer was talked about, and many people expressed strong expectation, that soon something remarkable would take place. Before the week was out, a vessel came in, wherein five or six captives among the pirates had risen on them, and with much bravery, killed the captain and chief pirates, and made prisoners of the rest.

Great notice was taken of this *prophetic prayer.* This fact shows the impression made on the public at the time of the prayer, and the immediate capture of the pirates. Dr. Mather makes this note: " I would feel no elation in it, but be humble in the dust, as any would not be amiable in the sight of God."

These pirates were confined in the prison, in Boston, until their trial and execution. The following entry in the diary will be read with interest : —

May 31. One of the first things which the *pirates* who are now so much the terror of them that haunt the sea, impose on their poor captives, is, *to curse Dr. Mather.* The 'pirates now strangely fallen into the hands of justice here, make me the *first man* whose visits, and company, and prayers they beg for. Some of them under sentence of death, choose to hear from me the last sermon they hear in this world. Being desired for publication, it was given to the printer with the title : " The Converted Sinner ; or, The Nature of a Conversion to real and vital piety." To this was added, a " more private conference of a minister with them," making forty nine pages.

Capt. Phillips and company, in about one year and a half, robbed no less than thirty four vessels. Some of the crews were murdered. Andrew Harradine and John Philimore [ancestor of the late President Fillmore] with six others, subdued the pirates. Watching their opportunity, they threw the master overboard, cut down the captain with an adze, and killed both cockswain and gunner. The rest were terrified, and made their submission.

Their trial came swiftly on the twelfth of May. It was found that some of them had been forced into piracy, and those were acquitted. The really guilty were condemned, and two of them, Archer and White, were hanged. The subject of the sermon was : " A Necessity, a tremendous necessity, that the sinner turn to God." The conference was intended faithfully and kindly to lead the guilty to repentance.

Governor Gurdon Saltonstall, of Connecticut, and Dr. Mather were intimate friends, and the sudden death of the former, in September, drew from the latter a fitting expression of friendship. He wrote, September 27 : —

> The sudden death of my intimate and time-honored friend, the excellent Gov. Saltonstall, who was a few years younger than myself, — how much must it awaken me to be *always* ready, and as fast as I can, do with my might, what my hands find to do, and what I would wish to have done before I die. O my God and Saviour, quicken me, assist me, and let an easy death (oh! for an easy as well as a happy death) conclude my labors and my sorrows.

On the first of October Dr. Mather preached a funeral sermon, in which he gave the governor his "deserved character." He does not overrate one who stood in the front rank of divines and statesmen in the colonies. The sermon was printed with the title: "Decus ac Tutamen; a brief essay on the blessings enjoyed by a people that have men of a right character shining among them." He styles Governor Saltonstall "that great and good man." The double text was: "The king said unto his servants, Know ye not that there is a . . . great man fallen this day in Israel?" "By the blessing of the upright the city is exalted."

The "Stimulator for a soul walking in darkness" and "Light in darkness, showing that days of darkness may be changed into marvellous light," and " The Nightingale" were among the printed sermons of the year. The last has one of those poetical titles of which we have already spoken. Who but Cotton Mather would have written "The Nightingale: an Essay on Songs among thorns"? It treats of the "supports and comforts of the afflicted believer, by one that has had experience of them."

The origin of the discourse on the words : "Unless thy law had been my delight, I then should have perished in mine affliction," was as follows : "A godly woman having been carried through many afflictions, thought herself bound in duty to invite her friends into a consort with her, in the praises of God her Saviour ; and having had a more particular experience of the truth in that word, *Ps.* 119: 92, she desired me to furnish her with a discourse upon it. I did so, and she published it."

Young ministers in modern times are not fond of being settled with elder ones as colleagues ; but this was common in the first century of our churches, and the plan seems to have worked well and happily. The Mathers worked in perfect harmony, to all appearance, and the relations of Cotton Mather with Mr. Gee appear to have been very harmonious. The following citation is made, to show how two ministers may work in useful fellowship : "Consult with colleague about putting in act, what has been proposed before ; i.e. a society of persons who shall consider what further service may be done for the church, and who may serve as eyes to us, to look out for us, and report to us what we may have missed."

Dr. Mather was far from well in the early part of the year, yet not to such a degree as to be kept from pastoral work ; but in November he had a severe attack, which lasted five weeks, or through December. He was debarred from his pulpit, and Samuel, now eighteen, preached part of the time. A cough and asthma and a fever came as a triple affliction ; but he was "gloriously supported by the Comforter, who caused him to triumph over the fear of death."

He styled this December as a "month of vanity," on account of his inability to perform his customary duties ; and yet it is almost laughable to read that he "read over several considerable books," went through "much of several folious," which made some "addition to his little stock of erudition"; read proof of his essay in the French tongue, and prepared for the press several discourses growing out of his afflictions.

Dr. Mather had not felt reconciled to the treatment received by his father at the time of his retiring from the presidency of the college; but he never made any demonstrations of hostility. By the death of President Leverett, there was now a vacancy, and many were expecting the elevation of Dr. Mather to that position, and perhaps he himself had some such expectation. On the seventh of May, the day after the funeral of President Leverett, at which he was one of the pallbearers, Dr. Mather wrote in his diary : —

The sudden death of that unhappy man, who sustained the place of President in a Colledge, will open the door for my doing of singular services to the best of interests. . . . I do not know that ye care of the colledge will be now cast upon me ; tho' I am told it is what is most generally wished for. If it should, I shall be in abundance of distress about it. But if it should not, yett I may do many things for ye good of ye Colledge more quietly and more hopefully than formerly.

He had reason to expect the offer of the presidency, because of the public sentiment in his favor. Dr. Eliot states that "the voice of the people cried aloud for Dr. Mather, and it was declared even in the General Court that he ought to be president." There is reason to believe that the members of the house of representatives were nearly of one mind in his favor.

But the trustees made choice of another, which is referred to as follows : —

Aug. 12. I am informed that yesterday, the six men who call themselves the corporation of the colledge mett, and contrary to the epidemical expectation of the countrey, chose a modest young man, of

whose piety, (and little else,) every one gives a laudable character. . . .
I always foretold these two things of the corporation: first, if it were
possible for them to steer clear of me, they will do so; secondly, if it
were possible for them to act foolishly, they will do so.

This is followed by a prayer, and an exhortation to
himself: "Lord, help me to a wise behavior. Hasten,
hasten, O slothful Mather, in despatching thy Treatise of
advice to the candidates of the ministry. Thou mayest
thereby do more good than twenty presidents of colleges."

A few days later he wrote down the pros and cons of
his relations to the college. It was a "dispensation of so
much mixture," that he desired a right understanding of
it, and a right behavior under it. He was desirous to find
out "what sentiments and what actions his God and
Saviour called him to."

1. The care of the colledge, with other causes, and duties, and trials,
would have been too much. Could not have lived a year through; yet
perhaps I am to die immediately at home, and God may have, mercifully, diverted the college from a choice which would have immediately
terminated in fresh troubles to them.

2. The care of the colledge would have given precious opportunity
to do good to all the churches in the country, and in a way of living
inexpressibly agreeable.

Yet, he wrote, "Light may arise in this darkness.
Who may tell what opportunity to do good may yet be
reserved for me?" Besides, the "grace he had already received in that kind, especially considering his prodigious
unworthiness, might well be sufficient."

Finally, the preferring a child before me, as my superior in erudition,
or in capacity and vivacity to manage the government of an academy;
or in piety and gravity. — This is what, for several reasons, it would be
a crime in me to be disturbed at. I hope my Saviour, who has taught
me, will help me to take all possible satisfaction in it.

Later in the season, Mr. Sewall having declined the office, Rev. Benjamin Colman was chosen; but he followed Mr. Sewall's example. Rev. Benjamin Wadsworth was the next choice, and he accepted.

In reference to the action of the corporation in choosing Dr. Colman, Dr. Mather, on the twenty-second of November, wrote : —

> The corporation of our miserable colledge do again, (upon a fresh opportunity) treat me with their accustomed malignity. But oh! may I take pleasure in the opportunity I have to glorify my God and Saviour, with a disposition he may delight to look down upon.

This is one of the passages in Dr. Mather's life which those who like to belittle him are fond of recalling. He is represented as a disappointed man ; as bloated with vanity, as swollen with envy, and as malignant in his feeling towards the corporation. Why, it may be asked, did he not take the result with equanimity, and be still about it, with a dignified silence ? That, it may be replied, is just what he did. There is no proof that he gave utterance to any impatient, unseemly, or complaining words. There is no evidence, that I have seen, that he spoke on the subject to wife or child or friend. All that is known of his feelings or thoughts was committed to a private diary, which was kept from the fire for his own review, and for the use of his sons (only one now remaining), if it might not be destroyed before the writer died.

It is not by any means certain, as even some who are not his admirers have allowed, that Dr. Mather would have accepted the place if it had been offered to him. In his pros and cons, he seems to have drawn the line quite fairly. He was too old and too much worn to expect many more years of life ; it would have been both hard to leave his church and of doubtful wisdom to have done it. If he had been offered the presidency, on the terms by which his father held it, namely, preaching in Boston and presiding at the college, his strength would have given way at once. And to yield his pulpit was to abdicate his throne. Probably, if the choice had been given to him, he would have decided to remain in Boston.

Nevertheless, he felt the action of the trustees in passing him by keenly. Though he gave no outward sign, it is evident that he felt himself deliberately slighted by their selection of another, and of three in succession. In this connection it is pertinent to give a quotation from Dr. Pierce, author of a history of Harvard College : —

> With all the defects and blemishes which marked the character of Cotton Mather, it will not be denied that he was a most extraordinary man. . . . It is equally evident that his judgment was not equal to his other faculties; that his passions, which were naturally strong and violent, were not always under proper regulation; that he was weak, credulous, enthusiastic, and superstitious. . . . His contemporaries appear to have formed a very correct estimate of his abilities. They saw his weaknesses and eccentricities, and therefore would not choose him president. . . . They saw, at the same time, what posterity sees, that he was a man of wonderful parts, of immense learning, and of eminent piety and virtue.

We have here a generous appreciation of the ability, learning, and piety of Cotton Mather, but dashed with the charge of being weak, eccentric, passionate, and enthusiastic, credulous, and superstitious. He was, doubtless, enthusiastic, but always in a good cause, and not beyond the bounds of reason. In the matter of credulity and superstition, he was in advance of his age. Naturally of a warm temper, he made most prayerful efforts to refine his passion from all mixture of enmity or malevolence. His contemporaries did indeed form a "very correct estimate of his abilities," and they would have placed him in the president's chair almost by acclamation, if the power of choice had not been in the hands of a few who disliked him. Forty-five years of active life taught him to know his own superiority, as a scholar, as an author, as a teacher, and as an administrator, to any man in the colony. In regard to the first of three points, there can be no question. There need be none in regard to the last. He was not only great in the pulpit, but his management of his parish had been a great success. It was indeed phenomenal. And the sense, shrewdness, patience, ingenuity, enthusiasm, and piety that he exhibited in the one position would have stood him in stead in the other. If he had been elected president at the age of thirty-five, he would, in all probability, have raised the college to a greater height than it attained for many years after. But the policy of a coterie of men who had the college in their hands, and knew that the inauguration of Dr. Mather would work a kind of revolution, refused him the opportunity to decline the honor. That injustice did not weaken his influence, hinder his doing good, or lessen his fame. Nor did he abase himself before those who had the power to grieve him by their neglect. So far from it, or from harboring feelings of enmity or revenge, he silently resolved, and publicly lived up to the resolution, to "take no step [as he easily could many], to throw confusion on the men who would make him low, in the eyes of all the country." This was the triumph of goodness. A reference to this matter, on the thirteenth of September, will reveal to us anything but enmity or revenge. His glorious Lord called him, as he supposed, to the "trial of being despised and rejected of men." In reference to the action of the corporation in not selecting him to be president, when he had "such a testimony in their consciences, as well as with the whole country, to the erudition, and capacity, and activity for doing good, and fidelity to the religion of the churches," he said : " It caused town and country to be inquisitive as to the cause, and to conjecture something to his disadvantage. Yet he would not complain, but be silent."

In concluding this matter, it is to be regretted that Dr. Mather made use of certain expressions derogatory to the good fame of President Leverett. In one place he calls him a " drone," and in another calls him a " wretch." The reputation of President Leverett was high in his time, and his administration is spoken of in terms of praise by all the historians of the college. He was not a " drone," in the common acceptation of the term, but a good scholar and able teacher. His fidelity to the duties of his office is unquestioned ; but, compared with the intense activity of Cotton Mather, he might almost be styled a " man of learned leisure." But the use of the word " wretch " in application to such a man, as generally understood, is inexcusable. Dr. Pond, in his work on the Mathers, raises the query whether Dr. Mather used that epithet. Possibly, he suggests, the word in the manuscript may have been different. It would be pleasant to find the query to be fact. But the probability is that the writer of the letter in which the word is found, in haste, and with a sense of disapprobation of some of the president's conduct, wrote the word as it reads in print. How much he meant by it we cannot determine. He called himself by viler names than " drone" or "wretch," when reviewing his own conduct or searching his own heart ; but a man has a better right to abuse himself than his neighbor. It is more pleasant to remember that Cotton Mather was quick to censure himself for any injustice of the kind; that he was sincerely grateful to President Leverett for kindnesses to his son Samuel, as one of his pupils, and that he was one of the pallbearers at the president's funeral.

One of the events that gave Dr. Mather great pleasure and encouragement at this time was the gathering of the children and youth around him as their pastor. On the twenty-fourth of August he wrote as follows : " The little damsels of the flock have so deserted the catechising, that I have now, for several months, intermitted the exercise, yet I will make one experiment more ; and accordingly, this week I have desired their attendance on me; declaring my purpose to take my measures according to what appearance they now make at the time and place appointed." Two days later he met the "little damsels," and treated them with " some very moving thoughts on the words : ' I will delight myself in thy commandments, which I have loved.' " There " appeared nigh one hundred." It must have been a large congregation which could present so many young girls.

Following up this effort, he entertained his youthful flock, on the fourteenth of September, with "two sermons on our Saviour, gathering the children of men as the affectionate bird, the chickens under his wings," and applied it to the young. He continued to catechise the "lovely children," the " little maids," the "dear children," as he styled them, and to preach to them from time to time, and they attended in a way to cheer his heart.

The college grievance being over, the remainder of the year, and also of his life, was comparatively tranquil, as the other afflictions that had beset him for years were in the process of alleviation. The clouds were breaking, and light was shining as the evening came on, and his heart felt the cheer.

True, he had causes of solicitude in his family. Hannah was obliged to leave home for a while, on account of the recurring distractions of her second stepmother. Elizabeth was about to be married, and this was of necessity a cause of anxiety, though the prospect was agreeable. Near relatives were sick or bereaved, and the state of the country was made unpleasant by several causes; among others, the Indian war.

Samuel was now his reliance, since Increase had disappointed his hopes. He had graduated with high honors, and had since studied for the ministry. He had been on a visit to Connecticut, stopping with friends — Saltonstall and Winthrop, at New London, and others in New Haven. At the latter place he had received much attention, on account of his ancestry, and, as it would seem, for his personal merits. Though only eighteen, the college conferred on him the master's degree. His preaching had given satisfaction. Returning home, he had preached in several churches, including those of his father and his grandfathers. An offer had been made him of a free passage to England, which he was inclined to accept. This threw his father into a fit of distress, when it might have been expected to gratify him, as giving his son an opportunity for great improvement as well as pleasure, in visiting the mother country and relatives dwelling there. But the father did not, perhaps, hold the privileges of foreign travel so high as others. Possibly he saw what is sometimes seen in our day, that young people learn more of evil than good in their sojourn abroad. Probably he feared that his beloved Benjamin might never return. The perils of the sea were great. An opening for service in England might be found. However that might be, the father could not endure the thought of his going. He prayed against it with great fervor, though he put no constraint on the young man. To his great joy the affair took such a turn that the voyage was cheerfully abandoned.

The next event which added comfort to the good man's heart was the settling of his "wretched administration." We shun all the particulars of this settlement, except the result. Dr. Mather had been involved in the debts of other people, in a case where he was under no obligation, for which he had received no consideration, and from which he never could obtain any advantage. It would seem that in all he was mulcted about £400, though the amount is not certain. He was poor. All his real property had been sold. Nothing but furniture remained, except his library, and he was fearful of the necessity of parting with that. His children suffered. He was in fear of bankruptcy and of consequent disgrace. In his distress he cried unto God. At length kind friends learned the facts, and a few of them united in presenting him enough to meet all his indebtedness.

The relief came on the sixth of July, when he wrote: —

A part of my flock have newly signalized their kindness to me, and shown me the kindness of God, in privately collecting and advancing a sum of considerably more than two hundred pounds, to pay a debt of wife's former husband, which I inconsiderately had made my own: and was now in the course of law, ready to have execution sworn upon me for. I cannot perceive a sense of gratitude unto me, in those for whom I have been such a sufferer. But my soul is filled, and even fainting with a sense of gratitude unto the kind people who thus lay me under very uncommon obligations. I must think of some singular, transcendent, uncommon way to express my gratitude unto them. Teach me, O Thou good Spirit of God, and lead me into the way of gratitude, and land of rectitude.

Dr. Mather expressed his gratitude to the friends who had rescued him from pecuniary distress in his own way, by preaching a sermon on "*The Unsearchable Riches of Christ*," printing it, and dedicating it to those friends, and sending a copy to every friend, with their names written with his own pen upon the front of the dedication.

The mental condition of Mrs. Mather had been a still keener affliction than the "wretched administration," but here relief also came suddenly, and as a blessing from heaven, after one of the most furious paroxysms in her whole experience. Under date of August 23 the diary says : —

In the evening of this day, my poor wife, returning to a right mind, came to me in my study, entreating that there might be an eternal oblivion of everything that has been out of joint, and an eternal harmony in our future conversation; and that for the expressing, and further obtaining of this felicity, I would now join with her in pouring out our supplications to the Lord; and resolve to pray oftener with her than ever heretofore. I did accordingly; and the tokens of the greatest inamoration on her part, ensued upon it.

The change seems to have been permanent, from several grateful references to it. A single extract from the diary, October 20, will happily close this painful subject : —

What shall I do that my carriage towards my consort may have in it yet more conformity to my lovely Saviour? I think of many instances wherein I will endeavor to it unto the utmost; especially for compassion to her with regard to the things which threaten her comfort. And that I may improve to the highest in the matter, I would pray much oftener than a monthly action of that importance.

Some days later he wrote : "By a marvellous operation of the Divine Providence, all things are come to rights in my unhappy family."

But the sorest affliction at this time, and indeed in his whole life, was the conduct and fate of Increase. This boy had been his special hope and pride. The failure of this son to take the studious, scholarly, and pious way of living was a great grievance to his father. But when to this was added the positive misconduct of levity, slothfulness, dissipation, and the choice of bad companions, the cup of grief was full and running over. The story reaches over years, but we shall make it brief. For two or three years since 1721 we have scarcely come upon his name, because of the loss of diaries ; but in 1724 he reappears very often. The grief over him becomes the monotony of woe. Increase was now at sea, and at last accounts on a voyage from Barbadoes to Newfoundland. No advices had come from him, but the father believed that he had intimations from another source. July 1, he exclaims : " But oh ! what advice from· heaven is come to me this day, about my poor son *Increase ;* yea, how many times have I been, of late, overwhelmed with afflations which told me that " —· This is enigmatical; it seems to intimate that he had received desirable suggestions about his son.

Before the month was out, he wrote as follows : —

My son *Increase*, my son, my son! *Aug.* 20. I am now advised that my son Increase is lost, is dead, is gone. The ship wherein he was bound from Barbadoes to St. Peters, has been out four months, and has not arrived. Ah! my son Increase ! my son ! my son! my head is waters, and my eyes are a fountain of tears. I am overwhelmed, and this at a time when the domestic — — are so insupportable. O my God, I am oppressed ; undertake for me.

But the soul of a Child! If the papers which he left in my hands, were sincere, and his heart went with his pen, — all is well! Would not my God have me to hope so? . . . My Saviour yet affords me this light in my darkness, that he enables me to offer up all the sacrifices that he calls me to.

It will be recollected that relief this very week came to his wife. Again he writes : " The death of my son Increase — Ah, my son ! my son ! What fruit could he bring forth upon it for the awakening of the young people betimes to turn and live unto God ? " This now became his burden — a comforting one, though sad — to make an " Essay to the end that the death of his son Increase might be for the awakening and quickening of early piety."

But on the fifth of September he had some probable advice that Increase was living; that the vessel, after a long, sad passage, had reached Newfoundland. "If it be so, Oh! may the distresses of the poor prodigal bring him home to God."

Dr. Mather did not place much faith in the report, for he proceeded to preach, on the 6th, a sermon in regard to the death of his son, and thought to print and scatter it especially among the young people. The good news was followed, as he had feared, with a confirmation of the first report. On the 7th, late in the day, he wrote: "Lord, thou hast first lifted me up, and cast me down; Oh! let there be no *indignation and wrath* in what is done unto me! To-day the good news of poor *Creasy's* being rescued and revived from death, is all come to nothing! 'T was another vessel. O my Father, thy will be done!" In this state of mind he prayed for direction about the sermon preached on the death of Increase, for his death must be made the means of good; "that at, or by his death, a poor child who did no good in his life, may do good in the world; that the child may be an instrument of good after he is dead."

A hearer wanted the sermon on the death of Increase, wherefore it was printed, with the title "*Tela Prævisa;* A Short Sermon on troubles to be looked for; a wise expectation of, and preparation for troublesome changes, recommended unto the strangers and pilgrims in this present evil world." This was on the last day of October; but another record, dated December, gives further information. Dr. Mather was very desirous that the death of his son should be the means of usefulness to others, and specially to the young. So the sermon was published

with "another that was agreeable or similar in character."
These caused considerable expense ; but while the volume
was in the press, "a strange hand of Providence made
such an accession from others to my own disbursements,
that I could add a third sermon to the book, wherein I
may yet more notably serve the interests of piety." All
these made a bound book, entitled " The Words of Understanding." Each sermon had a separate heading, as 1.
"The Philomela; with the Notes of Morning Piety."
2. "The Ephemeron ; or, Tears dropt on dust and ashes."
3. "Jonah ; or, The Dove in Safety, occasioned by some
early deaths which require such notes to be taken of
them." To these was added an "Instrument of a son's
repenting and returning to God, which is a copy of a
penitent and pertinent writing left by ye poor child, on ye
table in my study, before his going off." The reading of
that paper could not fail to be a balm to the father's heart,
and it cannot be read now without a thrill of sympathetic
joy. It is as follows : —

*Copy of a paper written by Increase Mather, and left in the study of
Cotton Mather, his father, when he left home the last time.*

In the first place, I have endeavored to make my peace with an
offended God ; and unto that end, besides what I do more than twice
every day, I have set apart *whole days for secret prayer*, to bewayle my
many and mighty sins before him ; and that, not with lukewarmness, but
in the agonies of a terrified conscience. I have confessed those sins,
and with a broken heart, have pleaded the benefits of the great sacrifice
to wash them away in his own most precious blood. And I have also
pleaded his own handwriting for it ; him that comes unto me, I will
in no wise cast out. And I heartily hope the God of all grace will
hear me in my distress, when I call upon him. And then also I have
bewailed, with a fountain of tears, my fighting and refusing a lovely
Saviour, who has died for me, and whom I have so often crucified over
and over again ; little thinking that every time I committed any evil
thing, I was acting the tremendous tragedy over again. But Oh! the
astonishing love of that Saviour, who is yet willing and ready to save

me, if I will but consent unto it! O Lord, I am willing; do thou make me willing. I fly to that blood which cleanses from all sin, and I plead his righteousness for me, to reconcile me unto his Father; and I renounce all other hopes, but through him to be brought into the favor of God, and yet be made one of his children. O my dear Saviour, do thou do this for me, and then I shall have *all my desire*. And, Oh my Saviour, do thou make all my sins grievous and hateful unto me, and let me now die rather than sin against thee any more. Oh! be the death of those things which keep me at a distance from thee; and especially that root of all evil, *original sin*, with which I am so horribly defiled, and which hath broken forth into many horrible transgressions. Lord, keep it under the restraints of thy grace; chain up that devil, that he may not break out as he has done! my continual cry is, O Lord, let all those afflictions which thou hast, in thy justice, laid upon me, be sanctified unto the salvation of my soul. For I had rather get good by afflictions, than get out of them. These are the real and deliberate sentiments of my soul. And I hope all sin is become so odious to me, that had I rather suffer anything than sin; and I would not, for a thousand worlds, commit any one sin against the glorious God who has marvellously rescued me from the jaws of ruin.

I. I resolve, by the help of God, not to let one day pass me, without secret prayer to God, and reading his sacred oracles, with meditations on them.

II. I resolve, by the help of God, to follow my secular business, out of obedience to him, with industry and faithfulness, having an eye to a glorious God, who, I know, sees all my ways; and if it please him to prosper me in my endeavors, I will study to do good with what my God shall entrust me withal.

III. I resolve, by the help of God, to steer clear of evil company, and have none but sober and godly companions.

IIII. I resolve, by the help of God, for the future, to live a life as much to the glory of God, as I have done heretofore to the dishonor of him.

V. I resolve, by the help of God, never to give over crying and prayer unto God, until I hear him say, Son, be of good cheer, thy many and heinous sins are forgiven thee.

VI. I do also resolve, by the assistance of God's Holy Spirit, that I will repel the temptations wherewith I may be assailed in an evil world, with that glorious word, (which I pray God I may always keep in my mind,) how can I do this wickedness, and sin against God?

VII. And then, with his help, I will keep continually praising and adoring the matchless love of my Saviour, who has triumphed over me in his grace after all my wanderings from him, and affronts to him, and after I have so often crucified him over and again, and grieved his Holy Spirit; being astonished that he has not left me to my ruin, when I have been upon the very brink of perdition.

The father followed this paper with the remark: "Ah, poor child; ah, dear child; if thy heart were in such recognitions, thou shalt be saved in the day of the Lord. Jer. 31 : 18, 19, 20 : I have surely heard him bemoaning himself thus, —, 'I have been as a bullock unaccustomed to the yoke. Turn thou me, and I shall be turned; for thou art the Lord my God. . . . I was ashamed, yea, even confounded, because I did bear the reproach of my youth.' A pleasant child. I will surely have mercy upon him, saith the Lord."

In the diary of this year, so full of sorrows and mercies, is a statement, highly characteristic, wherein Dr. Mather sets in order a series of "Dark Dispensations," followed by a cluster of "Consolations." This statement fitly closes the record of 1724. He introduces it in the words following: "It may be of some use for me to observe some very *Dark Dispensations*, wherein ye *Recompences* of my poor *Essays at Well-doing* in *this Life* seem to Look a little Discouraging, and then to express ye Triumphs of my Faith over such and all Discouragements."

He then refers to "twice seven instances," when things looked "darkly," and notes what a "gracious Lord helped" him to do and bear. Instead of giving these at full length, it will be sufficient to abridge them as specimens of the self-torture of a depressed spirit. Mr. Peabody says that "he had anxieties and trials which were enough to irritate the best temper in the world." We have seen what these trials were. One was the "wretched administration," and his involvement in a burdensome debt, on account of others. In a letter to John Winthrop he states that he had been obliged to pay near four hundred pounds which he never ought to have paid. He was poor to suffering, and feared that his library would have to go. His health was poor. His wife, a superior woman, whom he highly prized, was often in paroxysms of insanity. His son, on whom his hopes had been built, and to whom his heart clung most fondly, was a cause of grief and shame. In view of all these griefs and woes, his power of endurance almost gave way. He became moody, and looked on the dark side of things till well-nigh driven to despair. In this state of mind he penned these "Dark Dispensations." Dr. Sibley and Mr. Peabody err in ascribing his wretchedness to disappointments about the college, or loss of consideration with the general public. He was doubtless disgusted with the treatment he received from the circle who had got the college under their control; but he knew that the voice of the public would have made him president, if that had been admitted to decide the election. And the notion that he had sunk in public estimation is a vapory myth. It is inferred from passages in his diary, and not from authentic evidence.

It will be seen, also, by those who have read Dr. Mather's life, in these pages, that these "dark dispensations" were mostly the exaggerations of his own morbid imagination when under temporary excitement.

1. He refers to his exertions in behalf of sailors and seafaring men; yet says that "there is not a man in the world so reviled, so slandered, so cursed among sailors." These pages have shown how much he felt and did for sailors and fishermen, and all men who did "business on the great waters"; and also, how he tried to comfort their anxious friends at home, during their absence.

Doubtless his labors were thankfully appreciated, if the seamen did not always signify it. But he incurred the enmity of the base men whose guilty indulgences he tried to check, whether officers or common sailors. A lieutenant in the navy named his dog Cotton Mather, and sailors of lower rank cursed him. It was to his honor. If he heard of a house for guilty association in the north end, he at once organized an effort to close it. Hence the curses of base men.

2. Next, his uncommon and continuous exertions for the benefit and elevation of the negroes brought insults upon him. But these were not from his beneficiaries. Some men named their colored boys Cotton Mather, to affront him, because he was laboring to raise the poor creatures from their degradation. Such enemies are unwittingly the glory of good men.

3. The next grievance raises a smile. No man had done so much to elevate them in the respect of the community, or to "hold up the lives of excellent and distinguished women, as an example to others," he says, and it is true. But yet, he continues : "Where is the man whom the female sex have spit more of their venom at ? I have cause to question whether there are twice ten in the town, who have not, at some time or other, spoken basely of me." Could delusion further go ? In the time of the smallpox inoculation, it is true there was a spasm of almost insane rage shaking the great body of the community ; but in general, Cotton Mather was their favorite preacher and author, and trusted counselor.

4. He speaks also of having been tormented with "monstrous relatives," though he was always laboring to be a blessing to them. These "monstrous relatives," who seemed to fill his whole horizon, were two brothers-in-law, and a few connections of his third wife ; but what man

was ever more leaned on, and loved, by parents, brothers, sisters, nephews, nieces, and cousins, than Cotton Mather?

5. He claims that he had "unceasingly labored to vindicate the reputation and honor of the Scotch nation." We know that he befriended the poor Scotch, who, by means of banishment or other causes, sought a home in our country; but he states that no "Englishman was ever so much reviled and libeled by Scotchmen" as he. Yet we hear of no Scotchman abusing him but Dr. Douglas, whose abuse was eulogy.

He had labored to secure the best interests of the country, but had been "loaded with disrespect and calumny," and he had endeavored to strengthen and maintain the government; "yet nothing could excel the discountenance he had always received from the government." By the "government" he must have meant Edmund Andros and Joseph Dudley, who were opposed and hated by the friends of civil and religious freedom generally, while Dr. Mather was always in the confidence of the house of representatives, and the great and honest public.

And so on, through the whole list. He was suffering a sort of nightmare, with his eyes open; for he immediately considers his "Dispositions and Consolations." And not long after he wrote : —

'T is a thought full of consolation to me, and what carries an animation of piety with it; that the sad things which appear to me, as punishments of my offences, and I accordingly accept them, and I don't complain, but say, I will bear the indignation of the Lord, because I have sinned against him; — They really prove benefits unto me, and I find them intended for such; and they have those precious effects upon me, which proclaim the everlasting love of God unto me.

In a word, the great troubles of Dr. Mather, which seemed gathering into a portentous cloud, charged with desolation and woe, soon "dissolved into thin air," and the skies were serene, and the sunshine of divine favor gladdened his heart. His debts were paid, he was surrounded by troops of friends ; his audience was large, his church was increasing ; the little maids — "dear children" — came to his teaching by the hundred; his reputation as a benefactor was great ; his wife, restored to soundness, was his solace and joy ; and his son, though dead, had gone, as he believed, a renewed soul, to heaven.

CHAPTER XXV.

DR. MATHER returned to his study on the first day of January, 1725, and began the record with such "recollections and supplications as a New Year should be entered withal." His book, "A year well-begun," has described them.

In regard to the preceding year, he writes : "A fruitful year beyond any that ever I saw." He had preached sixty times, notwithstanding interruptions by sickness. Surely no year has come into review in which so many heavy loads of trouble and grief had been lifted from his heart. In regard to these mercies, and the interior experience in them, the year was fruitful, and the things recorded which he had done, and others not specified in the preceding pages, warrant his remark. The number of individuals and of classes of people befriended by him would make a long list, composed of relatives, friends, strangers, negro slaves, Indians, and students. He had heeded the admonition : "To do good, and to communicate forget not."

On the 2d he wrote : "In the time of my sickness I dispersed *alms* to the poor, and especially to some that were languishing under sickness." And the next day : "Must become more diligent than ever." His remnant of "life's pilgrimage must be carried on with new measures. No time is to be lost." He could not give so much time to recording "good devices." For his purposes to do good, he would make a very brief record every Saturday evening. One purpose was, on returning to his pulpit, to "entertain his people with two sermons on Philippians 1 : 21." "I.

How *Christ* is the Christian's Life; and II. What *gain* such a Christian shall have by his death."

It appears that Samuel had been "exceedingly and passionately set" upon going to England: but that, having been prevented by various causes, his "calm resignation and satisfaction" greatly pleased his father, and was taken as a token for good.

Young Thomas Walter, so full of gifts and promise, was now on his deathbed, and "full of distress and darkness about his future state." Says his uncle, "With much impatience and importunity, he calls for me to be fetched over to him in his agonies. I have the satisfaction to strengthen him in his agonies, and advise him, and comfort him, and leave him with a sensible satisfaction, and a good hope through grace. The prayer-hearing God enabled him to die, next day, with joyful triumphs over the last enemy."

It is said that Mr. Walter derived a large part of his vast store of knowledge from conversation with his uncle Cotton Mather. The sermon preached at his funeral by Dr. Mather was entitled "Christodulus: A Good Reward of a Good Servant; or, the Service of a glorious Christ, justly demanded and commended, from a view of the glory with which it shall be recompensed; with some commemoration of Mr. Thomas Walter, lately a pastor to a church in Roxbury, who had an early dismission from what of that service was to be done in this world."

Some of Dr. Mather's "precious thoughts" recorded at this time, and a few culled from previous months, may be inserted here. He states that his mind was often "enlightened and enlivened with such views of Christ as had heart-melting efficacy." One was this: "Christ is an Advocate with the Father in the Heavens, and by his potent intervention, saves us to the uttermost. He receives those of our petitions, which have an approbation with him, and presents them to the Father, and undertakes to prosecute them, and accomplish them; and him the Father heareth always. My petition for myself is, to be made a partaker of the heavenly life, and be fruitful of good during life."

The sentiment which enriches a poem of one of our admired writers is in the following "thought" of Mather. Alluding to the griefs and woes brought upon him by the ordering of Providence, he writes that in all the "worst that God will do unto me, he will not hurt me."

Again he says, it is "a marvellous consolation and encouragement in prayer, to think that there was a voice in all the acts of obedience which my Saviour paid unto the Divine law; especially, a voice went from the words of my suffering Saviour, as with open mouth demanding the blessings of goodness for his people. And all my prayers to the glorious God are nothing but the repetitions of that voice; and so they reach to heaven with a marvellous concomitance of efficacy."

Once more; he would preface seasons of prayer thus: "I am now making a visit unto the heavenly world. I am going where my Saviour is making a continual intercession for me. I am going where I hope, ere long, to be received into everlasting habitations."

Again, he tells us one of the "artifices" of his preaching, in these lines. He says that he "contrived, with abundance of artifices, to spread the nets of salvation for them [his hearers], that if, at the moment of delivery, they receive them with acts of compliance, and come into the language which I get ready for them, they are, unawares, taken in the nets, and they shall be found among the saved of the Lord."

Here is an encouragement to pray: "Certainly there

is a disposition to give in one who desires, and who directs
to have a gift asked of him. It may especially be supposed of a Father, that if he bids his children to ask a
good thing of him, he is disposed, yea, resolved, for the
bestowing of it. My most gracious God has advised me,
invited me, yea, commanded me to come and ask for his
blessing. His word is, 'Ask, and it shall be given unto
you.'"

Dr. Mather's habit of devotion, at. this time, was as
follows : —

Call on God seven times a day, in this order. 1. Rising prayer in
the study; daily petitions to the Lord; 2. Family sacrifices; 3. Near
the hour of 12, pray in secret in reference to the condition of the
family and the country; 4. After dinner, between 2 and 3, pray for the
success of my ministry. Also, for an *easy* and a *happy* death; 5.
About the shutting in of evening, acknowledged and celebrated the
glories of the Redeemer; 6. Towards the time of going to rest, sing
something of a Psalm to my domesticks, — a family or evening sacrifice; 7. A private prayer before going to rest. Thanks for good;
bewail sins; pray for pardon; commit myself and all mine into the
hands of the Lord.

Another "thought" comes in here. "The holy frames
and thoughts we have, were first of all produced in our
holy Jesus. The Saviour is the first recipient in these
gracious influences with which his whole mystical body is
to be animated, and whatever holiness is produced in his
people, is first in him." And here he found the reason
why any holy thoughts in himself found acceptance with
God, as follows : "Here I see the meaning of having the
Face of God shine upon me. It is the Christ of God that
is the *Face of God*. He shines upon me when he forms
holy frames and thoughts in me. I have him in me when
I have these from him in me. He withdraws, he hides
himself, he keeps at a distance from me, in the withdraw
and ceasing of these. The continual presence of hope

may cause me to sing with joy. Now I have Christ within me *the hope of glory.* The method of having holy frames and thoughts when in distress, is *to look up unto my Jesus* for them, in prayer for them through the ministry of the Spirit."

On the tenth of January, Dr. Mather had these matters to consider:— 1. Bereaved relations at Roxbury; the Walter family. 2. Decaying nephew in Boston. 3. The redemption of a captive. 4. One of the flock fallen by excessive drinking. 5. Several poor widows.

Among the occupations of a busy day, here are a few of the minor acts and devices. He recommended to Samuel many things, but especially "Antiquates Biblicæ." To Nancy he commended Baxter's "Poor Man's Family Book." He sent "agreeable books to a nephew coming to practice in the neighborhood." By "agreeable" books and things, he often meant those that were adapted to the person. Objects of charity were relieved, and "books of piety were sent to several parts of the country." These were things done ; now for the devices.

One was something to be done for the satisfaction of his consort. Another was to give "seasonable and effectual stops" to some "foolish steps taken to draw the civil government into interposing and inhibiting ecclesiastical censures upon offenders." The government was quite disposed, at times, to intermeddle with matters pertaining to the churches. Again, he speaks of "dealing with a very wicked and vicious gentlewoman," wherein his "admonitions to repentance had been frequent, but too oblique." He now proposed to try a "nameless letter," in which she might be dealt with more "directly and faithfully."

On the 30th he composed a sermon, describing a "soul wherein piety is flourishing." Such a "soul can sing in the valley of the shadow of death, and find it but a shadow." He was taken ill in the night with a relapse of the cough and fever, and confined for a week; diverted from public services; but he used all the "methods of piety" he could think of to glorify his "faithful God and Saviour, under this new visitation."

Dr. Mather attempted several services during his confinement, one of which had reference to the strenuous exertions then making to build up Episcopacy in the town, college, and province. To counteract this movement he published a brief history, in fifty-eight pages, of the "persecutions of the church of Scotland by an abjured prelacy." He gave it the title of "The Palm-bearers: a brief relation of patient and joyful sufferings, and of death gloriously triumphed over, in the history of the persecution which the Church of Scotland suffered from the year 1660 to the year 1688." Nothing could more fitly have served his purpose, as that persecution was one of the most cruel and senseless in history. In the history of Harvard College by President Quincy is a curious account of the efforts made by Rev. Timothy Cutler, D.D., formerly president of Yale College, to get a seat for himself and another Episcopal clergyman in the board of overseers of Harvard College. While in New Haven, he had renounced the Congregational ministry. He then went to England, and in 1723 he was ordained deacon and priest. Returning to this country, he became rector of Christ Church, in Boston. With all the zeal of a convert, he labored to build up the system which he had adopted. Dr. Mather was, very naturally, opposed to the methods of a man who denied the validity of ordination in the Congregational way and who disdained all fellowship with non-prelatical churches.

The diary has the following lines under date of February 7: "While sitting alone in languishments, unable to write or read, I often composed little Hyms, and sung them unto the Lord. I made vast numbers of them, which were immediately forgotten." He gives the following, composed when he was without such impressive thoughts of God his Saviour as were the life of his soul :—

> Oh glorious Christ of God! I live
> In views of Thee alone.
> Life to my gasping Soul, O give!
> Shine Thou, or I'm undone.
>
> I cannot live, my God, if Thou
> Enlivenest not my faith.
> I'm dead; I'm lost; Oh! save me now
> From a lamented death.

This stanza was added :—

> My glorious Healer, now restore
> My health, and make me whole;
> But this is what I most implore,—
> O for a healed soul!

Several funeral sermons were put to press this year. One was preached on the death of a son of his friend, Hon. Isaack Winslow, with the title "Edulcorator; a brief essay on the waters of Marah sweetened ; with a remarkable relation of the deplorable occasion afforded for it, in the premature death of Captain Josiah Winslow, who, with several of his company, sacrificed his life in the service of his country, engaging an army of Indians, May, 1724."

The character of Mrs. Abigail Brown was given in "Virtue in its Verdure : A Christian exhibited as an Olive-tree in the house of God."

The death of Mrs. Katharine Willard, a "vertuous gentlewoman," called forth a discourse entitled "El Shaddai: All supplied in an all-sufficient Saviour."

An abridged edition of the life of his father, with a preface by the Rev. Edmund Calamy, D.D., was published in London.

Other publications were : — 1. "An Essay on a Soul passing from death to life, in a translation from the first Adam to the second Adam"; 2. "Vital Christianity; the Life of God in the soul of man"; 3. "Deus Vobiscum, for a Sacramental occasion"; 4. "The Choice of Wisdom"; and 5. "Zalmonah, the Gospel of the brazen serpent"; in all 106 pages. The whole product of the year was nearly 500 pages.

As written above, at the beginning of the year Dr. Mather referred to the year preceding as the most fruitful in his life. He probably had in mind, among other events, a remarkable revival of religion in his congregation. The record states that fifty-three were added to the church in 1725. It is probable that the work began in 1724, and continued into this year. In the diary, Dr. Mather, in 1724, notes that he and his colleague were interested in the examination and instruction of persons who were preparing for their first communion. This "work of grace" surpassed any event of the kind for a generation in the preceding history of the church, or of any other church in Boston. About 1680 there had been great ingatherings into the churches, and additions had been constant, though in lesser numbers in the intervening years. But this new outpouring of the Spirit was phenomenal to the generation on the stage; and it was the harbinger of greater displays of the Spirit's power that were coming.

This seems to be the place to give the results of Dr. Mather's labors, as measured by the additions to the church, on confession of faith, during his ministry. It will be pleasing to some readers to have the results in successive years : —

```
1682–88, 28
    1689, 22      1699,  7      1709, 21      1719, 15
    1690, 27      1700, 28      1710, 19      1720,  7
    1691, 49      1701,  4      1711, 13      1721, 10
    1692, 12      1702, 16      1712,  6      1722, 14
    1693, 31      1703,  7      1713, 10      1723, 11
    1694, 23      1704,  9      1714, 35      1724, 10
    1695, 14      1705, 24      1715, 24      1725, 53
    1696, 21      1706, 21      1716, 21      1726,  9
    1697, 14      1707, 10      1717, 18      1727, 71
    1698,  9      1708, 20      1718, 26      1728, 18
```

Total in 47 years, 876; average per annum, 18 1-2.

In addition, Mr. Mather, at different dates, notes numerous cases of apparent conversion following his labors, outside of his parish.

The following letter comes in at this date. It is from Dr. Mather to John Winthrop, of New London: —

SIR, — Having passed through a winter of much feebleness, (and some employment) it appears high time for me to renew my acquaintance with a Friend, who would have been in my debt, for I know not how many letters, if his vast civilities to my son had not much more than cancelled it.

He would have joined with me in the acknowledgments I am now making, if he had not been at this time at seventy miles distance from me.

Such is my penury that I have nothing to send you, but first a few of our latest publications.

And then my humble request and advice, that you would not let your mind be disturbed, much less your health impaired, by the base usages you may be mal-treated withal.

I know not how better to address you on this occasion, than by letting you see how one you love well, is used; and if the Best Man in Connecticut Government will use a poor minister as I have been used, you will not wonder if inferior people treat you as I have heard they do. With the help of heaven, I [bear] all with patience. And I shall find the God of patience, to be the God of consolation.

I *know not how better*, — yes, I do. Sett before yourself the example of the glorious Lord, who was as the sheep before the shearers.

We have no Intelligence, worth a straw. I was going to say No Intellect. We are like to continue one year longer as we are, — inexpressibly happy in our Lt. Governer's wise and good Administration. You know what I wish you; and that I am

S'r. Your most cordial Friend and serv't,

Co. MATHER.

BOSTON, May 1, 1725.

MR. WINTHROP.

The year 1726, on which we now enter, was filled with hard study and fruitful toil, the record of which is chiefly to be found in the issues of the press. There is no diary. Not a letter is in print. The records of the church are silent. Dr. Mather was not in robust health, but he continued his services in the pulpit most of the time. Though his colleague was a man of great capacity, yet his senior found much to do in the parish as well as in the sacred desk.

In the matter of publishing, the product of this year is almost fabulous. I count over 900 pages of print. Research, composition, and proof-reading demanded a large amount of time; and much of this over and above pulpit and parish duties; for two of his volumes, each filling about 300 pages, were not in the line of preaching.

Three of the sermons were funereal; one of them was occasioned by the death of his daughter Eliza, Mrs. Cooper; and another by the "execution of pirates."

The sermon entitled "Ecclesiæ Monilia; or, The Peculiar Treasure of the Almighty King opened; and the jewels that are made up in it, exposed," was among the three. One jewel was "more particularly exhibited in the character of Mrs. Elizabeth Cotton, who *was laid up* a few days before." To this were added "certain instruments and memorials of piety, written by that valuable and honorable gentlewoman." Mrs. Cotton was the wife of Rev. Roland

Cotton, and sister of Governor Saltonstall, of Connecticut. Dr. Mather speaks of her in high terms. After noticing her early piety, he proceeds : —

The uncommon prudence of her economy, the large number of well-educated children that she has presented to the public, whereof this happy mother in Israel had the consolation to see several become well-esteemed pastors of churches ; the generous assistances that she often gave to the neighbors in their various afflictions ; the relish she had for the enjoyments in the house of her God ; and indeed, her whole behavior has bespoken a grateful remembrance of her, and a name in the enumeration of those whom our God, when he shall make up his jewels, will doubtless allow a place unto.

Another piratical crew were brought to justice, and like those before mentioned, they had the privilege of Dr. Mather's counsels and prayers. His sermon, preached before their execution, was printed in a pamphlet which bore the title, " The Vial poured out upon the Sea. A Remarkable Relation of certain pirates brought unto a tragical and untimely end. Some Conferences with them after their condemnation. There Behavior at their Execution." A paraphrase by Sir Richard Blackmore ; and a "Remarkable Relation of a Cockatrice crushed in the Egg," were added, making fifty-one pages. It is readable now, and must have been a magazine of wonders and horrors in its day. Dr. Mather had two interviews with the pirates, in which he dealt faithfully with them, closely pressing them to "repentance for their heinous crimes" and sins. Their names were William Fly, Henry Greenville, and Samuel Cole. The two latter gave more hopeful indications of a sense of guilt than Fly.

"The Choice of Wisdom " was a lecture given at Roxbury, valuable in its time, and designed to be left in the hands of those on whom pastoral visits were made. It is valuable also as showing the practical theology of the author. He received the Westminster Catechism as a sound expression of the teachings of the Bible, and was under the influence, though hardly the dominion, of the current mental philosophy in regard to the freedom of the will and its relation to the divine decrees; yet he felt no limitations in addressing responsible men. The full title shows this. "A brief and plain essay on the best of blessings, to be obtained by the choosing of them, and asking for them."

The "Diluvium Ignis," or, "Deluge of Fire," was a short treatise in Latin, on "the second and desired advent of Jehovah-Jesus, and the second and dreadful deluge attending him, and the instant end of all things." It contained "Scriptural, salutary, and very necessary admonitions to a world in deep sleep." Dr. Mather was a believer in the second advent of Christ, and he expected it in his day, or soon, without fixing the time. Among his manuscripts is an elaborate work, "Tri Paradisus," or "Three Paradises." The second paradise was to be planted at the second advent.

His "Fasciculus Viventium; or, All Good Wishes in One," treated of a "Soul bound up in the bundle of life; as the best thing, and all the good that can be wished for." Such a soul was "a bouquet, a nosegay, and a fragrant incense offered to God."

The "Glory of Aged Piety" was commended unto those whose "arrival to, or near, sixty, ranks them among the aged," and was printed with the title, "A Good Old Age." As a sexagenarian he appealed to those of about his own age, with his usual ingenuity and unction.

The full title of his "Hatzar-Maveth" exhibits the purport of the treatise, and in the poetical strain to which allusion has already been made. "Comfortable Words, in a short essay on the comforts of one living to God, but walking through the valley of the shadow of death, and finding it no more than a shadow of death."

Some good men and women, in every generation and country, have dark hours, when their souls are in deep waters. One such, to whom the light of God came when in darkness, desired Dr. Mather to compose his " Lampadarius" to show the "light which good men have, in dark hours, arising to them." This was published as a "monument and instrument of gratitude unto heaven," at the expense and desire of a man whom God graciously appeared for, under a dispensation full of darkness."

Another paper treated of the "Kindnesses of God to the Poor," accompanied with "seasonable advice." The drinking habits of the time called out a "Serious Address to those who unnecessarily frequent the tavern, and often spend the evening in public houses, by several ministers." This was signed by the author and twenty-two other ministers, and followed by a "Private Letter on the subject from the late Rev. Dr. Increase Mather." In our day, many spend their evenings in saloons, clubs, lodges, and open or secret societies. Almost the only resort of those whose homes did not attract them in old times was the tavern.

In the "Terra Beata," Dr. Mather set forth the "blessing of Abraham, even the grand blessings of a glorious Redeemer, which are given in the promises of the Bible, foretelling a happy time for all nations, for which they are to hope and pray." The "promises" pertaining to the subject are "explained with some uncommon illustrations."

About the same time his picture of the condition of the "Protestant interest" was anything but cheering. His "Suspiria Vinctorum," or "Sighs of the fettered," exhibited the desperate condition of evangelical Christendom; the oppression under which the Reformed suffered in different countries, and the duties which all true Christians were called on to undertake. This is said to be "briefly laid before the churches, by several ministers of the gospel desirous to do the work of the day." The pamphlet is ascribed to Mather, and probably was mostly written by him, with the advice and sanction of other ministers.

The "Ratio Disciplinæ Fratrum Nov-Anglarum; a faithful account of the discipline professed, and practised, in the churches of New England, with interspersed and instructive reflections on the discipline of the primitive churches," is too well known to need further description. The last edition was edited by Professor T. C. Upham, and published in 1829. It was an authority for more than a hundred years, and is now historically valuable. Indeed, it is a safe guide now, except in a few changes, which the growth and spread of the denomination have made convenient if not necessary (pp. 207).

The "Manuductio ad Ministerium" is one of the productions of this year which merits special notice. The whole title is, "Directions for a candidate of the ministry, wherein, first, a right foundation is laid for his future improvement; and then rules are offered for such a management of his academical and preparatory studies; and thereupon for such a conduct after his appearance in the world, as may render him a skillful and useful minister of the gospel." A most fitting running title was, "The Angels preparing to sound the trumpets."

The intelligent reader will be prepared to see the table of contents : —

1. Death realized. Good for a person intending for the ministry to realize that he is a dying man. 2. The true end of life answered. 3. Conversion to piety accomplished. 4. A zeal to do good betimes enkindled. 5. The right end of studies fixed. 6. Studies of the languages directed. 7. Study of the sciences. 8. Of poetry and style.

9. Of natural philosophy. 10. Of the mathematics. 11. Of theology. 12. Some useful proposals to students. 13. The sentiments with which the evangelical ministry is to be undertaken. 14. Of reading the Sacred Scriptures. 15. Study of divinity entered upon. 16. The pulpit, and the work of it. 17. Employments for a vigilant pastor. 18. The genuine and catholic spirit of Christ, described and commended. 19. Rules of health. 20. Rules of prudence.

The work is well worth reading, both for its matter and style. The contents show the wide range of study, the deep spirit of piety, and the great prudence inculcated. The progress of. scientific discovery, and the developments of history, and the better methods of exegesis have made old textbooks obsolete; but the training, the mental discipline, was as good then as now; and in the line of divinity, we have no abler ministers than those who instructed our ancestors.

Several editions have been printed. One with the title, "The Student and Preacher," was put out by John Ryland, of Northampton, England, in 1781, and another in London, in 1789. The latter contained a "literal translation of the author's famous Latin Preface," and an abridgment of Mr. Ryland's preface to his edition.

Two or three extracts from Judge Sewall's diary give us glimpses of Dr. Mather at different dates in this year: —

March 28. Dr. Cotton Mather dined with us after Lecture.

July 9. Dr. Cotton Mather was a bearer at the funeral of Madam Cotton.[1]

Aug. 7. Mrs. Elizabeth Cooper died. At her funeral, the bearers were six ministers of the town, viz., Sewall, Prince; Webb, Cooper; Foxcroft, Gee. She was a daughter of Dr. Mather.[2]

Aug. 13. Gave judges, attornies, etc., each of them, one of Dr. Mather's sermons of the " glory of aged piety."

The discourse of Dr. Mather in relation to the decease

[1] She was the widow of Rev. Roland Cotton, and sister of Governor Saltonstall.
[2] Her husband was Edward Cooper.

of his daughter, Mrs. Cooper, was preached early in August. She was a young wife, only twenty-two years of age, and much endeared to her father and friends. Her brother Samuel informs us that she had many of the traits of her "excellent mother." The title of the sermon was "Pietas Matutina:— One Essay more to bespeak and engage Early Piety, made on occasion taken from the early departure of Mrs. Elizabeth Cooper. By her Father." The theme "The piety of the morning" evinces the poetic piety and beauty so often noticed before. The sermon was followed by a poem, written by her brother Samuel, two years younger. The volume, of nearly fifty pages, is not found in any public library, which is to be regretted, because it might give clearer light respecting her religious character. The title and topic of the sermon, however, suggest the possession of early piety.

The death of Mrs. Cooper was the last event of the kind which Dr. Mather was called to mourn. That was the thirteenth time he followed a child to the tomb. Five of the children of his first wife died before their mother. Their names have been given in a preceding chapter. Three of the remaining four, namely, Katharine, Abigail (Mrs. Willard), and Increase, died before their father. Of the six children by his second wife, five preceded him in their death. Hannah, a daughter of the first wife, and Samuel, a son of the second, survived their father.

No correct and full list of Dr. Mather's children has ever been printed. The following is more nearly complete than any I have found, and this has been collected from many sources, and at different times : —

CHILDREN OF ABIGAIL [PHILLIPS] MATHER.

1. Abigail, born, August 22. 1687 ; died before the birth of the next child.

2. Katharine, born, September 1, 1689 ; died, December, 1716. Buried, December 20.

3. Mary, born, November, 1691 ; died, October 6, 1693, "near a month short of two years old."

4. Joseph, born, March 28, 1693; died, April 1, 1693.

5. Abigail, born, June 14, 1694; died, September 26, 1721. Married Daniel Willard, and had four children.

6. Mehitable, born, 1695; died, February 28, 1696.

7. Hannah, born, February 7, 1697; "a very healthy and comely infant." Outlived her father.

8. Increase, born, July 9, 1699. Lost at sea in 1724.

9. Samuel, born, December 13, 1700; "a lovely and lusty infant"; died, Friday, February 7, 1701.

CHILDREN OF THE SECOND WIFE, ELIZABETH.

(10.) 1. Elizabeth, born, July 13, 1704; married Edward Cooper; died, August 7, 1726.

(11.) 2. Samuel, born, October 30, 1706; died, June 27, 1788.

(12.) 3. Nathaniel, born, May 16, 1709; died, November 24, 1709.

(13.) 4. Jerusha, born, April, 1711 ; died, November, 1713.

(14.) 5. Eleazar, ⎰ twins, born, 1713; died, November of the same
(15.) 6. Martha, ⎱ year.

Two children survived the father; Hannah, born in 1797, was about thirty years of age at the time of her father's death. There are many references to her in the writings of Dr. Mather, which evince his delight in the child and his tender regard for her comfort and welfare. Though of a healthy constitution, she had frequent ills, by accident and sickness, and by the crazed aversion of her second mother-in-law. All the diseases that beset children came to her in succession. She was brought low by measles and to the gates of death by the smallpox ; but escaping these perils, she lived to rejoice her father by coming into the church in the last year of his life. Her subsequent history, and the date of her decease, have eluded my notice.

Samuel Mather, the son, was worthy of the name which belonged to so many of the family. The first, and perhaps the most distinguished Samuel, was the eldest son of Richard Mather, the patriarch. The youngest son of Increase Mather was the Samuel who was settled in the ministry, in Witney, Oxfordshire. Samuel, grandson of Richard, and son of Timothy, "the farmer," was the pastor of the church in Windsor, Conn., for the long term of forty-five years. He was a Doctor of Divinity, and an author of note in his time, and one of those wise old-time ministers who stamped their character and fastened their influence upon the people of their parish. He was also the father of one and the grandfather of another Samuel, who were respectable physicians, the one at Windsor and the other at Northampton. The fourth minister bearing the name of Samuel was this surviving son of Cotton Mather.

At the age of twenty-seven he was chosen as colleague of Rev. Joshua Gee, in the ministry of the Old North, the church of his father and grandfather. This was in 1733. Here he remained about nine years, when a disaffection sprang up which led to his secession, with a considerable following. This company was organized into the Tenth Congregational Church, and they built a meetinghouse on the corner of North Bennet and Hanover streets. This church dates from July 19, 1742, and continued its existence, with Dr. Mather for its pastor, till his decease, June 27, 1785, or forty-three years. At his request, they disbanded, and went back to the Old North Church.

CHAPTER XXVI.

COTTON MATHER IN THE SPHERE OF HIS AFFECTIONS.

I. LOVE OF NATURE. We have seen, in frequent quotations, Mather's delight in the beauties of natural scenery. These have been noted as they were found, in reading, but we have a more distinct expression in a passage which has been reserved. The reader will observe that nature led him up to nature's God.

It is not known when the following paragraphs were written; but they were printed in The Panoplist, sixteenth volume, which contains extracts from the diary of 1715–1716.

Desideria Vernalia, or Petitions in Spring. — Lord, let the Sun of Righteousness draw near unto me and let me be quickened, and revived, and made a new creature; and be made very fruitful by his benign and blessed influence.

Lord, let a glorious Christ return like the sun, to a miserable world, and bring a new face upon it, — produce upon it a *new creation*, and fill it with the fruits of righteousness.

Lord, let the hours of darkness grow shorter, and grow shorter with me.

Lord, let the "time of singing of birds" come on. Let thy Spirit fit me for, and fill me with, the Songs of the Redeemer. And let the songs of piety replenish the whole earth with a heavenly melody.

Lord, enable me with diligence to prosecute a divine husbandry, and with patience to wait for a good harvest of my endeavors to serve the kingdom of God. O, let light and joy be sown for us.

Supplications in Summer. — Lord, let me be as fruitful as any of the trees in the fields, which now yield a grateful spectacle. O, let me abound in the fruits of righteousness.

Lord, let my dear Jesus be to me as the shadow of a great rock in a weary land; and may I also drink of what flows from that wonderful rock.

Lord, let me be entitled to, and prepared for, the blessedness of that world in which no uneasy heat will molest thy children.

Autumnal Supplications. — Lord, let me see a joyful harvest of all my poor endeavors to glorify thee. Let me reap with joy. Lord, let me arrive at my grave, and thy floor, as a shock of corn fully ripe, in the season thereof.

Lord, affect me and the rest of mankind, with a sense of our mortality, for *we all do fade as a leaf.*

Dr. Mather's "Christian Philosopher" is replete with illustrations of his interest and delight in the works of nature, whether viewed merely as objects of beauty or from a scientific point of view. The same is evinced by his letter describing the "great storm," his little volume on the "volcano" in the Mediterranean, his sermon during a violent thunderstorm, and all his communications to the Royal Society.

II. LOVE OF ANIMAL LIFE. Dr. Mather's observations on the delights of animals, already quoted, attest his own pleasure in witnessing their enjoyments. Whether sporting on the earth, in the water, or the air, he rejoiced in their gay and infinitely varied movements. But he cherished a higher feeling in relation to them. It is thus written of him : —

He had often an opportunity to express a benignity to brute creatures, either to feed them, or make their condition easy to them. He would do it with delight, and raise two meditations upon it. I am now the instrument of God unto these creatures ; his kindness passes through my hands to them. And will not the blessed God be as beneficent unto me as I am unto these creatures? Especially if, as they look unto me to be kind unto them, I always look up to him.

III. LOVE TO MANKIND IN GENERAL. The "love of human kind" was a conspicuous trait in the character of Cotton Mather. It showed itself early in his life and seemed to grow to the very last. In boyhood he was helpful to other boys in their lessons ; he incited them to good conduct, and he wrote prayers for their private use. This love for boys — and girls also — was strong during his life. A curious statement is in point. It is said of him, that in passing through a place, he would drop words of caution and encouragement to the boys whom he met, and would solicit for them a playday that they might enjoy themselves. His love for the "little damsels of his flock" was equally evincive of a kind and gentle spirit.

But his affections were not limited to the young and lovely. It was soon evident, after his leaving college and coming into connection with the outer world, that his desire to be of service to all classes and conditions of men was an active principle. He loved the city of his birth, the college where he was educated, and the province, with fervent and patriotic ardor. His attachment to everything good in old England, whether in her people or her political and religious institutions, was ardent. But what was peculiar to Mather was his regard for the unfortunate, the miserable, the despised and degraded, the criminal and the base. Poor debtors, orphans, and widows had his sympathy, of course, and as a matter of ordinary benevolence; but his Christian regards embraced negroes, Indians, French prisoners, female criminals, bewitched persons, thieves, murderers, pirates ; in a word, malefactors of every sort found in him a friend. He visited, in filthy prisons and poisoned chambers, people whose souls were more foul than the jails, and with true kindness of heart ministered with Christian fidelity to their eternal interests, told them of their sins, led them to repentance, and preached to them an Almighty Saviour and a forgiving God. At their request, men who had hated and reviled him were attended by him to the place of execution, and often he was blessed by pirates who had cursed Cotton Mather.

It goes without saying that such a man had a warm place in his heart for relatives and personal friends. He could have used the words of Daniel Webster, in regard to the same class of friends : " Dear, dear kindred, how I love you all ! " But had he no antipathies and enmities? That depends on the meaning of the words. He had antipathies, but no malevolence. Dr. Arnold said that he had boys enough who said they loved God, but not enough who hated the devil. There is no doubt that Cotton Mather hated the devil and all his works. In the same sense, he hated wicked men and their evil ways. But it was a passion perfectly compatible with benevolence. He would do all that was possible to defeat their wicked schemes, to reclaim them from their evil ways, to bring them to condign punishment ; but he would labor and pray to make them good members of society and heirs of the kingdom of heaven. As for malice or revenge, they were not in his composition. He would have a personal quarrel with no man — no enemy. If he were misused, abused, or injured, he made it a point of duty to do the man a favor in some silent way, and to pray for him in secret. He studied to obey the precepts and follow the example of Christ, in the treatment of enemies. His feelings were grieved too easily by unkind and unfair treatment, but his heart was not made hard by abuse or soured by malicious tongues. There is no proof that he ever failed to appreciate a kindness or that he ever rendered evil for evil. The following lines show the pleasure of Dr. Mather in doing good to mankind in general : —

I am not unable, with a little study, to write in seven languages; I feast myself with the sweets of all the sciences, which the more polite part of mankind ordinarily pretend unto. I am entertained with all

kinds of histories, ancient and modern. I am no stranger to the curiosities, which by all sorts of learning, are brought unto the curious.
These intellectual pleasures are far beyond any sensual ones. — Nevertheless, all this affords me not so much delight as it does, to relieve
the distresses of any one poor, mean, miserable neighbor; and much
more, to do any extensive service for the redress of those epidemical
miseries under which mankind in general is languishing, and to advance the kingdom of God in the world.

The amiability of Mather was shown in his treatment
of transient callers and visitors. This is a test of character, or at least of temperament. Easy, luxurious men
find such callers a nuisance. If reading a pleasant book,
or idling away the time in some amusing occupation, their
temper is tried by interruption. Men of business do not
wish to be interrupted in their busy hours, unless the caller
has come with some proposal in the line of business.
Studious men sometimes fence off their studies by fixing
hours when they cannot be seen. But Cotton Mather was
free to all comers, whether children or men or women,
whether beggars or gentlemen, scholars or ignorant men,
negroes or strangers from across the water. One of his
rules was : " The man who wants to see me, is the man I
wish to see." He was covetous of time. Every minute
had a value in his estimation. The following lines show
how his days were crowded full of service : " This day I
performed the service of my general calling, instructed
the scholars under my charge, underwent the diversion of
meals and company, with whom I was a considerable
while ; I made a long sermon and preached it; I spent
more than a little time at the private meeting, where I
preached, and read over ' Knox's Historical Relation of
the Island of Ceylon.'" What time could such a man bestow upon visitors ? They were indeed a trial, but his
good nature and generosity triumphed. How will be seen
by this statement of his son Samuel : —

Because he did not love to be disturbed with tedious and impertinent visitors, and because his friends (Amici Temporis Fures) might sometimes unseasonably interrupt him, he wrote over his study door, in capitals, BE SHORT. And yet, let him be ever so busy when a friend came to see him, he threw all by. He was perfectly easy, with pleasure communicated the observations he had lately met with, and was so very obliging, although his friends knew his hurry and great business, they knew not how to leave him.

Nor was this amiability confined to scholars or genteel and respectable people; for it was one of his maxims that "a mean person with grace is more amiable to me, than another who. is otherwise never so well qualified, but graceless."

Dr. Mather's benignity to his enemies was remarkable, and sometimes had its reward. Here is an illustration of his disposition, and of his conquest of an enemy. Late one night, in October, 1704, several came to him, telling him that a very wicked man in the town lay a dying, but was anxious to see him before he died. The story is told by his son in the words following : —

When the Doctor came to him, (who wondered at him that he would so readily do it,) he told him to this purpose. That he had been a very profane person; that he had given himself a great liberty to abuse good men; but had abused no man in the world so much as Dr. Mather, and that he could not go out of the world without confessing it, bewailing it unto him, and beseeching him to pardon it. The Doctor asked him if he had received any particular prejudice, or ever had been informed, or could have pretended any particular matter of fact, upon which his abuses might have been established. He gave him to understand that there was nothing of that, but all was downright malignity; for he took him to be a man that did more good that others, and that was all the reason why he had vilified him more than other men.

The Doctor, after his well-known mild way, told the man, that there was no occasion for any pardon because of his speaking diminutively of him; for, says he, you may speak so of me, and do me no wrong. But, continued he, for your speaking injuriously, falsely, calumniously

a son could bestow on a father so worthy of honor and veneration.

In the conjugal relation Cotton Mather was a model husband, and his wives were worthy of the respect and tenderness which he lavished upon them. The first two made his home happy, and the last, except during a distressing aberration of mind, was to him a helpful and affectionate wife, and a tender mother to his children. Katharine, the daughter of his first wife, it will be remembered, would not call her "mother-in-law, but mother-in-love," and her stepson Samuel wrote of her in these words: "She is a lady of many and great accomplishments, and is the Doctor's disconsolate widow."

But the love of his children was one of the brightest elements of Dr. Mather's character. It combined authority with the utmost tenderness. Children were not to him as human animals or as pets or as objects of pride or as upper servants; but he respected their minds, their feelings, their wants. He appealed to their moral convictions. He treated them as the children of God. He won their respect, their veneration, the love of their hearts.

Some of the rules by which he was governed in the education of his children will make this matter clear and instructive.

In the first place, he prayed for them, and by name, that "God would be a Father to them, bestow his Son and grace upon them, guide them by his counsel, and bring them to glory."

When quite young they were entertained with delightful stories, of which their father had a bountiful store. He made great use of Scriptural stories, which are unequaled in their power to hold and delight the minds of children. And "every day at the table, he used to tell some entertaining tale before he rose." And when his children accidentally met him, he always had some sentence or remark that might be of use to them. His son writes that "this matter occasioned labor, study and contrivance."

He taught his children to pray when very young, giving them directions how to pray and what to pray for, and explaining the need and duty and privilege of prayer. "He would often call upon them: 'Child, don't you forget every day to go alone and pray as I have directed you.'"

He sought to form in the children a kind and pleasant temper. They were taught to do kind acts to one another and to other children. When he saw them do such deeds with pleasure, he would applaud them. They were cautioned against all acts of revenge, and urged to return good for evil. "He would show them, how they would by this goodness, become like the good God and the blessed Jesus." He was not satisfied except when the children had a "sweetness of temper shining in them."

In education the children were early taught to write as well as read. "When they had the use of the pen, he would employ them in writing out the most instructive and profitable things he could invent for them." As they became older they learned to express their own thoughts in writing.

In family government he sought to establish in the minds of the children "principles of reason and honor."

He secured their confidence in his wisdom and his love for them, so that they did not question his commands or disregard his advice. They were taught that it was "*shameful* to do amiss." Welldoing was "*amiable.*"

Both his father and grandfather discarded and abhorred the ancient way of punishing in family and school.

Cotton Mather followed their example.   Says Samuel
(page 17) : —

The slavish way of education, carried on with raving, and kicking,
and scourging, (in schools as well as families) he looked upon as a dreadful judgment of God on the world. . . . The first chastisement which
he would inflict for any ordinary fault, was to let the child see and hear
him in an astonishment, and hardly able to believe that the child could
do so base a thing; but believing that they would never do it again.
. . . He never gave a child a blow unless in cases of obstinacy, or
some act that was very criminal.

He made his children feel that to be banished a while
from his company was the sorest punishment, and that to
"learn all great things was the noblest thing in the world."
He did not reward obedience or studiousness by giving
play spells, because that would teach them that "diversion
was a nobler and better thing than diligence." Rather the
child would do well, saying to himself, "I have done well;
and now I will go to my father, who will teach me some
curious thing for it." They regarded the refusal to teach
them as a punishment. Eagerness to learn something
curious, entertaining, or useful from their father was an
inspiration to duty.

The children were not only taught to be ruled by the
dictates of honor and reason, but also by the filial and ennobling fear of God, whose benignant eye was ever upon
them. "He would show them how they must love our
Lord Jesus Christ, and how they must demonstrate it, by
doing what their parents require of them."

Dr. Mather used to tell his children of the "good angels,"
and of their kind ministrations, and to incite them so to
act as to please those blessed messengers of God. On
the other hand, he "would not say much to them of the
evil angels, because he would not have them entertain any
frightful fancies about the apparitions of devils." It was

enough to know that evil spirits as well as wicked people sought their harm, so that they might be on their guard. " Heaven and hell he set before them clearly and faithfully, as the consequences of their good or bad behavior here."

Such were the methods, the principles, and the spirit by which Cotton Mather sought to make his children obedient, useful, amiable, pious and happy. He had his reward. Some of the children died in infancy, and he gave them up to God, in the hope of meeting them again in a region where neither sin nor death ever come. One little two-year-old child died while expressing her assurance of going to her Jesus Christ. All who grew up came into the church, except one, and he gave evidence months before his early and violent death of deep and sincere repentance.

Here this chapter might be closed if it pertained to the life of an ordinary Christian ; but Cotton Mather embraced in the sphere of his affections *superhuman beings;* he cherished a personal love for the holy angels of God. To his mind they were real, personal, individual, and they were " ministering spirits " to him. They kept him from evil ; they were the medium of blessings from heaven. God used them to do his will in his servant's behalf. He kept vigils in which he believed that he had the presence and the influence — yea, the inspiration of angels. Samuel writes of this as " something singular and instructive," and quotes the following from the diary : —

On this day, I considered, that as by the praises of God, I should become like the good Angels ; thus it was a very reasonable thing that I should offer my extraordinary praises to him for his Angels. I saw that the Scriptures mentioned the ministry of the good Angels, about the heirs of salvation, with frequency ; and I saw that my life had been wondrously signalized by the ministry of those Angels. Wherefore loth to be guilty of such an unthoughtful neglect of the Angels, as the generality of the faithful who enjoy the assistances of those heavenly guardians are, I devoted this day to glorify the God and Father of my Lord Jesus Christ for the ministry of Angels, which has notably befriended me unto this very day. And I expected in this way not only to render myself more agreeable to those excellent spirits, but also to obtain from their and my Lord, a more signal share of their influence than had ever yet been granted me. 'T will be needless to relate how many Hymns I sang referring to the Angels.

This was in the morning of a day devoted to worship, and to a special consideration of the subject of angelical ministry. He continues : —

My chief exercise in the forenoon was, to consider exactly, and with as much of Scripture and learning as I could, the existence, the properties, and the relations of the good Angels ; and the honor, but not worship, due to those benign spirits ; and then to run over the marvellous references to their ministry which I have here and there found scattered in the oracles of God ; whether towards particular saints, or towards the church in general. . . . I cannot fully express the elevation of soul with which I went through these noble exercises ; which exercises at last I concluded with assurances that I should one day come to praise him that sits upon the throne, and the Lamb, in the company of his holy Angels forever.

Later in the day he made a catalogue of mercies received from heaven through the ministry of angels, and concluded as follows : —

Such things as these I did, with multiplied Hallelujahs, acknowledge on my study floor before the Lord. And in the midst of my rapturous praises, I could not forbear saying, " Bless the Lord, O my soul, and forget not all his benefits ! And if any good Angels of the Lord are now nigh unto me, Do you, also bless the Lord, ye heavenly ministers ; And, Oh, adore that free grace of his, which employs you to be serviceable to so poor, so mean, so vile a wretch as is here prostrate before him."

The *love of God-in-Christ* is the source and cause of all true love to holy angels and good men. In the estimation of Dr. Mather, all the beauties and excellences in all the "spirits of just men made perfect," and in all the holy angels, though exalted and refined through countless ages of service and worship, would amount to very little in comparison with the spiritual loveliness of the God-man, Christ Jesus. He is the "chiefest among ten thousand, and the one altogether lovely." His own words must be used in conveying his meaning : —

Having entertained a right and clear apprehension of my great Saviour, and his glorious Person, as the eternal Son of God, incarnate and inthroned in my Jesus, being somewhat understood with me ; and beholding the infinite God as coming to me, and meeting with me in this blessed Mediator ; the thoughts of him are become exceeding frequent with me. . . . I have learnt the way of interesting my Saviour in the thoughts. And I feel an impatience raised in me, if I have been many minutes without some thoughts of him. I fly to him on Multitudes of occasions every day, and am impatient if many minutes have passed without some recourse to him.

Now and then I rebuke myself, thus : "Why have I been so long without some thoughts on my lovely Saviour? How can I bear to keep at any distance from him?" I then look up to my Saviour ; O my dear Saviour, Draw near unto me : Oh ! come down to dwell in my soul, and help me to form some thoughts wherein I shall enjoy thee.

Mather then writes of his meditations upon the glories, the merits, the pattern of his "amiable Saviour," finding the subject infinitely inexhaustible, with this result : —

After I have been in the day thus employed, I fall asleep at night perpetually in the midst of some meditation on the glory of my Saviour ; usually on a Scripture where that glory is mentioned. So I sleep in Jesus ! And when I wake in the night, I do on my bed seek him that my soul does love. Still in the night the desires of my soul carry me to him in thoughts on the subject which I fell asleep with.

There is more in this lofty and seraphic expression, but the few following lines shall bring our quotations to a close : —

I find that where Christ comes, a wondrous light, life and peace comes with him, together with a strength to go through services and sufferings. The holiness and happiness to which I am introduced by this way of living, 't is better to me than all the enjoyments of this world.

CHAPTER XXVII.

THE BLESSED CLOSE OF A USEFUL LIFE.

WE now enter on the last year of Dr. Mather's working life, for though he lived to the thirteenth day of February, 1728, his last sickness came on in December of this year (1727). He was sick in April, but with his usual persistence, the weakness of his body was not allowed to impede the action of his mind; and this last year was filled with the products of authorship to the amount of five or six hundred pages, in addition to preaching and pastoral labors.

The first sermon that was given to the press was probably the one delivered about the middle of January upon the "special and mournful occasion of the death of a pious gentleman, Mr. Samuel Hirst," son-in-law of Judge Sewall. The title was "Ignorantia Scientifica," showing the great advantage of our not knowing the time of our death. "Instruction fetched from ignorance" expressed the topic of the discourse.

This was soon followed by "Signatus, — the Sealed Servants of our God, appearing with two witnesses, to produce a well-established assurance of their being the children of the Lord Almighty." The two witnesses were the Holy Spirit with the spirit of the believer.

The "Victorina" was published soon after the death of Katharine Mather, but a new edition came out this year. It was a choice piece of biography in its time.

From the following item taken from Sewall's diary, April 27, it appears that Dr. Mather was considered dangerously sick at the time : —

After Lecture, several ministers met at Mr. Gee's to pray for Dr. Mather. Mr. Thacher, Webb, Cooper, Gee, Sewall, prayed.

It is a reasonable conjecture that the volume entitled "Restitutus," in fifty-four pages, was the outcome of this sickness. The title intimates as much. "The End of Life pursued, and then the Hope in Death enjoyed, by the faithful; both of them described in a discourse made upon a recovery from sickness; or, the declaration of our returning from the gates of the grave."

The death of King George II called out a sermon on "Christian Loyalty." Dr. Mather was loyal to the House of Hanover, as before remarked. He knew how great perils the colonies, as well as the mother country, had been freed from by the establishment of that family on the throne of Great Britain.

"Agricola, or the Religious Husbandman," was a volume of great value, in 221 pages. Its interest will be seen from the following words: "The main intentions of religion served in the business and language of husbandry." It was a family book and was a treasure in the home.

"The Balance of the Sanctuary," preached in the audience of the general assembly, October 5; "The Marrow of the Gospel," showing the "union between the Redeemer and the believer"; the "Hor-Hagidgad," a happy departure, occasioned by the death of a brother minister, Rev. William Waldron; and "Juga Jucunda," containing a "relation of the glorious peace and joy which brightened the dying hours of Mrs. Abigail Goodwin," addressed to young people, were a part of the publications which appeared in the summer and autumn of this fruit-bearing year.

The "Baptismal Piety" is in two brief essays. Their simple but beautiful titles would seem enough to charm parents into offering their children to the Saviour. 1. "The Angel of the Waters, instructing the spectators of the sacred baptism, administered in our assemblies, how to make it a most profitable spectacle." 2. "The Angel of the Little Ones directing the aims and the frames wherewith parents are to bring their infants unto the holy baptism."

The earthquake that shook New England in the night between October 29 and 30, 1727, was the occasion of an address, soon published, with the title, "The Terror of the Lord." Text (2 Cor. 5: 11): "Knowing the terror of the Lord, we persuade men." The following account of the earthquake, and the meetings following, are from Dr. Mather: —

The night that followed the 29th of October, was a night whereto New England had never, in the memory of man, seen the like. The air never more calm, the sky never more fair; everything in all imaginable tranquillity; but about a quarter of an hour before 11, there was heard in Boston, passing from one end of the town to the other, a horrid rumbling like the noise of many coaches together driving on the paved stones with the utmost rapidity. But it was attended with a most awful trembling of the earth, which did heave and shake so as to rocque the houses, and cause here and there, the falling of some smaller things, both within doors and without. It cannot be imagined but that it gave an uncommon concern unto all the inhabitants, and even a degree of consternation unto very many of them. The first shock, which was the most violent, was followed with several others, and some repetition of the noise, at sundry times, pretty distinct from one another. The number of them is not entirely agreed; but at least four or five are allowed for; the last of which was between five and six of the clock in the morning. It extended for scores of miles, west and south. [In fact, several hundred miles.]

What added unto the terrors of it, were the terrible flames of light in the atmosphere, which accompained it. . . . The vessels on the coast were also made sensible of it by shivering that seized on them.

No time was lost by Dr. Mather and his brother ministers, in the effort to derive good results from an event so impressive, as appears from the following : —

In the morning, the pastors of the Old North Church directed the bells to be rung, that such of the people as could and would, might assemble immediately unto some suitable exercises of religion. The pastors of the New North joined with them in sending up unto heaven the supplications which the solemn occasion called for. And the pastors in the other part of the town, made a speedy and a hearty appearance; and most affectionately united in a concurrence with them. The assembly that came together, did more than crowd and fill the most capacious of our meeting houses, and as there was a multitude of serious Christians, who are acquainted with real and vital piety, so the whole auditory expressed a devotion which was truly extraordinary.

These exercises, beginning at eight A.M., closed about two in the afternoon. After an hour or two, say at four in the afternoon, "several churches in the other part of the town followed the example, and with vast congregations, continued the proper exercises of religion until about eight o'clock in the evening." The ministers were animated alike, and the Lieutenant-Governor, — Dummer, — "whose piety ever discovered on every other as well as this occasion, disposed him to direct that the Thursday next, which was the Lecture day, should be a day of supplications in all the churches in the city."

Dr. Mather, judging that the word should accompany prayer, and hoping that hearts softened by the voice of God would receive good impressions, seized on the "uncommon and tremendous occasion" to address the throng. What he said was at once desired for publication, and he gave it as he could remember. It was written out the next Saturday, November 4, just as he had spoken it, so far as possible. He intimates that probably some remarks were omitted, in the haste of writing, without regard to style or authorship. He began with prayer for a blessing on the word: "O! may the Holy Spirit of our God make it come with efficacy."

As the primitive outpouring of the Holy Spirit was attended with an earthquake, so he hoped that the earthquake would now be attended with "such an outpouring of the Holy Spirit as would make a holy and so a happy people." Proceeding he said:—

We find the hill, on the north side whereof Joshua was buried, had the name of Har-Gayash, which word signifies the *Mountain of trembling*. The Jews have a tradition that at the time of his burial, the mountain trembled with an earthquake, to testify the displeasure of God against the people. My friends, we approach as to an Har-Gayash, in what is now to be set before us.

His text was Micah 6: 9: "The Lord's voice crieth unto the city." He referred to other earthquakes in the town, in the country, and in other countries, as in Sicily, where thousands perished; and in Old Testament times. Next he spoke of the natural causes of earthquakes, as understood in that day; and then of God as the great, first cause. Then he inquired:—

What may be the voice of the glorious God unto us in the earthquake wherein we have had the earth just now trembling under us?

1. The voice of God in the cry is, "O glorify the perfections of the glorious God which are displayed in the earthquake."

2. Let the crimes that cry to the Holy God for all the vengeance of an earthquake upon you, be generally and thoroughly reformed among you.

3. The voice is: "immediately get into such a state of safety, that no earthquake may cause a heartache in you."

He then urges "repentance, and a speedy flight unto the only Redeemer." Doing this, one could say, "And now, O earthquake, do thy worst. Thou canst not make me miserable. My Saviour is my friend. I will not fear; what can an earthquake do unto me?"

Two other editions were immediately called for, that is, before the year closed. But this was not all. Dr. Mather saw that fear was passing off, and the unhurt people were growing careless in a reaction from their fright. He strove, as he had done in the morning after the shock, to appeal to higher and deeper considerations than mere bodily fear, or fear of any kind, however natural and useful in its place; and to fix the public mind on duty to God, and a wise regard to their own immortal interests. In this he acted with his ministerial brethren. In December he addressed his "Boanerges" unto the whole people of New England who were terrified with the late earthquake. This was an essay based on Psalm 78: 34, 36, 37, to "preserve and strengthen the good impressions produced by the late alarming providence."

This narrative brings before us the great revival of 1727–1728, with which and in which the life of Cotton Mather came to its translation. A large number — fifty-three — became members of his church in 1725. The next year there were nine. In this year, including January and February, which then belonged to the old 1727, seventy-one confessed faith in Christ. And what heightened the joy of the senior pastor, his own and only remaining daughter, Hannah, was one of the number. Samuel and Hannah were now in the fold, and the other thirteen, he hoped, were gathered into the fold above. Then, having welcomed a great accession to the North Church, and rejoicing in the like happiness of the other churches, he could use the words of the aged Simeon: "Lord, now lettest thou thy servant depart in peace, according to thy word: for mine eyes have seen thy salvation."

Thus we come to the eve of the departure of a faithful servant of God to his reward. We have seen already, in a quotation from Judge Sewall's diary, that Dr. Mather was sick in April. This is more fully referred to in Samuel's life of his father. At that time the good man, believing death was at hand, wrote and said many things. At one time he said : —

Lord, thou art with me, and dost make me to sing in the dark valley of the shadow of death. I perceive the signs of death upon me, and am I not affrighted? No, not at all! I will not so dishonor my Saviour, as to be affrighted at any thing that can befall me, while I am in his blessed hands.

To some gentlemen he said : "I hope I shall not be found a fool, but here I lie and sing, 'Soul, take thine ease ; thou hast good laid up in store tor many years, for endless ages; but another sort of goods than what this vain world puts off its idolaters with.'"

He wrote as follows : —

I feel the life of God begun in my soul. . . . Here is a life begun which can terminate no otherwise than in an endless life with my God. There is a well of water in me that will spring up into everlasting life.

Death, do thy worst ; there is no killing of the life to which my God has begun to raise me. Have I had a glorious Christ living, acting and working in me, and quickening me for living unto God ; and will he ever lose his hold of me? No, no ; I am sure of living with him forevermore.

Have I, to animate myself unto holiness, in all manner of conversation in my contemplations, often endeavored to affect myself with the holiness of the purified spirits in the paradise of God ; their flaming devotions ; their delight in God ; their hatred of sin ; the contempt with which they look down on the high things of this world ; and the goodness with which they treat one another? Done this with earnest desires to be as like them as this mortal state may attain to, and will admit of ? And shall I not now be fetched away to join with them in the praises of God ?

The following is inserted to show in what sense a famous and much-decried opinion or sentiment was understood by Dr. Mather ; and to raise the query whether the phrase, "willing to be damned for the glory of God," carried any other meaning.

But! what if after all, a Sovereign God will have me to be a castaway, and I shall be cast into hell, where the divine justice will be forever scourging of me? I desire it should be so? — Faulty tho'ts! fiery darts! — In the horror of darkness I now humble myself as clay before the potter, and I feel my heart so filled with the love of God, and so satisfied in his doing all things right as they should be done, that if it should be so, yet I desire that no scourge upon me may produce anything from me worse than this : O, love, and serve, and praise the glorious God who does all of this! Let none resist the will of the glorious God who does all this! Let me undergo all of this, rather than ever entertain one hard thought of the glorious One! — But my soul being thus disposed, the Holy Spirit of my God immediately shoots the rays of his light into it, and most powerfully says to me, " these dispositions were never made for a hell, the fire whereof is for the enemies of God. If it were possible for a soul to go to hell with such dispositions, it would carry heaven thither with it. No, no ; thou art a pleasant child unto me. I will surely have mercy on thee."

And now, vain world, farewell! Thou hast been to me a very uneasy wilderness. Welcome, everlasting life! The paradise of God stands open for me. I am just entering into a world where I shall be free from sin, and from all temptations to it; a world where I shall have all tears wiped from my eyes; a world where I shall be filled with all the fulness of God. The best hour that ever I saw, is what I am hourly and gladly waiting for.

But he had to wait a little longer ; and surely his heart was happy in waiting, when he found what the Lord had in store for him before going. The great awakening in the last months of the year gave him loved employment and filled out his life's work most honorably and happily. It would seem as if a gracious God reserved him for this work, or the work for him, to put a stamp of divine approbation on his servant. Besides his address after the earthquake, he was busy in pastoral duties and in fraternal ministries.

Late in December, Dr. Mather preached a funeral sermon for an aged friend. His usual felicity attended his selection of a title to the discourse : "The Comfortable Chambers opened and visited, upon the departure of that aged and faithful Servant of God, Mr. Peter Thacher, who made his flight thither on December 17, 1727." Samuel said in a note that this sermon was the "last that was ever preached by the Author, who was willing it should go to the press, that the world might have a lasting testimony of the sincere friendship, value and honor, he had for the person commemorated in it." The author died before the printing was finished. The sermon was republished seventy years later.

And now the worn-out servant of God had finished his work. Worn-out, I say, because his natural tenacity of life promised many years in addition. His grandfather lived seventy-five years. His father was eighty-four at his decease. He died the day after he became sixty-five, February 13, 1728; but though his honored progenitors lived longer, and were hard workers, he probably had performed as much work and had filled as many hours with care, suffering, and devotion, as either of them. His mind sped as the "swift ships." Like Raleigh he could "work terribly." He was aglow with thought, feeling, and emotion. No moments were wasted in idle reverie, and so he filled out the full measure of his days. His general health was better as he grew older. "As with Drusius, so with Mather; his old age was better to him than his youth; and he was generally more healthy in his later years than former." But now his vitality was exhausted nearly, and the causes that would end his life were at hand.

When the last sickness came on, late in December, Dr. Mather expected to die. In a note to one of his physicians he wrote : "My last enemy is come; I would say, my best friend." A few hours before his decease, he said : " Now I have nothing more to do here; my will is entirely swallowed up in the will of the Lord."

Says his son : —

He was entirely above the love of life, and the fear of death, assuring us that he was going to eat the bread of life, and drink the water of life freely; that all tears would soon be wiped from his eyes; that everything looked smiling about him; that it was impossible he should be lost; that he had a strong consolation, and that his views of the heavenly world were all glorious.

Very tender was his parting with his nephew, Mather Byles; and yet more so with his only surviving son. Omitting some personal remarks of appreciation, the son records that when on bended knees the patriarch's blessing was asked, he said : —

You have been a dear Son, and a pleasant child unto me, and I wish you as many blessings, as you have done me services, which are very many. I wish, and pray the God of Abraham, Isaac and Jacob may be yours, and his blessing rest upon you. I wish that, as you have the prospect of being serviceable in the world, you may be great and considerable, as the patriarchs were, by introducing Christ into the world. The grace of the Lord Jesus Christ be with you. Amen.

And being asked what sentence or word; what πύκινον ἔπος he would have Samuel think on constantly as he desired to have his father before him, and to hear him speak, he replied, " Remember only that one word *fructuosus* " (fruitful).

He died on Tuesday. From the Thursday before to that time, he was " dying of a hard *cough*, and a suffocating *asthma*, with a *fever;* but he felt no great pain." He had the " sweet *composure* and *easy departure*, for which he had entreated so *often* and *fervently*, the sovereign Disposer of all." At the last he said : " Is this dying? Is this all ? Is this all that I feared, when I prayed against a hard death? O! I can bear this! I can bear it! I can bear it!" And when his wife wiped his eyes, he said, "I am going where all tears will be wiped from my eyes."

Six days later, on Monday, the 19th, was the funeral. The sentiments of respect and veneration in which Dr. Mather was held by the community were shown by one of the greatest funeral processions ever seen in Boston. Judge Sewall's diary for February 19 reads:—

Dr. Cotton Mather is entombed. Bearers, the Rev'd Mr. Colman, Mr. Thacher; Mr. Sewall, Mr. Prince; Mr. Webb, Mr. Cooper,—who supported the pall. The church went before the corpse; first, Rev. Mr. Gee [colleague] in mourning, alone; then three deacons; then Capt. Hutchinson, Adam Winthrop, Esq., Col. Hutchinson. Went up Hull street. I went in a coach. All the council had gloves. I had a pair. Mr. Walter prayed excellently. Several gentlemen of the bereaved flock took their turns to bear the coffin. After which followed, first, the bereaved relatives in mourning; then his honor, the Lieut. Governor, the honorable, his majesty's council, and house of representatives; then a large train of ministers, justices, merchants, scholars, and other principal inhabitants, both of men and women. The streets were crowded with people, and the windows filled with sorrowful spectators, all the way to the burying place, where the corpse was deposited in a tomb belonging to the worthy family.

The tomb is still preserved, in the northeast part of Copp's Hill Cemetery. This is the tomb which was given to Cotton Mather by friends after the decease of his first wife.

The sentiments of the North Church in relation to their pastor, during his sickness and at his death, were expressed in the following votes:—

January 26, 1727-8. At a meeting of the brethren of the church, the following proposal was offered and approved; notice of it to be given to the whole assembly in the afternoon. Whereas, in the holy providence of our Lord, his aged servant, our Rev. and dear Pastor, is visited and brought low by sickness, which takes him off from those exercises of the pastoral care, whereby God has greatly endeared him to us, and threatens his removal from us, by death, which we would deprecate as a most awful frown of heaven; we do therefore desire and appoint, next Wednesday afternoon to be set apart and employed in humble, penitent, and earnest supplications to God our Saviour, that our Pastor may be restored unto usefulness, and continue to be a rich blessing.

They invited the Rev. Messrs. Colman, Thacher, and Sewall to assist in the service. Soon after Dr. Mather's decease the church voted as follows : —

Whereas, under the awful and humbling providence, wherewith the great and good Shepherd hath visited his flock, the united pastors of the town are in a course of preaching with us, according to the usual method of expressing their pious regards to a deceased pastor, and his bereaved flock and family; it is therefore ordered and appointed, that as a token of the like Christian regards, the salary should be continued to the family while the ministers supplied the pulpit.

In April it was voted that the " sum of 100 pounds be paid to Mrs. Lydia Mather, at the rate of five pounds per month, till the whole be paid, if she live so long."

The sentiment of the general public was expressed in the following paragraph, which appeared in The New England Weekly Journal, on the day of the funeral : —

Last Tuesday, in the forenoon, between eight and nine o'clock, died here, the very Reverend Cotton Mather, Doctor in Divinity of Glasco, and Fellow of the Royal Society in London, Senior Pastor of the Old North Church in Boston, and an Overseer of Harvard College; by whose death persons of all ranks are in concern and sorrow. He was, perhaps, the principal ornament of this country, and the greatest scholar that ever was bred in it. But besides his universal learning, his exalted piety, and extensive charity, his entertaining wit, and singular goodness of temper, recommended him to all that were judges of real and distinguished merit. After having spent above forty seven years in the faithful and unwearied discharge of a lively, zealous, and awakening ministry, and in incessant endeavors to do good, and spread abroad the glories of Christ, he finished his course with a Divine composure and joy, the day after his sixty-fifth birthday.

The Mather Tomb.

Dr. Mather's eminence as a man, a scholar, a minister, and a Christian was attested by his brethren in the sacred office. A few passages from their writings will exhibit their high appreciation.

The Rev. Peter Thacher, pastor of the New North Church, pronounced him "the glory of learning, and the ornament of Christianity."

The Rev. Joshua Gee was graduated at Harvard College in 1717, and settled as a colleague of Dr. Mather in 1723. He had opportunities to know him before his own settlement, as well as after; and being a man of superior gifts, his judgment carries weight. In a funeral sermon he thus spoke of his senior pastor : —

The capacity of his mind; the readiness of his wit; the vastness of his reading; the strength of his memory; the variety and treasure of his learning, in printed works, and in manuscripts which contain a much greater share; the splendor of virtues, which, from the abundant grace of God with him, shone out in the constant tenor of a most entertaining and profitable conversation; his uncommon activity in the service of Christ; his unwearied application to all the different exercises of the pastoral function; his extensive zeal and numberless projections to do good on all occasions; these things, as they were united in him, proclaimed him to be truly an extraordinary person; and united to make it difficult to find his equal, among men of like passions with us. He was pious, but not affected; serious without moroseness; grave, but not austere; affable without meanness; and facetious without levity. He was peaceable in his temper; but zealous against sin. He was a strenuous non-conformist to uninstituted ceremonies imposed upon conscience, as terms of communion among saints; which he considered as violations of Christian liberty, and snares to the souls of men. He strictly adhered to Congregational principles of church order and government; but he was catholic in his charity to all good men, though differing from him in circumstantials and modalities; desirous to have churches resemble the kingdom of heaven; willing to receive all men, as Christ receives us to the glory of God; and pleading for no terms of communion among saints, but the terms of salvation.

Dr. Benjamin Colman had been settled now twenty-seven years in the neighborhood of Dr. Mather. The Brattle Street meetinghouse was nearer to the Old North than any other outside of the "island." From all we know of them, the two ministers had been cordial in coöperating, during all these years, in all measures for promoting the interests of religion. There had been a difficulty in the founding of Brattle Street Society, because a party in that organization had adopted new views; but there is no evidence that Colman sympathized with the "new departure" men of that day. They were under the necessity of abating their designs, and the new church was placed on the old Westminster Catechism basis, and Dr. Colman had adhered to the ancient symbol of the faith with no sign of dissent. The following words of Dr. Colman were therefore not the result of an effort at magnanimity, but the cordial utterance of his sentiments. It is evident that he weighed his words, in order to be just and discriminating, and at the same time brotherly in his eulogy. An extract from his funeral sermon will be read with pleasure. He speaks of Dr. Mather in the following terms: —

The *first minister in the town;* the first in age, in gifts, and in grace; as all his brethren very readily own. I might add, (it may be without offence to any), the first in the whole Province, and Provinces of New England, for universal literature, and extensive services. Yea it may be, among all the *fathers* in these churches, from the beginning of the Country to this day, of whom many have done worthily and greatly; yet none of them amassed together so vast a treasure of learning, and made so much use of it, to a variety of pious intentions.

He then becomes more specific in his commendations, after which his recognition of Dr. Mather's human frailty gives added force to his eulogium. Read the following sentences: —

His printed works . . . will not convey to posterity, nor give to strangers, a just idea of the real worth, and great learning of the man.

. . . It was conversation and acquaintance with him, in his familiar and occasional discourses and private communications, that discovered the vast compass of his knowledge, and the projections of his piety; more I have sometimes thought, than all his pulpit exercises. Here he excelled, here he shone; being exceeding communicative, and bringing out of his treasury, things new and old, without measure. Here it was seen how his wit, and fancy, his invention, his quickness of thought, and ready apprehension were all consecrated to God, as well as his heart, will and affections; and out of his abundance within, his lips overflowed, dropt as the honey-comb, fed all that came near him, and were as the choice silver, for richness and brightness, pleasure and profit. But here love to Christ and his servant, commands me to draw a veil over every failing; for who is without them? Not ascending *Elijah* himself; who was a man of like passions with his brethren the prophets; and we have his mantle left us wherewith to cover the defects and infirmities of others, after their translation in spirit. These God remembers no more, and why should we? And he blots out none of their good deeds, and no more should we.

A citation—in the first chapter—has already been made from Dr. Thomas Prince, pastor of the Old South Church, to show the extent of Dr. Mather's reputation in foreign lands, during his life. The following paragraphs are taken from a writing of Prince, in 1729:—

By his learned works and correspondence, those who lived at the greatest distance might discern much of his superior light and influence; but they could discern these only by a more mediate and faint reflection. They could neither see nor well imagine that extraordinary luster of pious and useful literature, wherewith we were, every day, entertained, surprised, and satisfied, who dwelt in the directer rays, in the more immediate vision.

The following lines agree well with a part of those selected from the sermon of Dr. Colman:—

Great abilities, an insatiable thirst for all kinds of knowledge, an extraordinary quickness of apprehension, liveliness of fancy, with a ready invention and active spirit, seem to be the chief ingredients of his natural genius; and all these being sanctified in his early days, imbued with a Divine bias, and turned to the noblest objects; he became inflamed with the most ardent desires to amass unto himself, from all sorts of writings, an unbounded treasure of curious and useful learning, and to find out all imaginable ways of employing it for the glory of God, the good of men, and the advancement of his own perfection; that as he grew in knowledge, he might increase in goodness and usefulness, and become a greater and more extensive blessing.

Some distinguished men are great in one or two specialties, but not above mediocrity in other regards. Dr. Mather did not belong to this class. He was superior in many directions, and he appreciated men and books of every variety, from which useful knowledge or noble inspirations could be drawn. Says Prince, in continuation : —

By a transient acquaintance with him, one would think that, being sanctified from the birth, he had made the utmost improvement of his time in the *pursuit* of *knowledge*; but upon a further view of the social part of his life, the continual resort of visitants, with his gentle and easy entertainment of them, at all hours, and how he would scarce let the meanest and youngest of them pass him without instruction; it seemed as if almost all his time was swallowed up with *conversation*. And yet, being let into a more intimate discovery of his numberless and perpetual contrivances and labors to do good in the world, one would then be ready to conclude that he had no time left for either, but must have spent it all in *action*.

In regard to Dr. Mather's habit and mode of study and acquiring knowledge, we have this instructive passage : —

He early made himself master of the learned languages, as Latin, Greek and Hebrew. He read and wrote French and Spanish, with limited proficiency, and published several productions in the Iroquois tongue. He also kept to the constant study of the Holy Oracles in their inspired originals. As to other books, he gave no time but to what could give him *something new*.

What follows next must refer to his method after some years of experience in reading and study. A mature student finds but little *new* in the issues of the press, whether periodical or in volumes, except in the records of travel and of scientific research. A late New England physician and surgeon, considered by many as second to none, used to supply himself with the best publications, though having no time to read them. He requested his students, in their reading, to mark the passages which related to new experiments and discoveries, which he could glance at, when occasion offered. Dr. Mather had no students to do this office for him ; but he had a most expeditious mode of extracting the contents of a book.

In two or three minutes turning through a volume, he could easily tell whether it would make additions to the store of his ideas. If not, he laid it by, reading very little for pleasure, or as a matter of taste. If the book had something *new* to him, he skipped along from point to point, seizing on the new, and penciling passages to be reviewed. Of these he made a brief digest, and so laid the volume aside. As he grew older, the less time he needed to give to new books, and the more pages he could exhaust in a rapid reading.

Among his treasures as a speaker and writer, he had a vast store of "commonplaces," stories, incidents, anecdotes, sayings, that he could use at the moment, with ready application.

Nor was he less prompt in writing than in learning. He had the "pen of a ready writer, that knew not how to falter in his swift career."

In regard to the proper attitude of Christians toward each other, and their reciprocal rights and duties, as in other things, Dr. Mather was in advance of his age. Says Dr. Prince : —

He was an utter enemy to religious tyranny and impositions. He never valued any particular forms of worship, unless they were of Divine appointment. His heart was set on the spirit, the power, the practice of the great duties of the religion in Christian institutions. And this he was for propagating by convincing and moving arguments, warm persuasions, bright examples, and by every winning way that could be thought of, agreeably to its truly primitive and noble simplicity, and to human liberty.

But the chief ornament, and the vital spirit of his character, was his desire to be like his Master, and his intense zeal in serving him. Says Dr. Prince in this connection : —

He invented and pursued various and surprising methods for the advancement of vital piety. His glowing charity and piety spread a further luster on his other excellencies. His burning zeal for God, and fervent benevolence and love for men, were constantly working in him, employing all his talents, thoughts, and cares, by night and day, and breaking forth into numberless projections, and intense endeavors, which wasted and consumed his life.

INDEX